# HIGH TECH START UP

The Complete Handbook for Creating
Successful New High Tech Companies

REVISED AND UPDATED

## JOHN L. NESHEIM

THE FREE PRESS

THE FREE PRESS
A Division of Simon & Schuster Inc.
1230 Avenue of the Americas
New York, NY 10020

First Free Press Edition 2000
Originally published in 1997 by John L. Nesheim

The Free Press and colophon are trademarks
of Simon & Schuster Inc.

Designed by Carla Bolte

Manufactured in the United States of America

10   9

Library of Congress Cataloging-in-Publication Data

ISBN 0–684–87170–X

# Contents

*Preface   vii*

1   Introduction to Start-Ups and Their Funding   1

2   Historical Overview   15

3   The Process of Forming the Company   23

4   Getting Started Legally   53

5   Preparing the Business Plan   68

6   The Team   91

7   Ownership, Dilution, Negotiation, and Valuation   98

8   Personal Rewards and Costs   126

9   Venture Capitalists   170

10   Leasing as a Source of Capital   200

11   Bankers and Bootstraps as Funding Sources   212

12   Angels and Other Sources of Venture Capital   222

13   Wall Street and the Initial Public Offering   232

14   Mergers, Spinouts, and Corporate Venture Capital   267

*Appendixes*

A.   *Saratoga Venture Tables   283*
B.   *Resources for the Entrepreneur   317*
C.   *Three Venture Capital Firms Describe Themselves   325*
     *Bibliography   331*
     *Index   333*
     *About the Author   343*

# *Preface*

Why bother trying to help more entrepreneurs succeed? Start by listening to an icon of venture funding, Don Valentine, founder of Sequoia Capital (that funded Apple, Cisco, Yahoo , MP3.com and more):

> Sequoia is focused on the concept of *bigness*: big thinkers, big markets, big companies. Employing thousands of people paying millions in taxes and hundreds of millions in salaries. That's bigger than people who just want to become millionaires.

Too many new businesses fail to become successful, including high-tech start-ups. If we could improve the proportion of successes, the economic benefits to nations stagger the mind.

In *The Winning Performance*, which reported the results of research on 525 of America's midsize companies, Clifford and Cavanaugh (1985) say that "If just 1% of the companies in existence today had had the will and the skill to reach mid-size—$25 million in sales—the American economy would be more than double its current size. Yet the fact remains that more than 999 of every 1,000 companies stay small."

Peter Drucker, in his book *Innovation and Entrepreneurship*, reported that America created 40 million new jobs over twenty years since 1970. The jobs came from small and new enterprises.

Professor David BenDaniel, professor of entrepreneurship at Cornell University's Johnson Graduate School of Management, explains how the world has been impacted by high-tech start-ups:

> High-growth ventures have emerged as economic power houses in the United States, generating thousands of jobs, diffusing technological knowledge, and creating a culture of innovation that has ripple effects through out every type of business organization, and indeed their impact has changed business around the world.

The typical venture-backed high-tech start-up has a 60 percent likelihood of going bankrupt. What are the areas in which start-ups need help, and what are the payoffs for helping them?

- *High cost of capital.* Venture capital investors take high risks and require high compensation. Most founders have little idea how to value their start-ups and how to negotiate with suppliers of capital.
- *Increased competition between more numerous, similar start-ups.* Large influxes of billions of dollars to venture capital pools have increased competition between start-ups in any given business sector.
- *Big companies react more quickly.* In response to changes in market conditions, the billion-dollar companies detect and act on business opportunities faster than they used to.

This book is intended to help the leader of a high-tech start-up improve his or her odds of success. It also aims to help the corporate venture capitalist evaluate start-up candidates for acquisition, as well as the new "internal start-ups" that are emerging. We will analyze successful and unsuccessful high-tech start-ups and the techniques their management use to start, finance, value, and launch a new business from seed financing through initial public offering. We will provide data on the financial rewards of equity ownership and dilution by venture capitalists of famous high-tech start-ups.

This book has six goals:

1. To prepare the CEO for the surprises yet to come.
2. To prepare the CEO for negotiations.
3. To make clear the personal cost of leading a start-up.
4. To improve the CEO's odds of success.
5. To assist corporate development managers work with new ventures.
6. To help new venture capitalist partners and associates get off to a running start.

# Conventions and Practices Used in This Book

Most case studies use disguised names. Each case is based on actual events. Research for this book was conducted regularly since 1984, during which more than 300 interviews were done with over 200 individuals in more than 150 companies in the United States and abroad.

# Introduction to Start-Ups and Their Funding

The research on which this book is based provided a lot of data about start-ups of all kinds that use technology, from semiconductors to Internet sites. The findings include their probability of success and how they are typically organized. Let's begin with thirty-one facts about typical high-tech start-ups—many of them contrary to popular stereotypes.

1. The chances are 6 in a million that an idea for a high-tech business eventually becomes a successful company that goes public.
2. Fewer than 20 percent of the funded start-ups go public.
3. Founder CEOs own less than 4 percent of their high-tech companies after the initial public offering. Boom periods like the early Internet years often raise that to 10% and higher.
4. Founder CEOs can expect their stock to be worth about $6.5 million if the company succeeds in going public. Boom periods like the early Internet years produce billionaires.
5. Successful venture capitalists expect to personally earn about $7 million (in addition to cash wages) over five years for each $50 million pool of capital they share in managing.
6. Business plans are typically poor and are not well received by venture capitalists.
7. "Unfair advantage" and "sustainable competitive advantage" are missing

in most business plans but are considered by investors to be critical if the high-tech start-up is to have an acceptable chance of succeeding. Plans lacking such an advantage rarely receive venture funding from experienced, successful venture capitalists.

8. On the average, a venture capitalist finances only 6 out of every 1,000 business plans received each year.

9. Venture capital investors own a large 70 percent of the start-up by the time it goes public: 70 percent of hardware companies, 60% of software companies and 50% of Internet companies.

10. The personal costs of doing a start-up are high, affecting families and friends as well as individuals. Fear and burnout are common. However, many CEOs have balanced those costs with the rewards of personal and professional satisfaction and the potential financial paybacks, which can be more gratifying than the rewards of working for a large corporation.

11. Bankruptcies occur for 60 percent of the high-tech companies that succeed in getting venture capital.

12. Mergers or liquidations occur in 30 percent of start-up companies.

13. A vice president's stock is worth about $2.5 million or one third of what the CEO is worth at the time of the initial public offering. Boom periods can increase the wealth tenfold.

14. The average worth of the stock for each of the employees (not including vice presidents and other key employees) on the date of the initial public offering is about $100,000.

15. Investors in venture capital pools aim to earn in excess of 25 percent each year on their money, about 8 percent more than if they had invested in all the stocks of the companies making up the Standard & Poor's 500 company index. In boom periods they can triple their returns.

16. The 10 percent of the start-ups that succeed compensate for the other 90 percent of the poorer performing companies in the venture capitalist's investment portfolio. In essence, the successful founders are paying for the substandard performance or bankruptcies of the bad investments.

17. Cash compensation for U.S. start-up managements remains below levels offered by larger corporations in spite of the scarcity of start-up talent and tax law reductions in the United States. Technical talent is paid near or at the going rate for such employees.

18. The median annual starting salary for a founder CEO in 1990 was about $120,000. By 1998 it had risen to about $150,000. Pre-IPO cash bonuses had become common by 2000 and increased total pay to $190,000 by the time the company went public.

19. The vice president of sales in a start-up often earns more cash compensation than the CEO. This occurs when incentive compensation plans are linked to sales that exceed those of the business plan.

20. Of the start-ups that get to an initial public offering, the median company takes at least three and typically five years to get to the public offering stage. Internet and biotech companies have been able to go public based on their "stories," that is, without earning profits by the time of the initial public offering.

21. Equipment lease financing and leasing of facilities and leasehold improvements have proven to be reliable and competitively priced sources of capital to augment equity raised to finance a start-up.

22. Having as a founder a person experienced with the responsibilities as CEO greatly increases the chances of getting a start-up funded. A close second is having a complete management team ready to go to work, with experienced people for each of the key functions, including the first CEO willing to step aside for a new, experienced leader when the business begins to grow rapidly.

23. About $100 billion is committed to pools of venture capital. It is managed by more than 2000 actively venturing individuals in over 500 firms, mostly in the United States, mainly in Silicon Valley, with a few in Europe and Asia.

24. The intensity of competition between venture capital firms has swung back and forth. It favored the entrepreneur at the height of the boom days of the personal computer, biotech, and Internet eras. However, whatever the trend, venture capitalists still end up owning the vast majority of the stock of a start-up, typically in excess of two-thirds of the company.

25. Mergers and acquisitions of start-ups increase when the market for initial public offerings cools off and when initial public offering valuations are historically very high.

26. Investors' interests in new issues rises and falls depending on the interest of institutional investors in the stocks of public companies traded over the counter, as well as in blue chip stocks traded on the New York Stock Exchange. In general, windows for IPOs open and close, based on whether there is a hot market for stocks in general. E*Trade and other Internet era financial service firms have brought access to IPO offerings to the general public. By 2000, "day traders" were a factor in moving stock prices.

27. Pricing of private rounds of venture capital by investors follows the same financial guidelines and measurements used to price securities of publicly traded companies. Investors translate risks and rewards into acceptable levels of expected return on investment, which becomes the basis for the dilution of founders' shares.

28. Competition for the shares of a start-up is the best way to increase its valuation and to reduce dilution for founders. Competition is enhanced by careful planning of the strategy for the capital-raising campaign. However, such deliberate planning is noticeably absent among founders of high-tech companies, especially those started by engineers.

29. Venture boom-to-bust cycles have become a way of life. The boom times of the personal computer of the 1980s ended. Biotech arrived and ended. The Internet boom arrived in the 1990s. These caused wide swings in the financial return on portfolios of venture capital firms. Many firms failed and closed their doors, leaving nothing to their investors. Other venture firms survived and some thrived. This resulted in a hierarchy of venture firms, interrelated deal-making ("deal flow"), and politics. Portfolio returns have dropped as low as single digit ROIs and a few have risen above the 60 percent range.

30. Mixed sources of venture funding have become a way of life. As a number of venture firms died out, a need and opportunity was created for funds from other sources. One new source of venture funds is large public corporations whose business development leaders became very active in the Internet boom. There continues to be funding from non-American sources. Angel investors grew and were prominent in the early years of the Internet. Friends and family funding, as well as bootstrap funding, has continued since the earliest days.

31. Internal start-ups within established corporations are now a frequent phenomenon; they have allowed emerging growth companies to sponsor an entrepreneurial spirit while retaining an uninterrupted focus on the parent company's bread-and-butter business. For internal start-ups to be successful, special attention must be paid to the unique characteristics of such new enterprises, particularly freedom and compensation.

## Critical Issues

There are a number of key economic forces driving the venture capital funding of high-tech business.

- *ROI—return on investment—drives the start-up business.* It is measured in two ways: (1) A crude measure is that of how many times the value of one share invested rises by the time the initial public offering is over. This is called the "multiple." (2) A more sophisticated measure—the only number that really counts—is the annual compounded return, or percent per annum (p.a.), that the general partners in the venture capital firm return to the limited partners, pension funds, university endowments, and so on. To put it another way, how long the limited partners had to wait for the multiple to be returned determines the true percent annual ROI.

■ *Cash flow (the "burn rate") is what is managed.* All the accounting in the world does not matter to the founder who is struggling to meet payroll while launching the start-up's first products into a very competitive jungle.

■ *The IPO (initial product offering) is the holy grail.* Everyone has their eyes on that final goal. Mergers stand a poor second in attraction, because companies can generally negotiate higher valuations for a public issue.

■ *Liquidity ("exit strategy") is everything for the VCs (venture capitalists).* Anyone inhibiting attainment of liquidity quickly learns why VCs have earned a reputation as "vulture capitalists." A business plan must have an acceptable "exit strategy" that converts the investors' shares into cash.

Those are the economic laws that govern a start-up. The CEO who understands them will win more often and will survive to savor the grand IPO day.

## Venture Competition

Venture capitalists are driven by competing venture firms to maximize their return on investment. The general partners share in about 20 percent of the profits of a pool of money provided primarily by huge institutional funds, such as pension plans for Fortune 100 megagiants and billion-dollar university endowment pools.

If VCs earn a high enough ROI on their first pool of institutional funds, they will have a chance to bid for more. They are competing against the alternatives— such as the stock and bond markets—that are open to institutions. The economic and business factors that drive stocks and bonds also drive the VCs, and therefore must drive the start-up CEO.

## Venture Money Surge Leads to Problems

Venture capital partnerships have been a successful way of investing institutional money over long periods of time (ten to twelve years) for at first a limited number of investors. But with success, more money and more investors have followed. This in turn has led to serious competition between pools of venture capital. Since the surge of funds began in 1984, there has been a dramatic alteration of the risk-reward ratio for high-tech start-ups.

The *Venture Capital Journal* reported that during the ten years since 1977 the total of annual additions to venture capital partnership pools rose fifteen times, from a rate of about $200 million per year to more than $3 billion annually. This produced an excess of available venture capital and failures by many venture firms, which was followed by recovery, the arrival of the Internet start-ups, and more than $6 billion invested per year in the 1990s.

The $40 billion venture pool of the 1980s grew rapidly the following decade. By 2000, the venture capital pool was estimated by some to measure nearly $1 trillion, certainly $100 billion. The firms representing the pool continue to be flooded with business plans. Such increases intensify the simultaneous competition among start-ups that aim their technology at the same new perceived market opportunities. One example was the personal computer disk drive business, which boomed in 1984 and then went bust along with many start-ups. Another example is the minisupercomputer market; Convex and Alliant made it to IPO, but veteran venture capitalist partners say that another dozen companies or so were floating around at the same time the managers of those two founding groups were knocking on doors seeking seed rounds of venture capital. Internet start-up plans have flooded venture firms since 1995. In 1995, *Forbes* magazine reported that at least thirteen business plans were circulating in Silicon Valley the same month to do the same thing: sell pet food and products over the Internet.

Another effect of the success of venture capital investing is that big corporations have vastly improved their ability to see, decide, and act on new market opportunities. The giants have learned to invest their own "corporate venture capital." Since 1981, the number of acquisitions of venture-backed companies has more than tripled. And pioneering leaders of established public high-tech companies have invented a new form of internal venture capitalism dubbed "internal start-ups" or "start-ins." These have created successful new enterprises, attracted top managers, and proved to be successful in competing for already scarce high-tech talent.

# Result: Dilution, More Risk, Less Stock, Lots of Work

All of the forces just mentioned have increased the risk of failure of a high-tech start-up. Few if any other trends have emerged to offset this increased risk. Accordingly, investors have been following a trend of requiring higher and higher returns on the monies they have invested on behalf of their institutional clients. This means that less wealth is available to be shared by the founder and employees.

In modern portfolio terms, these trends have raised the cost of capital for the start-up. In more ordinary parlance, the founders have to give up a lot more of their companies today than they used to. Boom times appear to favor the founders, but over time the investors own the largest portion of the start-ups. In the 1970s it was not uncommon for investors to be in the minority. In the boom days of the 1980s start-ups such as Altos, Ashton-Tate, Microsoft, and Televideo went into business and retained 80 percent or more of their stock for employees and founders. After the bust of the 1980s, investors became the largest percentage owners. The explosion of Internet start-up deals in the boom time of the 1990s appears to have again changed the trend. Start-ups like Netscape and Yahoo went public very quickly, in less than three years, with investors owning less than 50 percent. Like the biotech boom days, some say the Internet IPOs were in essence a case of the public funding venture capital deals. With fewer employees, the founders ended up owning a larger portion of the company in the race to go IPO as soon as possible to fund the high cash burn rate of money-losing Internet start-ups.

The amount of stock given up by founders is spelled out in Chapter 7 in more detail. Research of Securities and Exchange Commission (SEC) documents by Saratoga Venture Finance revealed that, over the long term, CEO founders should expect to get to IPO owning not much more than 3 percent of their companies. That share of stock will be worth about $6.5 million at that time. They will have to work very hard for four to five years or more, and must have a lot of good fortune and big breaks to be able to cash all their chips in within two years after the IPO. Three years to IPO is rare, five is more common. And few get there (see Figure 1-1).

Is a start-up worth the personal cost required? That is among the key issues for the CEO considering a start-up and is discussed in Chapter 8.

And before a would-be founder can answer the personal questions, he or she must focus on another question: "How should I plan and control the venture capital formation process, from seed through multiround financing to IPO, so that I have an unfair advantage in getting the funds I need in order to succeed?"

## The Everlasting Process of Raising Capital and Other Stresses

The entrepreneur must realize that the process of raising venture capital never ends. From the first to the last of the fourteen stages of the venture capital formation process described in detail in Chapter 3, the CEO is continuously occupied with problems of how to raise needed capital. Experienced start-up staff members of both successful and unsuccessful companies said the same thing: "You never have enough money, things always take twice as long to do as you think, and there is never enough time to stop raising capital while you focus on running the company."

Figure 1-1. Chances of Success for a High-Tech Start-Up

Analysis of more than 300 start-ups since 1981 revealed the extra strains put on a CEO. Stress begins with the wide range of outside professionals—twenty categories can be cited—with whom the CEO must be in continuous contact, beginning almost immediately upon launch of the new enterprise. This puts a new kind of pressure on managers whose careers have typically been strictly "insider" executives. Such leaders are usually not experienced at dealing with lawyers, board members, bankers, leasing companies, landlords, Wall Street, and shareholders. Extra stress is added in boom times when investors and intense competition push the founder to run faster to the IPO in order to retain the "first mover advantage." More stress is added to the lives of founders who have never managed much if anything before in their lives. They are subject to extra pressures of "learning-on-the-fly" and how to deal with advice (what one wag called "adult supervision") from board members, venture capitalists, and others.

## Sources of Capital

The sources of venture capital are varied and often colorful and creative. For example:

- "Bootstraps" like eBay, of San Jose, California, get their first funds from personal savings and friends and relatives.

- "Angels" get start-ups rolling with their own seed money and hands-on help preparing for next-round funding from venture capitalists.
- "49er" start-ups like Netscape get seed money from their wealthy friends and founders (Jim Clark, prior founder of Silicon Graphics).
- "Classics" like Exodus Communications of Santa Clara, California, raise their monies from the usual VC gang at 3000 Sand Hill Road in Menlo Park, California, and other centers of venture capital such as those in Boston, New York, Dallas, Minneapolis, Denver, Seattle, and Los Angeles.
- "Creative" start-ups like Chips and Technologies and Worlds of Wonder get money from suppliers, landlords, and business partners who are acquainted with their skills as managers.
- "Hybrid" start-ups like AirFlash of Redwood City, California, get seed money from a mixture of angels, venture firms, and corporations like Intel and Lucent.

There are other unconventional sources of funding. Equipment lease firms provide substantial funds to augment equity capital of high-tech start-ups, and wealthy individuals continue to emerge as supporters of start-ups. Megabuck luminaries like Ross Perot are called professional "angels," and independently wealthy founders of start-ups are angels dubbed "49ers"—a term harking back to the gold rush successes in California in the 1849 era. Both represent unofficial pools of funds that go to work backing start-ups.

And the creative list goes on and on. Later in this book we will provide lists of venture capital sources.

More important than lists are techniques for planning and negotiating with money managers who are responsible for investing venture capital. Details are provided in case studies in later chapters.

## Some Findings About Rewards and Risks

Saratoga Venture Finance has carefully dissected the prospectuses of IPOs to extract the facts on the ownership, ROI, and sharing of the wealth among famous high-tech start-ups.

We found that CEO wages ranged widely, from base salaries of $65,000 per year to $230,000. The median in the nineties was about $150,000 for base salary plus significant bonuses prior to IPO. The trend is for cash compensation to rise as the number of start-ups grows and thus makes good management scarce. A good resource is www.advanced-hr.com, which publishes stock and pay compensation for venture-backed start-ups.

Investors dominate ownership; their proportion often exceeded 70 percent just before the IPO. There was no correlation between percent sold to investors versus the amount of capital raised. Boom to bust cycles greatly alter the ownership portions.

Return on investment of famous VC firms was slashed at the end of the 1980s after the shakeout following the personal computer–era boom. It became tough to repeatedly earn the 50 percent annual "slam dunk" of the boom days of 1978–1983. Kleiner Perkins and a few others managed partnership pools in the better days that returned nearly 65 percent p.a. In 1987 a portfolio return in excess of 25 percent p.a. would be among the top performers, according to private sources we polled, and average returns were around 17 percent p.a.

By 1990, we found that most portfolios had single-digit returns. "The turkeys hatched since 1983 have come home to roost," said one venture capitalist. Some pundits, major VC players themselves, said that there were some VC pools that lost all the investors' money by the time the partnerships were liquidated.

As 1990 arrived, along came the Internet boom and once again the ROIs jumped. By 2000, venture partners had returned to quoting 75 percent to 90 percent and higher returns on their investments!

Over the past two decades VCs have formed a vision of a "typical" portfolio of investments in start-ups. About 60 percent of the companies funded by VCs can be expected to go bankrupt. Fewer than 15 percent even get to IPO, and less than 10 percent is typical. Our database shows that 9.7 percent reach IPO. The remainder are either merged into large companies, sold off as "fire sales," or go on eternally as "zombies"—companies too small to get to IPO and not interesting enough to sell to other companies.

These and many other details about the companies studied are shown in the Saratoga Venture Tables in Appendix A; the tables include wages, options, founders' shares, venture capitalists' multiples earned, and how much the Wall Street firms got in fees to take the start-up public.

## The Personal Costs

Coping with political power plays is just one of the factors that contribute to the psychological and emotional costs of leading a start-up. There are many more, including the effects on the CEO's physical health and family. Some CEOs said they loved it anyway, while others said they hated every minute of it and would never do it again.

Some of our research in this area sharply contradicts popular myths. Here are highlights of what we found:

- *Hours worked per day for start-up CEOs are long, but are no more than those worked by an aggressive manager in a growing division of a much larger public company.* This surprised us, as it did most of the people we interviewed and analyzed. No one said that a start-up was *less* work than their last job as an employee.

- *Terror is a constant companion.* CEOs with experience often say "entrepreneurs should run scared." Based on our surveys, they do! *Inc.* magazine and other surveys and testimonials support the belief that fear of failure is a constant companion.

- *Founder CEOs seldom last as employees for more than three years.* This is universally lamented by all parties, including the VCs. We will discuss the reasons and cures later in this book. Silicon Valley psychologists report that few founders make it to the IPO without personal emotional trauma.

- *Burnout and heart attacks, marriage problems, and divorces are no more frequent than in other high-tech jobs.* Employees of start-ups may actually be a bit less prone to such problems if the CEO sets a good example of a balanced personal life, including regular exercise, enough sleep, proper diet, and time for family, friends, and spiritual matters.

- *Honesty and integrity (or a lack of them) are as common as in bigger companies.* Contrary to the expectations of some observers, no evidence could be found that the stress of a start-up produced a pattern of especially immoral, or moral, behavior.

# Future Trends

It is interesting to compare the predictions made by Saratoga Venture Finance in the first edition of this book and to make observations regarding the actual outcomes:

- A shakeout of venture fund managers will continue to occur, leveling out by the mid-1990s.

  *This has happened and the venture industry has settled down, led by the survivors, followed by growth in the form of fresh firms formed by former partners of the leaders.*

- The trends of the 1980s indicate a significant slowing of the flow of fresh funds into the earliest stages of new ventures. This will continue as surviving VCs spread their investments across all rounds of funding for new enterprises.

  *This occurred and continues today as venture firms pursue specialized strategies on funding different stages in the life of high-tech start-ups.*

- $2 billion to $3 billion of new venture capital will become available each year, sustaining the $40 billion pool at work in 1990.

  *The pool stabilized at $40 billion, with new funding running at $3 billion annually until the Internet boom arrived, then doubling to more than $6 billion invested annually from a pool that had more than doubled in size.*

- Some funds will never return. Others will diversify more, into low-tech and leveraged buyout investments. Offshore investing will be done by several, attempting to get away from intense U.S. venture competition. The remaining VC leaders will converge and dominate.

  *This is now the form of the venture community.*

- Specialization of venture sources will continue: biotech, electronics, and other segments of industry and technology.

  *This is how the venture industry segmented until the Internet boom added electronic commerce and related Internet companies as the newest addition.*

- Merger and acquisition activity will rise and fall in cycles that are the reverse of those of the U.S. stock market.

  *This has happened until Internet mergers arrived and grew with the stock market boom.*

- Business plan screening by VCs will remain generally quite tight. Those that best articulate the unfair advantage of the proposed business will get funded.

  *This remains one of the most important things a founder should know and respect.*

- Extra caution by VCs will require CEOs to be better prepared for their launch strategies. A candidate with successful prior experience as a CEO will be sought after first by investors.

  *The experienced CEO as founder is the number one concern of venture investors. Such leaders are very scarce.*

- More favor will be placed on deals with complete, first-class, experienced management teams with a long-run or "marketable" CEO in place. Inexperienced teams will find it very difficult to get money.

  *This is the rule; the exceptions come during boom times, such as in the Internet explosion, when "stand-in" managers are called upon to provide "adult supervision" and angels become very useful.*

- Attracting as complete a start-up core team as possible will be even more essential to success.

*Concept start-ups are difficult to fund; the key people should be in place on day one for technology, marketing, and management.*

- Corporate venturing will continue, mostly for secondary-stage funding. And the corporations will use more "internal venturing" structures.

*This is now a steady trend.*

- Foreign venturing, especially from Europe and Asia, will continue and even accelerate.

*Venturing from Europe and Asia is in place, but is not yet a dominant force.*

- The U.S. IPO market will continue its cyclical strength, subject to ups and downs resulting from excesses and from trends in the broader equity market.

*The steady growth of the U.S. stock market has fueled a record run of an uninterrupted IPO market.*

- New overseas markets for IPOs, the way London was in the 1980s and Taiwan was in the 1990s, will emerge and be tested during the remainder of the decade.

*This has been tested, but is still in its infancy. Europe continues to experiment with NASDAQ-type stock markets such as the Neuer Markt. Asia is working on the same.*

- Intense pressures will continue from investors for an exit strategy that gets them liquid within five years of investing.

*That is a rule and way of venture life.*

- VCs will be delighted to invest in deals whose prospects can get investors ten times their money in five years. VCs will compete even more aggressively for cream-of-the-crop deals.

*There now seems to be an annual phenomenon centered upon a small crop of "designer" start-ups in a category which the top-tier VCs all rush to fund simultaneously.*

- Investment banking desires for high-tech IPOs will not abate but will result in reshuffling the rankings of the leaders in that intensely competitive business.

*All of Wall Street now competes aggressively to do the best IPOs, from the smaller firms specializing in high-tech to the giant firms. Acquisitions and new e-firms have scrambled the rankings.*

- Employers and giant corporations will be more predatory in legal action aimed at preserving company proprietary intellectual property and key employees.

*There are now established legal guidelines to follow to stay out of trouble as a start-up.*

■ Tax uncertainties and trends toward more changes in accounting rules make the careful choice of a CPA firm more important in the 1990s.

*Software start-ups are especially affected by fresh accounting rules.*

■ A greater percent of ownership will be retained by founders who deliberately plan a capital-raising campaign complete with strategy and alternative sources of venture capital.

*Founders say they won more by being better prepared.*

■ The proportion owned by the CEO will decline a bit over the next decade as intra-VC competition wanes.

*The results show this has happened. Boom times cloud that general trend.*

■ Venture equipment lease firms will continue to bid for financing of the better deals done by the top VC firms.

*This has continued.*

■ CEOs will have more of an opportunity to set an example of a balanced personal life for the start-up culture, as the scarcity of qualified CEOs adds to their power.

*CEOs have become even more powerful as a result of the Internet boom and scarcity of experienced talent.*

## Strategies and Implementation

This book presents a classic strategy for starting a high-tech company and securing multi-round financing. The case studies provided in each section were chosen carefully to reveal how the classic strategy can be modified to fit the special objectives of the founding team.

The focus of the book is on how to use ROI know-how as an anchor in developing a start-up strategy, especially for pricing each round of venture financing.

The author hopes that the information provided here will allow the CEO to spend more time doing strategic thinking and finding and improving a sustainable competitive advantage for the company's long-term well-being.

If there are fewer failures, more jobs, and better lives as a result, the author will be very satisfied.

# 2

# Historical Overview

Start-up high-tech capital formation is the process that results in sufficient cash to fund the growth of a new enterprise. The entrepreneur should obtain this funding at a price low enough to continue to motivate the personnel talent that is needed to get the work done on time.

- Capital formation is a process.
- The process is ongoing for the start-up; it never ends.
- The process must be deliberately planned and managed.
- One measure of whether it is being successfully managed is the financial flexibility or adequacy of funds that the start-up survives on during the process.
- Another measure of success is how motivated key employees remain after they learn how much their holdings have been diluted by the latest round of funding.
- A final measure is how much the process has strengthened the company's "sustainable competitive advantage," also known as its "unfair advantage."

## How Entrepreneurial Capital Formation Has Evolved

In the twenty years up to the 1950s, venture capital was almost a hobby for the genteel rich: a game for those with inherited wealth, a small portion of which was invested in the revolutionary ideas of a few entrepreneurs. ROI was long in coming; seven to ten years was common. IPOs were rare and seldom reported in the *Wall Street Journal*.

During the 1960s, a few observant individuals talked some holders of wealth into pooling their funds in the form of limited partnerships for the specific purpose of regular investment in new companies, particularly those claiming to have made a technology breakthrough. This decade spawned Digital Equipment Corporation, Data General, and people like Arthur Rock, Tommy Davis, and Fred Adler, as well as Hambrecht & Quist—and a few dozen now-defunct companies in businesses like keyboard data entry, video records, custom mainframe software services, hang-on-the-wall TV, and undersea farming. Investors made money and lost some. And the name "venture capital" was launched.

The favorable results of the 1960s, particularly the high-tech boom of 1964 to 1969, led to a venture capital spurt in the early 1970s. It was short-lived and entrepreneurs soon saw the slowdown become rampant: Congress made changes that boosted the tax on capital gains; the U.S. culture went through the painful years of Vietnam; soaring inflation shot ROI (and dilution) requirements up to record levels. The result: Not enough new funds were attracted to replenish the fully invested venture pools.

By 1979, the annual additions to the limited partnerships under the management of independent private venture capital firms had sunk to less than $179 million, according to *Venture Capital Journal*. But good times were ready to stage a comeback. Political lobbying by electronic company alliances of venture capitalists and the CEOs of their start-ups were successful in attaining changes in tax laws. The changes favored high-tech companies engaging in intense amounts of R&D. And the capital gains tax was lowered significantly.

In 1980, the new funds rose to $681 million, and by 1983 they had soared to more than $3.4 billion for one year alone. Some economists said that the inflows were simply a result of lower ROI hurdles attributable to reduced inflation and the end of domestic turmoil over Vietnam. Others were adamant that the tax changes were critical in getting the new-funds faucet turned on again.

By the end of 1986 a total of $24 billion had been placed in the hands of general partners whose private venture capital firms filled a one-inch-thick directory of sources of venture capital. There were two major U.S. venture capital industry associations, complete with staffs who lobbied Congress and the White House.

Names like Microsoft and Lotus had become familiar to the general public, along with Gates and Jobs, Sand Hill Road, Silicon Valley, and Route 128. IPO was a set of initials known to most college graduates, and the word entrepreneur hit the covers of books on the *New York Times* best-seller list. And people had invested and lost in companies like Eagle and Visicorp.

Wall Street firms that had become contenders for high-tech IPOs included smaller, specialized firms such as Robertson, Colman & Stephens and large, widely diversified firms such as Goldman Sachs. The massive influx of competing money caused a scramble (some called it a shark-infested feeding frenzy). Venture firms began actively positioning themselves to be differentiated from the crowd. Some began to specialize. Fresh monies had already spawned the first generation of medical and biotech start-ups. The Genentech blockbuster IPO made it official: It was now legitimate to include the initials M.D. in the title of a CEO of a high-tech start-up. Electronic sectors like telecommunications were now large enough to attract venture firms committed to focusing most investments in a single sector. And a venture fund of funds called Crossroads was started successfully by Hal Bigler to invest in the best of the best venture partnerships.

After a short period of attempts to spin off defense technologies into start-ups, the next wave that triggered another boom was the arrival of the Internet in the 1990s. This kicked off yet another wave of fresh companies and IPOs of companies yet to earn a profit. Netscape represents the arrival of this new Internet era, and Yahoo became a household name. Cisco and Ascend were delivering the equipment to build the infrastructure of the Internet and every college student was building a personal homepage on the Web (and several were dreaming of starting their own new enterprise—many did). Small-cap stocks pushed the NASDAQ to record levels and Internet stocks climbed to valuations that no one had dreamed about. Venture firms were offered more capital to manage than they had room for. Another boom had arrived.

## Corporate Venture Capital

Meanwhile, back at corporate headquarters, the CEOs of the giants of the 1970s began to become more active in the high-tech start-up business. Venture investors had learned of the high prices that pharmaceutical giants were willing to pay for medical, biological, and genetic-engineering firms. Now they saw companies like Analog Devices, Apple Computer, Kodak, and Raytheon begin to invest directly in start-ups.

The corporate investors said they were mainly seeking access to new technology—that it was faster and cheaper to buy it than to invent it internally. Even IBM made forays in venture investing in the 1980s, using its own brand of investment. Its deals included the acquisition of Rolm.

Acquisitions accelerated during the late 1980s as corporations committed more funds to acquire start-ups, particularly before the new companies got past the IPO stage. Venture Economics reported that the number of such acquisitions of venture-backed companies rose from 32 in 1981 to 101 in 1985. Venture capitalists said the rate of deals continued high in 1986 and was even higher after the October 19, 1987, Wall Street crash.

Venture firms welcomed this additional channel for liquidity. The many floundering start-ups of the boom years of 1982–1983 were on the auction block for whatever they could fetch. The glory days of easy 50 percent annually compounded returns year after year were gone. Good and bad acquisitions were made. As one investment banker said, "Every company is worth something at some price."

By 2000, the large corporations of the 1980s wave mostly had ended operation of their own venture funds and instead were selectively investing directly in venture-backed start-ups. This in turn contributed to a new wave that included the hiring of VPs of business development at Internet companies like Yahoo and even Intel. Cisco and others began buying start-ups. A few corporations began creating "internal start-ups" or "spin-ins," using phantom stock for equity rewards. Lucent went public and creatively began forming new enterprises (from the ideas formed at their Bell Labs). People heard news daily about business partnerships between large companies and start-ups. Such commercial commitments had become part of the way of life for the giants.

## Wall Street and Investment Bankers

In the early days of venture capital, a few Wall Street firms made good money focusing some of their efforts on underwriting the few initial public offerings available in the 1950s and 1960s. They were dubbed "The Four Horsemen." Why this was so is not clear, although during our interviews the reference was often made to a recasting of the biblical four horsemen of the Apocalypse. Investors and CEOs beware? Anyway, the industry has always had a sense of humor.

The four firms were, in the approximate order of their power and influence in the decade of the 1970s:

Hambrecht & Quist, San Francisco, California
Alex Brown, Baltimore, Maryland
L. F. Rothschild, Unterberg, Towbin, New York, New York
Robertson, Colman & Stephens, San Francisco, California

These firms specialized in emerging high-tech growth companies and became well positioned to make a great deal of money in the boom of IPOs in the 1980s.

Until the PC boom legitimatized the high-tech venture capital and new issues industry as a place for serious investors to put part of their funds, high-tech stocks were left for the more unusual investors. The volatile stocks were mostly shunned by conservative equity investors from giant institutions who control the trillions of dollars invested daily on the stock exchanges of the United States.

Consequently, the main-line investment bankers, firms like Goldman Sachs and Morgan Stanley, also stayed on the sidelines, leaving the four horsemen to do most of the IPOs.

The PC boom of 1981–1984 changed all that.

By 1986, *Forbes* mixed into the "IPO Top 20" investment banking names like Goldman Sachs, Merrill Lynch, Kidder Peabody, and Morgan Stanley. Aggressive sales personnel from these firms, known as "new business managers," could be counted on to knock on any start-up's doors within weeks of its round-one funding. The competition had grown so fierce that, of the four horsemen, only Robertson, Colman & Stephens (renamed Robertson Stephens & Company) was ranked in the top ten that year. Rothschild was virtually out of the IPO business. Montgomery Securities took their place, only to be absorbed in the merger of the giants Bank of America and Nationsbanc.

The 1990s Internet boom bought even more change: Bill Hambrect left Hambrecht & Quist LLC to form a novel Internet-centric investment banking firm, W. R. Hambrect & Co. Sandy Robertson teamed with E*Trade, which formed E*Offering. Goldman Sachs put funds into Internet-based Wit Capital. After-hours trading started. Day traders began pushing the stock market. The old world of investment banking was entering another shake-up. Then Chase Manhattan bought Hambrecht & Quist LLC in 1999.

These Wall Street trends have reduced the cost of capital to start-up companies (competition to fund a start-up is said to be an entrepreneur's best friend) and are keeping the wealthy, powerful investment banking firms on their toes. It has not been uncommon for CEOs to drop a leading firm and pick a different one after their company's most recent financing was poorly handled.

A noticeable new-issues trend during the 1980s was the sharp drop in the number of years a start-up was in existence before it went public. Pressures for liquidity are always intense for all parties—venture capitalists, limited partners, founders, and employees. Venture Economics generated the comparative data on the number of years to IPO for start-up companies shown in Table 2-1. Several Internet start-ups went public in less than three years: MP3.com went public 16 months after inception at a valuation in excess of $1.8 billion!

According to several seasoned investors, premature offerings can kill companies and fool investors. The SEC knows this all too well. Each year a large number of opportunists attempt to bilk investors by offering securities of shaky start-ups. The well-known VCs and investment bankers shun such deals.

## TABLE 2-1. Trend in Years to IPO for Start-Up Companies

| IPO Year | Median Age of Companies at IPO |
|---|---|
| 1980 | 9.4 |
| 1981 | 6.0 |
| 1982 | 4.0 |
| 1983 | 4.0 |
| 1984 | 4.6 |
| 1985 | 3.7 |
| 1986 | 5.5 |
| 1987 | 5.4 |
| 1988 | 5.2 |
| 1989 | 6.4 |
| 1990 | 6.2 |
| 1991 | 6.5 |
| 1992 | 5.6 |
| 1993 | 6.6 |
| 1994 | 7.1 |
| 1995 | 7.2 |
| 1996 | 5.2 |
| 1997 | 5.6 |
| 1998 | 4.2 |
| 1999 (first half of year) | 4.1 |
| Median All Years | 5.6 |

*Source*: Venture Economics Information Services

The classic venture-backed firms have maintained good reputations. Most have yet to be involved with a major scandal on Wall Street. An exception was the legal harangue over Osborne Computer in the 1980s and a settlement in the 1990s between a top-tier venture fund and some disgruntled founders. Nonetheless, *Fortune* and *Forbes* constantly warn investors that IPOs represent dangerous waters for the naïve investor.

The Internet era has been great for investment bankers. They brought a record number of IPOs to market during the 1990s. And the fresh stocks did well, overall, for investors. The Internet stock feeding frenzy boomed and cooled and heated up again. Along with stratospheric rises in Internet valuations, Wall Street investors keep closer watch on the companies behind the stocks, particularly speculating on the rate of revenue growth and when each company would finally turn a profit. Will the boom continue? Well, for that we will have to wait and see.

# 2000 and the Next Century

So where has the capital formation process brought the start-up CEO and the venture capital business? For one thing, the start-up industry has arrived at a new stage in its maturity. That is a certainty. The implications of this new stage are very important for the budding start-up CEO to be aware of. Details follow in the next chapters. Here are a few items to keep in mind as you begin to form your start-up plans and look into entering the next century:

1. *Venture capitalists started taking more time, being much more thorough in doing their "due diligence" checking of a start-up, until the Internet boom came along.* They remember all too well when their portfolios returned single-digit rewards to their investors. By the time the feeding frenzy of the 1980s ended, the turkeys came home to roost. VCs became more careful about the intensely higher-tech start-ups in the 1990s. But our research revealed lots of Internet investments being made quickly, with some VCs bragging they made decisions in ninety-six hours.

2. *Complete management core teams are more eagerly sought after by investors, but are reluctantly conceded as inevitably missing.* The lack of adequate managers for start-ups has become the number-one lament of the investor. Start-ups beginning with a couple of young people with an idea are very unlikely to get any funding unless the idea is amazing and the founders are ready to step aside immediately for a new CEO supplied by the investors.

3. *Having a well-validated market was more necessary to attract capital until the Internet boom arrived.* The "cross your fingers and hope" days seemed to be over after the personal computer boom ended. Investors began to demand a more measurable quantification of the market with at least a plausible five-year forecast of revenues. Start-ups needed a want-to-be customer reference list of companies eager to buy the first product or service when it is ready. But the Internet "first mover advantage" motivated—some say panicked—many VCs into "story" or "concept" investing, and once again they began to make faster and faster investment decisions.

It all boils down to a contrast in investment philosophies. In the one camp is the investor seeing the need to move as fast as possible with the first good idea. In the other camp the investor sees the need for a better, well-planned business idea and a more thoughtfully prepared campaign for raising capital. Picking the right route is the primary responsibility of the founder CEO. This book is written to help you, the CEO, create and succeed with a better plan. The new century represents a time when the venture pools are full of capital looking for homes in exciting, promising start-ups. It is your job to tell the venture capital sources why your team should be funded next—at the price per share you are asking for. Chapter 3 will get you started with that process.

*3*

# The Process of Forming
# the Company

The founders can dramatically increase their chances for successfully raising the capital they need to start a new high-tech company if they understand the venture capital formation process. This chapter examines in detail the fourteen stages of this process, which is summarized in Table 3-1.

Each of the fourteen key stages has a main focus activity that must be adhered to. We will talk about the most likely amount of time required for each stage.

We will identify typical participants, along with the motivations of each, and suggest tactics for negotiating with them. We will describe what kind of help is needed to succeed at each stage.

Major costs are given for each activity of a key stage. Those numbers can be used to plan budgets. We will analyze the risks at each stage and make suggestions for reducing potential problems to manageable tasks.

For all fourteen stages we will present the output and the related ROI. Two case studies are included in the discussion of the stages. The first, Sigma Designs, Inc., provides a good illustration of bootstrapping; the second, Compaq Computer Corporation, illustrates stage 5, creating the business plan.

The initial stage is getting the idea for the company, while the last stages include the IPO and new relationships with Wall Street investors. The stages in between are equally important, each with its unique characteristics.

**TABLE 3-1. The Start-Up Capital Formation Process**

| Key Stages: | 1<br>Idea | 2<br>Kitchen<br>Table | 3<br>Founders'<br>Commitment | 4<br>Pullout from<br>Employer |
|---|---|---|---|---|
| *Main Focus<br>Activity* | • Secure a vision | • Solidify a dream | • Get firm<br>commitments<br>from key people | • Leave current<br>employer:<br>"stay clean" |
| *Elapsed Time<br>Required* | Months to years | 2-6 Months | 1-2 Months | 1 Month |
| *Typical Time<br>Schedule Cumulative* | — | Month 6 | Month 7 | Month 8 |
| *Typical Participants* | • Yourself | • Friends and<br>founders | • Founders only | • Founder<br>• Lawyer |
| *Help Needed* | • Creativity | • Confidentiality<br>• Business<br>judgment<br>• Technology<br>• Strategic thinking | • Commitment<br>of 1 to 3 founders | • Good legal<br>counsel:<br>intellectual<br>property and<br>labor law |
| *Major Costs* | • Own time | • Time of several<br>people | • Nerves to<br>commit | • Nerves to start<br>to live on own<br>savings |
| *Main Risks* | • Lacks<br>commercial<br>realism | • Secrets leak out | • Cold feet of<br>founders | • Counteroffers<br>or threat of legal<br>action by former<br>employers |
| *Results:<br>ROI & Output* | • Inspiration<br>and vision | • Crisp view of<br>risk-reward<br>tradeoffs | • Yes or no from<br>founder<br>candidates | • Clean, legal<br>separation from<br>former employers |

# Stage 1: Getting the Idea

One question that people often ask is, "Where do I get a good idea from?" Research shows that the sources are as varied as the activities of the human mind. Hobbies and personal pastimes rank high in the most often cited category. The personal passions of Steve Wozniak and Steve Jobs, and of Bill Gates and Paul Allen, resulted in two new companies, Apple and Microsoft. Other founders simply decided to leave a current employer and walk across the street to start a

| 5 Business Plan Creation | 6 Filling Management Team | 7 Raising Seed Capital | 8 Closing Capital & Incorporation |
|---|---|---|---|
| • Write fresh business plan | • Attract vital talent | • Get $ cash commitment from lead venture investor | • Get $ cash into bank account |
| 2-6 Months | 2-9 Months | 2-12 Months | 1-2 Months |
| Month 14 | Month 18 | Month 27 | Month 28 |
| • Founders<br>• Consultants<br>• Lawyer<br>• CPA Firm<br>• Patent lawyer | • Friends<br>• Consultants<br>• Media<br>• CPA Firm<br>• Recruiters | • Venture capitalists<br>• Consultants<br>• Founders | • Lawyer<br>• Venture capitalists<br>• Founders<br>  Commercial banker |
| • Wise business judgment, especially marketing and financing<br>• Sustainable ("unfair") advantage | • Candidates<br>• Compensation plan<br>• Wise people selection | • Whom to contact<br>• Coaching on presentations<br>• Judgment on pricing and valuation | • Good negotiating tactics<br>• Financial counsel<br>• Legal advice |
| • Time<br>• Personal computer<br>• Spread sheet<br>• Word processor<br>• Copy machine | • Lots of time for interviewing | • Time<br>• Patience<br>• Copies<br>• Deliveries<br>• Telecom<br>• Travel | • Legal fees |
| • Plan is not worthy of being funded<br>• Plan lacks distinctive competence | • Compromise<br>• No money, no hire<br>• Leaks of secrets<br>• Distractions from business plan | • No lead venture capitalist<br>• Get shopworn | • No cash, so must start over |
| • Inspired document<br>• Sustainable advantage<br>• Clever strategy | • Recruitment of top notch managers | • Firm commitments of seed venture capitalists | • $ Cash in the bank |

*continued*

new company in the same business, as was the case with SEEQ and Linear Technology.

The ideas are described monthly in a vast variety of magazines such as *Inc., Business 2.0,* and *Forbes.* In addition to being fascinating reading, the articles are provocative and can stimulate the entrepreneur looking for a good idea.

One thing is certain: Creative minds keep coming up with lots of fresh thinking. "There is no shortage of ideas!" exclaimed Regis McKenna, the public relations

**TABLE 3-1. The Start-Up Capital Formation Process (continued)**

| Key Stages: | 9<br>Finding a Home | 10<br>Start-Up | 11<br>Secondary Capital Rounds |
|---|---|---|---|
| *Main Focus Activity* | • Rent working quarters | • Hire people<br>• Get started building first product | • Raise more $ cash<br>• Leverage expensive equity |
| *Elapsed Time Required* | 1 Month | 6-18 Months | 2-6 Months each round |
| *Typical Time Schedule Cumulative* | Month 29 | Month 30 | In Years 2-4 after Seed Round closes |
| *Typical Participants* | • CEO<br>• Real estate broker | • Board of directors<br>• Investors<br>• Employees<br>• Suppliers<br>• Strategic partners | • Venture capitalists<br>• CEO<br>• Equipment lessors |
| *Help Needed* | • Real estate broker<br>• Facilities consultant | • Start-up experience | • Venture capital leads<br>• Equipment lessors |
| *Major Costs* | • Time<br>• Rental deposits | • Burn rate:<br>  $ per month | • Time of top management |
| *Main Risks* | • Bad choice: size, location, $ per month, wrong length of lease | • Short of good people<br>• Product completion slips<br>• Competition starts too soon | • Lack of management focus<br>• Run out of cash, miss payroll<br>• Bankruptcy |
| *Results:*<br>*•ROI & Output* | • Place to work for a year | • Live company in action | • Sufficient $ cash in bank<br>• Price per round higher than last round |

| | 12<br>Launch first<br>Product | 13<br>Raise Working<br>Capital | 14<br>Initial Public<br>Offering ("IPO") | Overall |
|---|---|---|---|---|
| | • Get customers | • Leverage equity | • Gets shares liquid<br>• Cash in some chips<br>• Celebrate | • Create and grow a viable, exciting, successful high-tech company |
| | 1-2 Years from start on work | 3 Months for each banking or leasing round | 4 Months including road show | 4-8 Years from start to IPO |
| | 24-36 Months | After first quarter of profitability | Goal: IPO ready at end of Year 3 | Aim at 5 years start to finish |
| | • Customers<br>• Whole company<br>• PR firm | • CEO<br>• CFO<br>• Commercial banker | • Investment banker<br>• Securities lawyers<br>• Wall Street analysts<br>• Industry media<br>• General public | • Many risk takers |
| | • Strong marketing skills<br>• Positioning of company and first product<br>• Cash reserves<br>• Quality of execution of plan | • Profitability<br>• Savvy banking and leasing contacts | • Timing<br>• Pricing of shares | • Lots of effort<br>• Several big breaks |
| | • Burn rate:<br>  $ per month | • Time of CFO and CEO | • Underwriters' fees<br>• Legal fees<br>• CPA fees<br>• Printer fees<br>• Travel costs<br>  Road show slides | • $3-$50 million of investors' capital |
| | • Lack of focus<br>• Product slips<br>• Poor market acceptance<br>• Big competitor counter-punch | • Have to use precious equity instead of cheaper loans | • Bad price per share<br>• Market window closes<br>• Business sours | • Company survives but is too small, not able to get public |
| | • Finish first product<br>• Begin first sales to customers | • Funding for growth in working capital needs | • Funding capitalists:<br>  × 5 to × 10 investment<br>• Founders: $ millions each<br>• Employees: × years of wages<br>• Image as successful company | • Viable company<br>• Great place to work<br>• Created $100 million of wealth<br>• Growing, high ROI business |

pioneer of high-tech, speaking to a newspaper reporter who had speculated that after the boom of 1982 to 1983 the gold vein had run out.

One other thing is certain: The VCs said they will continue to be willing to listen to fresh ideas of enthusiastic people. There are more than $100 billion in funds gathered by venture firms that are committed to financing new enterprises that use technology. Venture capitalists want to find good companies to invest their funds in.

**Main Focus Activity.** In stage 1, the founder-to-be with an idea should focus on this: *Secure a vision for a company.* The soul of a new company is born at this time. Without sufficient belief in the vision, the new idea for a business usually ends up as just a discarded dream. This vision becomes especially important later, in the formation of the company culture. And it shapes the sustainable competitive advantage.

**Time Required.** We have found that stage 1 usually takes shape slowly, over a period of at least a year, and commonly more. However, ideas that are formed quickly also can be successful. Bill Gates and Paul Allen were in college when a computer they saw on the cover of *Popular Mechanics* magazine set their juices boiling and led to the Microsoft success story.

**Typical Participants.** Stage 1 is the lonely stage, with the entrepreneur sitting alone contemplating the alternatives until they are either discarded or built into a structure ready to be discussed in secret with a trusted friend. This loneliness will not last—many other people in many roles will become involved as the process continues. Table 3-1 outlines who will be involved as the fourteen stages proceed, and in what order.

**Help Needed.** The most help needed during stage 1 is in the area of emotions. Psychologists tell us that this is a delicate time in one's personal life, when an individual does an immense amount of soul-searching. Emotions stored for years surface in surprising and often awkward ways. And one asks deep questions of oneself: "What do I want to do with my life? Do I want fame or financial success? Can I cope with the stress of leading a start-up? Will my spouse be willing to support me if I try to do a start-up?" Dealing with these questions at this time will increase the odds of success later. Stage 1 is a profound decision point, equivalent to deciding whether to have a first child or not, and why, and when, and at what cost; it has the same importance as deciding to become a parent.

**Major Costs.** The major cost at stage 1 is time—the founder's time. We found few if any out-of-pocket costs at this stage. Good thinking time was the major requirement for doing a good job at stage 1.

**TABLE 3-2. Participants in the Capital Formation Process in Typical Order of Involvement**

| | |
|---|---|
| 1. **The Person with the Idea** <br> The Leader | 11. **Commercial Banker** |
| | 12. **Real Estate** <br> Broker <br> Landlord |
| 2. **Key Followers** <br> Buddies <br> Founders | |
| | 13. **Key Suppliers** <br> Telephone <br> Insurance <br> Furniture <br> Utilities Benefits |
| 3. **Family** <br> Spouse <br> Children <br> Mom and Dad <br> Relatives | |
| | 14. **Recruiters** <br> Contingent <br> Retained <br> Buddy System |
| 4. **Friends** <br> Personal <br> Business | |
| | 15. **PR Firm** |
| 5. **Business Consultant** | 16. **Media** <br> Local <br> National <br> Industry |
| 6. **Lawyers** <br> General counsel <br> Patent | |
| | 17. **Customers** |
| 7. **CPA Firm** <br> Accounting <br> Taxes | 18. **Wall Street Analysts** <br> Securities and Exchange <br>    Commission <br> Wall Street analysts <br> Investment bankers <br> Investment speaking forums |
| 8. **Venture Capitalists** <br> Venture firms <br> Corporate investors | |
| 9. **Board of Directors** | |
| 10. **Equipment Leasing Company** | 19. **General Public** |

*Source*: Saratoga Venture Finance

**Main Risks.** There is one major risk in stage 1: lack of realism. Realism is a must, if only to help the founder focus on obstacles and create out of them a sustainable competitive advantage. This is the time when the would-be entrepreneur must quickly get away from dreaming and into the realm of possibilities.

However, a vision is necessary, if only to sustain an individual who is up against seemingly impossible odds. Here is how one veteran of the personal computer era put it to Paul Zachary of the *San Jose Mercury News* in 1987: " 'We were damn fools,' says [Lee] Felsenstein, who designed the pioneering Sol computer in 1976 and later the Osborne 1. 'We just ignored the dire predictions that it couldn't be done.'"

**Output and ROI.** The founder's main output and return on investment in stage 1 will be these:
- *Enjoyment.* At the very least, there is the fun of dreaming.
- *Inspiration.* One's creativity will have been stretched.
- *Personal profile.* Would-be entrepreneurs will know much better who they are and what their source of purpose and fulfillment in life is.

And the individual who decides to go on to stage 2 will have constructed that precious "vision for my own new company."

# Stage 2: Meeting Around the Kitchen Table

Now the excitement starts to rise. The founder thinks he or she has a good idea and must take the vision to the next step. Stage 2 is the first testing ground and involves a brief, intense burst of private activity.

**Main Focus Activity.** The main focus in stage 2 should be: *Solidify a dream.* This is the time to start refining the vision into the stuff that successful new enterprises are made of. It takes dedicated blocks of time to do it and requires openly sharing the vision with a few trusted friends, in familiar circumstances. Our interviews revealed that *it was true*—most of these meetings took place around kitchen tables!

**Time Required.** Stage 2 took most start-ups from two to six weeks to complete. The discussions varied in intensity; some of the CEOs we spoke with had only a couple of meetings; others went to four- and eight-hour sessions on weekends.

**Typical Participants.** At stage 2 entrepreneurs first share their vision with a trusted friend or two. In our interviews we found that this person often became an active participant later in the life of the start-up, often as a cofounder. Stage 2 also included contact with a respected new businessperson, former start-up leader, lawyer, or start-up consultant experienced in doing venture capital deals. As Mike Phillips, formerly of the Palo Alto law firm of Morrison & Foerster put it, "My firm and others with venture experience in Silicon Valley see all kinds of people in a week who are trying out a new idea. The person is understandably quite cautious and needs to talk confidentially with someone connected to the venture capital world, someone who can help steer the founder's vision, usually toward more realistic thinking about what makes a successful start-up, the kind of thinking that can increase the likelihood of the founding team getting their seed round of venture capital."

**Help Needed.** Stage 2 requires help in maintaining confidentiality and getting good business judgment. The only way to have confidentiality is through personal trust and discipline. We found no one who used nondisclosure documents in stage 2.

Good business judgment came from the quality of the professionals and veterans that the founders talked to.

**Major Costs.** Like the prior stage, stage 2 costs time—of at least one more participant. Some lawyers will work for brief periods of time without charging a fee. It is important for the founders to ask how the attorney will charge them. (See Chapter 4 for details on how to select the best legal counsel.)

**Main Risks.** The top danger in stage 2 is that the secret could leak out. It is dangerous if one's current employer gets word that an employee is forming a new company—before the employees have prepared for departure (see "Ethical Departure from an Employer" in Chapter 4). It is even worse if the idea gets snatched up by someone else, including another start-up group or even that same current employer. Founders told us of the extraordinary efforts they used to conceal the proprietary nature of their ideas. And we heard a few sad stories of people who lost their ideas and never got started at all. Others got started but were stopped by lawsuits disputing rights to intellectual property and people.

**Output and ROI.** When stage 2 is done, the founders will have sorted out the risk-reward trade-offs. Paperwork was rare at this stage, probably because of the intense need to keep ideas confidential.

## Stage 3: Getting the Founders' Commitments

Stage 3 is next, and the excitement grows. This is a delicate phase in the life of the start-up, one that begins to separate the doers from the dreamers.

**Main Focus Activity.** In stage 3, the successful start-up CEOs should focus on this: *Get firm commitments from key people.* That sounded easy to us, but the CEOs said this was hard. Even worse, however, several said they got into trouble because they skipped over this step.

This was the problem: When the pressure rises, the core team quits. It is difficult to stand up to rough personal negotiations and nerve-racking waiting time. Employers fight to retain good people. The CEO who has not obtained *firm* commitments from the core team is very likely to find his company melting before his eyes like butter in summer heat.

A sense of reality is crucial. It is better to find trusted friends dropping out at this early stage than see them quit later, when keeping the core team intact affects capital funding. Such last-minute dropouts can kill a venture capital deal before it is funded.

**Time Required.** We found that start-ups spent one to two months getting personal commitments from the core team. This was often done in parallel with the stage 2 kitchen-table talks, but successful CEOs preferred not to proceed to stage 4, pullout from employer, until stage 3 was completed.

**Typical Participants.** In stage 3 the work is concentrated on the founders. Other key personnel, such as good circuit designers and software programmers, are put on hold for a while. This is done to solidify the core of the team, the core that would be presented to the venture capitalists as competent, qualified, and able. It is also the team that will share the most in the financial spoils and be directly involved with presentations and negotiations.

**Help Needed.** The original founders need help from additional founders, typically one to three other people. Each will be needed to help assess the others, particularly the likelihood of their actually joining the start-up when the CEO tells them that "now is the time."

**Major Costs.** The major cost in stage 3 is to the nerves. The entrepreneur must confront people and get them to either commit or drop out. There may be key people whom the founder senses may drop out if they get cold feet after their employer threatens legal action. The founder must now be able to count on the core team that is so necessary to get the company off the ground.

**Main Risks.** The major risk is not doing this step and finding out later in a critical moment that the team consists of a bunch of people that are only half committed to the founder's vision of a start-up.

Cold feet on the part of cofounders are dangerous; this can sink an enterprise later on, just when raising seed capital seems to be going well. We heard several sad tales of exactly that happening.

**Output and ROI.** Go/no-go decisions and firm handshakes are the precious outputs in stage 3. That sets the foundation for a shared vision, one that has a core of committed, enthusiastic founders to lead it.

# Stage 4: Pullout from Employer

Now the test of nerves begins as pressures mount. It is time for the founders to break away from current employers and begin working full-time on the new enterprise. Here is where a lot of different approaches to start-ups appeared in our research.

Venture capitalists were overwhelmingly consistent here; all said, "Leave your current employer before you write your business plan." Venture capitalists hate investing in a start-up that gets bogged down in lawsuits that drain precious time and cash resources. The case histories of the SEEQ and Linear Technology lawsuits between former employers and the founders are classics that formed this rule of venture capitalists.

Some venture capital firms will actually lend the core team a room, telephone, and computer to support them in writing the business plan.

However, the founders of one class of start-up, called "bootstraps," argue against leaving employers until later on in the life of a start-up, in order to continue earning wages until the last possible minute. This breed of start-ups is exemplified in the following case study.

---

## *Case Study: Sigma Designs*

Sigma Designs is a classic example of a bootstrap. Here is how the founders did stage 4, as reported by Steve Kaufman of the *San Jose Mercury News*:

> The Sigma story started in February 1982, when several engineers at Amdahl Corp. tinkered with an add-on, PC memory board in one of their homes in Sunnyvale. The venture started out as a hobby, but the thing worked, and they realized it might generate a lot of business. They displayed it at the annual PC Fair in San Francisco, advertised a little in a personal computing magazine, and added a so-called multifunction board to their product line.
>
> A year later, they were selling one hundred boards a month at $500 to $600 a shot, and Jimmy Chan, the vice president of product development, became the first to leave Amdahl to work in the business full-time. Tran, the president, followed him eight months later, at which point the company was producing $125,000 in monthly sales. When Jason Chen, the vice president of manufacturing, joined the company in June 1984, monthly sales had skyrocketed to $800,000.
>
> Sigma went public on May 15, 1986.

Most well-known start-ups are not bootstraps, but follow the more classical process outlined in this report.

---

**Main Focus Activity.** In stage 4, the focus is this: *Stay clean.* The objective is to avoid being sued by a former employer. And the goal is to leave with a "win-win" solution. When Sierra Semiconductor founders left National Semiconductor, they left with a cordial relationship, and contracts were soon signed that gave both parties access to technology, products, and production. Jim Diller and his core team took Sierra public in 1991. That was quite different from the lawsuits that transpired between Linear Technology and National in the early days of Linear. Linear's Bob Swanson and his core team were pioneers, and legal precedent was set by the outcome of this core team's departure from National. Linear went public in 1986. The 1990s were relatively free of lawsuits from former employers.

**Time Required.** It took about one month on the average for founders to clear out of their employment situations. Anticipation of this event can speed up the departure time, especially for engineers and other personnel who can get tied up in longer projects that they feel obliged to complete before joining the start-up. Jerry Anderson, founder of the computer-aided engineering start-up Valid Logic of San Jose, California, said he lost six precious months to hard-charging competitors Mentor Graphics and Daisy Systems because the technical founders were tied up in completing work at Lawrence Livermore Laboratories and finishing their Ph.D.s.

**Typical Participants.** The main concern is to get the founders away from their employers and on the job with the next stage of the start-up. CEOs advised against becoming distracted at this time by attempts to also get the next wave of employees out of their jobs.

**Help Needed.** Founders should be getting top legal help at this stage. We studied several start-ups that simultaneously engaged two law firms: one for general legal counsel and the other for intellectual property. This reflects the growing importance of creating and protecting companies' intellectual property.

**Major Costs.** It is at this stage that the first cash costs start. If founders leave their employers before the seed round is raised, they must live off their savings or do some part-time work such as consulting.

Some law firms ask for a small retainer; $1,000 per month was often cited. Many others, particularly the veteran firms familiar with start-ups, did work on contingency in this stage, some risking $30,000 in fees that the start-up would get funded.

**Main Risks.** The number-one risk is a lawsuit by a founder's former employer.

The number-two risk is losing a founder to an employer's counteroffer.

The number-three risk is a lawsuit by a company for which a founder is doing part-time consulting.

**Output and ROI.** The gold medal in stage 4 is that the members of the founding team achieve a clean pullout from all their employers.

# Stage 5: Creating the Business Plan

Stage 5 is the time when the founder's vision goes on paper in the form of a business plan. This is where hard decisions are made, ideas discarded, and fresh breakthrough strategies documented. It is hard work.

**Main Focus Activity.** The focus at this stage is on *writing a well-conceived business plan.* It is more than words or a financial forecast that shows yet another $100 million start-up in five years. Rather, it is a written plan that tells how the founders plan to turn their vision into a sustainable competitive advantage. Tips from the pros are presented in Chapter 5, "Preparing the Business Plan."

**Time Required.** Founders reported that they needed a lot more time than they thought to prepare their business plan. Two to nine months must be allowed. Most start-up personnel underestimate the time requirement of this phase by a factor of two. The following case study reveals how that happened to one of America's most successful start-ups.

---

## Case Study: Compaq Computer

Here is how *BusinessWeek* reported Compaq's experience with the stage 5 process in its cover story of June 29, 1987.

> But after 13 years, Canion tired of [Texas Instrument's] bureaucratic style and its emphasis on technical excellence at the expense of marketing. The turning point came in 1980. After he set up a disk drive manufacturing unit, Canion was abruptly transferred to another business unit because management considered his job finished. The job just begins when you start selling product, he contends. You need to continue the marketing focus. The last straw was his assignment to the group designing TI's first office microcomputer. Canion quit within 18 months because he felt management misunderstood personal computers. His biggest gripe, ironic in light of Compaq's present market battle: TI wouldn't accept the importance of IBM's products.
>
> Canion and TI buddies William H. Murto and James M. Harris set up Compaq—

and promptly got off to a slow start. Contrary to its early advertising, the company did not spring to life one afternoon when the founders sketched the idea for a portable PC on a napkin at a Houston pie shop. According to L. J. Sevin, Rosen's partner in Sevin Rosen Management, Canion called with a plan for building circuit cards to expand the storage capacity of IBM PCs. Sevin was underwhelmed. He felt that the product was "a little too easy to do. We made him go back to the drawing board."

Canion's fourth or fifth idea clicked. It was for an IBM-compatible portable. With $1.5 million in seed money, Canion and his crew began designing Compaq's first PC in February 1982. By early 1983, when Compaq began shipping its portables, the company had raised $30 million. In late 1983 it raised $66 million more in a public offering, then finished the year with sales of $111 million.

---

**Typical Participants.** Now enters the "herd of helpers." They are used by the CEOs of successful start-ups to prepare a better business plan. This list includes:

- *Founders.* The founders meet as a group to talk, write, and edit.
- *Consultants.* These local consultants specialize in work for a fee in the risky, pre-seed-round stage of a start-up. Several also stand in as CFO, or even CEO or VP of marketing. Some are also angel investors.
- *Lawyers.* Both general and intellectual property counsel can make important contributions.
- *CPA firm.* CPAs help with the numbers, but a quality firm will act as a great business advisor as well. (See Chapter 5's section on "The Role of a CPA Firm" for advice on how to pick a good firm.)

**Help Needed.** The most help the founders will need will be in the strategic thinking area, principally in marketing and financing. And no matter what skills exist in the founding technology team, observers were firm in their insistence that there were never enough effective results in the area of working out a sustainable or unfair competitive advantage. (For tips on how to solve this thorny, critical problem, see Chapter 5's section on "The Importance of Unfair Advantage.")

**Major Costs.** Major costs will be kept low if the founders can convince the herd of helpers mentioned above to work for free for a while longer. If not, the CEO must start adding up the hours per helper and multiplying by hourly billing dollars. Top venture capital law firms in Silicon Valley bill senior partners at $250 per hour and higher. Top CPA partners are billed at slightly lower rates. For contrast,

New York lawyers cost at least $100 more per hour, frequently $300 more per hour and higher but have less start-up experience.

Most veteran legal and CPA firms will work out a custom arrangement. An introduction through a close friend or consultant can be very helpful.

Other costs to be covered are typing and copying, secretarial, and supplies. The fledgling group will need a personal computer and spreadsheet software. Saratoga Venture Finance has created a special software package called QuickUp™, which forecasts financial statements running on a spreadsheet like Excel. It includes a handy set of tools to get the CEO of a start-up off to a flying start with a complete set of financial projections. (See www.startupweb.com for details on what QuickUp contains, how it works, and how to obtain a copy.) The purpose of the software is to encourage the entrepreneur to do more strategic thinking and less time-consuming modeling and financial forecasting.

**Main Risks.** The number-one risk is that the founder will produce a plan not worthy of pursuing, and that the hard work up to this point will appear to have been for naught. That has happened to the best of the start-ups, as Compaq's founders learned.

The number-two risk is that the plan will not be worthy of being financed but will be funded anyway. This strange phenomenon was encountered in several of the start-ups we interviewed. VCs often said they bet on a team of experienced managers much more than on their business plan. The risk in this situation is that no one is very sure what is going to happen.

**Output and ROI.** The gold medal is for a business plan that is an inspired version of the founder's vision, built on a foundation of a well-thought-through sustainable competitive advantage.

# Stage 6: Filling the Management Team

By this stage there is a business plan in which the founders have confidence. There is also a set of projections showing the head counts needed to set the new company in motion. Now comes the task of filling out the rest of the team, particularly key managers. Who, when, and for how much stock?

Chapter 6, "The Team," discusses in detail what venture capitalists look for in the people involved in a start-up.

**Main Focus Activity.** Focus in stage 6 is this: *Attract the vital talent.*

Some investors will bet almost solely on the people leading a start-up. They argue that if all else goes wrong, top people can recover and at least make something of what otherwise would be a wipeout. The key to success here is to gain an understanding of what vital talent is all about.

**Time Required.** This is a very time-consuming step. Our interviews revealed that from two to nine months can be expected to elapse before the CEO assembles a complete team of talented leaders who will pass the tough scrutiny of the best venture capitalists' secret checkouts of chosen personnel.

**Typical Participants.** Start-up CEOs used about every conceivable means to find and attract top personnel. Interviews showed that the primary method was the buddy system. Through word of mouth, friends pass along the news that someone is forming a start-up and needs certain talent.

Second was the use of the "herd of helpers" from stage 5. The CPA firms were surprisingly helpful in finding marketing and sales candidates as well as accountants. They are careful to avoid recruiting from among their clients. The top high-tech CPA firms consist of very well-connected businessmen.

The third method was use of the media, either in the form of "leaked" PR or in recruiting advertisements. Some start-ups received a great deal of response to an ad that announced that a start-up was in formation. More common, however, was an interview with the business editor of the local newspaper, who was given an exclusive on the story of the entrepreneur leaving a famous employer to start his own company. The published articles attracted a lot of attention, including that from venture capitalists.

The fourth method was engaging recruiters. This method was used almost exclusively after the seed round, and especially when the founders needed a strong CEO. Not all founders want to be the CEO of a start-up; instead they prefer to become chairman *and* CEO, leaving daily tasks to chief operating officers (COOs) and presidents. Needless to say, recruiters are very expensive for a start-up, with or without seed capital in the bank. (See Chapter 6 on more pros and cons of the use of this and other methods of hiring needed talent.)

**Help Needed.** Help in making wise judgments is what is needed most in this stage. It is worth more than gold.

Finding scarce talent is the second area in which help will be needed. Founders should remember that A-quality players attract A-quality players.

A thorough compensation plan will also be needed, prepared in advance of actual recruiting. Wages, bonuses, and stock (founders' shares and incentive stock options) must be ready in writing, in terms of dollars, formulas, and number of shares. Sadly, good plans for distribution of shares beyond the core team are typically nonexistent.

**Major Costs.** Everyone agreed here: Recruiting takes enormous amounts of time. This will be the entrepreneur's greatest cost at this stage.

Only rarely did start-ups recruit from out of town and thus incur the related high cost of such travel expenses. Relocations of families did occur, though rarely.

**Main Risks.** Here are the major risks, listed in the rank order mentioned in our interviews, starting with the most significant and most likely:

1. *Compromise.* CEO after CEO said "Do not, under any circumstances, compromise your high standards in order to attract a warm body to complete your team."
2. *No dough, no deal.* If your company is not funded, candidates often say no. Yet such people are needed to help attract funding. This Catch-22 was commonly the lament of founders in this stage. Chapter 6 details techniques used by CEOs to deal with it.
3. *Leaks of secrets.* CEOs told horror stories about marketing and technical candidates who said no to offers of employment, then returned to their employers and disclosed a great idea that they had discovered during interviews at a start-up.
4. *Distraction.* Not only does recruiting not advance any product development work or market research, but it can even threaten a business plan if a series of experienced candidates tell the CEO they think it will fail for very plausible reasons, some of which the CEO had not yet thought of.

**Output and ROI.** At the end of this stage, the CEO will have all vital talent committed to joining the start-up, at various agreed-upon dates.

# Stage 7: Raising Seed Capital

The founders must have a strategy for attracting investors. They must decide which VC firms to contact, how to get ahead of all the other hungry business plans on the VCs' desks, and how to demonstrate convincingly that they have an unfair advantage.

**Main Focus Activity.** Here the focus is: *Get a firm commitment from a strong lead venture capital firm.* Once the lead firm provides backing, other investors will follow.

**Time Required.** According to our research, this phase typically takes a long time, much longer than the founders anticipated. Anything from two to twelve months can be expected, with nine months the median.

**Typical Participants.** There are three categories of participants at stage 7:

1. Venture capital partners and their technology and market consultants.
2. The entrepreneur's own coaching consultant, if one can be engaged.
3. The start-up's core managers, whether or not they've left their employers.

**Help Needed.** The founders will need help in three main areas:

- *Who to contact.* (See Chapter 9 for help here.)
- *Coaching on presentations.* Founders need to understand the ways and wiles of venture capitalists; see Chapter 9.
- *Valuation, dilution, and deal pricing judgment.* Here is where millions of dollars of potential wealth are negotiated. Chapter 9 provides special case studies of two start-up deals. Saratoga Venture Finance has researched how much of the company the start-ups had to sell, at what prices, and for what percentage of the start-up. The shares are accounted for and presented later in this book in the form of the Saratoga Venture Tables™ to assist the CEO in negotiations with experienced venture capitalists.

**Major Costs.** Major costs at Stage 7 will be these:

1. *Time,* to pitch to a lot of venture firms, some several times.
2. *Emotional stress,* particularly trials of patience and fear of failure as personal cash dwindles, as a spouse doubts the company will ever get started, and as the founder goes through the first roller-coaster ride of a venture deal.
3. *Cash expenses for travel to VCs* (rarely have VCs paid for a founder's travel to see them), copying expenses for reproduction of business plans, Federal Express charges (everyone seemed to send every business plan by overnight mail), and telephone bills. At least $1,000 must be reserved for these expenses.

**Main Risks.** The number-one risk cited was *getting no lead VC.* Someone must step up to take the lead.

The number-two risk is *getting shopworn.* This is tricky to avoid and quite important. (See Chapter 9 for help.)

The third risk is *selling stock too cheaply.* Valuation work was typically done naively, without adequate facts or detailed calculations. Chapter 9 will help the CEO plan this strategy.

**Output and ROI.** The founders want four things at the end of this step:

1. A committed lead venture capital firm backing the start-up.
2. Firm dollar commitments for a percentage of the start-up company.
3. A fairly priced deal.
4. A timetable for getting to the closing date, with cash in the bank.

# Stage 8: Incorporation and Cash in the Bank

This is the stage at which the founders must select an attorney to close the deal with the funding sources and to incorporate the company. A commercial bank must be selected so that the funding sources' money can be deposited. When this stage is complete, money is finally available to do the work that until now had been just a powerful vision.

**Main Focus Activity.** In this step, there is one and only one focus: *Get the money in the bank account.* Salespeople call it "closing the deal."

It is insufficient to get a venture capital firm to say it will do the deal. The founders must get cash in the bank. As the ancient proverb puts it, "There is many a slip 'twixt the cup and the lip."

**Time Required.** It always takes longer than anyone believed likely. One should expect one and sometimes two months for the lawyers for the start-up company and those for the venture capitalists to do their work—that's how long it will take until the negotiating work results in a deposit slip in the new company's bank account.

**Typical Participants.** The people the CEO and other founders will work most closely with at this stage are:

- *Lawyer.* A good attorney is needed for incorporating the company, distributing founders' shares, and the considerable other legal work. (See Chapter 4 for more details.)
- *Commercial banker.* A good bank—one whose focus is servicing business accounts—is needed for a place to park the cash, invest it, set up a checking account, and do the company payroll. (See Chapter 11, "Commercial Bankers," for the services of a banker in this phase of a start-up's life.)
- *Founders.* Founders will participate in negotiations. For the first time, founders will see one another behaving as a group around the negotiating table. We were warned to expect anything from such participants in this

phase, especially in discussions on how much of the company to sell to the venture capitalists.

■ *Venture capitalists.* VCs will be the heavies at this stage, for obvious reasons. Chapter 9 reveals how successful CEOs negotiated with the VCs and got good deals.

**Help Needed.** Most of all in this stage, the founders will need good negotiating skills, street-smart tactics, and strategy.

**Major Costs.** The major cost will be for legal services. It can be hard to get a law firm to do the work on a contingency basis, but several CEOs succeeded in doing so because the likelihood of funding appeared so good. The founder should plan to incur at least $3,000 to $5,000 in legal and related expenses by the time the seed-round deal is completed successfully.

**Main Risks.** The main risk is *getting no cash*. This happens to successful start-ups, however. Compaq was mentioned earlier. Another example is Gordon Campbell, who, after getting no venture funds, changed strategy. He raised funds for the amazingly successful Chips and Technologies, Inc., of San Jose, California, without a penny from the classic venture capital firms.

The next biggest risk is investors dropping out of the funding. We were told of many, many cases in which the lead venture firm suddenly bowed out without any warning. Chapter 9 discusses why CEOs believe this happens and how to handle it.

The final major risk is the notorious *creeping close*. This is a dread disease that all CEOs feared the most. It happens when everything is done, but the money is not yet in the bank. Everything seems to take "just a few more days" and the requests for information seem endless. A CEO of a minisupercomputer start-up in southern California told us, in gripping detail, how his team finally got their seed round and celebrated at the president's beachfront home. People resigned from their employers the next day. And the following Monday afternoon the lead VC firm called to announce its pullout from the deal due to unforeseen internal problems of the firm. (See Chapter 9 for more stories of intrigue.)

**Output and ROI.** Getting the cash in the bank. After it is counted—then, and only then, should the founders and managers celebrate.

## Stage 9: Finding a Home

Now there is money in the bank! The time has come to spend some of it and get a place to work—other than around the founder's kitchen table.

**Main Focus Activity.** In stage 9, the focus is simple: *Get appropriate working quarters.*

**Time Required.** This usually takes a month or two—the time to look for working quarters, sign the thick lease documents, and get the place cleaned up before you move in.

Getting a facility for heavy manufacturing can take longer, although most CEOs said one month was all it took for them to make up their minds. The paperwork can take a few weeks to finish. The landlord may have to paint and clean up before you can move in.

**Typical Participants.** The lead participant at this stage is a real estate broker. However, going direct may be better and can produce some surprisingly favorable benefits. Chapter 10, "Leasing as a Source of Capital," presents a fascinating case study involving the landlord as venture capitalist. And the founders at one manufacturing-intensive start-up hired a financial consultant to help them attract venture leasing funding because of the large amount of capital equipment that the factory would tie up.

**Help Needed.** A real estate broker experienced in the special needs of start-ups was very helpful, according to several CEOs. A founder benefits most from a broker's hands-on experience with a start-up in this phase. CEOs told us about lots of tricks to save on capital and cash flow. These included complex terms and conditions in the lease with respect to flexibility in future moves to other quarters.

Furniture, cubicles, phones, and computers eat up about $2,000 to $4,000 per employee, more for engineers with workstations. Leasehold improvements used up large, unplanned chunks of the budgets of several start-ups that we spoke with. Unused rented space is a terrible waste of capital. And the CEO must decide how long a lease to sign, for how many square feet, of what kind of space.

**Major Costs.** The major cost will be the CEO's time to find the home. The broker's fee is passed back to the start-up but is buried in the monthly lease of the facility.

Some start-up CEOs deliberately rented facilities and furniture on a month-to-month basis until round one funding was completed. Their strategy was to buy time and cash savings until the full-time start-up team could refine the business plan to a greater degree.

**Main Risks.** Your biggest risk is: *Picking a bad facility.* There are a number of things that could make your new quarters a bad investment:

- *Bad location.* You can't attract the new hires. It could be a poor commute, for example.
- *Wrong image.* Again, you can't attract new hires if your quarters project a cheap appearance.
- *Wrong size.* Too small is as bad as too large.
- *Monthly rent too high.* This wastes precious cash.
- *Too long a lease.* Yes, it is tough to predict the speed of the start-up's growth, but someone must pick a number.

**Output and ROI.** The result is simple: The start-up now has a good home. A great home will increase the ease of attracting fine employees and impressing good customers.

# Stage 10: Starting Up

With a home of its own (for the next three to five years), the new company is now ready to *officially* get started.

**Main Focus Activity.** Our CEOs were about equally split on priorities at this stage, so we list both of them as equally important:

1. Hire the necessary people.
2. Get started building the first product.

Some CEOs remembered getting burned by starting work too soon or by losing many months in launching the first product because they put off hiring extra people until much later. Hiring almost always falls behind plan.

**Time Required.** It takes from six to eighteen months to get the first product ready to ship to the first customer. CEOs said that six months meant that either: they had done some of the product development with their former employer's support (Sierra Semiconductor is a good version of this arrangement), or they had built the prototypes in their garage before leaving their employer (see Case Study: Sigma Design Systems).

CEOs also said that VCs get very nervous if the first product takes much longer than eighteen months to get to market. Closing of market windows is a constant threat. Chapters 6 and 10 discuss this problem in more detail. Medical, bio, and genetic engineering start-ups have taken the longest time to develop their first products, while software and Internet portals are expected to take the shortest time to get to market. Electronic hardware-based systems fall between those two categories.

**Typical Participants.** At this stage the CEO is confronted with a new—often frighteningly new—set of participants. These include the new boss: the board of directors.

Others include investors not on the board, all the new employees the CEO is responsible for managing, and a bevy of suppliers of services and hard goods, not to mention industry media, technology newsletter writers, and local press, as well as neighbors who never before spoke to the CEO, and doting parents and relatives.

**Help Needed.** The best help is prior start-up experience. No two ways about it. Perhaps that is why VCs told us that they are about as happy to have a CEO on his second start-up (even though the first one failed) as they are to have Mr. Ever-Successful-in-Every-Situation who has never done a start-up before.

**Major Costs.** The CEO's mind will now begin to focus night and day on a single financial number: the *burn rate*. This is the amount of cash used each month to pay for anything and everything.

The company now has employees. Who are expensive. And who can spend a great deal of money in a day. Soon the CEO grows rather more miserly in salary offers than he or she used to be at the old Fortune 500 employer.

Costs per month mount up quickly as telephones, voice mail, lobby furniture, plant service, security service, and so on are added. It is easy to spend $400 to $500 per person per month just to open the doors for work each morning.

And then the engineers start submitting their purchase orders for computer-aided design equipment, and the manufacturing people present their budgets for test gear, etc. This is when the CEO must start adding zeros to all numbers forecast for cash expenditures.

The smart CEO should think about all of this when preparing the business plan financial forecasts. The value of such forethought is obvious.

**Main Risks.** The successful VCs and their start-up companies said that these were the main risks in this phase of the fledgling company's life:

1. *Slips in product completion schedules.* More than anything, this made everyone the most nervous. Gene Kleiner, originator of the Kleiner Perkins venture capital firm, calls this the risk of "repeatable technology."
2. *Insufficient market and too much competition.* As a mindboggler, a famous university study showed that sixty-nine disk drive start-up companies got rolling during the heyday of the personal computer, around 1983, each predicting a 5 percent share of the market for itself. Customer acceptance

45

can be lackluster for many reasons. Competition can come from unexpected sources, either from a giant company that has set an industry standard, or, more frequently these days, from other start-ups.

3. *Shortage of good people.* This was a lament by everyone, from entrepreneur to entrepreneur.

**Output and ROI.** The end result is a hustling, bustling company of enthusiastic people eager to transform the founding vision into a commercial reality.

A company with a heart.

And a high-cash burn rate.

# Stage 11: Raising Secondary Rounds of Capital

The joys of operating a new company last for a brief moment, until the reality sinks in that there is no way for the founders to complete the first product and get sales started with the cash that remains in the bank.

**Main Focus Activity.** In stage 11, the main focus should be this: *Raise enough cash and leverage precious equity.*

**Time Required.** About 25 percent of the CEO's time and 20 percent of the time of those reporting directly to the CEO will be consumed just by raising needed capital during the next one to four years. A major regret of numerous first-timers was that they did not realize this axiom of start-up companies. It is especially a problem if the CEO is also the chief technology manager.

**Typical Participants.** Each round of financing will be very closely managed by the start-up's lead venture capital firm. The reasons are explained in Chapter 9. The CEO and the CEO's key communicators will be deeply involved.

And a new participant will appear on the scene: the equipment venture lessor, whose role is explained in Chapter 10.

**Help Needed.** The CEO will need the most help from the lead VC. But note carefully: *CEOs said that they felt the fund-raising leadership* had *to come mainly from the CEO to avoid disasters such as missed payrolls.* CEOs warned never to count on anyone except the CEO to raise the money.

Equipment lessors as middlemen can help raise millions of additional dollars of capital for start-ups. And experienced consultants can save time, effort, and shares for the company's management and employees.

**Major Costs.** Time is the major cost. Lots of it. Personal stress levels also rise in this stage.

**Main Risks.** There are three main risks at this stage:

1. *Running out of cash.* A surprising number of CEOs missed payrolls before secondary rounds of capital were in the bank.
2. *Lack of management focus.* This was the lament of every operations person we talked to, particularly those with little prior "outside" experience (with Wall Street, public relations, news media, or treasury operations such as banking, financing investments).
3. *Bankruptcy.* Yes, it can happen even to the best of them, for both good and bad reasons. That *is* one of the risks of doing a start-up. According to our research in 1987, about six in ten start-ups went bankrupt and that statistic has continued since then. Not all start-ups survive to the second round of financi

**Output and ROI.** A successful stage 11 results in two vital signs of start-up health:

1. Sufficient cash in the bank.
2. Equity at a significantly higher price per share than in the last round.

For guidelines on pricing the successive rounds of venture capital, see Chapter 9 and the case studies in the chapters that follow.

# Stage 12: Launching the First Product

By now the CEO and managers have built up a head of steam and are racing to meet deadlines. The cash is burning rapidly, and the first product is nearing its alpha test milestone.

**Main Focus Activity.** Here is the most important activity: *Focus.* Focus is number one to most of the successful entrepreneurs we spoke to. It is a mistake to spread out into other products, technologies, or customer segments. The important thing is to uncover the big market opportunity and stick to the original business plan in order to exploit that opening and be the best at doing it.

A close number-two priority is: *Find customers.*

Customers spell relief and hope. Most of all, they spell cash *inflow.* To find good customers, one needs good products, starting with the first one. Some start-ups never get more than one chance to try with other than their first product. Therefore, it must be the best the company's people know how to make, consistent with what the targeted customers say they want.

**Time Required.** The launch of the first product takes place in a rollout, usually from one to two years.

**Typical Participants.** There are three major players at this stage:

1. Customers
2. PR firm
3. The whole company

**Help Needed.** This is the time to flex your marketing muscle. All that you've got. You will need wisdom in positioning the company and its first product, consistent with the founder's plan for sustaining the company's competitive, unfair advantage.

**Major Costs.** The major cost is the boost in marketing and sales expenses needed to roll out the first product. Meanwhile, the burn rate is growing as new hires come on board each month. And the cash balance drops daily.

This stage requires amazing human fortitude. The CEO's emotional highs and lows will increase in amplitude. Entrepreneurs who doubt our findings can check it out when they get to this stage by asking their spouses or closest friends for a description and evaluation of their recent behavior, before and after this stage gets under way.

**Main Risks.** Here are the major risks at this stage, listed in rank order:

1. *Lack of focus.* Everyone must concentrate on getting the first product launched ASAP.
2. *Product schedule slips.* Every management and personal behavioral technique available must be used to keep on schedule for the launch date—without burning out employees and their supervisors.
3. *Underperformance.* The worry of every entrepreneur is that the product will not perform up to initial design specifications. *Overperformance,* also known as "creeping elegance," is a close cousin to this risk. Tight coupling of marketing and engineering will help reduce such problems.
4. *Poor market acceptance.* It is a common worry of CEOs who aim at a new, unestablished market.
5. *Jaws, or Big Company Counterpunch.* This is becoming more common as the world giants learn to react faster. And they can always use their muscle to change an industry standard they set, and they can use lawyers to slow down a delicately poised, vulnerable start-up.

**Output and ROI.** The first fruits of the CEO's labor will be the first product and a very excited, confident company of hardworking, competent employee-owners.

The CEO's boss, the board, will be handing out pats on the back, and the industry media representatives will be lining up to do stories on how the founders and the company became successful so soon.

# Stage 13: Raising Working Capital

The founder CEO might think that by now all the capital-raising days are over. But in fact, they never end. Like teenage boys at dinner, start-ups are amazing in how much they can consume.

One very successful start-up showed us its original business plan. The company had grown twice as fast as predicted and reached its public offering two years earlier than planned. The one shocking oversight in the underlying assumptions was that the company required *double* the originally predicted capital base per dollar of revenue. The founders (and their first-tier venture capital backers) had failed to realize that the engineering staff alone would tie up as much capital as total inventory. The R&D and customer support staffs used the company's own manufactured systems to do their work, but in much larger quantities than anticipated. Success breeds its own brand of capital problems.

**Main Focus Activity.** During this phase of life, the company's financial focus should be this: *Leverage equity.*

**Time Required.** Starting in the first profitable quarter, the CEO will be continuously involved with raising working capital. This will supplement the prior rounds of venture capital.

**Typical Participants.** At this stage, the lending officer of the company's commercial bank will visit the office for the first time. The company's chief financial officer will get much more involved with leading this phase of capital raising.

**Help Needed.** The most help will come from having the company's *first profitable quarter.* Banking savvy and experience will be required.

**Major Costs.** The major cost—other than the cost of the actual loans—is the CEO's *time.*

Debt is a lot cheaper than equity and is worth millions in value to the founders because it does not further dilute equity.

**Main Risks.** The main risk is that the loan may have to be repaid at the worst time—that is, when the company is waiting for large collections from customers but is short of cash for the next payroll.

**Output and ROI.** The test of success at Stage 13 is how much extra cash the company has in the bank at the end of the effort. Financial flexibility is the main objective.

# Stage 14: Initial Public Offering

At last The Day has arrived: The founders have decided to go public!

**Main Focus Activity.** Here are the priorities: (1) *Get the shares liquid (registered)*, (2) *Cash in a few chips,* and (3) *Celebrate!*

**Time Required.** Start-ups usually take three to five years to get to this point. However, the median number of years required has dropped noticeably, from an average of nine years for IPOs in 1979, to below four years in 1985, and back to about five years in 1990 but dropped with the Internet boom.

Chips and Technologies set an early record, going public in seven quarters from date of inception. Since then several start-ups have beaten that record during boom days.

**Typical Participants.** Enter the Wall Street clan: investment bankers and security analysts—and their lawyers. Joining them will be the securities law expert from the start-up's law firm and the start-up's CPA firm.

And now the CEO gets to deal directly with institutional investors who will come to hear the company's story during the CEO's road show.

Finally, the CEO gets to cope with all those members of the general public who now know his phone number and who feel they are owed a personal explanation for the company's $1.25 stock price drop yesterday.

**Help Needed.** The CEO needs help from experts in investment banking, Wall Street, and securities law. Each expert will get a share of the money that is raised.

**Major Costs.** An IPO is the most expensive cost measured in both absolute and percentage terms. The company can count on spending at least $500,000 and usually much more on lawyers, accountants, printing, travel, etc. The underwriting syndicate gets about 7 percent of the total capital raised (in other words, millions of dollars).

*And not a penny of these expenses is tax deductible.*

All the details are spelled out in Chapter 13, "Wall Street and the Initial Public Offering." This information will help the CEO's negotiations with the investment banker.

The amount of time required of the company's finance staff is high, as is the time required of top management for due diligence and road shows.

**Main Risks.** The main risk is *missing the window.* CEOs warned us of coming out too early—or too late. This is discussed in detail in Chapter 13.

Related risks include a stock price that is too high—or too low, selling into a souring stock market, hitting an unpredicted quarter of soft sales.

The ultimate risk is that the offering may have to be pulled off the market and offered another time—or never at all.

**Output and ROI.** Successful IPOs produce all of these things:

- Image of success in the high-tech industry. This can help salespeople sell credibility more easily.
- Investors increase their invested monies from 5 times to 200 times or more.
- Founders become multimillionaires (on paper).
- Employees increase their net worth by a nice multiple.

## Managing the Post-IPO Stage

Most of this is covered in detail in Chapter 13; suffice it to say here that this is territory calling for experience. It is a dangerous stage to tackle without good advice and much experience.

Dealing with skilled Wall Street security analysts and little old lady investors on the same day calls for an experienced, dedicated expert. The specialized securities laws must be understood and carefully adhered to.

And the CEO and founder must remember to work out a personal strategy for dealing with underwriter lockups, Rule 144, and other regulations that greatly limit the amount of stock that they can sell during the years soon after the initial public offering.

## Overview of the Entire Process

In summary: The entrepreneur chose to focus on converting an idea to a vision that became a commercial success. It took somewhere between four and eight years to get to the IPO.

The entrepreneur learned to deal with a vast array of participants, all of whom earned something because of their dealings with the start-up.

The help the founders needed was half effort and skill, and half taking advantage of big breaks, good and bad.

The founder got strangers to believe in his or her vision to the tune of $3 million to $50 million of invested cash, and spent it all.

The core team worked very hard and incurred a significant personal cost for such success. And so did many other fine employees.

The founder took a chance—on becoming a small, going-nowhere company, on going bankrupt.

The reward is a cornucopia of satisfaction: Seeing a viable company alive and doing business well; working in a great place with terrific people; earning investors $100 million to $1 billion; becoming personally worth millions; gaining more self-knowledge about one's identity and motivation and purpose in life; drawing closer to one's spouse and family; learning to balance one's life and still be the leader of a very successful high-tech start-up.

*4*

# Getting Started Legally

I t is critical for start-ups to have good legal assistance from a very early stage. There are two general categories of legal help that the entrepreneur needs to get started: legal assistance with intellectual property issues, which means assuring that the core team members depart from their employers in an ethical and legal manner and protection of the start-up's own intellectual property; and general legal work, including incorporation.

The attorneys you hire can help you more effectively if you understand what their job is and how to select the best ones for your needs.

## Kinds of Legal Help Required

First of all, prospective entrepreneurs need a careful plan to avoid trouble when departing from their employers. Changes in the U.S. Patent Court since 1983 have increased the value of fighting to protect proprietary intellectual property. Established companies have changed from passive to aggressive protectors of their intellectual property. Furthermore, the now-classic cases of SEEQ versus Intel and Linear Technology versus National Semiconductor have taught the legal community where the lines of battle are to be drawn. The Internet era opens up uncharted legal territory requiring wise legal advice.

Experienced legal counsel will help the entrepreneur sidestep potential problems and greatly reduce the chances of a court battle. In addition, the start-up company's intellectual property also needs protection.

The start-up's law firm must be skilled at patent work and the many specialized tasks associated with managing intellectual property. For example:

- Business contracts for specialized start-ups such as genetic engineering joint ventures and computer software companies require special experience not possessed by all law firms' staffs.
- Licenses to and from other companies require customizing and understanding of the business purpose behind the deal being negotiated.
- Nondisclosure agreements require advice on how to incorporate them into company policy.
- Engineering notebooks and the procedures for administering them should all be part of a deliberate strategy worked out with counsel.

Incorporating the company involves administrative tasks that are more effectively done by a law firm than by a layperson. The founders need guidance on the number of shares to issue, the class of shares, and the number of shares to assign to each person in the core group. Good counsel is knowledgeable in these areas and provides guidance based on experience with similar undertakings. Stock options require state government approval, and counsel will help the founders avoid the pitfalls in the rules attached to this important area.

Experienced and savvy attorneys can be of immense assistance when the time comes to negotiate each round of financing. They will look out for the best interests of the founders.

Finally, U.S. securities law is a specialized area that requires wisdom and intimacy with the procedures and practices of Wall Street.

Mario Rosati, of the law firm Wilson Sonsini Goodrich & Rosati of Palo Alto, California, says:

> I think the founder should get a lot more than a lawyer. I meet with the person who calls me. I tell them to come in and to talk, no charge for the meeting. I look for character and credibility. I ask about their work experience and education and training that is relevant to the start-up they are talking about. If I decide to take them on as a client, I fully back the company, helping them with more than legal matters: help them select the right accountant, draft a good business plan, find the best fitting sources of funding, and negotiate terms of the deal. The best legal help understands how to be a good businessman with the founder. In some cases our firm even does some early stage financial backing of the start-up.

Here is advice from a veteran of Silicon Valley, Mike Phillips, formerly of Morrison & Foerster of Palo Alto, California, who became senior vice president and chief counsel of JDS Uniphase:

In selecting general counsel for a start-up, the entrepreneur is essentially taking on a business partner who will play a key role in many of the company's important milestones. The entrepreneur should focus on the following factors in the selection process: competency, integrity, personal fit, and availability. Besides the obvious, competency requires substantial experience in connection with high-technology and start-up businesses. As to personal fit, make sure you pick a lawyer that you are comfortable with at a personal level, someone with whom you can communicate and who listens to you. Availability is also important because you want the lawyer you pick to be the one that actually does the work and not one that disappears after the selection process.

Founders told us they learned to look for start-up experience in the partner and his supporting group and to be sure to pick wisely, interviewing legal counsel as carefully as a prospective employee.

## Choosing General Legal Counsel

Law firms that are experienced with start-ups handle both general legal work and intellectual property matters. However, we found that two different attorneys are often engaged, one for special patent work, and one for regular legal work. Here is what our research revealed an entrepreneur should look for in a good attorney:

- Look for firms that are experienced with start-ups. Particularly valuable is the law firm that has lived with a start-up from seed-round days through IPO.
- Avoid using a law firm that does more work for venture capital firms than for start-ups. The problems are different and the start-up's needs are different. There is also the possibility of mixed loyalties if the attorney continues to provide representation for the entrepreneur's investor group.
- A friend who will have to subcontract most of the work is a poor choice. VCs want to deal with experienced partners from an experienced firm.

    Avoid automatically using the largest firm in town. Bigness is not necessarily goodness.
- The law firm to choose is an experienced firm that is smart enough to provide a workable solution rather than the ultimate, costly solution, one that provides nuts-and-bolts how-to advice instead of lots of theory.

After selecting the right law firm, the entrepreneur should select an individual attorney or group of attorneys after determining who he or she is most comfortable with. The relationship with the particular counsel who will handle the legal work is more important than the size of a law firm or any nuances in community reputation.

Fellow CEOs, venture capitalists, and investment bankers are good sources of referrals to attorneys with relevant experience. Over the years several of the law firms have focused on venture and start-ups. They have the experience you need. They will discount their fees until your start-up reaches the IPO.

The entrepreneur should think of the long term and pick a firm that can go all the way to IPO with the start-up. Changing firms along the way is difficult and expensive.

## Choosing Patent Counsel

Competent patent counsel is not easy to find. The work is specialized and requires both technical and legal skills. Recent shifts in patent law and the sudden increase in the number of lawsuits mean that even more attention must be paid to issues of intellectual property law. Trademark skills and a knowledge of copyright law are also required.

Your candidates should be familiar with such landmark cases as Texas Instruments versus NEC (memory chips), Polaroid versus Kodak (instant cameras), Lotus versus 1-2-3 clones (software), and so on, even into the Internet era of business process patents. Close ties of the chosen patent counsel to even more specialized counsel in Washington, D.C., can also be important.

## Ethical Departure from an Employer

Driven by threats to their success in setting an industry standard, established companies have recently added legal strategy to their corporate long-range plan.

For instance, Microsoft and Intel regularly use PR to deliberately rattle legal swords, threatening any upstart who might even be thinking of building a new product to compete head on with one of theirs. The large companies have spent hundreds of millions of dollars to create an industry standard. They mean to reap the fattest reward they can from that precious investment.

**The Intellectual Property Issue.** The issue is how the founder and members of the core team can leave their current employers and not get sued. We found that most engineers were vaguely aware that this question was important. However, several start-up founders said that they later came to realize that doing something wise and practical about this issue was much more complicated than they realized. Several had found themselves in trouble with their former employers.

After this issue continued to surface regularly in our research, we spent time with leading venture capital attorneys to analyze it further. Lois Abraham of Brown & Bain in Palo Alto, California, highlighted the fundamental issue this way:

> Individuals should be especially aware that there are two groups whose intellectual property rights are protected. One is composed of the employees, whose knowledge and skills belong to each person to do what needs to be done to earn a gainful living. The other group is the employers, who are to keep the fruits of labor of employees for the benefit of the shareholders. Both groups are strongly protected by the law. Finding the line that cannot be crossed is difficult. Good legal counsel is very important.

Here is a typical problem: After the seed round is closed, the CEO discovers that the start-up's lead design engineer has three schematics of his last employer's related products in some old, forgotten file boxes that are buried in the junk in his garage. The engineer says the products never got to market, but the start-up's counsel sees red flags everywhere. What should the founder tell the venture investors, who performed their due diligence last month and asked about this issue?

**Potential Problems and Pitfalls.** There is a long list of headaches to watch out for; here are some examples:

- Members of the start-up's technical staff have taken boxes of work home from their former employer over the past three to nine months, particularly in the past four weeks. Included in the boxes are:
  —Copies of a few overhead transparencies that contain the bold capitalized header: CONFIDENTIAL—COMPANY PROPRIETARY—XYMEX CORP.
  —Articles copied from electronics magazines that include these handwritten notes: "Good idea for new product"; "Should be feature added to Xymex 6141"; "Tell Mike and marketing staff."
- The founder cannot remember what he did with the last three backup tapes and box of diskettes. The former employer has just called with the information that these items cannot be found.
- The start-up's marketing guru has just shown the founder a copy of a copy of a copy of the proposed pricing of Big Corp's Model 9999. An interviewee (still employed by Big Corp) left the pricing copy with the start-up's marketing vice president.
- Your attorney turns green when told that the new company's core team has been designing product and writing their business plan at night and on weekends during the long-term planning session at Big Corp, where they are still

**TABLE 4-1. Nine Commandments to Follow When Leaving an Employer**

1. Take *nothing* with you.
2. Take no notebooks, meeting notes, schematics, drawings, business plans, or portions thereof.
3. Make no copies of anything, not even magazine articles with your handwritten notes in the margins.
4. Tell your supervisor of the whereabouts of any mag tapes, diskettes, or other electronic information storage devices that you had access to or used.
5. Do not write any portion of a business plan until well after you have left your employer, preferably months afterward.
6. Do not meet with cofounders until after all of you have left your employers.
7. Do everything you can to prevent the possibility of a lawyer twisting your actions into a story that makes you look like a sneaky thief.
8. After leaving your employers and upon your first meeting as founders, get your patent counsel and general counsel to write a letter to your former employers stating what business you plan to enter and asking what specific proprietary information the employers may feel you possess.
9. *Talk to no one* from or at your former employer until your legal counsel gives you the all-clear signal.

*Sources*: Skjerven, Morrill, MacPherson, San Jose, CA, and Saratoga Venture Finance

employed. The start-up's first product will be bus-and-socket-compatible with Big Corp's top-selling model 2219.

Given any of the above circumstances, an opposing attorney can skillfully present a damning case, twisting the facts to paint a picture of evil, scheming people who violated their employer's trust and stole company secrets.

**Practices and Policies for Successful Prevention.** Table 4-1 lists some important rules to follow when leaving an employer. The secret to success here is advance planning. The founder's actions will leave a trail that will paint a picture of his character. An opposing counsel will seek to use—disadvantageously—every detail of the founder's actions and those of the start-up's key employees.

The advice in Table 4-1 provides an overall plan that maximizes protection for the founders. Table 4-2 lists steps that should be taken that will increase the value of the start-up's own intellectual property. The key factor to success here is discipline.

Successful CEOs insisted from day one on establishing and following selected policies and practices. The objective was clear: to make it clear to all employees and visitors that this company places the highest priority on retention of propri-

**TABLE 4-2. How to Protect a Start-Up Company's Intellectual Property**

---

1. Have all employees sign upon first day of employment an "Employee Proprietary and Confidential Information Agreement." It will help keep the company's secrets secret.

2. Install and enforce a written patent notebook procedure. It will strengthen your company's claims that its intellectual property is very valuable, as well as improve chances of obtaining desired patents.

3. Issue to all of the company's technical staff written patent notebook recordkeeping instructions. Be sure your people respect the importance of these instructions.

4. Be sure your VP of engineering strictly manages the issuing and tracking of all notebooks given to the technical staff.

5. Keep on hand a good stock of the kind of notebooks required by your instructions. Do not use the kind of notebooks commonly found in stationery stores.

6. Issue to all employees and all managers Confidential Disclosure Agreements that cover the following areas and instruct them to use the documents in dealing with nonemployees:
   a. START-UP, INC., and a third party exchanging confidential information.
   b. START-UP, INC., receiving confidential information from a third party.
   c. START-UP, INC., disclosing confidential information to a third party.

7. Require that your VP of finance and administration issue and control all Confidential Disclosure Agreements.

8. Prepare a document called "Submission of Inventions and Suggestions" for the use of third parties, typically nonemployees but also often nontechnical employees of START-UP, INC.

9. Prepare an "Invention Disclosure" form that will clearly identify the holder of any proprietary information that START-UP, INC., may be interested in using or developing.

---

*Sources:* Skjerven, Morrill, MacPherson, San Jose, CA, and Saratoga Venture Finance

etary information. Sloppiness was not tolerated. New hires were carefully instructed on policy and procedures in their first week of employment. VPs were expected to set the example for the company.

# Case Study: Newtech Company

In October, Bill and Kim committed to creating their own start-up. They quickly formed a core group of four and started drafting their business plan. They had worked closely together at Radco and they both had outstanding track records for creating the top three products that literally saved Radco from bankruptcy as a start-up five years earlier. Radco was still trying to get to IPO. Their shares were fully vested, and neither liked the latest leadership of the company.

Bill had resigned from Radco earlier that month. He had contacted Kim, who had been consulting for nine months while working at home on prototype product designs. They decided they needed a CEO as a leader in order to attract any venture capital and called Mike at Tech, Inc. They had gotten to know and respect Mike seven years earlier when all three of them had worked together at Tech, Inc., before Bill and Kim left for Radco.

After some consideration, Mike agreed to lead the start-up. After two months of work on the business plan, he contacted his first venture firm, which immediately scheduled a presentation at Tech Ventures.

During the presentation, the venture partners became quite excited about the Newtech strategy. However, as the due diligence questions got around to technology, it became clear that nobody at Newtech had given much thought to the problems and pitfalls that might arise with intellectual property issues.

Moreover, an embarrassing moment of silence occurred when one partner asked how the shares were divided. Mike had not yet settled that with the other founders.

At the end of the all-day session, the senior partner told Mike in frank terms that he had handled the intellectual property issues very poorly. He gave Mike the name of a local law firm, and Mike was in its office the next afternoon.

Cathy represented the law firm and was the expert in technology problems. She began by asking Mike for a retainer, which Mike paid out of his personal funds. She started questioning the founders in her office the next morning.

Cathy soon uncovered the following:

1. Mike had created no problems with his way of handling the departure from his last employer. However, there was some related general product marketing information that might be a problem. He had obtained it at Suma, from a friend. Newtech would compete with Suma. Cathy put that problem aside for the time being.

2. Kim had indeed left Radco nine months ago; that was true. However, she had not told Mike she was still on retainer to Radco. Nor had she told Mike that she had signed a nondisclosure agreement the day she left, and that the related information was vital to the technology strategy of Newtech. Kim's Southeast Asian cultural background always led her to withhold troublesome information until the last minute. Cathy had to pull the facts out of her using the best inquiry techniques she could muster.

3. Bill thought he had departed from Radco in a very professional manner, on good terms with the president and his boss, the VP of R&D. Cathy soon learned that Bill had cleaned out his office the day he departed. He had tossed four cartons of paper into a trash bin himself and had left six mag

tapes in the cubicle of an MIS operator who was gone at the time. In addition, he had put two bookcases of materials of all sorts into cardboard boxes that he had obtained from the copy room; these were now stacked in his garage at home. He had little idea of exactly what was in those boxes. Cathy told him to bring the boxes to her office for an inventory of their contents.

By Friday of that week, Cathy had a list of the contents of Bill's boxes. They contained copies of presentations to top management, clearly marked CONFIDENTIAL and COMPANY PROPRIETARY. There were several old engineering notebooks and many copies of technical articles and papers on products that were related to Radco's leading-edge products.

That same afternoon, Cathy received a phone call from Bill. He sounded quite shaken. His friend, the head of R&D at Radco, had written him a letter containing some legal-sounding wording, including this sentence: "It has come to our attention that you may have in your possession six mag tapes, two schematics of Radco Model 34340, and other proprietary documents that belong to Radco."

Cathy met with Bill on Monday morning. Bill wanted to call the president, talk to him, and straighten things out in person. Cathy advised him to wait until the following day and turned her attention to learning from Bill the basic technology and strategy behind Newtech's fundamental business plan.

She learned that Newtech intended to design its first product, the Newtech 1, to be pin-and-socket- and board-compatible with the Radco 34340, except that it would run on a mega-bit bus and be four times as fast. The speed advantage would come from Bill's and Kim's design skills. The next products would become an ultra-high-speed family of products designed around the Newtech 1.

When Bill left at 4:00 P.M., Cathy firmly told him not to talk to anyone at Radco until further notice.

On Monday evening, the regular weekly meeting night for the Newtech core team of eight people, Kim did not appear. Calls to her home got only the telephone answering device. Mike became concerned. Bill said he would try to have lunch with Kim on Tuesday and find out what was happening.

At 6:30 P.M. the next day, Mike met Bill at a local restaurant. He was shocked to learn that Kim would not be joining Newtech after all. The president of Radco had made Kim a counteroffer and told Kim to accept it or face years in court with tons of legal bills, a ruined reputation, and all her friends angry at her. Besides, he had argued, Newtech would never get funded with a big lawsuit facing it. And the president had gone on to say he knew all about Newtech's plans and the technology belonged to Radco and its hard-nosed venture capitalists. Mike and Bill left at 7:05 P.M. in a very despondent mood.

The next morning, Mike got his third call from Tech Ventures's senior partner. How were things going? When would Mike have the intellectual properties issues resolved? Mike stalled him, said, "Soon," hung up, and went to pick up the day's mail.

He sorted through the stack while he slowly walked back down the driveway to the house, but he stopped short as he immediately recognized the Radco logo on a business envelope. He tore it open on the spot and read a detailed description of the general technology direction that Newtech was planning to take; that Radco considered its patents and products to be proprietary; and that any hiring of Radco employees or of those who had recently left Radco would result in immediate, severe legal action by Radco's law firm against Mike personally, since Newtech was not yet incorporated.

Mike called Bill to talk things over. During the conversation, Bill slipped and told Mike that he had gone over to Radco on the previous Friday to try to talk to the president. (At the meeting on Monday, Bill had only talked about wanting to talk to Radco's president, whereas in reality he had already done so! ) The talk had ended with an offer to consider some sort of joint venture, and Bill had then told the president about the product plans and strategy for Newtech.

At 10:30 A.M. on Thursday, Mike decided what he had to do. He called the senior partner at Tech Ventures and told him that the founders of Newtech had decided not to proceed at this time.

---

# Protecting Your Own Intellectual Property

To what degree is it important to protect a start-up company's intellectual property? One experienced venture capitalist answered that frequently asked question in these terms: "We realize that the new business enterprise could go bankrupt. And while we do not plan on that sad event, we do seek to have something, something of worth, something tangible to offer for sale if all else fails. That is why we shy away from companies that get their worth mainly from intangibles such as services. We much prefer to invest in companies that will generate a new technology, a real and valuable way of doing something better and something very valuable to customers. The CEOs of the companies in which we invest had better protect that asset with all of their diligence, or we will find someone else who will."

**Procedures and Practices.** We found that all start-ups kept their secrets closely held to some degree. The consistency varied widely. Enlightenment came for a few on the shocking day that they received the IBM "SWAT" squad, who told them what secrecy really meant and how to build secure rooms, etc., before IBM would deliver its latest computer for alpha testing at the start-up's new-products development lab. Microsoft was among those companies.

However, we discovered that any security problems were not in the companies' physical defenses; rather, they were in the legal area, where most CEOs lack experience. In addition to the personal inexperience of founders, there have been shifts in the U.S. Patent Court, and court or trial results in areas such as copyrighting microcode and patents related to the Internet that affect the security of intellectual property.

Table 4-2 lists nine practical steps for protecting a company's intellectual property. Allen MacPherson, a patent attorney in a San Jose, California, firm, was good enough to share these steps with us. He has developed customized programs, policies, and practices for his start-up clients based on these recommendations. According to Mr. MacPherson, "The key is to develop a documentable practice that is followed by your employees as a matter of daily habit. You want to be able to demonstrate to a judge that your actions showed how vital and valuable to the company was its intellectual property."

Ken Allen, of Townsend & Townsend, Palo Alto, California, told us how important it was to "start right from the beginning with a foundation built on guidelines established up front by the legal counsel who will have to represent the company in related legal actions."

Barry Evans, of Whitman Breed Abbott & Morgan, New York City, tells entrepreneurs: "Secrecy at inception is an absolute prerequisite! You must begin there and use the tools of law to protect your valuable intellectual property."

## *Case Study: Extro Electronics, Inc.*

Just how practical legal advice is was demonstrated to an electronics start-up CEO who recently recruited a top star from another start-up that was floundering. Sam, the engineer, had impeccable credentials, an excellent track record, and a good cultural fit.

Jack, the CEO, was elated and greeted Sam personally when he saw him report to work at Extro on Tuesday. All went well until Sam failed to report to work on Friday.

After a few phone calls, Jack learned that Sam was at work at his desk at Discus Systems. And Sam was not returning phone calls, either at his office or at home.

Jack called in his longtime assistant and had her pull Sam's personnel file. He found, to his great surprise, that the file was practically empty—no signed acceptance of the offer of employment from Extro, no signed nondisclosure agreement, nothing but a copy of Sam's résumé.

"Now what do we do?" he lamented to his assistant. "We told Sam about our plans and technology, and Discus Systems could use that information to scoop us in the marketplace!"

At the time of this writing, the case remained open, with Sam still not answering phone calls and Jack still worried.

---

**Patents, Trademarks, Copyrights, and Trade Secrets.** Each of these—patents, trademarks, copyrights, and trade secrets—plays an important role in the start-up's overall intellectual property strategy. Each calls for special expertise, to which good legal counsel can direct the CEO.

What we found missing most often was an overt, conscious plan to use these legal elements to construct a thorough effort to use intellectual property as part of the start-up's overall plan to succeed.

And these elements fit nicely into a complete legal plan that reinforces the company's plan to build and reinforce a sustainable competitive advantage.

## Incorporating the Company

It is always a pleasure to see the joy on the faces of the founders of a start-up as they say enthusiastically, "We're a company, a real, live company." In legal terms, they are now a registered entity, a thing called a corporation. And they are subject to operating within all the state laws and regulations that govern such a business entity. Good legal counsel is a must.

**The Role of an Attorney.** Although it is technically possible to save a few dollars by doing one's own incorporation, we found that most start-up veterans advise against it.

The start-up's counsel will help choose a company name, file all the papers with the secretary of the chosen state, and pay all required fees. There are also tax documents and filing papers to be created before the company can go into action as a corporation. In addition, the attorney must draft closely related legal documents for incentive stock options, and they must be scrutinized by the secretary of state of the state in which the start-up is incorporated.

It all goes together as a package that good law firms have set up as boilerplate on word processors. Their clerks are ready to move the paperwork through the bureaucracy and pay the fees on time. And the good firms do not charge much for this; they negotiate a custom deal with each founder that recognizes the risk of the new enterprise.

**Picking a Company Name.** We found a great deal of chaos in picking the start-up's final name, especially with the Internet URL name becoming so important. We were given dozens of ways to select one and as many reasons for picking a certain kind of name. In the end, few people even cared.

What is important is picking a name and getting on with life—with raising the money.

For the less experienced, here is a summary of the consensus on picking a good name:

- Do not spend much time or money on it. The CEO should decide on a name if the founders cannot reach consensus in a day or two.
- Do not pay professional name finders to get you a name. Only if a product or company needs a lot of differentiation—as is usually the case with consumer-intensive companies—should the principals expend a great deal of effort on name choosing. A name earns its reputation over time, no matter which one is chosen.
- There is about a 75 percent chance that the first name will be changed within eighteen months, according to start-up company veterans.

**Reserving a Name.** Each state has a method of checking to make sure a proposed company name is not being used already and of letting a start-up reserve that name for a few weeks. This procedure allows the founders to work out incorporation documents with their attorney. It is possible to call a telephone number in many states, pay a fee for an extended holding time, and thus get the name the founders have fallen in love with.

**Cost to Incorporate.** It should not be expensive to incorporate a company. A reputable law firm will charge around $3,000 to get the incorporation job done and to do more work (bylaws, option plan, etc.) to finish up the related documents. The start-up should use the legal firm it chose for general legal matters.

Several top law firms familiar with venture capital start-up companies said they used young attorneys and paralegal talent to do routine incorporation work, which allowed them to charge a lower than normal fee for it

**Typical Agreements.** Each state has its own set of documents that are needed to incorporate. The firm of Morrison & Foerster in Palo Alto, California, gave us a list of the more important documents needed in that state. These are typical, and are listed in Table 4-3.

**TABLE 4-3. Typical Start-Up Incorporation Documents**

---

Memorandum of Action of Sole Incorporation of START-UP, INC.

Closing documents and personal checks for purchase of shares by founders

Unanimous Written Consent in Lieu of the first Meeting of the Board of Directors of START-UP, INC.

Proprietary Information and Inventions Agreement

Letter to Internal Revenue Service for Election Under Section 83(b) of the Internal Revenue Code of 1954, As Amended

State form called: "Commission of Corporations: Notice of Transaction Pursuant to Corporation Code Section SYZ3333(f)"

Statement by Domestic Stock Corporation, to be filed with the Secretary of State

---

*Sources:* Morrison & Foerster, Palo Alto, CA, and Saratoga Venture Finance

The stock shareholder documents are closely interlinked with the other legal papers.

Some CEOs thought it advantageous to postpone incorporation until the seed round was completed. They wanted to avoid pressures from VCs on founders to contribute a lot of personal cash to the founding capital of the new company. The founders must put in capital, and the attorney will explain how much is necessary.

**Problems and Pitfalls.** The number-one problem cited to us over and over was picking the wrong legal counsel. Nothing beats experience in working for start-ups.

The next often-cited problem was getting the general counsel to do specialized work for which they were not well qualified, such as intellectual property work.

A regular headache to founders was not getting quick access to their lead attorney, being sent instead to inferior junior attorneys of the firm.

Other pitfalls high on the most often mentioned list included:

- using a giant law firm lacking in practical street smarts needed by start-ups
- picking a firm for its reputation and not for its know-how with the specialized technology in question
- finding that the start-up company is a second-class citizen compared with the other clients serviced by that law firm
- switching attorneys in midstream. It is important to pick the best firm and stick with it.

# Summary

Remember: Your choice of lawyer will be with you for a long time, so pick carefully! True, the CEO can fire a law firm, but that is much more awkward to do than it sounds (we found no start-up that had decided to fire its legal counsel, in spite of some black stories about poor advice and expensive, low-grade service). So do your best to pick the best the first time. One CEO told us he thinks his choice of lawyer saved him millions in negotiations with investors. Another CEO said he grew to appreciate the business advice he got from his lawyer.

The start-ups also said what a pain it was to have to work with an inexperienced lawyer; one such member of the bar forgot to check off the tax form box that would have prevented the CEO from having to pay taxes on his shares each time they vested! A veteran investment banker said that going public without the best lawyer experienced in securities law was like going through hell.

Law firms, like CPAs, specializing in venture-backed start-ups will deeply discount their services, making up for it at the time of IPO and thereafter.

We are convinced that the choice of a good law firm is one of your most important decisions. The choice of the particular partner is even more important, whether it be for corporate law or intellectual property advice. In addition to helping to get your firm incorporated, the lawyer will be experienced with business plans and able and willing to read and comment on your first drafts. Our next chapter will help you get started writing a top-quality business plan that will not only impress your lawyer but, more importantly, impress the people with the money to invest in your start-up.

# 5

# Preparing the Business Plan

When you prepare a business plan worthy of being financed, it will stand out. Venture capitalists told us time after time that most of the plans they see are "just plain bad."

CEOs who succeeded in obtaining the funding they wanted told us why their plans were funded. Our research revealed that the heart of their secret for success was their ability to document the start-up's distinctive competence, the company's competitive advantage, and the management's plans to *sustain that advantage*. The greatest danger was in creating a plan without advantage. In other words, investors want to see a lot more than exciting technology.

In this chapter we have incorporated the work of leading business thinkers. Peter Drucker classifies entrepreneurs' strategies; Donald Clifford and Richard Cavanagh of McKinsey identify what to look for in winning companies; Michael Porter of Harvard helps top management focus on doing useful strategic thinking; and Tom Peters talks about how to test your company's uniqueness. The best from the venture capitalists is included.

This chapter provides an outline to show the start-up CEO what a venture capitalist looks for in the body of a written business plan. It explains how to create financial projections using a personal computer and spreadsheet software, so that the budding entrepreneur can get off to a good start, save valuable time, and have more days available for strategic thinking.

This chapter analyzes a new participant—the CPA firm. Picking a good CPA firm is analyzed based on interviews with start-up CFOs and CEOs.

This chapter is devoted to helping the founders of a new enterprise create the core of a business plan that will have a better chance of succeeding than the other one thousand business plans it is competing with.

Unlike most of the literature on start-ups, this chapter will not spend much time on the outline; that is not where the heart of success lies. Rather, we will focus on the findings of successful people: venture capitalists, CEOs, and some of the giants who have dedicated their careers and personal lives to analyzing and improving the practice of modern business management who have published research findings regarding successful and failed new companies. Their findings may shock you.

The diligent reader will be able to apply this chapter's pragmatic suggestions and significantly improve his or her chances of raising needed capital.

## Required Material

Like a résumé for a job interview, a business plan is required material. And just as a résumé alone does not get the applicant a job, neither will a business plan get a founder financing; the funding will depend on how well the founder manages the process of high-tech capital formation. A business plan is expected to cover certain details, which we will spell out later in this chapter.

Opinions on when and how to use the business plan to raise capital varied considerably among those interviewed. CEOs who were successful said that deciding *when* to use the written plan was a key element in their tactics. The founder must know when to submit the business plan, to whom, and how to present it. (We found several clever methods used.) *Do not start by mailing business plans to a lot of venture capitalists.*

## Confidentiality

Confidentiality was of concern to all CEOs. But venture capitalists told us it was impractical for VCs to sign nondisclosure agreements; they see so many deals that to do so would invite legal trouble. And we were told in confidence of business plans clearly marked CONFIDENTIAL AND COMPANY PROPRIETARY that were handed out by venture capitalists to other start-up companies.

Participants strongly advised careful control of the number of copies made and to whom they were given. Several CEOs required VCs to return the business plan, without being copied.

## Timing

When should you submit your business plan to a venture firm? Many CEOs told of sending copies to ten to twenty venture capital firms, but receiving virtually no response. The reason for this is simple: A three-man venture capital office receives about one thousand business plans a year, or about four per day. At that rate, the office could be doing nothing but reading plans, if it chose to do so. Instead, the VCs work out a method of screening the plans and read only certain ones. The rest are scrapped, returned to the sender in one to four months, or, in a few cases, filed.

An entrepreneur's goal is to avoid such a fate and instead get the start-up's plan to the top of the hot-deal in-box for careful scrutiny by the managing partner of the venture firm.

## Attention Getters

How is this accomplished? Here are some tactics that worked for successfully funded start-ups:

- *Always start with a personal introduction.* This was the *major* recommendation by everyone, including the people with the money to invest.
- *Visit first. Do not send a plan until after at least one personal meeting.* This saves everyone time. The VC will not go further if he or she has decided to keep out of a particular kind of business. And the founder can ask how many competitors the VC firm has invested in or is about to invest in.
- *Be frank and find out.* Some CEOs had extensive sessions with a certain venture firm that resulted in a "No, thank you," then later read in the paper about that firm funding another directly competing start-up. "Be sure you do not get pumped for the wrong reasons," said founders who learned the hard way.
- *Present the plan; tell your story.* Marketing CEOs especially recommended this be done as soon as possible, preferably in the second meeting. The CEO can control the flow of information better and can be specific in how it is presented in response to the questions of the venture partners present. More information can be kept confidential this way than if you mailed the business plan.
- *Negotiate, don't teach.* One CEO put it this way: "After weeks and weeks of work, several presentations, and reference checks galore, the venture firm said 'No'! I got angry when I realized they were learning our business on our nickel!" He went on to say he'd never again spend time with a venture capitalist who had no hands-on experience in his or a related business.
- *Treat every contact as part of the overall negotiation for money.* Put each question into the context of pricing a deal. Then you will not be surprised later when the lead partner says, "We think we need *n* percent (which is 10 percent

more than you had anticipated) of your start-up, because you said a few weeks ago that you did not have much [management experience or whatever] and that is critical to your company's success or failure, in our opinion." In other terms, focus on doing a deal from day one; never assume that the venture capitalist is just being a nice guy, talking to you about your neat ideas. After all, he is in business and is just as short of time as you are.

- *Realize that business plans are everything and nothing.* This paradox is easy to understand. History favors the reality that the successful start-up usually abandons its original plan in some significant way as it gets into business. "People, we always start with the people," was so often said by VCs that one wonders why a plan is even necessary. Yet the plans are agonized over, read, and reread. And the final funding decision depends a great deal on how it impresses the venture partners. We concluded that what is really going on under the surface, consciously or unconsciously, is a search for the missing sustainable competitive advantage. (More on that later in the chapter.)

- *Write a super executive summary.* Because that is all most readers take time to read. They then attend the first presentation meeting to take the rest in. One partner will take on the role of lead partner and will read the plan in detail. He will be the founder's primary contact, and the deal's life or death will depend upon his degree of responsiveness during the course of the investigation.

- *Write well.* Most plans are awful, say the luckless readers. Use a word processor with a spelling checker. The goal of the start-up's founders is to stand out—but not for bad composition. The poor VC has an in-box piled high with unread business plans and will appreciate one that is concise, clear, and informative.

- *Be neat without overdoing things.* In this day of desktop publishing, documents can be stunning. However, a great strategy is worth much more than beauty.

- *Keep the packaging crisp, not drenched in gold leaf.* Like school term papers, content is what counts. We've seen VCs tear off and throw away expensive, bulky covers and binders, fancy pictures, and fat sections of copies of magazine articles.

# Deal Flow

Deal flow is the behind-the-scenes power game that can suddenly turn a CEO who has worked hard into a star or result in a soft, "Sorry, but we have decided to pass on investing in your deal—in this round." Deal flow is a kind of Monopoly game of venture capitalists: "Sam, we'll let you in on Super Corp.com. run by Dr. Wunderkind—if you let us in on your next super deal"

Any deal becomes one of the playing cards. And if Power VC Firm drops a hot deal in the lap of the start-up's lead VC, the CEO may suddenly find the phone ringing with the "Sorry . . ." response. Not surprisingly, the substitute deal could be with a direct competitor. It happens, and increasingly so, with more than two thousand venture firms competing with more than $40 billion of venture funds to invest annually.

How can such an outcome be avoided? We asked that question of our interviewees and they summarized their strategies as follows:

- *Get hot and stay hot.* In the end, deals are decided on emotion. A CEO must not let a deal cool down or lose momentum.
- *Always have alternative sources of funds.* The sharp CEOs were able to create competing groups, all vying for the deal. But there is the danger of becoming shopworn. Avoiding this requires sophistication and skill. The start-up's legal counsel, CPA, and start-up consultant can help immensely here.
- *Never count the cash until it's in the bank.* CEOs lamented about the closing party that took place before the funds were in the bank—and the funds never got there. Closings are delicate. A CEO needs all the help available to secure a solid closing.
- *Always remember that deal flow is at work.* The CEO should not be too disappointed when the "Sorry . . ." call comes in. It should be expected. Even great salespeople expect mostly "no's." It's not the end of the world.

## Due Diligence

The founders must assume that *everything* written in their business plan will be checked, particularly details of marketing assumptions. The VC is looking for hidden traps, oversights, oversimplifications, hidden competitors, and upside opportunities. When the weeks and months of due diligence work are finished, the VC will try to find the silver thread woven through the business plan: It will be in the form of a simple, one-sentence line that will become his or her reason for saying yes to your invitation to invest in this start-up.

## What Investors Look For

Now let's concentrate on the perspective of the venture capitalists, so that you can better see what they are looking for, and looking out for, based on their successful and unsuccessful experiences.

The experienced investor looks for many things. We found a long list cited by the people with whom we spoke. (We'll go into this in more detail in Chapter 9, "Venture Capitalists.")

Our findings have been categorized into five sets of things venture investors look for in a start-up. They are, in order of importance:

1. a large, rapidly expanding market
2. people/management that can get the job done
3. a brilliant idea or technology that can be commercialized
4. a strategy that has a strong "unfair advantage"
5. a reasonable price per share

When asked which is their biggest headache, venture capitalists answered in resounding unison: *People management is number one.*

**Management Experience.** Ideally, investors want a *complete* team, with a CEO, and VPs for each function. (The possible exception is a VP for finance; the reasons for this are presented in Chapter 9 in the section "How a VC Firm Controls Its Investment.") Chapter 6 discusses the team requirements in more detail.

The general rule is: *The more complete the team, the more likely the start-up will get funded.*

Investors consider it a valuable asset to their funding if a start-up is run by a team that has been working together for five to ten years. One timeless example is Linear Technology, who walked out of National Semiconductor as a unit (sans VP, finance) and started in business with the key functions filled. That is the good news.

The bad news is that Linear was sued by National. For guidance on how to avoid this kind of lawsuit, see Chapter 4, in the section called "Ethical Departure from an Employer."

Next in importance after completeness comes *competence.* The president must at least have a proven track record that has demonstrated the likelihood of success in the new venture. This does not require experience in a prior successful start-up. Bob Swanson, president of Linear, had no prior start-up experience; he had been with National as a manager for most of his career. Prior to the start-up, he was the general manager of National's linear business.

After competence comes *maturity.* It is very common to begin with an incomplete team, putting individuals lacking adequate experience as managers of people in the position of being corporate officers. One Internet-intensive venture capitalist said, "We have to provide a lot of 'adult supervision' these days!" The first management problem that venture investors look for is people in positions for which they are not qualified. A former salesperson in the role of president will not be well received if he has no prior track record as a general manager, no matter how well he has succeeded as manager of a national sales force; such people are viewed as looking for something other than financial business success. Consequently, the VCs carefully scan the management section of the business plan that contains all résumés.

A core group of high-tech people frequently label themselves vice presidents, with one becoming president, creating a problem later when there are personnel to be managed and business goals to be met. In the raw-seed stage of funding, VCs investing in that portion of the life of a company may reluctantly accept an existing set of self-assigned officers, but with the proviso that such people step aside when the seed venture capital firm recruits experienced leaders who are more satisfactory to investors. Yahoo is a classic example of how to do this right: Founders stepped aside, became "Chief Yahoos," and a fresh management team was hired quickly to grow the business.

**Emerging Incompetence.** Emerging incompetence is a common malady in start-ups; it is hard to avoid. What happens over time is that the founders and early hires are almost always outgrown by the exploding growth of management problems in the expanding company. This commonly happens before the initial public offering.

It is especially evident when times of trouble inevitably come. The board of directors, dominated by the venture capitalists, will try to talk such managers into stepping aside, but all too often intense personal emotions and egos enter into the fray, especially by founders, and a fight then becomes bitter:

*Founder:* I started this company; I want to remain president!
*Venture Capitalist:* If you don't step down, this start-up will never get another nickel of the capital it needs to survive!

However, the fight is usually quite brief; eventually, the board members have a brief squabble behind closed doors, agree to act as a single united body, and emerge with their unalterable decision. And out go the (often not fully vested) resisting employees, regardless of their titles, personal sacrifices, or prior contributions to the start-up.

We only hear about the start-up management heroes, the giants on the cover of *BusinessWeek* such as Hewlett and Packard, Sporck and Noyce and Sanders, billionaire Bill Gates, and Jim Clark, who started two famous companies, Silicon Graphics and Netscape. For each one of those, there are probably a thousand stories of founding managers who fought and lost as their start-up outgrew them. There are also successful stories of early team members who stepped aside and stayed, at least for a few more years.

In general, the management team will be incomplete at first. Because of this, the investor looking at the start-up will want to hear a plan for filling out the team with people having the skills necessary to help the start-up succeed.

**Brilliant Idea or Technology That Can Be Commercialized.** Simply put, can the idea become a commercial reality? Can the high-tech team convert it from a laboratory success into a device that can be manufactured by the thousands at a low cost? How high is the risk in the technology?

Ben Rosen (venture investor in Lotus and Compaq) was asked what his firm looks for in a start-up. He told the *Wall Street Week* television audience, "We look for blinding technology!" He quickly added that there must be a reasonable chance to convert a brilliant flash of an idea into a wave of manufacturable product that customers are eager to buy.

**Large, Rapidly Expanding Market.** It is almost obvious that investors are looking for a rapidly expanding market. Yet, exceptions create the color—as well as a clarification—of this fact. For example, there are often the "as-yet-not-yet-started" markets: The Sony Walkman was an amazing success, but it was started even though market research showed very little consumer interest. Biotechnology engineering spawned Genentech even though investors and industry analysts were unable to predict the future potential. And consider successful Linear Technology, whose analog integrated circuit market was well established and grew more slowly than the digital IC market. VCs have committed millions to superconductor start-ups without any existing applications or markets.

In the case of Linear, the sustainable competitive advantage was founded upon a unique phenomenon of analog technology: The designers of linear-integrated analog circuits are generally much more experienced and more scarce than digital designers. By attracting the top analog designers to a single, analog-only company, a case was made to create a start-up company in a mature industry.

As for new, untested markets: That is what most start-ups are all about. In fact, it is probably the single greatest challenge to a start-up marketing leader, which is why hiring a VP of marketing with prior start-up experience is so valuable. The VCs are familiar with this reality and go about testing the realities of business plan claims by various means, including sessions with Dataquest, IDC, and other market research firms.

However, we found the VCs most favored method was to telephone a couple of potential customers and ask them about the likelihood of their buying the proposed product. A CEO should have a prepared list of such potential buyers for the venture capitalist to call. It may ensure that the VC says yes.

**Strategy.** Cutting across all the above investor concerns is a priority considera-tion of how the start-up management plans to get ahead and stay ahead. We were told that the VCs spend the most time on this issue. Because of its importance, we have devoted two sections later in this chapter to strategy: "Sustainable Compet-itive Advantage" and "Creating Your Company's Strategy." The individual who understands those sections is well on the way to success.

# Overview of a Business Plan

There is no magic about what should go into a good business plan. Table 5-1 pro-vides a generic outline of the eight sections that should be included. Following is a brief outline of what should be covered in each section.

**Executive Summary.** It should be brief, and it must be *great*. This is about all most readers will ever scan, let alone read. It must catch their attention, answer their key questions, and entice them to read further. It should be treated as a comprehensive miniplan. Your unfair advantage must stand out clearly.

**Customer Need and Business Opportunity.** What is the start-up going to build and how? Why would a customer want it? How well will it perform? Include your product technology here. Marketing strategy discussion starts in this section. Start building your unfair advantage in detail.

**Business Strategy and Key Milestones.** This chapter summarizes the start-up's strategy. It includes a one-page chart showing sequential, cumulative head count and cash flow at each significant milestone.

**Marketing Plan.** A great deal of time should be spent on this section. When the VC finishes reading it, he or she should be confident of how the start-up will po-sition its first products and why customers will value them relative to the compe-tition.

**Operations Plan.** This section should contain enough detail to show how the start-up will design and manufacture its first products. The VCs will grill founders on the realism of the schedule to get to first customer shipment. Show total head-count and facilities requirements.

**Management and Key Personnel.** This should be kept as short and focused as possible. The emphasis should be on directly related experience, especially track records as managers. Irrelevant experience can be omitted.

**Financial Projections.** Use a simple spreadsheet model to project the start-up's financial success and need for capital. Include forecasts by month for years one

## TABLE 5-1. Outline of a Business Plan

**Executive Summary**

Purpose of this plan (amount of funding, uses)

Business opportunity, business model, market, product/service, technology, management

Summary of five-year income statement, profit, head count and capital requirements

**Customer Need and Business Opportunity**

Product/service idea and technology description, end users and customers

Value proposition

**Business Strategy and Key Milestones**

Plan to out-maneuver the competition

Show each milestone with cumulative cash need and head count

**Marketing Plan**

Basic need and company solution

Ideal customer and value proposition

Market segmentation and size of markets

Channels of distribution

Strategic partners

Business model, branding plan

Sales strategy and plans

Customer support

Five-year sales forecast

Competition, positioning, and unfair advantage

**Operations Plan**

Engineering plan

Web site plan

Manufacturing/outsourcing plan

Facilities and administration plan

**Management and Key Personnel**

Organization

Staffing plan and head count projections

Detailed résumés of leadership

Incentive compensation program

Company culture plan

**Financial Projections**

Overview and key assumptions

Five-year forecasts

Income statement

Balance sheet

Cash flow statement

*Source:* Saratoga Venture Finance

and two, with annual summaries for years one through five. Build in conservative assumptions. Details of revenue by product line, average selling prices (ASP), and so on, should be kept in backup files in case they are called for.

**Appendices.** These are not often used. They can contain photographs or copies of market research projections. Appendices should not be filled with bulky backup data.

**Presentation.** A total of thirty to fifty pages is typical of what is written. Try to cut it to fewer than fifty pages. The shorter the better, although short ones are hardest to write. Make a few copies of your plan at the copy shop, and bind about half in some kind of neat, sturdy folder—nothing gaudy. You will soon be making a lot of changes, so there's no need to run up a big copy bill for soon-to-be-obsolete business plans. Each grilling by the VCs will uncover weaknesses that need fixing, which allows the founders to build a better plan as they go along. Be prepared to submit electronic versions (on short notice) via e-mail.

**Resources.** There are some very good free resources for preparing a business plan. Some venture capitalists have guides on their web sites. There are others available from the best large accounting firms. Some commercial Internet sites also make suggestions. Surf to find the latest suggestions.

# The Importance of Unfair Advantage

"What do you do better than any other company?" will be a question the CEO must be well prepared to answer. A vague answer is as bad as no answer at all. Potential investors are looking for that special ingredient that will give them confidence that a start-up company will have an advantage over its competitors, an advantage that will survive copying and reverse engineering and brute-force attacks by giants with a lot more money. An advantage that can produce enough products to make the IPO dream thinkable. An unfair advantage. A distinctive competence.

Because of the high failure rate in start-ups, the investor is a born skeptic. Critical comments from the sea of doubting venture capitalists are thus common. As our research shows, about 60 percent of the funded start-ups go bankrupt, so they are right to be skeptical. A very high proportion of start-ups rely solely on their technology as the backbone of their distinctive competence. Yet history shows that a lot more than technology is required to be a long-term success in a new business enterprise.

"What do you have that will enable you to switch gears, shift, and sidestep if the market is a lot different than you plan on?" That is the question in the investor's mind as he or she listens to a CEO explain the start-up's strategy. The CEO's responses must be well thought through.

# Shooting Stars

Every investor shudders to hear the words "shooting star." That is the phrase used to describe the company that got off to a flying start, but failed soon after reaching the headlines. According to our interviews, a large proportion of emerging companies fall into this category. The goal of a start-up's CEO is to avoid the mistakes that lead to such a demise.

"But who cares?" some said to us. "All anyone wants is to get through the IPO or be acquired as fast as possible and get out as a millionaire or billionaire." We asked that question of many participants in the venture business, and they had a similar response: "Institutional investors make up our largest source of capital. They are also the investors in IPOs. We can't sell them all the turkeys and expect to be in business for long."

Thus the venture capitalist takes the longest-term view when reading a business plan, asking a number of related questions at the very beginning:

- "Is this a product or a business?" The VC often sees ideas from high-tech personnel that are best suited to be sold or licensed to an established company. Single-product ideas are good candidates to become shooting stars, and VCs tend to shy away from them.
- "Can the market support a company that will grow to more than $100 million in revenue in five years?" The venture capitalist cannot afford to invest in anything less and must plan on becoming liquid in order to succeed in his investment business.

Lawsuits from investors who lost money are one consequence of going public too soon, on a song and a hope that everything will turn out all right. In 1991 the courts were still working on the rash of investor class action suits that broke out after the IPO frenzy of the 1982–1983 personal computer boom. The same concerns exist in the Internet era of high stock valuations.

*Forbes'* **Study of Shooting Stars.** Why does it happen? How can it be avoided? One watchdog of IPO shooting stars is the self-appointed guardian of the capitalist scene, *Forbes* magazine. It published a timeless review of this kind of company in its issue of January 28, 1985. The article makes good reading and opened with this salvo:

Were you one of those investors enticed into believing that small companies—"emerging growth stocks"—were the only game in town? If so, you probably have a long disaster list of your own. There are plenty to choose from. American Software down 21% in the last year, to under $16 a share. Hawkeye Bancorp off 51%. Lee Data Corp. down 69%. LJN Toys off 59%. Oak Hill Sportswear down 36%. Reeves Communications down 57%. Sandwich Chef off 40%.

Face it, you can't blame this on just a fickle market. The profits, indeed the revenues, of many hot little companies suddenly turned cold.

Why does it happen? Why do so many small, promising companies peak so early? Why doesn't success breed success?

The simple answer is that the thin capitalization and narrow product lines that permit spectacular growth also permit overnight disasters.

That a young firm should have problems is not surprising. To succeed, it must do five things:

- Get an idea that can be funded.
- Market that product or service.
- Maximize efficiency.
- Extend that idea through add-ons and variations.
- Come up with another viable idea.

Obviously, entrepreneurs can stumble in any of the five areas, but the last step—coming up with another idea—seems to be the killer. *Forbes* has been chronicling the rise and fall of small companies since 1979, and we are always surprised at how few fast starters turn out to have staying power. Of the top 100 companies from the *Forbes* Up & Comer Class of 1979, 25 were acquired, leaving 75 still independent. Of those 75, only 25 qualified for the 1984 list of top-performing small companies. So, even if one charitably assumes that the best companies were acquired, it seems reasonable to say that the odds against staying on top are, at best, only 50/50. Little wonder so many investors get burned on the stocks of hot little companies.

Here are the headlines of *Forbes'* mini–case studies that followed the above introduction. They suggest what to look out for:

- "THE MARKET SOURS"
- "THE FLUKE FACTOR"
- "OUTFLANKED"
- "LAST YEAR'S MODEL"
- "THE GRASS LOOKS GREENER"
- "THE SKIMMING TRAP"

- "Dropping The Baton"
- Me-Too'ed by the Mighty

The writers closed with these words:

> Why do so many emerging growth companies peak so early? Because in addition to facing decisions as difficult as those at IBM or General Motors, their slender resources often force them to bet the company.
>
> There are two morals to be drawn from all this. One is for entrepreneurs: Don't get carried away by your own success; overconfidence is as dangerous as excessive timidity. The other is for investors: There is a depressingly high chance that just about the time the insiders are offering you a ride on their fast-rolling bandwagon, that bandwagon is poised to go right over the cliff. The maxim that follows for entrepreneurs: Always run scared. For investors: Be skeptical of super-high growth rates.

What you need is something to lean on, at all times, in all circumstances. That is what sustainable competitive advantage is all about.

## Sustainable Competitive Advantage

The two hardest things about a sustainable advantage are that few are very sustainable, and few have many real advantages.

When a business plan contains a sustainable competitive advantage it is like the little girl: when it is good, it is very, very, good, and when it is bad, it is horrid. So let's examine how to develop an outstanding sustainable competitive advantage. A venture capitalist with one of America's top twenty VC firms had this to say about what he called "the company's compelling advantage":

> We start looking for the technology or idea that is the core to the advantage of the start-up. This has become much more important to us because of the sharp increase in competition for funding start-ups which has arisen in recent years.
>
> In past years, we used to be able to count on calmly reviewing business plans, picking the best with a high degree of confidence that our $2 million total investment would be invested in a start-up that had a two- or three-year lead on the competition.
>
> However, today we are having to deal with much different circumstances, something our partners call "the steeplechase effect." The VC community has so much money chasing so few deals that we are actually seeing six or seven start-ups launched over the same six-month time period to do the same thing.
>
> As a result, venture capitalists are much more sensitive to the competitive threat to a start-up. And that threat now comes from very large corporations, many

of which have become much more responsive and alert to where technology and markets are going. They are much quicker on their feet than they were five or six years ago. We look for all the sources of competition: from start-ups funded by other venture capitalists, from large companies, from other businesses, from other technologies, from other markets. . . .

All this increase in competition results in a shortage of good management. It gets back to the basic problem of how the start-up plans to fill its needed team.

Closely linked to good management is proprietary advantage. We examine it closely in our due diligence. The proprietary advantage is very important to a venture capitalist. We have to see clearly what the company's compelling advantage is. Venture capitalists are looking for the revolutionary—not the incremental—advantage. Incremental technologies build incremental companies—usually with a short life cycle—unless there is an outstanding management team that can continue to pursue incremental advances with few dollars of investment. The big wins are where you pursue a major new development that blasts you into a new market.

The proprietary advantage does not have to be technology: it can be in a new concept; for instance, in how to market a business in a large, established marketplace. We ask lots of questions about marketing and its relations to the proprietary advantage: How are you going to get to market? Is it a large, established market or a brand-new, untapped one? Is it splintered, served by a collection of small mom-and-pop companies? Why will you have access to customers?

The business plan does not have to be long. We see all too many generic business plans that extrapolate poor thinking into financial forecasts of a $100 million company in three years. Instead, the plan should spend more time on addressing the issues surrounding competitive advantage, the pros and cons of the key issues facing the start-up.

In our final decision, we are very selective. The entrepreneurs must learn that and not be so disappointed when we say "no," which is most of the time. We are sent close to four thousand business plans a year, including a few referred to us by people we know well. We fund only ten to fifteen of those, with more these days going to low tech than prior to 1983. And as for ultimate success—the IPO achieved by a good start-up—we believe there are only ten to twenty such deals in a given year in the entire U.S. among all the venture capital funds. We fund only the best plans we can find. And there are too few of those.

That advice has stood the test of time and is as relevant today as it was then.

The best analysis of sustainable competitive advantage we could find is contained in a classic (out of print) *Business Horizons* article entitled "Sustainable

Competitive Advantage—What It Is, What It Isn't," by Kevin P. Coyne. Coyne (1986) dissects the advantages of a competitor, presents what to look for to test the sustainable edge, and adds a section on how to think through other competitors' possible reactions to a strategy. We strongly recommend that prospective entrepreneurs read it. Here are some of the key points of the analysis:

- Sustainable competitive advantage (SCA) is:
  1. a consistent difference in product attributes
  2. that is a direct consequence of a capability gap
  3. that endures over time.
- SCA is based upon delivering superior value to the customer (not necessarily the lowest price).
- The product attribute differences must be the customers' key buying criteria.

The article is rich in lessons on what else to look for in an SCA. A CEO can use it to prepare a checklist and then test the start-up's own business plan against that list. Coyne concludes with these sobering words:

> Although an SCA is a powerful tool in creating a successful business strategy, it is not the only key ingredient. In fact,
> - Possessing an SCA does not guarantee financial success.
> - Producers can succeed even when competitors possess an SCA.
> - Pursuing an SCA can sometimes conflict with sound business strategy.
>
> Although its attainment is the goal of competitive strategy, sustainable competitive advantage is not an end in itself but a means to an end. The corporation is not in business to beat its competitors, but to create wealth for its shareholders. Thus, actions that contribute to SCA but detract from creating shareholder wealth may be good strategy in the competitive sense but bad strategy for the corporation.

He goes on to cite examples of bad strategic thinking, including one very familiar to high-tech people: "Aggressive learning-curve pricing strategies that sacrifice too much current profit."

## Creating Your Company's Strategy

This is how Tom Peters summarized the characteristics of an effective strategy in his column "On Excellence":

> What is your organization's uniqueness? Can you state it in 15 to 25 words or less? Does everyone in the organization buy in? Is the strategy statement printed on wallet-sized cards that are given to everyone? Is it immortalized in granite?

VCs seldom find that in business plans. The point is that too often the only foundation on which a company is proposed to be built is technology. That translates to phrases often spoken by technologists, such as "faster X4" or "six times the price performance," all of which some other high-tech group will be copying just as soon as they hear of a start-up's funding. "What else does a start-up have besides technology?" The answer is a good test of how deep a company's strategy is. Venture capital investors want as much depth as they can get before parting with their precious funds.

Geoffrey Moore added perspective when he remarked (*Inside the Tornado* and *Gorilla*):

> [W]e began. . . . explaining what makes high-tech markets and the high-tech stock markets so volatile. The short answer to that question, as we saw, is *tornadoes*. What we learned at the same time is that, in the eye of these tornadoes, a *gorilla* is often born. That gorilla is destined to enjoy competitive advantages unlike any others in the market place. And those marketplace advantages, in turn, generate stock market returns that are also unparalleled.

The next sections are designed to help founders sort out their strategy.

**Classification of Start-up Strategies.** There are several types of strategies followed by successful companies. Some follow strategies based on the work of the great management consultant, Peter F. Drucker, which are digested in his book *Innovation and Entrepreneurship: Practice and Principles* (1985). A careful study will help the reader sort out the kind of strategy the start-up founder's plan could best use. The risks vary with each strategic type. CEOs may be surprised to find their strategies are not very strong. If this is the case, the weaknesses must be confronted and the business plan revised.

As Jerry Crowley of the start-up Gazelle Microcircuits explained to us, "Remember that a business plan is a living thing. It gets modified, shifts, and is altered along the way as the company progresses, hits barriers, fixes things, encounters competition, discovers opportunities, and gets a big break or two."

Another help is the classic book *Marketing Warfare* (1986) by Al Ries and Jack Trout. Its timeless tips work well in the Internet era.

We have also found helpful the strategic thinking in *Building Strong Brands* (1996) by David Aaker, *New Positioning* (1996) by Jack Trout, and *The 22 Immutable Laws of Branding* (1998) by Al Ries & Laura Ries.

**Positioning.** Practice can help the CEO assess the strengths and weaknesses of the start-up's major competitors. When these exercises are completed the CEO must next position the company and its first products against its prime competitors. If the CEO avoids this step the venture capitalists will expose the start-up's softness in their rugged due diligence question-and-answer sessions. They will have no mercy on founders who have not adequately prepared their chosen strategy.

Positioning is very hard work and many good books have been written about it, so we will not go into the details here. Suffice it to say that a CEO who is uncomfortable with this work should call for help—from a start-up consultant, a sharp marketing expert, or an experienced general manager.

No matter who is selected, the CEO should remember that the goal is to do top-notch strategic thinking as a whole company. The CEO and founders should not expect to succeed in raising capital by leaving this vital work to a marketing person working solo.

**Strategic Thinking.** Practical help in doing strategic thinking comes from Michael Porter, a professor at the Harvard Business School. Here is a summary of Porter's advice for CEOs:

> Every company, whether diversified or not, should have a strategic plan for each of its businesses. I favor a set of analytical techniques for developing strategy that have grown out of my research over the past 15 years. Whatever techniques one uses, however, a good plan should contain the following elements:
>
> - an analysis of the industry in which the firm competes
> - sources of competitive advantage
> - an analysis of the existing and potential competitors who might affect the company
> - an assessment of the company's competitive position
> - selection or ratification of strategy, built on competitive advantage, and how it can be sustained

Our research at Saratoga Venture Finance shows that start-ups that supply the above points in their business plans have a much higher chance of obtaining the funds they desire at fair prices.

## The Role of the CPA Firm

The help of a good accounting firm is needed next. That means more than a good accountant. What is required are the services of a vast number of financial specialists, who can assist with the following tasks:

- check the start-up's financial forecasts
- verify the realism of the start-up's key assumptions

- prepare the start-up's tax returns, which are required even though a company does not yet make a profit
- confidentially review the wisdom of key business plans and strategies, particularly the long-term implications of alternative actions the company could take today
- help set accounting policies for keeping books. This is particularly important in the area of setting policies that are consistent with those of other similar high-tech enterprises.
- arrange introductions to venture capitalists and investment bankers

It may sound trite, but a CEO should remember that this choice involves engaging a whole firm; therefore, the choice should be made thoughtfully.

We reviewed the high-tech practices of the most frequently mentioned accounting firms and ranked them in rough order of estimated annual billings for high-tech start-ups as follows:

1. Arthur Andersen
2. Ernst & Young
3. PricewaterhouseCoopers
4. KPMG
5. Deloitte & Touche

CPA firms can contribute much more than expensive bookkeeping—if a top firm is chosen. And a few strong regional CPA firms also have high-tech practices. Above all, avoid being the first high-tech start-up for the chosen CPA firm in your local area.

Start-ups outside the United States will find a local office of an American CPA firm eager to assist the new enterprise. Founders said that using them helped their later entry to the large market in the United States and got their financial forecasts into a format that the venture capitalists in Silicon Valley were most familiar with. Most start-ups will quickly be looking for customers overseas. A top CPA firm is already international. By comparison, venture capitalists are less helpful outside the United States.

**Choosing a CPA Firm.** Our research showed strong consensus here: the founder should go for a top name firm from the beginning. No one recommended starting with a small firm and later shifting to a larger one; the pain of change and the animosity generated were not worth the possible fees saved with such a strategy.

However, our confidants recommended looking not just for a large international accounting firm, but also for one whose local office contains the most high-tech experience in your area. Some firms have transferred top personnel into states that have lesser high-tech experience in order to get such a practice started. The founders should pick the firm with the most high-tech veterans in the local office.

The experienced high-tech chief financial officers emphasized this: A firm should be selected based on how well the accounting firm's manager and the start-up's CEO and/or CFO communicate on business matters. They told us, "It's tough enough to get all the work done with limited resources without having to struggle to teach the CPA firm's manager what is practical and theoretical about an accounting reserve or expense accrual."

**Accounting Fees.** New companies do not have to pay the expensive going rate for accounting services. All the top companies will discount their standard rates deeply—if they get excited about a start-up's long-term prospects. It is the CEO's job to sell them the start-up's vision for the future.

The CEO must be sure to get the fee agreement executed up front. This agreement must include: all offices worldwide (some firms cannot guarantee discounted rates in their independent offices in Europe and elsewhere) and all tax work. A CEO should be able to get a great deal of free time for the early days, particularly in the preseed stage.

A firm should not be chosen because of its low accounting fees. Other matters are too important, such as related industry experience. It is wise to get a commitment for the fees for an IPO. It is not too early and it is important to get the lower fee rates wherever possible. None of the fees related to raising capital are tax-deductible in the United States (surprise!).

# Making Financial Projections

The start-up's consultant and CPA firm should review the financial forecasts. They must be told to do more than validate the accuracy of the arithmetic.

Their experience is valuable in verifying the founders' underlying business assumptions. For example, how would you estimate the number of support engineers needed in marketing and engineering to care for customers who are spread out over the United States and the rest of the world markets? You need help to project dollars per head. Your CPA firm can help you do that.

**Modeling Financial Projections.** The CEO is about to do more numbers than anyone ever believed possible. A business plan is a document, a snapshot, of an ever-changing strategy. Change is a certainty.

To relieve the CEO of the bulk of the burden of building intricate formulas and basic structures of a financial model of a start-up you need a spreadsheet model of your business projections. The CEO can then start by plugging in his own revenue and head-count numbers and end up with a five-year forecast.

The objective is to redirect the CEO's time from cranking out lots of time-consuming numbers to increasing the time spent on strategic thinking. That is where the big payoff is.

**Calculating How Much Capital Is Needed.** Our experience showed that most business plan forecasts were off by a large order of magnitude in two areas:

- *Sales revenue.* Forecasts are particularly likely to be overly optimistic in predicting average selling prices and a larger-than-realistic share of the market. This is understandable in most cases—the CEO is forecasting into a new, untried market without much, if any, related track record to go on. Internet business models are largely unproven, further compounding the problem.

   Venture capitalists know this and will still grill the CEO about the numbers. The wide real-world misses have turned most VCs we spoke to into doubting Thomases who were apt to make remarks like "Your numbers are off by a large order of magnitude" or "There is no way you will ever come close to those unit projections"—as if the VC is the expert in the CEO's industry. The CEO must be ready to face this and respond wisely with a plausible answer. Pick your numbers and support them with your thinking. Everyone knows they are estimates. The issue is why you think they are the most likely and what is the upside, the possible huge dream that might come true?

- *Capital required.* We have been fortunate in being allowed to see original business plan forecasts years after the success of a start-up. We found that most of them grossly underestimated the capital needed to launch the business. Only a rare few CEOs proudly told us they were right on plan. We often found unrealistically low expectations for: how long it took (much longer than planned) for the sales cycle to close on business deals with large numbers of early customers (Geoffrey Moore analyzes this problem in his book *Crossing the Chasm*); and the cost of furniture, computers, telephone systems, and leasehold improvements.

Another great cause of trouble was the old nemesis, often called product slip. This condition occurs frequently when product development hits a snag and an additional six months to one year are required to finish the first complete prototype. This is almost a given for high-tech companies. Yet rarely did any financial projections address this serious possibility. Our experiences have led us to recommend—as a matter of policy—that forecasts include enough of a cash cushion for a major rework of the first major product of the company, at least six months' worth of burn rate.

One consequence of this failure to allow for product slippage is that VCs have a habit of "doing the double" in private: They quickly calculate the return on their investment in a start-up company at the best price they think they can get, then assume they will have to double the cash invested in order to become liquid through either merger or IPO. They then adjust their first pricing to be sure of getting a good ROI, even if extra capital is required. The founders' dilution is just part of the calculation. The CEO must decide how much capital will be required; the figure must be as realistic as possible. It is surprising to most founders how many VCs tell CEOs to raise millions more capital than they originally asked for.

**Other Capital Tips.** All the capital needed should be shown as one big number as a plug to the balance sheet and cash flow statement.

The financial structuring (preferred stock, etc.) details should be left to sessions with the start-up's consultant, accountant, and attorney.

Try to show all capital as equity. Bank borrowings and equipment lease-lines can be reconsidered after the company gets its first funding.

Do not forecast any bank debt until after one year of profitability. Thereafter, the start-up can borrow about 60 percent of U.S. receivables. Inventory financing should be forgotten. About half the value of equipment and cubicles can be leased.

Wages should be loaded by 25 percent to cover benefits and related taxes.

No more than about ten to twenty million total shares should be issued by the time the IPO is projected, unless the CEO anticipates a "blow-out" IPO worth billions instead of hundreds of millions. The number of shares includes all stock options. A per-share price in the low teens will be desired at the time of IPO.

The CEO should consult the CPA for advice on how to deal with the uncertainties of the tax loss carryforward of net operating losses in a start-up. After that the CEO can pick a tax rate.

# Summary

This is a good place to begin your serious work. First, try writing the initial draft of your executive summary in less than one hour; keep it to four pages or less. That will tell you what you are missing in your thinking about your business plan. It's always the hardest chapter to write. The toughest portion is the first paragraph, in which you should summarize in three sentences or less what your unfair advantage is all about. Once you have surmounted that hurdle, the rest is downhill.

Keep in mind the following tips from the veterans:

- Spend time on creating a great business plan.
- Build the plan on unfair advantage—one that is sustainable against competition.
- Prepare for tough questions from VCs.
- Create an adequate capital plan, with cash to spare for emergencies.
- Hire ("rent") the best help you can to advise you in this work.

After you finish a draft you are satisfied with, ask friends to read it and comment. Your advisers will be glad to get in a few words before you lock in your final version. Also keep in mind that this is not a business plan as an operations manager thinks of it. Instead, it is a document intended to help both the company and the investor to better understand the business to be financed. So adjust your writing accordingly and, as you write, keep the audience in mind: the people with the cash to invest. They are always looking for hidden gems to invest in. Try to help them avoid having to wade through a badly written business plan to discover you. Instead, take the time to do a job you are proud of, and enjoy the reward from such a big effort as this, communicating the most important business idea of your life.

Now let's turn to the number-one topic for investors—the management team of your start-up—and listen to what advice the veterans of start-ups give CEOs who are attempting to assemble their first core team of people.

*6*

# The Team

Investors start reading a business plan by skimming the executive summary; then they jump to the section in the back entitled "Management."

Our research showed that investors are extremely reluctant to invest without knowing their risk concerning "adequate management." The issue is what "adequate" means. This chapter will clarify this issue and will help the founders decide what additional talent they will need.

## The Core Team

Each group of people that starts a company has a core team around whom the company is built. Only a few of the original group are founders; most are additional talent that the leader feels will be needed soon after funding is closed. The core team should be picked very carefully, because its business and interpersonal style becomes the foundation for the company's culture and, like yeast, grows the value system that becomes the mark of that start-up.

The founders should pick the most outstanding talent that can be found. These people will represent the company to investors of the seed and subsequent rounds of funding. The company people must make an excellent impression—not from a slick, smooth point of view, but rather from their track records and skills and by their depth of experience in the areas most important to the sustainable competitive advantage of the company. Don't settle for a few average employees—this is the wrong place to compromise.

**Experience.** *Do I have a chance to attract venture capital if I do not have prior start-up experience?* We found that venture capitalists generally gave the same answer to that question: They say that if it's a good idea, a new enterprise will always be welcome, along with the person who thought it up, but the chances of raising venture funds will certainly be increased if the founder has prior experience with a start-up. However, most start-ups are not led by people with years of prior experience in new businesses. VCs will be frank and tell the leader if his or her experience needs to be supplemented by that of others with track records in start-ups: "How do you feel about being CEO?"

The CEO's goal is to stack the deck in the start-up's favor, and to get the needed capital at a fair price. If the founders believe that start-up experience will improve the company's odds significantly, they must find it. For instance, ask venture capitalists for leads to people wanting to be CEO of a start-up. Venture capitalists get hundreds of résumés from people who are looking for a start-up. Founders can benefit from those contacts, even before asking the venture capitalist for money.

*I am a technologist (or a young person), not a businessperson. I think my idea can be a big success, but I don't know if I should proceed or not. What should I do?* Start-up advisers and angels are asked this question by people from many backgrounds. They told us their answer is always the same: Get started on the trail to getting your business financed. Complete your business plan as soon as possible; let that be the pacing process that you use to answer your important questions. Follow our guidelines for the early stages and this will raise the key issues you need to deal with. You can always get good people to listen to a good idea. And during the process you can attract the management talent you will need.

Now let us address a key issue for investors—completeness.

## The Importance of a Complete Management Team

By the end of the first multimillion-dollar round one of financing, the CEO will be expected to have filled all the key functional positions that report directly to him. Venture capitalists are particularly concerned if VP of marketing or VP of sales or VP of business development positions are not filled at that stage, particularly if the CEO is the lead technologist or idea person with little business experience.

The investors see a race to finish the first product or service or web site as soon as possible. Incomplete management teams slow that race down and a window of opportunity may be missed. When a key person is missing, the CEO must take time to find, recruit, and train the new member of the executive team. That pause will probably delay introduction of the start-up's first product, increasing the risk for investors, who will in turn price round one accordingly, with more dilution to the founders.

*What is the best sequence in which to add people? When should we hire a salesperson and a finance manager?* The order in which start-up founders added to their executive teams varied, but we discerned this pattern:

- Most start with the inventor and a solid leader of engineering, often without an experienced VP of engineering. This increases the risk of not delivering a great product. Thus, investors look hard at such a technical leader's skills, doing a lot of questioning and checking of references while investigating the start-up. The investors much prefer a prior VP or at least a veteran technical leader of teams of engineers. This secures the technology and creates an asset for the investors in case the company goes belly-up.
- Most added an experienced CEO as soon as possible. This is preferred in all cases. Hopefully, that person can come on board in time to help close round one financing.
- The VP of marketing is the next most important position to fill. Most investors insist that this person be a part of the creation of the first product. Increasingly we find that investors are leery of placing any funds at risk in "a company in which technology is looking for a good market."
- The VP of business development is the next in line. This person sometimes is VP of sales for a while or also the VP of marketing in the early days of the start-up.
- The VP of sales was added about two months before first product was ready to ship. We were told that salespeople get cabin fever waiting for a chance to demonstrate their first product, live, to the first customer.
- The VP of manufacturing or operations must be on board in enough time to get the first product ready to ship or the web site ready to go public. Such people are responsible for meeting time, quantity, and quality commitments, all of which can be measured. This is not important for software companies.
- The VP of finance and administration position can be filled after the other positions are filled. This recommendation is controversial with some venture capitalists, and is discussed below.

Venture capitalists and the start-up's chief financial officer are seemingly in the same camp, with the same goals of success. However, an experienced CFO is frequently an antagonist to some of the venture capitalists. They are most likely to argue over the need for capital, the price at which it is to be sold, and the degree of control over spending and hiring; which investment bankers, attorneys, and new investors the start-up should do business with; what class of risk should be used to invest surplus funds; and how much leasing and borrowing the company should do.

In a nutshell, we found that many venture capitalists are reluctant to turn over control of financial policy to a strong CFO. As investors, they want to keep close reins on their new child, particularly when it (inevitably) starts to steer off course from its original business plan. That is understandable by most CEOs.

Such control by VCs is not necessarily in the best interests of the entrepreneur and his core team. Some angry CEOs told us that investors had pressured them into dropping R&D projects so that the company's financial statements would look good enough to get the IPO done. Others told us that venture board members virtually took over running the company's financial affairs when a weak controller succumbed under the pressure of bad times. Other CEOs told of being threatened with expulsion and blackballing if they did not go along with the terms and conditions of the proposed next round of financing (the dreaded "washout," which severely diluted the employees' equity but did less damage to the prior venture capitalists because of the antidilution clauses in the contractual clauses included in their preferred stock).

Needless to say, the founders and CEO had better be prepared to fight for the start-up's and their own interests. It is easier with a strong CFO on board as early as is reasonable.

Lately we have been seeing proportionately more CEOs adding a full VP of finance instead of a controller. And the CFO is being brought on more quickly than in prior years. This may reflect the experiences of successful IPO companies, many of which attracted an experienced CFO early, near round one time. This was noticeable for companies that raised more than $20 million of capital. And the shortage of experienced start-up CEOs may be shifting more power to them, allowing the CEO to choose a stronger VP of finance. Boom times call for quicker IPOs and thus quicker times to hire a CFO that can take the start-up public quickly.

**Completeness, Lawsuits, and Time.** Investors do like to see that two or three of the core team have worked together before. This reduces the risk to the investor by speeding the first product to market and reducing the time wasted in learning to get along with each other.

It takes time for people to learn to work together. We found all management lamenting how long it took for the culture to form, gel, and begin to function creatively. Few business plans acknowledge the slip time associated with this "working with strangers" phenomenon.

Investors do not like lawsuits or even the likelihood of legal entanglements.

Classic law cases of the 1980s set the guidelines for fair play. The complete Linear Technology team left National Semiconductor together, got round one monies almost immediately, and were promptly sued by their former employer. (Chapter 5 tells how to avoid this painful problem.)

## Outsourcing the CEO (and others): The Roles of Consultants and Contractors

Most start-ups begin recruiting by using the buddy system to recruit team members through the first three rounds of funding. This reduces the mistakes caused by hiring a stranger, takes much less cash than using recruiters, tends to cement the start-up's culture, and creates a spirit of togetherness and participation by new employees. Unlike the era of the 1980s, lots of recruiters, expensive newspaper advertisements, and for-fee-web-site hiring services are now being seen well before IPO time, reflecting the continuing shortage of qualified leaders.

By definition, all start-up companies are short of talent. Most start-ups solve this problem in part by the frequent use of contractors and outsourcing to experts such functions as public relations. These part-time personnel fill in for missing skill sets, and the company pays only for what it gets. Such personnel are widely available in the larger metropolitan areas and are regularly used in the life of emerging companies long after they go public. This phenomenon appears to have become a way of life for rapidly emerging high-tech companies. It is now common for the stock option plans of start-ups to allow shares to be granted to key contractors. As Don Valentine of Sequoia Capital put it, "Because of the start-up talent shortage, we now get the core management to focus on specific jobs in the business and, as venture backers, dig into our talent bank of related people to provide missing skills on an as-needed basis. It is an important way to use a venture backer, so pick your investor wisely and ask about their people resources."

Venture capitalists themselves make extensive use of part-time talent, often called "technology experts" or "due diligence associates." Venture firms can be helpful in recommending part-time consultants to fill any series of jobs that the start-up needs done.

Contractors are common in engineering; they get paid by the hour, day, month, or project. Consultants are more often used in other functions. Some open and close the financial statements each month. Some run the personnel department for the early months. Still others work on market research or sales training. These contractors are usually highly experienced former operations professionals. Their compensation often includes equity in some form, ranging from grants to purchase stock to issue of stock warrants, as well as cash compensation.

These part-timers range from the recently unemployed to the financially independent person. The latter are called "stand-in executives." They may have just finished a successful start-up and cashed in at IPO time. Saratoga Venture Finance calls such people "49ers" (from the idea of financial independence gained by American pioneers in the California gold rush of 1849). The part-time work schedule gives both parties a chance to look each other over, possibly for permanent employment (without an expensive recruiter's fee). This part-time-to-permanent arrangement is frequently done deliberately, both by 49ers interested in becoming start-up CEOs and the executives who hire them as contractors.

Recruiters are used as in larger companies—sparingly, but when the hiring is going to be hard or needs to be very fast and thus is critical to success. A growing number of venture firms are keeping an active roster of possible VP and CEO résumés in a personal computer database, just to be able to supply needed talent to their start-ups.

However, investors and founders have encouraged the use of recruiters in order to keep a start-up on plan. Bodies are needed—fast—to get the work done before a competitor arrives. CEO recruiting continues to be tense, due to the shortage of that pool of talent, and VP work is steady for recruiters who specialize in start-ups. Be sure to include their fees (15 to 33 percent of annual cash compensation) in your business plan financial forecasts!

## Impact on Valuation and Attraction of Funds

We believe that the pattern of high-tech start-up hiring practices we have described is commonly used. It is aimed at one goal: hiring as complete a team of competent professionals as the start-up can attract, as soon as possible, in order to execute its business plan on time and within budget.

The president of a very successful start-up was asked for advice on what to do to be a successful start-up, and he answered, "Hire the best people you can find!" Investors agree with him—the better the people, the less risk there is likely to be. The CEO should be able to translate management strength into negotiations that mean less dilution for the CEO and the founders, leaving more shares for more top people. As one veteran put it, "*A* players attract *A* players."

Interestingly, top-quality people often emerge from bankruptcies. Prior bankruptcy experience is valuable; failure has its rewards. Mature investors have seen six out of ten of their children go under. They know that it was not all the fault of every employee; the big breaks account for a lot of the outcome. Therefore, according to a number of wealthy, successful investors with whom we spoke, top managers from defunct companies are actively recruited to new start-ups. We would say, "It is better to hire a leader who learned from mistakes than it is to hire someone who was just lucky."

In the end, the CEO will want to be able to present a solid core team to attract the first rounds of funds, while avoiding the sacrifice of too much quality or too many shares along the way. Compensation (equity and cash) for this team is discussed in Chapters 7 and 8.

# Ownership, Dilution, Negotiation, and Valuation

T he question most frequently asked by entrepreneurs is: How much of our company should we give up to get the money? This chapter is dedicated to guiding the start-up CEO in answering that important question.

To assist the CEO in making this decision, we have done proprietary financial research on famous start-ups like Lotus, Apple, and Compaq, as well as on newer companies like Netscape, Yahoo, and others. Actual data from SEC records were processed and summarized using proprietary software that produced the Saratoga Venture Tables™ that are included at the end of this book. Examples of the tables and related charts are presented in this chapter and include these data:

- the percentages the founders retained and how much the other employees received
- the percentage that went to venture capitalists
- how much the investors really made
- data from the results of the initial public offering

We will also discuss the process for dealing with venture capitalists and suggest tactics and negotiating tips gathered from start-up CEOs—both successful and unsuccessful ones.

This chapter presents key actions that lead to success in each stage of the capital formation process, from seed to IPO. It also presents a surefire formula for pricing a start-up's financing and explains how, why, and when preferred stock is used. And we discuss the delicate process of closing on a venture-financed deal, including why it is so important to keep your mind focused on success. Remember: Success has been achieved only when the money is in the start-up's bank account.

# Summary of the Campaign to Raise Capital

There are thirteen financial stages in the process a CEO will go through to attract venture capitalists to a start-up deal. Each stage has its own special nature, risks, and activities necessary for success. In the descriptions of the stages that follow we have included the advice and insights that were cited most often in our interviews. There is plenty of room for creativity, yet the vast majority of funded deals follows this course of events, regardless of which round of financing is involved:

**Stage 1: Set Funding Objectives.** Certainly the number-one objective is to get the money in the bank. But the founders must also answer these questions:

- How long are we willing to go on looking for money? When should we throw in the towel? Refer to Chapter 3 for a review of the overall process of marching to IPO.
- What is the rock-bottom point for dilution (percentage drop in founders' ownership) in this round? Be sure all founders agree before negotiations start!
- What amount of capital should be raised in this round? What is the minimum, the maximum, and the amount to ask for in the first session? This figure will be challenged during the presentations to venture capitalists. The founders must be ready to answer in unison.

**Stage 2: Prepare the Plan to Attract Investors.** The founders must decide which firms to contact, how to get ahead of hundreds of other business plans that are ahead in the queue, and what to say to sell the firm of choice on taking the position of lead venture capitalist.

Founders need to plan this stage as carefully as any other critical business activity. It is a time for good minds to focus on how to succeed, given the resources on hand.

**Stage 3: Pick the Best Capital-Raising Strategy.** To get started here, founders should review Chapter 5 and focus on their company's strengths and weaknesses. Investors will be looking for the hidden winner—the company with the strong unfair advantage. And they will scrutinize the founders and their core team personnel closely.

The CEO should talk strategy with experienced business executives outside the start-up. Start with people who are avid supporters of the founders and leaders of the start-up, and people who are excited about the business plan. Most of our clients are surprised at how helpful this can be.

The money-raising strategy must eventually have the full backing of the lead venture firm, the firm other investors will follow. They can attract other venture firms.

*Warning:* Many CEOs and CFOs have told us of a big mistake they made in raising capital. After the seed round they assumed that their lead VC would raise the next rounds of capital while the CEO and CFO returned to running the company. This turned out to be a myth. The start-up organizations that realized this soon enough survived; the others suffered or even died. The CEO of several start-ups has this advice (learned in the school of hard knocks):

> Tell all the founders that the only way to succeed in raising the needed capital is to have the founder/CEO do it. Do not count on their well-intentioned lead venture partner to raise the cash. He cannot be counted on; he has too many alligators swimming around his fledgling promising companies, and he is frantically trying to help save his other drowning turkey investments. Raising your own capital is too important an event to be entrusted to anyone but yourself.

## Case Study: Crown Semiconductor

Here is an actual profile of the objectives, plan, strategy, and tactics used by two founders to get round one capital:

- Hire a household name veteran as CEO, someone highly competent whom we can respect and get along with.
- Add three friends from our two seed venture capital firms who are heavies in our industry; put them on as advisers to the board of directors.
- Present our company as the blue chip of the start-ups in this very new technology. Reinforce every word in the presentation with an image of top class.
- Use our (well-known) law firm's top partner to introduce us to five to seven other top venture sources, at least two on the east or west coast, whichever is opposite. Quickly follow those introductions with calls from our two seed sources.
- Negotiate for at least $10 million, fully expecting to accept only $6 million. Cut off at that amount [they built a reasonable spending cushion into their financial forecasts]. Induce scarcity; competition among funding sources is our best friend. That will keep the price of this round higher, reducing dilution.

- Make 30 percent for insiders (officers and employees) the minimum owner-ship dilution point at projected IPO time.
- Give up only one more board seat to investors in this round.
- Focus the sales pitch on: greatly reduced risk since seed capital came in: We got the first test part running, we got a top CEO (and other leadership from people out of some of the best companies in Silicon Valley), and we are only five months from shipping first product. And VCs, you'd better get in now, be-cause there may not be a tomorrow: Our business plan calls for this to be the last round before IPO.

For the record, the above plan was implemented to the letter. The start-up succeeded on all points and got the cash in the bank at a favorable price per share.

---

**Stage 4: Assign Tasks.** The CEO's job here is to get the start-up's little band all working to implement the capital-raising plan efficiently.

One person should be the keeper of VC contacts, appointments, and calen-dars. This gets quite complex if the CEO must get on planes and go around the country with a road show.

One person should be responsible for keeping the presentation up to date. This will be changed on the fly as difficult questions pop up from potential in vestors. These changes can drive the CEO wild unless there is a sole source re-sponsible for keeping order.

Practice your presentation, letting employees critique you. Practice makes perfect. Dry runs are necessary. Flops are created by people trying to wing it. VCs see the best every day; the CEO should make sure this presentation is in the top ten.

**Stage 5: Launch the Campaign.** Focus should be on how to get efficiently to the desired VC firms. It is a mistake to waste time teaching people about the start-up's business. If they aren't in genetic engineering yet, chances are they won't say yes to a presentation from a genetic engineering start-up, certainly not to be the lead venture firm.

A lot of people who have been through the process said, "It never goes fast enough, and you always get a lot of no's." Our interviews showed that there was seldom a group who found raising capital easy and swift. The founders must be prepared instead for a lot of presentations and door knocking.

If the company is already running, the CEO must beware of losing business focus in this stage. If the CEO cannot afford to spend up to 20 percent of his or her time pitching sources of money, then tasks need to be delegated to someone else. Yes, CEOs spend that much time being deliberate about raising new money—some even hire and organize with that job specifically in mind. For instance, an experienced operations executive joined an electronics start-up in San Jose, California, to run operations. As Mr. Inside, he freed time for the founder, born in Taiwan, to focus on his work as Mr. Outside, raising capital and managing the strategic alliances with Japanese and Korean companies.

**Stage 6: Make Presentations.** The CEO's goal in a presentation is to get his or her company distinguished from the dozen companies the venture partners saw last week. This doesn't mean that you should impress the VCs with your super-high-tech, but rather that you should make it clear that your company provides an opportunity for investors to earn a very high ROI in a short time. Yes, cover the high-tech bases, but remember that cash flow and ROI are the measures of success for the venture capitalist, so these must be presented as part of the pitch. A CEO who is not familiar with how to calculate the right numbers and present them can ask the start-up consultant, CPA manager, or attorney to provide these figures. Do not put the deal pricing in your presentation or business plan; rather, leave that for negotiations in person.

The CEO must wear a tough skin. The VCs are quite negative sounding in their questions. They have seen a lot of turkeys and have learned how to smoke them out. They are just doing their job, specifically the part called due diligence.

The first meeting is usually short, about one hour. Subsequent presentations are usually attended by more of the senior partners of the firm, in a large room where the CEO will be center stage. By then, one partner has decided the company is worth looking at seriously. This is the key person in that VC firm for the CEO from now on. This individual will be the start-up's champion and will pace the review process of that business plan within the VC firm.

The partners will expect to see a professional presentation, at least with overhead foils. Laptop computer–driven presentations are now the standard. Bring your laptop.

The CEO will get about two hours for the first formal presentation, including interruptions and many questions.

It is important to avoid presenting anything vitally proprietary, especially at the first meeting. VCs will not sign nondisclosure agreements. Their attorneys warn them that they see so many similar plans each day that the nondisclosure agreements may open the door to big trouble. Don't be surprised to meet your rival start-up arriving in the parking lot as you depart.

When the founders must open the door to reveal sensitive intellectual property, they can often do so instead under tight nondisclosure agreements from an expert hired for that purpose by the venture firm. That may happen anyway, particularly in the later stages when this VC gets serious about doing the deal.

A warning about hired experts: VCs do not always trust their own judgment on the technology or market, so they ask someone more qualified to be the technology judge. We have met several such experts, and a number of CEOs share our perceptions. Founders told us experts usually send in very negative reports, probably because they are hired not to be wrong. The use of experts is good in theory, but we have generally heard of mostly negative results. This is probably why VCs with operating backgrounds from a single technology tend to stick together and invest mainly in that area. We advise clients to go to the VCs who are personally familiar with the start-up company's technology and avoid the problem of negative experts.

The CEO must be prepared to answer questions about how the shares in this deal have been priced. Be ready to respond to a valuation question at any meeting, starting with the first meeting, even before things get serious. We found that start-up CEOs and veteran VCs treat this step as the start of negotiations. The CEO must therefore be prepared to quote on the high side. When asked how negotiable the price is, the CEO's first response should be "Negotiable." If pressed to name a figure, be prepared to start the negotiations with a reasonable figure (see Chapters 7, 8, and 9 for more specific help).

**Stage 7: Feedback from the Presentation** The goal in this stage is to answer this question: How real is the interest of the VC firm to which we just made a presentation? This is a delicate state of affairs; the investors are not yet hooked. They are just nibbling. The big risk is that their interest in the business may cool.

Tough persistence and everlasting confidence are needed. We reviewed our logs of client work to see just how persistent one must be to communicate during this stage of raising capital. We found that the typical venture partner takes at least six calls or e-mails before returning one. These are very busy people with a tall stack of unread business plans on their desks, five or six board meetings every other month, and another six investments that must be bailed out of real trouble. This is not the arena for the bashful or timid. A CEO seeking funds must be persistent, but polite.

However, many refusals should be expected for many good reasons, including the natural consequence of deal flow, which was discussed in Chapter 5.

Negatives can be turned into positives. When the CEO is told over the phone by the start-up's venture firm champion at Top Gun Venture Firm that "you're going to do just fine. The plan is great. But we're going to pass on this round, the deal is just not right for us at this time," the CEO should be ready to counter immediately with, "Tell me in more detail where to rethink our business plan." VCs like to give advice. Many of them are good at it, coming from years of operating experience in that industry.

**Stage 8: Modify Your Plan but Retain Your Vision.** Now the CEO must decide what and how much to change: the plan, the pricing of the deal, or even the entire business. Remember the success of the great Compaq: it took several *major* reworkings of the first business plan to close on funding.

A founder must listen carefully to close advisers here, but most of all must follow his or her dream. That is important for the long haul, both to the company, and to the founder's personal psychological well-being.

**Stage 9: Due Diligence Time.** Here the VCs find the nits and gnats that come out in their due diligence work. All references are checked, and then the VCs find references on the references. They call the market research firms, a half-dozen of their friends who might buy the start-up's first product, and attorneys who will be asked about every issue.

The start-up's attorney and consultant are very useful here. A savvy start-up attorney is worth a great deal during this stage. He or she knows the focus of the venture capitalists and can call VCs as a somewhat neutral party to detect any problem areas that may be bothering the VC. The start-up consultant can also walk the CEO through any land mines in areas such as preparing the references for the kind of questions the VCs will be asking.

Your goal is to get through this stage as quickly as possible. But beware, it can take months!

**Stage 10: The Lead VC says: "Yes, we will!"** The only thing left is for the VC firm to say one word: Yes. But that is easier said than heard. There is only one objective for the CEO during this phase: Get the VC with the money to say yes. But chances of influencing this stage are slim.

One reason is that VCs are very busy comparing alternative companies, looking for ways to invest their remaining funds wisely. VCs meet religiously every Monday in their partners' meeting; that can be counted on. And there they make their decisions. Any given deal is competing against a dozen on the table for consideration that day.

Another reason is that VCs are always hard to reach. CEOs crack jokes about how soon it became obvious that VCs usually returned calls from an airport on their cell phone or crackling from their car phone at 7:15 P.M. as they rounded the entrance to the driveway of their home. Try calling your VC champion at his office on Tuesday morning (after the closed-door, all-partners meeting the prior Monday) to learn how well your deal is looking to their firm.

**Stage 11: Closing the VC Funding Contract.** The goal here is to convert the verbal "yeses" into written contracts, which are known as closing documents. And to agree on the last VCs to be let into the deal.

The biggest risk is that a bad surprise may scare off the lead venture investor. This sometimes happens because of questions asked by a follow-on investor.

The herd instinct is at work, along with deal flow, which is working for the start-up at this stage. In a humorous way, CEOs said they felt their companies had become part of a venture version of a Monopoly game. Companies had become like the houses on Park Place and were being offered in exchange for a futures contract on the next deal going up on St. James.

To succeed here the CEO must cooperate fully with the lead VC, but must never assume that the VC is managing the deal for the CEO. The CEO is the one who must lead the deal to completion.

**Stage 12: Closing Week.** This is the week for the start-up's attorney to really show his stuff. The documents must be prepared and agreed to by all parties. It is a mess to those unaccustomed to the paperwork and logistics nightmares.

A bad start-up lawyer can kill a deal; we were told about several such cases. Also, weak lawyers take so much time to do things that they may easily double or triple their fees for the deal. Lawyers experienced with venture firms and start-ups should be used exclusively.

The CEO's goal is to stay out of the way, but to respond instantly to the attorney's calls. Needless to say, the attorney has to have briefed the CEO on the points to be negotiated well before this stage is reached.

**Stage 13: Cash in the Bank.** At last! This week the founders count it twice, shout for joy, and go celebrate. Next week they meet their new bosses, the VCs sitting on the board of directors.

# Roles and Goals of the Participants

Knowing what motivates each of the involved parties helps the founder reach a more satisfactory end result. Chapters 9 and 13 show how venture capitalists and Wall Street investment bankers make their money, how wealthy they can get, and therefore what they are eager to do with a start-up. This chapter focuses upon the motivations of other participants as well, such as the attorney and the accountant. The goal is to better equip the CEO and founders to negotiate the best deal they can get.

**The Start-up Consultant.** Some experienced veterans of start-ups earn a living assisting the founders along the way toward the IPO. This kind of business person makes money by providing the start-up with certain services at each stage of the capital formation process, in exchange for compensation in the form of some combination of cash and stock (either as outright purchase or as a warrant; that is, the right to buy shares over the next ten years at a fixed price per share). This compensation makes the start-up consultant desire the same success that the CEO and the founders do, thereby avoiding conflict of interest.

The start-up consultant should be able to give advice based upon firsthand experience in start-ups. The CEOs of the consultant's other client companies should be able to provide top-notch references. Some consultants make excellent "stand-in CEOs" until funding attracts the full-time CEO.

**Start-up Attorney.** The company needs an experienced start-up attorney as soon as it gets started. Chapter 4 discusses what start-up attorneys can do. In particular, during these stages the attorney must competently walk the fine line between the practical and theoretical practice of law. One experienced venture capitalist told us that an attorney with a heavy practice working for venture capitalists is the wrong firm for a start-up to use, mainly because the focus of the practice was very different from that of an attorney doing start-ups as his main practice.

The goal is to close on the financing. The terms and conditions can be real deal-busters, with the VC attempting to impose vetoes and other restraints on the CEO. The start-up's attorney should be experienced at countering the more exorbitant claims of investors' attorneys, and must be able to make counteroffers and do trade-offs on the start-up's behalf without losing sight of the goal: Get the deal done, now.

Attorneys charge by the hour. The CEO should expect a fee in the range of thousands of dollars—more if the opposing side's attorneys are not experienced with start-up law practice. This situation tends to create a larger fee if the deal becomes protracted, which is not in the start-up's best interests. Some law firms accept stock or warrants to keep their fees lower. We found IPO prospectuses that revealed stockholdings by the lead attorney in the law firm used by the start-up, as well as by the general fund or trust in which the law firm puts selected forms of compensation.

We found that top attorneys really get into their work, eager for the client's success. We found only one situation where the fees were considered outrageous, and in that one it turned out that the founder/CEO and the attorney were close friends.

Another important point: an experienced start-up attorney will know the latest pricing of the latest venture capital deal: which firms are toughest or softest; what degree of complexity and creativity is acceptable in structuring the deal; and what the CEO and founders should give up, give in to, trade off, and stand firm on.

**The Accounting Firm.** The accounting firm helps the CEO keep a good sense of the balance between the price on a deal and its relative worth in financial terms. It provides advice on tax matters that affect the CEO, the start-up team, and the company.

For instance, the accountant's estimate of changes in accounting conventions or in the tax rate will affect the after-tax earnings of the start-up, which in turn will affect the valuation of the company, which will affect the value of the percentage the CEO will own. But tax reforms have created large uncertainties about the operating loss carryforward and how much a start-up can expect to pay in taxes. The outcome of tax advice on that question is worth millions; an extra round of capital may be required if the tax treatment is wrong.

If the projections of the start-up's financial statements are realistic, the CEO can better control the pricing of the deal. When there is solid backup by a top CPA firm, investors are less likely to argue that there is a lot of uncertainty in the business plan, thereby requiring the founders to lower their price for the deal. Founders must insist on good *business* advice from the CPA, not just good *accounting* advice.

The accountant will also be able to advise about whether the deal is priced too high, too low, or in the middle of the deals it is competing with. And he or she will advise you of several ways to calculate and measure value, based on financial statements. Experienced start-up accountants have seen a lot of stock offerings of high-tech companies and have gained experience they can pass on to you, quickly.

The CPA firm also charges by the hour. Its fees should not be high at this stage, not until the start-up's books must be audited annually and examined closely each quarter. Advice sessions are usually not for a fee; they are used to nurture the relationship and the account for the long term. Accordingly, the CPA is motivated to help the start-up client succeed; he or she is on the client's side. It is anticipated that the IPO fees and annual work thereafter will make up for the low fees during the start-up phase of life of the company.

**Conflict of Interest.** It is important always to ask the consultant, attorney, and accountant whether they have any conflicts of interest. Some work very closely with venture capitalists—the very ones you are going to negotiate with. Others may be close to suppliers or customers that will be important to the start-up's business. And there is always the chance that they have worked with a competitor with whom they are still close. Get the cards on the table quickly, and get on with the deal.

**Venture Capitalists.** The start-up needs the venture capitalist. The VC firm has the money. The CEO's goal is to get the VC to give the start-up some of the money the VC has been entrusted to invest.

The VC is paid according to a formula spelled out in Chapter 9. The VC's share of the start-up's rewards comes after the VC firm's investors get back at least their invested principal. The VC gets his cash when the partnership that was formed to invest is terminated, that is, liquidated. That outcome will take several years; seven is normal, ten not uncommon, and top firms are extending terms to twelve years.

Accordingly, the venture capitalist wants the start-up to become liquid ASAP, if not sooner. That puts pressure on the CEO to "dress up the financials" to look good at IPO time, which in some cases may not be in the company's best interests long term.

Furthermore, the venture capitalists have a chance to attract new money to invest only if the last partnership has done well. Thus, the start-up will be under pressure to raise several rounds of capital at regularly increasing prices per share. Short-term performance pressures become a reality soon, well before the start-up goes public.

A pattern of higher and higher prices in a company is a delight to the venture capitalist, and to employees also. So where is the conflict? The answer is that the venture capital people want to start with as large a percentage of the company as they can: in case of a huge success, in which case their values rise rapidly in absolute terms; or in case of disaster, in which any forced dilution will be less painful to the investor trying to attract new capital under terrible company conditions.

The name of the game for the venture capitalist is ROI, return on investment, measured by percent per annum. The CEO's deal should also measure results this way. This should be pointed out in the business plan and emphasized strongly in presentations to investors. The accountant or start-up consultant can run the numbers for you correctly.

We asked several CEOs "What are the realities of negotiating with venture capitalists?" We obtained many answers, which we have summarized in the next section. The CEO must be just as analytical in negotiating for start-up money as for buying furniture or some other resource needed for the company. The CEO must test the quality, measure the availability, check out the post-sales service, and determine the fairness of the price offered; then decide and close the deal. After all, money is just like other necessities; it has a price. It should be treated that way.

# Negotiating Phases: Problems and Pitfalls

CEOs have to negotiate wisely at each stage of funding, but nobody is born knowing how this process works. For example, the first-time start-up CEO wants to know the answers to questions such as: When should I call the venture guy back? How much should I bother him (he hasn't called us back since last week)? These are not trivial questions—someone who is too pushy can make the deal sound like a loser, but the CEO who is too laid-back may lose the interest of the investor, who has a lot more fish to catch.

Here is a summary of tips for handling each stage of raising venture capital:

**Seed.** The earlier the stage of financing, the more risk there is for the investors, as well as for the founders and the start-up team. Accordingly, the CEO will have to work hardest to get the money at this stage. He can expect to call on twenty or more venture firms and make at least as many presentations, time after time after time.

The first goal is to secure a lead venture capitalist.

Usually the seed capital is planned to cover payroll through completion of the first working prototype. If the financial cushion planned into the seed funds is inadequate to cover expenses up to the next funding (round one), VCs can extract a heavy price per share (deep dilution) to provide an emergency round of funding (a "bridge loan") in order to keep the CEO from announcing to the employees that the company will miss its next payroll.

The main problem of negotiating at the seed stage is to get and keep the VCs' attentions long enough to convince one of them that this start-up is worth the investment risk. The special risks of a seed round have increasingly attracted specialists, firms that focus on investing in seed-round deals only (see Chapter 9). These specialized seed investors will be more likely to put up with incomplete management and will be sympathetic to the need to get some money to build a prototype to prove the technology works. Angels and "friends and family" are often used to seed fund deals not ready for venture capital firm funding.

A common pitfall is to rely on one source for the seed money. The best advice we found was: "Don't rely on getting all of your venture money from one source." Competition does wonders for a deal.

**First Round.** Often referred to as the first "real" round of venture capital, these funds will be about $2 million to $5 million, five to ten times more than the seed round. Stock will be labeled Preferred B, since the seed round took Preferred A. The price per share will represent a large increase over the prior round.

It all sounds simple, but problems are soon encountered. The first one is the problem of "business slip." This occurs when the start-up finds that product development or market positioning are deviating significantly from the original business plan. The start-up's first key milestone will be missed. Should the CEO expose the slip and admit it? Will this decision hinder or enhance closing of round one? What if the decision on disclosure should slow closing on round one?

The best response is to tell the truth. The bad news is better delivered by the CEO as early as possible. Otherwise, when it leaks out, the CEO's credibility will be badly damaged.

The cure for this dilemma is twofold: Plan for at least one redesign of the prototype (or retry of the first key milestone) and raise enough seed-round cash to do that; and hire competent *managers,* especially a VP of engineering, then closely monitor, encourage, and coach the development work. These two approaches will help avoid slips and help you achieve milestones on time.

The next problem is getting commitments from *new* investors. This will take a lot of time, especially if your lead investor is simultaneously fighting fires in three other investments. The start-up's management must be prepared to raise the money without any help from the lead, and still keep marching ahead on schedule with the business plan. (Suggestion: This is the time to go back to your business plan schedule and rethink what impact product slip will have on raising capital. You may want to reschedule your milestones and plan on raising more capital per round.)

The CEO and potential investors will haggle a great deal on pricing the deal, and the CEO must be prepared to justify the pricing. For a favorable round one, the CEO should have competing VC factions vying for his deal.

Incomplete management teams scare off a lot of investors at this stage of a start-up; a missing VP of marketing will probably bring the show to a complete halt.

The focus should be on demonstrating success early, with confidence that a lot more will be coming soon. And then it is time to close on the financing.

**Multiple Rounds.** Later rounds of financing will all be "fillers," capital needed to grow the business and get the company into shape to go public.

These rounds vary considerably in price per share, depending on whether management has succeeded or badly botched the original business plan. During these stages the CEO will have lived out the true meaning of what it is to operate with a "living business plan" that changes daily.

The statistics increasingly say that the CEO's time as a founder is drawing to a close. Rough moments will have come and gone at least a few times, with ups and downs much wilder than any roller-coaster ride. Our research shows that most founder CEOs have gone or have stepped aside to be replaced (Jerry Yang became Chief Yahoo) in the first three years.

And the start-up will still need more money. Venture capitalists told us over and over again that entrepreneurs are overly optimistic—they always underestimate the time needed to get the first product to market, overestimate the ease of getting the company operating, and need double the capital called for in the first business plan. The number-one error is underestimating how long it will take from the first sales call to shipping the first product.

Drops in prices per share are likely. Lower prices are needed to attract capital under conditions of duress. In times of duress a CEO quickly learns the meaning of all the boilerplate terms and conditions in the preferred-stock agreements, particularly the antidilution clauses. Antidilution occurs when a predefined formula gives VCs more shares because the subsequent round of financing was sold at a price lower than the VC has paid in previous rounds. Founders must be prepared to lose a large percentage of ownership in these cases.

"We waited too long before going after our next round of capital!" is an all-too-common cry from the start-up CEOs, several of whom never survived as CEOs beyond such fiascoes. It is never too early to start raising the next round of capital. The CEO should get set at least six to nine months in advance of missing a payroll and add three months of burn rate to the company's cash cushion for added safety. In other words, the CEO should start raising the next round just after closing the previous round. One Internet start-up founder planned three rounds of funding before he raised the seed round. He went on to raise capital successfully by using a pattern of beginning the next round of financing a month before the closing of the current round.

**Mezzanine.** This is the last round before the IPO, about a year or so before the big event. It is another name for the unplanned funding that keeps payroll flowing while everyone waits for a rotten stock market to perk up again.

It is tricky to decide how much to sell at this stage. Some start-ups that do large mezzanine deals survive, but pay a high price in terms of dilution. Waiting too long can be costly for management, but not for the investors (remember the antidilution clauses in the venture investors' contracts). And be aware that few investors are willing to do mezzanine deals; mezzanine results have often been disappointing to investors.

**Initial Public Offering.** By the time the multiple rounds begin, the first visits from the investment bankers will have begun. This interest initiates a game new to the

CEO: the public stock market game. It ushers in promises of liquidity, fame, and fortune—and a host of new problems, which are discussed in detail in Chapter 13.

The CEO must become an expert in pricing IPOs even before the seed round is raised. You must work backward from the IPO pricing to the seed-round pricing in order to make sense out of your VC pricing plans. The money markets that drive the venture capitalists are the same ones driving the IPO pricings. The start-up consultant, attorney, and accountant can help the CEO develop the required expertise.

## Structuring and Pricing a Venture Capital Deal

A venture deal is like any other financing, with a few special characteristics mixed in for good measure. The classic deals are based on experience acquired by a lot of people in America over more than fifty years of venturing. The not-so-classic deals reflect the creativity of the investors and entrepreneurs who make this kind of business so interesting.

We will now describe a classic venture capital deal and then some interesting creative alternatives that were very successful for all parties involved. Actual percentages and per-share amounts are analyzed later in the chapter.

It all boils down to answering this question: How much of my company will I have to give up in order to get the capital I want? The following process is what actually goes on in the classic deal.

**Use of Preferred Stock.** The CEO, founders, and employees will all own or get options to buy common stock. The investors will all own preferred stock. This is done to avoid a tax problem: As the per-share prices rise quickly, the United States Internal Revenue Service will try to attribute income to the prior-round investors and tax their sudden profit. Separating the shares into rounds of preferred stock isolates the rounds from one another and protects the investors from this problem.

All preferred shares are converted to common shares at the time the company goes public. A conversion ratio of one share of common for each share of preferred is typical practice. Whatever the ratio of exchange, the important calculation is what percentage of voting common stock everyone gets after the IPO.

Each round is accompanied by a thick set of legal agreements that contain the clauses so important to investors. Table 7-1 lists the common items in the agreements. The start-up's attorney will advise on which are to be deal busters, negotiated, or given up. Strategy must be planned early.

Each round of investors typically adds one more member to the start-up's

### TABLE 7-1. Typical Terms of Preferred Stock Issued to Venture Capitalists

Number of shares issued, price per share

Conversion price: number of common shares per preferred share

Antidilution formulas

Registration rights: mandatory; "piggyback"; number of shares

Veto rights: next financings, acquisitions, mergers

Veto rights:

    Sale and other disposition of assets

    Dividends

    Amount of stock issued

    Borrowing and leasing

    Compensation of executive employee staff

    Ownership, sale, or access of technology

Rights of inspection

Right to elect board members, attend board meetings

Vesting rights of employees

Receipt of financial statements

Closing expenses

*Source:* Saratoga Venture Finance

board of directors. There is a desire to "represent this round of investors" at the end of each round. The trouble with this is that it makes the board venture-capitalist heavy. Most CEOs we met found that bias to be unwise. The start-up veterans started out with a couple of strong venture capitalists on their boards and then insisted, as a condition of each successive deal, that no more investors be added to the start-up's board.

The founders will be expected to agree to some formula that takes shares out of their portion instead of the venture capitalists' percentage ownership if the start-up's share price sinks for the next round or two. The CEO and the start-up's attorney must negotiate hard on this provision.

Investors will want no obstacles to getting liquid. They will want to include clauses that get them cash or registered public shares if the founders ever sell the company to a giant. But such clauses can cripple the chance of even starting negotiations with a big company. Follow the advice of the start-up's attorney.

Veto rights or their equivalent are common. They usually appear innocent until the CEO is forced into some undesired action. For instance, CEOs told us they were urged in desperation to get money from the Super Venture Fund, whose partners were archenemies of the CEO and whose style and chemistry clashed with the CEO and core team. We have also witnessed cases where complete irrationality took over under veto conditions while the CEO missed payroll after payroll and developed ulcers.

Vesting limitations are imposed by preferred-stock investors. Vesting is a contractual agreement between the start-up and the employee. It limits the employee by connecting the number of days employed to the number of shares the employee may acquire through exercise of stock options. These days, typical terms are vesting over four years, with a one-year waiting period before the first day of exercising shares may begin. For instance, a new employee will have earned 12/48ths of his stock option on the first day of the second year. Thereafter he vests (earns) an additional 1/48th on the first day of each successive month over the four years following date of employment. These four years represent the whole vesting time. The CEO must get the best deal possible for his employees. Valid Logic, Netscape, and other successful IPOs used three-year stock option vesting schedules to attract more people from scarce talent pools in highly competitive times. Some venture firms try to insist on five-year vesting. Some founders get faster vesting.

Employees have the choice of exercising the granted stock option (buying the shares) or waiting until the IPO occurs, when virtually all employees exercise their options. If the IPO takes longer than four years, the early employees will have to exercise or lose their optioned shares.

How much cash will the respective founders put in? That varied a great deal among companies. Several issued stock to founders at less than 1 cent per share. Multiplied by 500,000 shares for a founder (that is, 10 percent of 5 million outstanding shares), that comes to $5,000. Founders should not expect a free ride— they must be prepared to sign a check as an investor, but the amount will be small. A minority of companies loaned the purchase price to key employees. This became the case most often when heavy management was added late in the life of the start-up. Finance is creative and is where the start-up consultant, attorney, and accountant will earn their keep. There are severe tax and liquidity implications for decisions to buy or borrow. The CEO and founders must get all the advice they can in these matters.

**Pricing Each Round of VC Funding.** There are several quantitative methods used to calculate the price per share of each round of funding a start-up. The methods most often cited by venture capitalists and investment bankers who were interviewed are shown in Table 7-2. All of them should be used by the CEO.

**Key Funding Issues.** We will now go through three case studies, each touching upon key issues for the start-up CEO who is learning to price VC rounds of fund-

### TABLE 7-2. Valuation Quantification Techniques

| | |
|---|---|
| MULTIPLE ROI: | "How many times our investment can we reasonably expect from the time we invest to the time we are liquid, i.e., when the start-up goes public?" (Used most often by venture capitalists in seed and later rounds of private funding of start-ups.) One dollar in today's money will be worth how many dollars at IPO? |
| ROI PER YEAR: | "How much will we earn per year by the time the start-up goes public?" (Particularly important for the investor in the earliest stages of a lengthy start-up.) If we put one dollar into the bank, how much interest would it have to earn each year to be worth the IPO price? |
| PERCENT CONTROL: | "How much of the voting stock will we control after this round of financing?" (More important for actively participating investors than for others.) What percent of the stock of the company will be owned by investors versus management and employees (counting all options as if exercised)? |
| NEXT ROUNDS: | "How much room is left for the next round of investors if the start-up needs another round? Will that be enough to attract them, especially if the start-up gets into trouble? Will we be able to avoid a write-down of our share price in the next rounds?" (Most important for strategy in funding a start-up that needs a lot of capital or one that has been disappointingly long in going public.) If we raise the price in each successive round of funding by a ratio of 2:1, can we hit the desired IPO price? |
| PRIOR ROUNDS: | "Will the pricing of this round make too high a profit for the last round since they have invested?" New investors do not like windfall profits for prior investors; instead, the new money tries to keep the markup of shares below 3:1; boom periods can increase that ratio. |
| HISTORICAL MULTIPLES: | "Using the start-up's historical financial statements, are the prices of this round reasonable when compared to equivalent companies? How many times revenue does this round represent?" |
| FUTURE MULTIPLES: | "Using forecasts of the start-up's financial statements, are the prices of this round reasonable when compared to equivalent companies? How many times revenue, profit, book value and cash flow does this round represent?" (This is used especially for pricing initial public offerings.) |

*Source:* Saratoga Venture Finance

ing. Each case has special characteristics and demonstrates how varied VC deals can be in real life.

---

## Case Study: Network Equipment Technologies

Network Equipment Technologies, Inc. (NET) went public on January 23, 1987, after starting business in August 1983. Here is how the private rounds of venture capital and the initial public offering ended up distributing the wealth.

After the IPO, the company had 12,568,987 shares outstanding and had reserved shares for and/or had issued to employees the right to purchase another 1,287,588, for a grand total of 13,856,575 shares. The ownership of those shares was as follows:

### EQUITY OWNERSHIP

|  | Percent | Shares |
|---|---|---|
| New investors at IPO time | 10.8% | 1,500,000 |
| Private-round venture investors | 57.7% | 7,992,000 |
| CEO and VPs | 9.6% | 1,327,555 |
| *Subtotal* | *78.1%* | *10,819,555* |
| All other employees' stock and options to buy stock | 21.9% | 3,037,020 |
| **Total company** | **100.0%** | **13,856,575** |

The venture capitalists had invested a total of $24,956,000, for which they got 7,992,000 common shares. Those shares at IPO time were worth $16 each, for a total of $127,872,000. Their ROI ranged from 67 percent to 85 percent per annum.

Over the space of seventeen quarters, the cofounder and CEO, Bruce D. Smith, sold NET stock to investors in three rounds of funding:

### FINANCING ROUNDS

| Seed | Preferred A | $4,332,000 |
|---|---|---|
| Round 1 | Preferred B | $7,499,000 |
| Round 2 | Preferred C | $13,125,000 |
| **Total** | | **$24,956,000** |

The IPO raised $24 million of new capital for NET by selling 1.5 million new shares of common stock at $16 each. An additional 1 million shares were sold by several investors, NET officers, and other shareholders during the IPO. The company spent $3.48 million, or 8.7 percent of the offering, for the fees and expenses (none of which are tax-deductible) necessary to accomplish the IPO.

The CEO owned 534,513 shares for 3.9 percent of NET; these were worth $8,552,000. The shares of several of the other nonfounder VPs were valued at an average of $2.4 million each.

On Thursday, July 21, 1987, NET shares closed in trading on the NASDAQ market at $23.25, up 45 percent in the six months following the IPO. And over the same six months, NET revenue per quarter grew and so did net income.

That is a classic start-up success story.

---

# Case Study: Chips and Technologies

A modified classic is the case of Chips and Technologies, known as Chips. Chips altered the classic pattern by taking only twenty-one months to get to IPO; it was an amazing business success.

Shunned by the venture community, the CEO and cofounder, Gordon A. Campbell, funded Chips first with personal bootstrap funds, next with a round funded mainly by Chips's landlord, William L. Marocco, and finally with corporate venture capital from Chips's key Japanese suppliers of chip foundry manufacturing services.

### FINANCING ROUNDS

| | | |
|---|---|---|
| Seed | Common | $97,000 |
| Round 1 | Preferred A | $1,705,000 |
| Round 2 | Preferred B | $1,528,000 |
| **Total** | | **$3,330,000** |

That was all the capital needed to build a very big business. By June 1987, Chips was selling millions of semiconductors a month and accounted for sales growing quickly toward the $100 million per year mark. Net income was running 16 percent of revenue and return on ending equity for the quarter ended March 31, 1987, was an annualized 34 percent.

The speed of getting the first product to market and the burst of sales helped insiders retain a large proportion of the company.

117

**EQUITY OWNERSHIP**

|  | Percent | Shares |
|---|---|---|
| New investors at IPO time | 13.6% | 1,750,000 |
| Private-round venture investors | 32.3% | 4,151,077 |
| CEO and VPs | 41.9% | 5,388,077 |
| *Subtotal* | *87.8%* | *11,289,154* |
| All other employees' stock and options to buy stock | 12.2% | 1,571,665 |
| **Total Company** | **100.0%** | **12,860,819** |

The CEO ended up with 23.3 percent of the company, worth $15.01 million at IPO date. The shares climbed, settling on July 21, 1987, at $24.75 per share. That made Gordon Campbell worth about $74 million at that time. His VPs' (several were cofounders) shares at IPO time were worth about $2 million each.

The investors' ROI soared! Using the IPO pricing of $5 per share, their return ranged from 266 to 284 percent per annum! At $24 they deserved a place in the Guinness Book of World Records.

Chips's success teaches lessons in how to modify, persist, and succeed. Campbell and his employees also deserve an award for sheer determination.

A footnote: Gordon Campbell later became a regular investor in start-ups through Techfarm. In 1999, his company, Cobalt, set IPO Internet-era records (once again)!

# Case Study: Netscape

Netscape began with Jim Clark leaving Silicon Graphics, which he had founded. Seeking an Internet start-up possibility, he contacted via e-mail Marc Andreessen, a graduate student at the University of Illinois and coauthor of the original NCSA Mosaic Web browser. Together they founded Netscape in April 1994. In seventeen months the company went public at a $1 billion valuation.

The prospectus filed with the Securities and Exchange Commission for the August 8, 1996, public offering tells the facts about how it was done.

This start-up funding is a special case involving an "angel" (in this case, Clark himself), a friend and very well-connected venture capitalist (John Doer of

Kleiner Perkins), and follow-on funding by strategic partners (including Adobe, TCI, Times Mirror, Knight-Ridder, and the Hearst Corporation).

Clark did the $3 million seed round of Preferred A in May 1994 by himself (including a small amount from a key manager, James Sha). A few months later came the Preferred B round for $6 million that brought in Kleiner Perkins. By June 1996 Preferred C brought in $18 million more and also—very important—the strategic partners.

Two months later the company went public, raising more than $160 million (new shares plus the underwriters' options).

The stock price exploded from $28 to above $70 before settling in a $30 to $40 trading range. This IPO "jump" and return down is the classic pattern of movement of initial public offerings. However, the Netscape range up and down is rare, except in boom times.

Note also how the "cascade" of deal making progressed: from a founder's own funds, then to a venture capitalist, and finally to corporations. That is the classical sequence. What is not classic is the amazing speed from founding to IPO.

- Explosive growth demanded that fast, very expandable working capital financing be provided almost immediately. Sales jumped to $16 million in the first six months of the first year!
- The stock market was "hot" for Internet stocks. The valuation per share—while unthinkable—was impossible not to take advantage of. The "window of opportunity" for a company without profits would close within two years (and other companies like *Wired* magazine had to withdraw their IPO offerings).
- At IPO time ($28 per share) a graduate school dropout (cofounder Marc Andreessen) was worth $112 million.
- Corporations made six times their investment ($4.50 to $28 per common share) in a few months.
- Employees raced to join the company, only to have large numbers of them find to their great dismay that soon their options were "under water" (public stock price far less than the price of their options).

### FINANCING ROUNDS

| | | | |
|---|---|---|---|
| Seed | Preferred A | $0.75 | $3,113,250 |
| Round 1 | Preferred B | $2.25 | $6,428,750 |
| Round 2 | Preferred C | $9.00 | $18,000,000 |
| **Total** | | | **$27,542,000** |

Note: One preferred share converted to two common shares.

**EQUITY OWNERSHIP (JUST BEFORE THE IPO)**

| | | |
|---|---|---|
| Clark | 30.0% | $272,160,000 |
| Andreessen | 12.3% | $112,000,000 |
| Company (All) | 72.8% | $660,660,000 |
| Investors (All) | 27.2% | $246,860,432 |
| **Total Company** | **100%** | **$1,068,520,432** |

**Pricing.** As these cases show, founders and investors did well in financial terms. The cases also show that the wide range of percentage owned by outside investors and the proportion owned by the CEO also varies widely. The general rule is simple: the faster to IPO, the less dilution. And if it can be done, timing and a bit of dumb luck in a hot stock market make a big difference in the final outcome.

Later in this report we present more details on how to translate all of this into the dilution the founders will have to accept in order to get money for their company.

In the meantime, a study of the Saratoga Venture Tables™ in Appendix A will provide information from the famous start-ups to help the CEO know what to expect when negotiating rounds of venture financing.

## Ownership and Control

"I'll never sell more than 49 percent of my company to investors. My fellow founders are committed to controlling this start-up. We do not want the vulture capitalists telling us when to jump and when to sit." As consultants, we have heard this often—from very well-meaning souls. And from some very naïve founders.

This section is intended to help the CEO gain a more realistic expectation of what will happen to the control of a company as the founders start to sell shares in it to outside investors.

**Conventions, Practices, and Expectations.** The facts of life are that as soon as more than one person gets some claim on the equity ownership of the start-up, the first founder rapidly begins to lose control as a sole proprietor.

First, state laws are quite strict about offering shares in new enterprises. The flimflam and bogus company hucksters have, over the centuries, bilked so many investors out of so much money that Americans are subject in each state to laws that are on the side of the new investor, the one who is in the minority. These are the "blue sky laws."

The phrase "blue sky laws" is popularly applied to state statutes regulating the offering and sale of securities within the jurisdiction of the respective states. "The name that is given to the law," said Justice McKenna in *Hall* v. *Geiger-Jones*, "indicates the evil at which it is aimed; that is, to use the language of a cited case, speculative schemes which have no more basis than so many feet of blue sky."

It is dangerous, to say the least, to simply start selling shares in a company. The entrepreneur needs a good attorney who is experienced in these matters and in the home state's laws. Otherwise, a founder could easily end up with a lawsuit later on when the start-up company badly needs classic venture capital. VCs shy away from companies with legal trouble.

**Effective Control and Preferred Stock.** Classic venture capitalists do not control a start-up in terms of shares voted. Even if they had the 51 percent of the votes, they would have to be very careful for the reasons noted above.

What really happens is demonstrated in this disguised case study.

---

# Case Study: Yourco, Inc.

The founder succeeds in selling preferred stock in his start-up, Yourco, Inc., to investors. He soon learns that the investment will be made via HiTech Venture Limited Partnership III. The general partner, Sam V. Enture, hands the start-up's attorney his usual preferred-stock contract, which calls for one seat on the company's board of directors because he must represent the interests of Partnership III.

When the founder reads the fine print, he quickly sees that Sam will now be calling a lot of shots; future financings are going to involve virtual veto power authority by Sam. (Table 7-1 describes some of what can be expected.)

Next, the founder finds that Sam requires that Sam takes over as chairman. After all, the founder has never run an independent company before, and Sam is a veteran of many. Anyway, Sam's name at the top will attract a lot more investors of similar world-class stature. Everyone will benefit, he postulates.

At the first board meeting, the founder learns that the board of directors will hereafter be setting compensation policy, including, but not limited to, wage scales, starting with the founders, cash bonuses, and, of course, all stock option grantings to new employees.

If the start-up doesn't already have one, Sam will advise (in a firm tone) using a top venture lawyer, and he'll have the attorney of his choice, Rick Jones, call tomorrow. Goodbye to the founder's friend, the less experienced guy who set up this whole deal in the first place.

And Jim, the founder's CPA buddy, will no longer suffice to do the books. Instead, Sam provides the phone number of Tom, downtown at the regional headquarters of one of the Big Six multinational accounting firms.

As the first board meeting comes to a close, Sam smiles and gives the founder his next assignment: At the board meeting next month, he is to present a summary of the progress of Yourco, comparing it to the original business plan, complete with head count and budget facts.

---

Welcome to the world of venture-capital-backed start-ups!

With a little better idea of what to expect, a founder can better prepare for what is to come. It is unrealistic expectations that cause many of the squabbles between the board and the founder/CEO. Like the Boy Scout motto says, "Be prepared."

## Typical Agreements

Like all contracts, agreements with investors can be customized to fit any need and circumstance. The practice of securities law can be very creative.

However, venture capital terms and conditions have evolved since the 1930s, when this form of investing became serious. The rules have made a lot of sense to a lot of people since then, and they have also enabled a lot of founders and VCs to become very wealthy. Companies were run within the bounds of the restrictions and many became successes. So we were not surprised to find CEOs telling us in interviews of the good results they had in spite of what sounded like onerous conditions.

The best advice the start-up presidents had for the prospective start-up leader was to get a good attorney, who will keep the founder from being subject to unfair restrictions and will help plan for the future. Dick Riordan, who founded the Los Angeles law firm Riordan & McKinzie, told us, "The start-up CEO needs to use a lawyer that will structure the deal today to take care of the events of tomorrow. That is why the lawyer needs to know venture capital well and also have a good sense of business."

The number of shares to be outstanding is aimed at somewhere between 10 million and 15 million at IPO time. Your goal is to produce a per-share price in a range acceptable to quality investors, at least $10 and no more than $25. And the agreement specifies the exact number of shares in the voting control of the new investor. This starts to put bounds on what can be sold to other investors.

The conversion price is usually one for one. At IPO time, all preferred shares are converted to common, share for share. Underwriters will be expecting that condition.

Antidilution terms are tricky. The CEO should work out each combination of circumstances and do the calculations to see what the VC is expecting will happen to the CEO's percentage when the company gets into trouble and has to have extra, unplanned rounds of capital added to keep it alive. The start-up's attorney will be familiar with what ranges are acceptable, a common practice among the latest venture deals.

Registration rights also become key when a company goes public. This gives you the right to have your shares registered with the Securities and Exchange Commission so that the shares may be traded publicly. Everyone wants their shares to become public as soon as possible so that they can be sold quickly, as desired. CEOs and founders do not want anyone in line ahead of them. Yet some investors try to get such a favored position. The common practice is to have everyone in the same boat, all getting registered together when such events arise.

The fights about registration rights are usually over how many of the founders' shares may be sold at IPO time. This is argued between the CEO and the underwriters as part of the underwriting agreement signed at the time of the IPO.

Veto rights are the implicit control items that were mentioned earlier. They are very real. A CEO must get to know them well. They fall into two categories: financings and stock related. In all cases the CEO must know what his authorities are under adverse conditions.

Rights of inspection are needed by investors so they can get into the accounting and legal books in case of trouble. Venture investors successfully sued Osborne and its auditor, Arthur Young, over accounting matters. Not many situations require such action. But since financial trouble can and does happen, a company's books must be open as soon as it takes money from the first investor.

Board member voting is where the power plays occur, particularly as venture partners vie for the top-gun position in hot start-ups. Being chairman of a raving success adds a lot of publicity and awe to the VC firm whose general partner is chairman. This VC hopes that exposure will get the firm a lot more first looks at great start-ups and will get it in on the few first-class deals over the next year or so.

As to the wisdom of having more or fewer VCs on the board of a start-up, we found a lot of mixed opinion. The only consensus pattern of response was from CEOs whose company had gotten into trouble at some time in the past. A clear majority said that at such times most VCs are a big hindrance, more trouble than help. Some CEOs were bitter and advised keeping as few VCs on the board as possible, and particularly to avoid the arrogant ones who have not had much recent operating experience in meeting the payrolls of struggling start-ups. The deans of venture capital speak often of the need for people who can become good board members. Those gray-haired VC veterans can be worth their weight in gold.

Vesting rights of employees is so commonly standard now that to compete with anything more stringent would put you at a disadvantage. The usual course is to have four-year vesting monthly after a one-year waiting period. Be more creative if you think it will help in your recruiting, but check with your lawyer first.

The company must mail financial statements to investors. Investors will commonly call at times convenient to them to inquire about the numbers. They expect a prompt reply, usually immediately (drop everything and talk to me), because their time is so constrained and they want to get this call off their mind. Some write short notes, mail them, and watch to see how fast the CEO responds. (They'll remind the CEO at the next board meeting, in front of the other members.)

Closing expenses are an area for haggling, concerning both the dollar amount and who will pay for expenses, particularly for the VC's legal fees. Attorney's fees (which are paid for out of the capital raised) should be reasonable (check with your lawyer for local rates and practice), with excesses paid for by the VCs themselves. The company's attorney will advise on what "reasonable" is in a given region.

Those are the major points—those that will be worth thinking about before the company gets started.

# Famous Start-Ups: Their Private Deals with Venture Capitalists

We conclude the chapter with a description of the Saratoga Venture Tables™ in Appendix A. The information they contain is hard to get; it will help you plan and prepare for negotiations with investors.

The information in the tables has been generated exclusively by Saratoga Venture Finance. The work digests and analyzes Securities and Exchange Commission documents, particularly the initial public offerings of famous companies. The result is a computerized database of private venture facts on new enterprises and their public offerings.

Selected results of selected companies are made available in the Saratoga Venture Tables™. The data included are:

- percentage owned by founders, employees, and venture capitalists
- pricing of rounds of stock sold by famous private companies
- cash compensation of executives
- mix of stock between top management and employees
- cost of deals charged by Wall Street investment banking firms
- amounts of stock option pools
- wealth of president and founders after going public

**Conventions and Assumptions Used.** The Saratoga Venture Tables™ are derived from SEC documents to which the reader can refer for exact details. While the Saratoga Venture Tables™ have been produced faithfully, they contain certain assumptions about some details of the private financings. Not all SEC documents were in complete enough detail to avoid making certain assumptions.

Note that the percentages of ownership are based on a special definition of the total number of shares outstanding; it assumes that all options in the option pools are granted and exercised. Using this convention helps CEOs to better plan their allocation of shares to employees. The data required in the SEC prospectuses do not offer this important calculation.

# 8

# Personal Rewards and Costs

I n this chapter we will examine the rewards of doing a start-up. And we will count the cost.

Our goal is simple: to help entrepreneurs realistically examine what they are about to get into and to better prepare them for achieving their personal best. The chapter contains some very frank statements by people we talked to. We have changed names and places to preserve the privacy of those who were willing to be open about their experiences. We thank them for their concern for others' success and for their participation.

The first section concentrates on financial return; the other sections review professional and psychological rewards. After that we analyze the personal costs of doing a start-up.

## Potential Financial Return

Over the fifty years or so that modern venture capital has been in existence there have been vast swings in the factors that affect the formation of wealth: taxes, wage levels, inflation, depression, recessions, wars large and small, the rise and fall of dynasties and governments, periods when business is viewed as the bad guy, and elation with business as the leader of all that is good for the world.

All this change adds risk. Yet the entrepreneurial-minded keep coming. The reward must be attractive, compared with the risk. That is what "equity" is all about.

The basis for wealth formation in venture-backed companies is equity. It con-

**TABLE 8-1. Ownership by Founders and CEOs Just After IPO***

| | Average per Founder (%) | Value at IPO ($M) | Employees excluding Founders (%) | Value at IPO ($M) | CEO (%) | Value at IPO ($M) |
|---|---|---|---|---|---|---|
| Chips and Technologies | 8.8 | $5.6 | 19.1 | $12.3 | 23.3 | $15.0 |
| Cypress Semiconductor | 1.1 | $3.4 | 16.6 | $53.3 | 2.1 | $6.8 |
| Netscape | 14.1 | $150.1 | 33.7 | $360.8 | 10.5 | $112 |
| Silicon Graphics | 4.6 | $6.7 | 29.4 | $42.7 | 3.1 | $4.5 |
| Yahoo | 10.8 | $52.0 | 29.1 | $139.9 | 2.8 | $13.3 |

* Includes all options granted plus available option pool

*Source:* Saratoga Venture Finance

sists of all the leftovers after everyone, including the government, has been compensated fully.

To take on the risks of a start-up for the reward of leftovers seems incongruous at best. To get a better handle on this strange phenomenon, we will start with the item that in the end is the only monetary thing that counts: cash—preferably, cash in the entrepreneur's personal account at the bank.

Then we will look at the cash value of being a founder or a later-stage employee, and how much CEOs and VPs are worth at initial-public-offering time.

Table 8-1 lists top guns of some famous start-ups and their equity and it shows what the founders were worth. Both the percent they owned and their absolute dollars of wealth from the start-up are measured in terms of the price per share at IPO time. Later, some stock prices rose and others dropped by large percentages, for many different reasons. The number of founders is shown and the average ownership per founder is calculated, as is the value of 1 percent of each company.

This table provides all the types of information any employee needs to measure the fairness of an equity offer:

- what percentage of the company the employee will own at IPO time
- what each share of stock will be worth at IPO time
- how many shares of stock will be outstanding at IPO time

The equation is simple:

$$\text{Employee's percentage} \times \text{Total number of shares outstanding} \times \frac{\$}{\text{share}} = \$\text{Wealth}$$

The CEO will be expected to predict these numbers for each employee hired, especially the key VPs and the veterans of start-ups. They will insist on being given these numbers. This chapter will attempt to help by explaining how the stock value calculations are done. In tables later in the chapter we will provide facts from famous start-ups so that the CEO can set realistic targets for rationing precious equity for sale to investors and attractive employees. But a word of caution: There is very little other factual information easily available about this important subject. Be very careful of your sources of information about stocks, options, and equity.

To get even more detail—for example, to find out what the vice presidents of each function got—carefully examine the Saratoga Venture Tables™ in Appendix A.

Now let us make some observations based on Table 8-1.

**CEO's Share.** There is a wide range of value in the worth of the CEO's wealth. And remember that we have included only the more famous start-ups in our table. A lot more leaders were worth a lot less at IPO time. A year or so after IPO the shares can rocket up, as they did in the Internet boom period, making millionaires into billionaires on paper.

Bill Gates of Microsoft represented a rare success (until the Internet era arrived). By start-up standards, Microsoft was very old at IPO time and thus was worth much more than a younger company. Famous start-ups in the early 1980s typically went public in less than three and half years, while Microsoft waited until it was eleven years old. By 1990, a wait of five to eight years had become common. With the arrival of the first Internet start-ups, the wait for hot start-ups to go IPO once again swung back to less than three years, some less than two years! As the next century arrived, the time began to lengthen once again! These swings are very hard to predict, so we recommend that founder/CEOs assume their start-ups will go IPO in about five years.

In an exploration of companies in the Saratoga Venture database over long periods of time, we noticed that there is a bunching of wealth in the $6 million to $7 million range for the CEOs of classical high-tech start-ups. This is so predominant that we wonder if this is a rule laid down by investors! Our research also showed the wealth rose during boom periods, particularly during the early stage of eras such as the personal computer or Internet.

Excluding Internet boom extremes, the median of our selected companies has the CEO worth $6.8 million. Internet IPO successes easily averaged more than $100 million! The pre-Internet era high was Bill Gates, worth $236 million (this rose to billions in later years and he became the wealthiest person in the world!). The low was seen occasionally, in companies where the leaders appear to have traded very high cash compensation for very low equity positions. Bill Gates and others who started their companies in the pre-1983 era took low salaries and got much larger percentages of their companies. CEOs of Internet-era companies are taking classical combinations of stock options and competitive salaries. However, this does not appear to have greatly reduced their equity portion of compensation. That may be due in part to the increased bargaining power attributable to the constant shortage of managers qualified to lead Internet start-ups as CEOs.

Until the Internet, seldom did the CEO own more than 3 percent of the start-up after IPO time. Yet here too there is a range of results. In our pre-1990 sample, the median CEO percentage at IPO time was about 5 percent; the high was 40 percent and the low was 1.6 percent. But several famous post-1990 Internet-era companies have CEOs owning much more than that for several reasons: One is because the CEO used personal funds to do the expensive, high-risk seed round of funding. Another is because of the buyer's market mentality that resulted in the 1990s rush of investors to be first to fund "the next Microsoft of the Internet era." By 2000, it was not uncommon to see founder/CEOs own 10 percent to 20 percent of their start-ups the day after the IPO.

**Founders' Shares.** Founders other than the CEO rarely owned more than 4 percent at IPO time. The founders are replaced by hired CEOs who get fewer shares for taking less risk.

Note that exceptions do occur: When the board of Silicon Graphics brought in a new employee to take over from the founder as CEO (the leader stayed on as chairman and chief technical officer), the new CEO ended up with less than the founding leader, but was nonetheless the number-two employee in terms of ownership ranking. The CEO hired to grow Yahoo to IPO got just under 3 percent after the IPO, compared with 10.8 percent for each of the two student founders.

Implicit is the obvious: Those who are founders get a lot more wealth than those who join later, even though people may join only a few months after the founding of the company. It seems that here the old adage is true: "The early bird catches the worm," or at least the fattest one by far. A late joiner cannot qualify as a founder nor get the same number of shares as the founders. Founders take extra risks, such as leaving employment before any money is raised. Their "extra" equity reward is compensation for those risks.

The competence and experience (or lack thereof) of founders compared with employees who join later seems to have little to do with these wide ranges of wealth, according to several of the start-up industry people we spoke to. The individual who joins a year later as VP of sales or finance, for instance, can expect to get a very small portion of the company compared with the founders.

One noteworthy exception occurs when the board of directors decides it is time to add operational leadership while retaining the high-tech guru who has been the company's leader but is struggling to cope as a manager. This appears to us to have been the case in Silicon Graphics (we are not picking on or criticizing its management, just using the organizational changes to make a point): Ed Mc-Cracken—a veteran and successful general manager from Hewlett-Packard—joined three years after the founding of the company and ended up with 3.1 percent versus 4.6 percent for the founder, Jim Clark (who later left to found Netscape). The successful Silicon Graphics chairman stayed on and continued leading the company's advanced-technology work.

Attorneys warned us that a big bite of stock for a new leader—and the attendant dilution—often comes out of shares controlled by insiders. And in some cases when the founder/CEO chooses to leave or is forced out by investors, because of buyback conditions in the company's policies on stock, the shares for the new leader come out of the holdings of the former CEO and the remaining management and employees. The VCs do not want to share in such dilution proportionately with the remaining management and employees.

**Employees' Shares.** After founders, the other employees share in the remaining pool of stock via incentive stock options. The median size of the ownership pool for all nonfounder employees in the companies analyzed was 19 percent of the company, with the high at 26 percent and the low at 3 percent.

Examination of start-up data over twenty years revealed a pattern. Hardware start-ups arrive at IPO time with a 70:30 split, with investors owning the 70 percent and the rest shared by founders and stock options for employees. However, software start-ups arrive with a 60:40 split. Internet start-ups were often a 50:50 split. The difference for software companies appears to be because software founders often use "sweat equity" to do their seed round, taking no salaries and working out of their homes or student apartments. Internet start-ups benefit from perceptions of vast markets in the future.

The option pool for employees is tricky to plan because so little hard data is publicly available. The pioneering study for option pool planning was published in 1997 by Dee DiPietro, president of Advanced HR in Saratoga, Californa. The study showed that start-ups follow a reasonably consistent pattern when planning options, that such plans could be methodical, but that care must be taken to not make costly errors in granting options. Our other research found that the founders and investors worked out various schemes for creating enough shares to attract a lot of new employees. A deliberate scheme is needed to avoid running out of enough shares to attract the top players that will be needed in the ranks of the middle management as well as in all the other positions in the company. Whatever scheme is chosen, be sure there is enough stock available, in terms of both percentage and absolute dollars.

The nonexecutive employees' pool of equity for pre-Internet IPOs ranged from a high of $145 million to a low of $12 million, with $38 million as the median. The first was in a mature company, eleven years old; the other in a company only a little more than twenty-one months old. Those pools were created in the form of options to be shared among all employees in each company. Each had a widely varying number of employees and per-employee distribution of stock, according to our analysis. It seems that here each company makes a significant statement about its culture and character. Some spread the wealth more widely, others focus shares in fewer hands. Internet companies had wider variances in wealth distribution, probably due to the many unknowns about the future size of the markets for the Internet start-ups.

---

# Case Study: Cypress Semiconductor

One example is a classic that has stood the test of time: Cypress Semiconductor. It used stock options to make Cypress stand out as a motivator, with equity for all. First, the leader, T. J. Rogers, shared founders' stock among six people, including himself (two or three founders is much more the norm; see Table 8-1). The founders were almost all of the required key functional employees at the VP level.

During the private years the company granted bonuses in the form of stock to all employees, tied to milestones that were a part of the culture at Cypress called "turbo MBO." Literally every employee worked daily with detailed goals for the week and month. Success resulted and the employees shared in the increase in the value of the stock.

Additional stock options were granted to all levels of the company along the way, including top management. To veteran investors this is rare; seldom are top managers ever granted more stock than the original amount they were granted when first employed by the company. The reason is not clear, based on our limited interviews. We have nonetheless formed the hypothesis that it happens because most start-ups go widely off their original business plan, go over budget, are late with first product, are profitable much later than first planned, and are managed poorly.

Cypress ended up going public quickly, three and a half years after starting in business. At that time the founders did well by most measures. The CEO owned shares worth $6.8 million; the average for the five other founders was $2.7 million, and the pool for its 336 other employees (including both the granted and the remaining available pools of options) was worth $53 million.

Cypress continued to perform well after the IPO. And the stock rose to close at $11 7/8 on July 21, 1987, up 32 percent from the $9 IPO price.

Rogers was paid a total cash package of $122,325 for the twelve months prior to the 1986 IPO. His VPs earned in the range of $91,000 to $93,000.

Just before the IPO the founders and employees had claims to stock accounting for 26 percent of the company. Private sales of stock had brought venture capitalists' holdings to the remaining 74 percent, including 3 percent owned by an important early corporate partner, Monolithic Memories.

## What Is 1 Percent Worth?

The final variable in the equity equation is the value of 1 percent of the company at IPO time. When using this measure, examination of selected companies shows a wide range of value among the companies.

The low was Chips at $0.6 million for each percentage point. Chips went public in twenty-one months. The value later rose by a factor of five, to $3 million, as the IPO price of $5—issued in a very soft IPO market—rose to $35. Within four months the stock had settled near $25.

The high was Netscape, which went public sixteen months after founding. A 1 percent share was worth $10.7 million (1 percent of Microsoft was worth $5.9 million after eleven years).

The median value is about $1.5 million per percentage point. This varied considerably among companies because of many variables, including maturity of the company and consensus by Wall Street analysts on projections of the companies' operating earnings, cash flow, and return on invested capital.

**Other Findings.** Here are some further observations based on our research:

- Our proprietary databank suggests that the greater the amount of capital to be raised, measured in absolute dollars, the lower the percentage retained by management and employees.
- What is not visible is probably as significant as what is. That is, how much did the founder/CEO *planned* on giving up, versus how much he actually gave up because he grossly underestimated the capital actually needed, or missed development schedules, or found out that the market was much smaller or slower to grow than he had expected, for example?

- In simple terms, start-up CEOs who get to IPO in less than five years can look forward to becoming at least multimillionaires—typically, they acquire about $7 million; tens of millions is rare, at least until the Internet arrived. Note that in the examples we chose, one does not see the wealth of those CEOs who left before the IPO, for whatever reason—because the board dismissed them, they got tired and quit, or they just wanted to get out of the stress and see more of their families and friends.

**Participants' Cash and Equity.** The name of the game is wealth formation in the form of equity. Cash compensation plays a small role relative to stock options. Cash bonuses do occur; prior to 1998 they typically occurred in significant amounts only after the company had been profitable for several quarters. Some venture capital firms were fiercely against large cash bonuses of any kind until after the IPO. We found most start-ups since 1998 granting some form of cash bonuses annually.

One trend we detected was that the level of cash and equity have reversed direction and relative importance since 1983. That year seems to have been a watershed:

- Prior to 1983, it was common to find CEOs working for $50,000 per year and ending up with a company in which outside investors owned less than 50 percent of the stock. Everyone hunkered down, lived on a lean and mean salary, and waited to make up for lost wages when the stock went public in five years.
- After 1983, salaries moved up much closer to those of employees of public, established corporations. More venture money meant more start-ups needing to pull more managers out of successful, well-paying, established companies. CEOs of the 1990s have shown up at IPO time earning in excess of $100,000 and even more, and VPs and those reporting directly to them have been earning salaries a lot closer to the going rate for people with their experience and skills in larger, already public companies.
- Equity showed a reverse trend. It has now become rare to see start-ups at IPO time with more than 35 percent owned by management and employees. Software companies seem to have more like 40 percent, perhaps because so much of the seed-round funding came from founders. Overall, investors typically took 65 percent to 75 percent of the company by the time the IPO was over. Prior to 1983, those statistics for equity were reversed, with the larger percentage going to founders and employees. In boom periods, such as the launch of a new period like the Internet era, the percentage owned by investors drops below 50% because valuations are much higher for much younger companies. As boom times calm down, the percentages are expected to settle back to the typical ranges.

**TABLE 8-2. Ownership by Employees and Investors Just Before IPO\***

| | Employees (%) | Value at IPO ($M) | Investors (%) | Value at IPO ($M) | Equity Capital ($M) |
|---|---|---|---|---|---|
| Chips and Technologies | 63 | $35 | 37 | $21 | $3 |
| Cypress Semiconductor | 25 | $74 | 75 | $176 | $40 |
| Netscape | 73 | $661 | 27 | $247 | $40 |
| Silicon Graphics | 33 | $49 | 67 | $78 | $22 |
| Yahoo | 55 | $443 | 45 | $199 | $6 |

\* Includes all options granted plus available option pool

*Source:* Saratoga Venture Finance

Our sample in Table 8-2 shows the holdings of common equivalent shares, including all pools of options, both granted and available, just before IPO time. The valuation is measured at the IPO price. The definition of employees includes everyone except the founders.

Netscape and Yahoo had the highest portion for employees in great part because they went public so quickly.

Chips had the highest portion for the CEO who bucked the trend, got the company going without classical venture funding, and went IPO very fast.

Notice in the cases of Netscape and Cypress Semiconductor the lack of correlation between the amount of equity capital raised and the dilution to management and employees. Each raised $40 million, yet the portion owned by employees was 3:1 higher for Netscape. Much of the explanation is due to Jim Clark, the founder, using his own funds for the seed round, and to the higher valuation for Internet-era companies.

Our research strongly suggests that the portion sold to venture investors ends up adhering in most cases to classical expectations. The mix of investors to management and employees is most likely to be in the range of about 60:40 to 70:30. Boom times move it to 50:50, or even more proportionately for noninvestors.

Companies with low venture capital requirements, like Chips ($3 million) and Microsoft ($5 million), sold proportionately less to investors. This seems to be a bias in the funding and makes common sense, yet, as noted above, the final percentages sold vary widely, for various reasons. So be careful not to accept too quickly rules of thumb thrown at you by investors and others.

# Big Fish, Little Fish

At this juncture we must bring up a familiar issue that we hear about quite often: Is it better to be a little fish in a big pond or a big fish in a little pond?

In the parlance of start-ups that is rephrased: Is it better to do a start-up that requires $3 million in capital and grows to $20 million in annual sales; or one that needs $30 million to get to $100 million? Will the dilution to me in the bigger pond outweigh my lower absolute wealth in the little pond?

The answer can, fortunately, at least be quantified with simple arithmetic (see Chapter 9). Then the entrepreneur must decide which strategy has the best chance for fulfilling the start-up's business plan. This of course focuses only on the financial aspects of such a decision.

Control seems to be a swing factor in settling this issue. Both small capital requirements and speed to market augur well for selling less to outsiders and retaining more control. However, as cited in Chapter 7, investors quickly get into control, regardless of percentage owned.

Most of the classical venture capitalists argue for the larger pond, which is in their best interests. They have a great deal of capital to invest, and it takes about the same effort and time to invest $1 million as $10 million. The venture capitalist is not in the business of getting the founder the best deal in town; that is up to the founder.

**Cash: Wages and Bonuses.** Venture capitalists approve of paying cash wages, but just not too much. The CEO's job is to determine how low a wage he can exist on personally, and then expect none or at least very little increase in cash compensation until the start-up becomes profitable years later.

Cash bonuses are more common today than in earlier days. Sales VPs all get commission compensation; marketing VPs less commonly so, even if they are responsible for sales. But the proportion of cash taken out by the top executives of a start-up as bonuses was rarely in the same proportion as in large, established companies.

High salaries did exist in some cases, typically in wildly successful companies with sales at IPO time already in excess of $100 million per year.

To generalize, the universal attitude is classically a "lean and mean" one toward cash compensation. The CEO should be prepared to step down by perhaps 20 percent or so from the nice base-plus-bonus package at his former BigCo Inc.

Day one wages for start-up CEOs in the seed stage were rarely over $90,000 during the 1980s. Nonetheless, there were important exceptions, and the trend in the 1990s was toward larger cash compensation. CEOs starting in the $150,000 to $200,000 range became common as the new century arrived.

135

**TABLE 8-3. Annual Cash Compensation Just Before IPO***

| | | | Range of VPs | |
|---|---|---|---|---|
| | | *($ in thousands per year)* | | |
| | Highest Paid | | High | Low |
| Chips and Technologies | $137 | VP Sales | $125 | $93 |
| Cypress Semiconductor | $122 | CEO | $93 | $91 |
| Netscape | $225 | VP Sales | $225 | $80 |
| Silicon Graphics | $156 | CEO | $138 | $105 |
| Yahoo | $69 | CEO | $65 | $65 |

* For the twelve months prior to IPO as reported to the Securities and Exchange Commission in the offering prospectus

*Source:* Saratoga Venture Finance

## Is It Worth It?

I wonder if I'd be better off staying at big IBM, or HP, or doing a start-up such as XYZ.com? Would the payoff be worth it? A quick calculation can show it takes decades of high-taxed salaries to earn the $3 million after tax that a VP gets for doing a successful start-up.

**Vice Presidents.** The compensations for vice presidents are not as varied as for CEOs but still require a lot of years of wages just to even out. A VP earning $180,000 a year at BigCo Inc., who gets 0.5 percent of a start-up, pays $50,000 for optioned shares, pays taxes at the marginal rate of 39 percent, and whose company is worth $1.5 million per 1 percent requires 8 years of wages to equal the worth of his or her equity.

Note that in neither case—CEO or vice president—is any credit given in the above calculations for the cash wages paid by the start-up.

Clearly the comparative financial reward is attractive to a manager who is interested in doing a start-up. The tougher aspect to measure is the risk of doing one.

**The Downside.** The CEO must be prepared to live for three to five years on the salary that he accepts with the first funding of the start-up. Most start-ups do not get to the successful heights shown in our examples of famous high-tech start-ups. Our research suggests that only about 9 percent of the companies that are funded get to those lofty levels of success.

As a consequence, the prudent individual must expect to pay bills and meet family obligations on wages earned or else formulate another plan. Here are a few of the more common personal plans as well as a few of the more creative ones we have encountered. All are real names, although some details have been changed for privacy:

- Sam saved enough to live without any income for two years. This provided enough time to resign, write a business plan, incorporate a start-up, and work at lower wages until three years later, when he got a raise at the point the start-up became profitable.

- Bob treated his reduced salary as an investment. He considered the incremental wages lost to be schooling in the world of the entrepreneur, regardless of the outcome.

- Charlie, an engineer, opened up a Chinese restaurant on the side with two cousins. His goal was to accumulate seed capital to start his own company. While his share of the profits turned out to be insufficient to start a company, the capital did give him enough to make up for the lower wages he settled on when joining the founding team of a new enterprise.

- After twenty years as an engineer, Jim found himself at the age of forty-five without sufficient funds for retirement. Although he had become a very successful engineering manager, his string of start-up company employers had not done well. Jim quit his latest job as an engineer and went into the real estate business. He bought and refurbished a five-apartment complex. After three years, he found the cash flow income to be enough for his eventual retirement. So Jim found yet another promising start-up and went to work again in his first love, engineering.

- Philip Huang, the founder of Televideo, worked a second part-time job at 7-Eleven convenience stores to help him save the start-up capital that he used to create Televideo.

- Jake and Sue were top salespeople who married to form a family and raise children. Both wanted to do a start-up. They agreed she would go first, and she joined her former boss in his new start-up. The company did fine. After nearly four years it went public. Sue emerged as one of the top salespeople. Meanwhile, Jake kept the bills paid on his salary. They saved his commission checks for rainy day emergencies. After Sue's company did their IPO, Jake left BigCo Inc. and joined a tiny high-tech start-up as VP for marketing and sales, taking a big cut in salary. Meanwhile, Sue got another raise and set another record as their top salesperson. Now they switched roles. Sue's salary paid the bills. And the couple sold half her shares to pay for the extra expenses of their first baby and the construction of an extra room on their home in Silicon Valley.

- Jack decided to go for broke. He took out a second mortgage, guaranteed loans to his start-up, and cut the family's spending to a pittance. This went on for nearly three years. Then his company went bankrupt. Although his wife is still with him, his kids remember every day of those three years, including the Christmas with gifts from the Goodwill store.

**Tables of Cash Compensation.** Table 8-3 shows how well paid top management was in start-ups that were successful. Shown is the total cash compensation that existed in the twelve months prior to the IPO date, including all bonuses and any other cash compensation. Equity-related compensation is excluded. In some cases we found that the board of directors approved significant increases just prior to the initial public offering. Such increases, however, were not a prevailing pattern.

Here are some of our findings:

- Cash compensation varies widely and appears related to several factors. The Advanced HR study showed 1997 top compensation ranged from a high of $500,000 for the CEO of a software start-up to a low of $50,000 for another CEO. The median for software was $200,000, Internet $175,000, and telecommunications $150,000. We noted that start-ups that are classically consumer-oriented compete for people in an industry well known to pay significantly higher cash compensation than electronics companies of similar size. Internet-era companies seem to be betting more heavily on the equity compensation than on cash. Hardware companies tended to pay the least cash compensation.
- The head of sales often earned more cash than the CEO in "hot" companies. This occurred in both Chips ($100 million annual sales run rate by IPO time) and many others since then. And the VP of sales was a close second to the CEO in several start-ups. Some start-up CEOs told us that they had paid their head of sales on a commission structure to encourage beating the business plan by a wide margin. They wanted the compensation to be the result of hot sales and not to be artificially limited to being a salary lower than that of the CEO.
- The salaries of VPs naturally followed those of the CEO. However, several chairmen said they had on occasion paid proportionately more cash to VPs than to CEOs because the VPs were not holding a large fistful of founders' shares. This was most pronounced when the company decided to bring in a chief operating officer to run the show. The new leader is often paid a lot more in cash than the CEO, who is a founder and wealthy stockholder.
- Here again, what is unseen is as significant as what is visible. Compensation rates for private companies are difficult to obtain. However, since 1981, Saratoga Venture Finance has monitored start-up CEOs' salaries and compared them to wage guidelines published by several popular compensation surveys. We found the closest correlation for high-tech companies was with

the start-up-focused findings of the Advanced HR surveys. Some lawyers and venture capitalists also keep some data. Or ask your start-up consultant, recruiter, or human relations adviser for assistance.

**Founders' Shares.** CEOs often have questions about founders' shares. Some of the honor given to founders is good, but also we found that they get tied up with a lot of restrictions. There is an awe, an air of extra respect, for "founders' shares," some of which is unfounded and misleading. We found that this is due to a number of misconceptions.

- First, pieces of paper labeled "founders' shares" don't exist. Everyone gets the same certificates for common shares as everyone else.
- The term "founder" is used in each prospectus as required by federal security law. In simplest terms it means the person(s) employed or holding office the company the day was incorporated.
- Founders get more shares than any other employee. Typically they are there in the first days, it is their idea, they took a big risk when they left their employers to start the company, and they worked very hard to create the business plan and convince investors to risk their money in the company.
- Founders lose a lot of privacy. Corporate laws identify a founder as such in the IPO prospectus and include compensation and shares compared with everyone else in the company.
- The founder has basically the same restrictions on shares as any other common shareholder has: Rule 144 and related rules limiting sale of stock.

**Rule 144.** Rule 144 is meant to prevent founders and investors from selling their shares soon after the IPO and running away as the company collapses in ruins shortly thereafter, leaving the latest investors holding worthless shares. The rules are, as usual with the law, complex. But here is an oversimplified explanation of it all. (Be sure to talk to a good securities lawyer if this pertains to you.)

A founder must wait a good part of about two years before selling his shares to anyone. The clock starts ticking only on the date the owner has paid for the shares in full; getting a loan from the company to buy the shares does not start the two-year countdown.

What a founder does not want is to wait to start the clock ticking the day after the IPO. But in order to own the shares he must have paid cash to purchase the shares. That is more risky than waiting. The trade-off between waiting to purchase and purchasing early will have tax consequences, too, so a talk with a good tax adviser is a must.

Rule 144 does allow some sales of private, nonregistered stock. However, the restrictions on who can sell and to whom are quite narrow. Advice from a good tax and securities adviser is mandatory. There are frequent proposals for changes in Rule 144.

**Employees' Stock Options.** For most employees, including everyone other than founders who buy their shares on day one, the means of getting stock ownership is through stock options. There are no special rules for options for a start-up. The option plan a company selects must comply with federal and state laws for such things.

How much the company grants to whom depends mainly on company policy. Most start-ups these days are granting options from day one to all employees, hourly employees included. It is necessary to calculate the size of the pool needed over five years. That takes some real finesse, and a computer model can help save a CEO's sanity.

The company's lawyer can explain about the two types of options: Incentive Stock Options (ISO) and Nonqualified Stock Options. The former has better tax consequences, generally, but is limited to an absolute dollar value that can be issued per person. Since that is a problem for a lot of VPs who will be hired later on, the nonqualified will be used for fixing that problem. The shares are the same, common stock, only the amounts and tax effects are different.

Vesting is now almost always designed to occur evenly over four years, with an initial one-year waiting period. The company gets the right to buy back any unvested portion, even if the employee has paid for the shares in full. This is the hook the investors use to keep the CEO at the office, working hard even when things seem impossible. And it is their main control on CEO performance: If the CEO does not deliver, they will probably fire him, buy back the unvested shares, and grant the remaining shares in an option as part of the new CEO's employment package. Other vesting schemes do appear, and they are usually in favor of the investors.

**Employment Contracts and Personal Loans.** Although they do occur upon occasion, employment contracts for high-tech start-up CEOs are rare. They are almost nonexistent before, during, or after IPO time. VCs hate them; most won't touch a round of financing for a company with contracts in place.

Personal loans are also very rare. The exception is in the form of loans to buy stock. But that is less and less common and is seldom done for anyone other than a critically important executive who must be assisted financially to attract him to work for the new company.

**Relocation.** Relocation loans are rare for start-ups, but do occur from time to time. It is hard for a tiny company with just $250,000 in the bank to squeeze out the extra money. Relocation of key employees is to be avoided. It costs a lot of time, takes a lot of emotional energy from your employee, and adds to the already high stress of doing a start-up. This is especially obvious for start-ups in the high-rent districts such as Silicon Valley, the Boston area, and metropolitan New York City. Another problem is that banks do not like to grant mortgages guaranteed by new enterprises of any size, especially those that may fail next year.

**Venture Capitalists' Shares.** Investors buy preferred stock that has the option of being converted into common shares under certain conditions or is required to be converted into common at the time of the IPO.

As noted in Chapter 7, the shares have certain restrictions and requirements. They are like a contract, and the CEO is the party that must perform.

Watch out for the conversion terms. A 1:1 ratio is almost always used, but special antidilution clauses may trigger a much higher ratio in favor of investors.

## Case Study: An Engineer's Offer of Compensation

A.W. had decided two years earlier to start looking for a start-up to join, and over the past eight weeks he had been talking seriously about joining one of two start-ups where he had been interviewed, PiTech and Saga Systems. Since immigrating to the United States from Taiwan he had put in ten years at two well-known companies. He held bachelor's and master's degrees in electrical engineering and had earned his Ph.D. at MIT thirteen years earlier. A.W. had developed a series of successful chips, had three patents, and regularly contributed IEEE papers in his field of expertise. He had just sent his last chip design to the wafer fabrication lab at BigCo, Inc., and was now ready to leave. He wondered what the offer from PiTech would be.

A.W.'s wife, Nancy, was a tech writer at Netscape. The profit on her stock option would be the reserves they needed to support his parents in Taiwan. They had both also talked about their dream house and decided they could never get it except through a big success in stock at a start-up. But Nancy's stock had done only well enough to fund the family reserve, and now A.W. decided to get the home by going to a good start-up in its infancy. He wanted the maximum stock he could get. They lived frugally and did not have a high lifestyle to support.

PiTech had been after A.W. for some time. Jim, the PiTech CEO and former director of engineering in the Logic Division of BigCo, had noticed A.W. during the past four years. In addition to being a very hard worker, A.W. was talented. He had pulled several key design projects out of the fire. This was important to the massive turnaround effort that Jim had been handed four years earlier.

During that time, Jim had been thinking of the value of his 30,000-share option at BigCo, which had a strike price of $3.25. The recent electronics industry slump had plunged the BigCo stock price from $12 to $6.75. His work had yet to be recognized on financial terms because the Systems Division had fallen into the tank at just the time the Logic Division was getting into black ink. The hours had been long, there was lots of travel to key customers, often with few results to cheer about. Key engineers had left for greener pastures over the past two years, and innovation was not as common as earlier. A.W. had been a sparkling exception.

After much personal consideration, Jim finally contacted Frank at Elm Ventures. Frank was a former executive at a successful start-up, Tecnic Corporation. Frank had met Jim at an evening seminar put on by his school alumni association. Frank took care to listen to Jim's guarded words and was impressed by the man and his track record. Jim left with confidence that some of his ideas for a start-up business plan would be attractive to Frank once they were down on paper. Nine months later, Elm became the lead investor in the seed round for PiTech.

A.W. liked Jim, who during interviews at PiTech had mentioned that a slot as director of advanced engineering was available. But A.W. would report to a new VP of engineering, Mike, who had joined as a founder and was a close friend of Jim's. In A.W.'s mind, this increased the risk of joining PiTech. Mike had only limited experience in managing engineers at Digital Equipment Corporation. According to the grapevine rumors in the Route 128 region of Boston where Mike had worked, he was reputed to be one of the greats as a solo inventor and much less successful as a leader of a group of design engineers.

Jim had prepared a written offer and had it waiting in a manila folder on his desk. He had decided long ago to make every offer of employment in PiTech, at least up to offer number 100. Jim had carefully calculated how much to give his first twenty top recruits. Six of the last twelve offers had been accepted with no hassle or haggling, and only one had not worked out and left. Jim was confident that his offer to A.W. was generous and fair, both to A.W. and to PiTech.

The receptionist called Jim when A.W. arrived. Jim ushered A.W. into Jim's small office, closed the door, and the two began the meeting. A.W. waited for the CEO to make the offer. After agreeing on a rather open-ended charter to design the next two logic chips, Jim got around to the offer.

"After careful consideration, we have decided to offer you $76,500 per year base salary and 30,000 shares," said Jim. He paused to see A.W.'s reaction. A.W. did not move a face muscle but tensed up inside. He had expected higher numbers in both base and stock.

"May I see the written offer?" asked A.W. Jim handed it to A.W., who read it carefully.

"How does it look to you?" queried Jim.

After a long pause that made Jim quite uncomfortable, A.W. replied, "Well, frankly, I am a bit disappointed." Pause again.

Jim groaned inside. "Why didn't I check with Sam over at NewCo? He would have helped me on this one. I haven't any support in human relations; I thought this was an attractive offer. His base is nearly that of our VP of engineering! How can I go any higher? But did I go too far below his old base of $83,000?"

"Well, perhaps I can answer any questions you have about your offer, A.W. All the guys want you to join us, and we thought the offer was really quite fair for a start-up." Jim knew he couldn't say that everyone had taken cuts in pay, because that just was not true; in fact, two people had to be offered raises to get them to join.

"How many shares do you have?" A.W. said.

Jim stiffened visibly. He hadn't expected this seemingly quiet person to be so aggressive. A.W. noticed it and sensed defensiveness. "I wonder if he gets that defensive about everything?" thought A.W., who began to doubt his initial attraction to Jim as a leader.

"Well, that's confidential, of course!" barked Jim. He was now angry inside.

What Jim did not know was that A.W. had done his homework. Friends had given him details about PiTech and its backers. His friends had spent a lot of time coaching him on how to measure the wealth in the stock offer, and a lawyer friend had obtained PiTech corporate records in the state capital. A.W. knew almost exactly how many shares Jim and the other founders each had.

"OK, how many shares are outstanding?" said A.W.

"About five million," replied Jim.

"Is that including the venture capitalists' preferred converted to common?" asked A.W.

At that moment, Jim sensed he was dealing with someone more experienced than he was.

"No, you need to add another 5 million shares or so for that," said Jim. He waited, nervously.

"About 11 million in total?" inquired A.W.

"Yes," answered Jim. But Jim did not tell A.W. about the one million shares granted as options to an equipment leasing company and a technical consultant. After all, they were not yet shares outstanding, at least not until the IPO time.

"What do you think the shares will be worth at the public offering date?" asked A.W.

"Oh, brother, this guy is sharp! I hope he designs as well as he does his homework!" Jim thought. "Well, the calculations I have made tell me we can get about $15 per share if we do our business plan," responded Jim.

What Jim did not know was that during the team interviews, Mike said one of the venture capitalists on the board of directors had let slip that they thought the company could do $10 at IPO time. Jim had decided to skip that number. After all, it was a wild projection, wasn't it?

The offer letter stated that the stock for A.W. would be priced at 10¢ per share. A.W. had learned that the seed round had gone for 50¢ each after the Preferred A was converted to common 1:1. Jim pointed out that "at those prices, and as employee number 14, you would be practically a founder!" A.W. liked that idea.

"How many shares will be outstanding at IPO time?" responded A.W.

Now Jim really got nervous. "If I tell him, he'll learn that we need three more rounds of venture capital to get the $35 million that our business plan calls for. And the total 23 million shares will make his wealth, before the cost of 10¢ per share, worth less than $300,000. I hope he buys my $15 per share!"

Jim eagerly said, "Remember, 30,000 shares makes you one of the top ten shareholders in the company!"

A.W. immediately revolted inside. "Who does he think he is kidding? I know what dilution is. I'll end up owning less than 0.1 percent of the whole company; that's next to nothing!"

Jim kept thinking he had revealed too much already. He disliked opening up with anyone, especially like this. Would A.W. get scared of the dangers of having to meet milestones in order to get the other venture capital that PiTech needed? "If I don't get this guy," Jim thought, "our first product ship will be set back six to twelve months!"

"OK, I'll give you $80,000 base and an extra 5,000 shares," blurted Jim.

A.W. decided he had enough, and said, "Could you put that in writing?" Jim immediately inked the changes and initialed them, handing the modified original to A.W. without making a copy.

"Thank you, I'll get back to you soon," said A.W., and he walked out the door.

As he started his car and eased out into the traffic, he thought about the meeting. By the time he arrived home he had made up his mind.

He would accept the Saga Systems offer from for the twenty-man start-up, reporting to the president as director of engineering at $85,000 and with an option for shares he figured would be at 0.2 percent of the company and worth about $800,000 at IPO time. He wondered why he had been so excited about Jim in the first place.

**Employee Benefits and Perquisites.** All start-ups have to be competitive with health benefits. That's a given. Several insurance companies focus on smaller enterprises and serve them well, with good rates.

Beyond medical and dental plans, the seed start-up seldom offers a lot more in benefits, but glasses and other extras are no longer only reserved for post-IPO companies.

Vacations are officially two weeks, but one should not count on having time for more than a week at a time. Spot vacations of a free day, or "comp" days as compensation for a weekend of work or long travel, are more likely.

Cars are not offered. Some field sales people get car allowances instead. Car allowances for executives are scarce.

Fancy offices are rare. Furnishings are usually spartan and often used. Even for the CEO.

Secretaries are nonexistent at most new companies. Instead, one person does every administrative job imaginable.

Several start-ups told us they offer free use of laptops and workstations in engineers' homes to encourage extra hours of design time. And several others offer either loans of personal computers or inexpensive purchases through the company. The idea is to encourage more work and productivity in staff personnel.

# The Professional Reward

Our research revealed that there are several nonfinancial reasons that people joined start-ups. Many people said that these were more important than the monetary reward.

**Being a Winner.** Becoming an early employee of a famous start-up like Netscape or Amazon.com, one that everyone talks about, is probably the most often mentioned motivator of those who think of start-ups. The next Intel, Compaq, America Online. "Wow! That would feel great," said people we interviewed. That overpowered the other responses of those we spoke to and observed. Venture firms also have this desire. "Everyone loves a winner," is how the saying goes. "So try for one," says the venture capitalist.

However, reality is sobering. Few are winners. Historically, only one in ten have made it to the fame of attaining the ranks of those companies that got to IPO. And only a handful of those that get funded become household names like Yahoo. Yet all the people who start out seem to have faith that their company will make it. That is the stuff start-ups are made of. Everyone has to believe in the dream, the vision of glory and success.

Some start-up veterans told us such dreams were unrealistic. A few said you just have to believe. Yet others were of the opinion that "it's better to have tried a start-up and failed than never to have tried at all."

**Hot Start-up Atmosphere.** We have learned firsthand how exciting it is to be a part of a company that is on a roll. When a start-up is hot it is *hot!* It was breathtaking to us to just a walk into the lobby of Netscape after its IPO and as it was ramping up to $20 million of revenue for the quarter. After we were greeted by the friendly receptionist, we looked around. The lobby was jammed with customers whose conversations were marked with accents from Texas, New York, Korea, Japan; suppliers' representatives were hassling the polite but very firm receptionist, who said they all needed prior appointments; two walk-ins who were having trouble with English were getting help filling out job applications; engineering interviewees were coming and going like patrons of Baskin-Robbins on a 100-degree July day; advertising and PR agents were zooming through the lobby, racing for cars to avoid being too late for the next interview with reporters; phone calls from the BMW, Porsche, Mercedes, and Ferrari dealers' salesmen were waiting for attention; repairmen with their shiny aluminum toolkits were getting immediate access to the inner sanctum. The switchboard wouldn't stop ringing. And the air of pride and hard work, and the look of confidence on the faces of the employees who swaggered through the lobby, were obvious.

Once ushered into the inner sanctum, we walked past cubicles housing people bent over PC screens and workstations, and meeting areas filled with people being interviewed. The chart of daily stock price changes was posted outside one cubicle; it looked like a rocket flight path. Talk in the aisles was over new orders, ship rates, the next browser that looked solid after alpha; how the development team had worked until 1:00 in the morning to get the final changes done before the deadline; that the president had been quoted in the *San Jose Mercury News*. T-shirts with various versions of Netscape logos were everywhere.

The air was filled with the feeling of success. Netscape had accomplished in less than two years what most start-ups, even the famous ones, typically took five years to do.

The last memory of our visit was the article someone had ripped out of a newspaper and pinned to his cubicle fabric with a bent paper clip. The headline said something about the move by Microsoft into Internet browsers. As we headed to our car in the hot afternoon sun, we recalled the familiar words from a classic article in *Forbes* on the "shooting stars" that so often are hot companies that quickly burn out; the writer had written that "entrepreneurs should always run scared."

**Patents and Creativity.** Regardless of which company we visited, engineers were quick to tell us they had confidence that their ideas would lead to several landmark patents. They talked about this a lot, especially since the U.S. patent court and the copyright laws had changed and were granting almost any patent applied for. The desire by engineers to get a patent was clear, even if the company had all the legal rights assigned to it. Framed replicas of granted patents were displayed visibly in cubicles of many of the technical staff members that we visited.

Clearly, many engineers felt they had a much better chance to get patents in a start-up than in a much larger company. When asked why, they cited fewer constraints on creativity or that the entire business plan of the start-up was founded upon the inventions (to be) claimed by the engineering staff. Their excitement seemed to stimulate ideas that led them to new heights of exploration, stretching the former limits of their technical capabilities.

**Papers, the Media, and Conferences.** Presenting papers at technical conferences ranked high on the list of reasons to do a start-up, at least for the technical staff. Marketing personnel talked about getting invitations to make presentations about their start-up at industry seminars and trade shows. Such highly visible forums were attractive to many people we interviewed.

Yet we found such visions in conflict with reality. Managers of start-ups lamented that their technical staff did not even have enough time to write the minimal technical collateral materials needed by the company's sales and marketing staffs. Papers on the company's latest new products, aimed by marketing departments for covers of magazines, usually lacked writers. And there was such intensity for finishing new designs that some engineers lamented they had to turn down trips to annual technical conferences they used to attend religiously.

However, marketing staffs flocked to seminars and conferences. They cited their need to be abreast of current trends, and they wanted to influence the newsletter writers and media people who were invited to attend. Public relations included such activity, and employees seemed to search each issue of their favorite magazine or newspaper for tidbits written about their start-up. If a competitor was mentioned but not a word on their own company, employees were quick to point this out to the VP of marketing.

Regis McKenna received top marks for pioneering and setting an early example for how to use public relations as an offensive marketing weapon for start-ups deep in the battles for setting industry standards. Since the winning companies so often included those that set and defended the standard, this partially explains why so many people on the marketing staff seek out the paper and seminar circuit with great intensity after joining a start-up.

**Industry Business Accolades.** Coverage in the local news, industry, and Internet media was clearly pleasing to the founders of start-ups. They said the interviews and resulting publicity were "part of the game." But the press promotes the good and the bad, making bums out of the heroes as fast as the rumor mills send out faint signals that "Mr. X May Return as CEO" or "Newco may not get its next model out on time" or "A former employee who refused to be identified said . . ." Bad press did deliver news that caused customers to hesitate or even forgo orders that the start-up counted on and needed badly. That simply reinforced the power of the public relations "PR push" needed behind the start-ups. And the drive for headlines was renewed with more vigor and desperation.

The winners got the personal fame that goes along with such success. The companies and management of the losers, the majority, were quickly old news and seldom mentioned in good headlines again.

**Personal Growth.** Many people said they joined a start-up to achieve much greater personal growth, to get out of a rut in BigCo. Our interviews revealed two very different groups of people in the realm of personal growth: One camp responded well to the demands of the start-ups they joined, learning on the job and adding experience after experience to their always-up-to-date résumés. The other camp was ground up, burned out, and left in worse shape by the start-up experience.

Escape from stagnation in a large company was the attraction for many. They were looking for less politics, less waste, less bureaucracy. Most start-up people believed they escaped from all that in a new enterprise. This helped them grow personally.

Some people seemed to thrive on the stress and difficulties that a small company inevitably encounters. Some claimed to possess more drive or determination. Others attached credit to a religious belief. Others said they were just happy to have made it through in one piece. Whatever the outcome, a start-up profoundly affects a person who becomes involved in it.

Some people picked up special skills on the job in their function, whether it was finance or manufacturing or whatever. But, compared with the formal classroom learning sessions conducted by large established companies, start-ups spent little time on such things. Predominant was the classroom of the school of hard knocks and lessons learned on the fly. A vast majority of the people with whom we spoke had mastered sophisticated tools and techniques well before joining a small start-up. New companies tend to use skills rather than create them, especially those skills requiring heavy blocks of time to learn.

**Management Climbing and Turnover.** Consensus was that promotion was a lot easier in a start-up than in a larger company. However, it also seemed a lot easier to end up without a job.

Part of the source of the problem of turnover lies in the hiring practices of start-ups. Veterans of start-ups kept telling us that management under stress tends to recruit the nearest warm body rather than incur an expensive and time-consuming headhunter fee to carefully search out the best person for a key regional sales position or product marketing job or whatever. "Sink or swim" was a common phrase bandied about, and a lot of new hires sank.

Our hypothesis is that this hiring practice contributes significantly to the troubles so many start-ups run into and never recover from. Firing people in a start-up has vivid, negative morale repercussions. Recruiting and retraining is dreadfully expensive for a company with limited resources such as the new enterprise. Low turnover probably has a lot more to do with success than it is given credit for.

# The Floundering Founder Phenomenon

One observation became so predominant that we think it is a rule of a start-up: at some level of sales or complexity or duress, the founding leader will find that he is failing miserably. This was first identified by Laurence J. Peter and Raymond Hull as the Peter Principle—he has risen to his level of incompetence. It is painfully evident in start-ups.

As noted in earlier chapters, the board of directors is dominated by VCs who very frequently fire the president founder who won't give up even though the company is in a real mess. Few people enjoy firing this person, or think it good. However, we did find several old venture capital salts with the reputation of believing that it was both natural and healthy to ax the founders, because the companies that succeed always got to a point where that was necessary.

The resulting bitter feelings are seldom forgotten. Spouses of such discarded employees told us of years of expensive legal battles behind the scenes that were intensely fierce, angry, and devastating. Former friends had to choose sides and close relationships were severed, never to be renewed.

On a more optimistic note, the experience gained and the value of any vested shares are worth a lot, particularly in the next start-up job, even if the first one does not work out. One budding manager left an outstanding career at a large computer company to take over the presidency of a start-up when that company was growing 300 percent a year just after going public. He inherited a lot more of a mess than anyone had expected and left after a short period of time. However, soon thereafter he was recruited to be the president of a small private start-up. Its sales soared and it shortly went public.

It would be an interesting and very useful study to learn how long founders last and why. Some leave because they have become independently wealthy. But few leave voluntarily; their lives seem to be so bound up in their start-up, their baby that they have given birth to and nourished from the first day they got the idea for the start-up.

# The Personal Cost

This section is dedicated to learning the truth from both the losers and the winners. Our goal is to enable a person considering doing a start-up to weigh—realistically—both the tantalizing rewards and the expensive costs of launching or joining a start-up. We recommend that you undertake such an analysis; the world of the start-up can be a jungle of terror for the wrong person. Table 8-4 compares the demands of a job in a start-up with a similar job in a large division of a very large company. We will discuss each of the eleven areas mentioned in the table in more detail.

The findings, observations, and case studies that follow are collections of personal experiences of people we interviewed. Accordingly, names usually have been altered to protect the privacy of the persons involved. Our contributors wanted to give some firsthand examples of how it really is in order to help others make up their own minds more realistically and avoid some of the pitfalls and pain they themselves encountered while doing a start-up. We thank all of our contributors for their courage and truthfulness.

Our conclusions can be summarized as follows: The toll of a start-up depends on how firm a foundation the employee has for his self-worth. A start-up is the most dangerous for the personality whose personal worth is wrapped up in the degree of his success or failure on the job. The more independent one's self-worth is from the success of the company or personal job performance, the less expensive a start-up is likely to be in personal terms.

The trick lies in predetermining what one's self-worth is actually founded on. This is not easy to do, even for the highly educated employees of high-tech start-ups. Professional counselors and psychiatrists lamented that this is particularly difficult for people who work and live in a technical world and are uncomfortable with people problems. But that is where you must begin. Then you will be able to consider doing a start-up realistically, with your eyes open.

Make a realistic assessment of yourself, of the possible personal cost to you of doing a start-up, and of the chances of a start-up adding to or detracting from your finding fulfillment in life. Our goal is to assist you in attaining your personal best for you and your family.

**Time Commitment.** How much harder do people have to work in a start-up? This is a question we are asked frequently.

## Table 8-4. Personal Costs Associated With a Start-up

As compared with job demands of a manager in a division of a large, public company with revenues exceeding one billion dollars, a core team member must face:

**An increase in the general level of stress**

There is more likelihood of burn-out, and the breakup of already strained relations between family and friends.

**A much larger time commitment required**

Startups require longer hours and have shorter vacations.

**An increase in the requirement to "do it yourself"**

No large backup staff to delegate work to.

**Additional reporting requirements**

The founders must now report to investors and the board of directors.

**Less time for exercise, fitness, diet, and health**

At a time of increased stress, the healthy stress-reducers are less available.

**Increased psychological pressure**

The weak points in personal character start to stand out and affect employees and families.

**Increased pressure to make right decisions, and to make them faster**

The founder's decisions now affect a small group of very close people.

**A heightened awareness of the risk of failure**

There is more personal exposure, and a greater chance of failure and of seeing the company go bankrupt.

**Increased pressure from peers to "succeed"**

Media and industry exposure grows noticeably, and with it the audience for success or failure.

**A sharply heightened test of love and intimacy**

The founder's family reacts to the conditions noted above, seeing growing evidence of the related problems in your shared lives; including less time, less cash, and more interpersonal irritability.

**A sharp boost in personal introspection**

"Who am I? Why am I doing this? Where can I find personal peace, contentment and fulfillment?"

*Source:* Saratoga Venture Finance

As for start-ups, we found that people generally work harder in a new enterprise than in a billion-dollar giant. We found that certainly there was no "9 to 5" behavior that lasted for long, if at all. We did observe that many of the start-up employees were the kind of people who were always going to work hard, regardless of the size of the company for which they worked. In fact, they did not work much harder in a start-up. This seemed to be especially true of the seasoned CEOs who set the pace for the rest of the employees.

To put our findings in perspective, consider this from a 1987 study of executive work patterns. The research was sponsored by Accountemps, the personnel company, and included 100 high-ranking executives picked from *Fortune*'s top 1,000 companies. The average executive rose at 5:49 A.M., getting about seven hours of sleep a night. On the average, the executives left the office at 5:52 P.M.

## Case Study: Bill's Style of Work

One start-up CEO—we'll call him Bill—never changed his style from the time he left his billion-dollar semiconductor employer as a division VP to the time he took his start-up public. Bill regularly showed up for work at about 8:45 or 9:00 in the morning, well after other company personnel were hard at work. He did help the whole crew move into new quarters on a Saturday and worked with the troops over the first July 4th holiday to get the first product completed. But he was rarely in the office after 6:30 P.M. and seldom dropped in on Saturdays. Bill took his bag of work home and did administrative tasks on his computer in his study on Saturday morning or Sunday evening. He used a couple of breakfasts a week to interview candidates, and dinners were mainly for customers who came to visit several days per month.

Bill traveled on Sundays for Monday meetings with customers and used Friday to fly home from Asia or Europe, as well as from most domestic trips. He did not object to other employees doing the same. He traveled by the cheapest coach fare, except that he flew business class on cross-ocean journeys, and chose leg-stretch-out lounge seats (at coach fares) for the red-eye from San Francisco to the east coast.

Bill began this pattern starting the first day on the job, and continued in that style regularly after the first year went by. Some employees told us they had kidded Bill about it one day (after they had been putting in long weekends of work without Bill). He immediately snapped back that that was his pace and that was how he always would work, no matter what company he worked for. He said he got his work done in that amount of time and maybe others were not able to.

As it turned out, Bill's start-up went on to grab a nice share of the market in the business segment it served. And when his company went public, Bill was worth in excess of $6 million. Which grew to $30 million in the next five years. His VPs also did handsomely with their shares at that time.

**Times of Trouble.** In times of trouble, however, we found enormous increases in the demands for the time of start-up employees. Engineering teams frequently worked past midnight, occasionally napping on cots at work, to meet vital cus-tomer and product delivery deadlines. Marketing and sales personnel slept five hours a night for weeks on end in order to get booths and products ready for demonstration at important industry shows. Even more pressing was the time demanded when the company came close to running out of cash; then the num-ber of hours put in by all employees rose enormously. In circumstances as des-perate as these, it becomes very clear that start-up employees are reputed to work much harder than Fortune 500 personnel.

**Fortune 500 and Other Executives.** We compared our findings with more formal surveys and concluded that start-up executives work about as hard as CEOs in low-tech companies and in America's largest corporations. A 60-hour workweek is the standard for high-tech executives, according to a 1986 survey by Heidrick & Struggles, the Chicago-based international executive search firm. That finding came from their survey of about 350 executives at independent, private, and public technology companies, all with annual sales of less than $450 million and at least fifteen employees.

And a 1987 survey of chief executives of America's largest corporations found nearly two-thirds claiming to work between ten and eleven hours a day, Monday through Friday. Most of them also reported working on weekends; nearly 60 per-cent claimed between one and five hours of weekend work. Half traveled seven or more days per month.

Discussions with large-company employees in the 1990s showed us that that pattern of work continued into the year 2000.

**Stress.** How different is the stress in a start-up from the stress in a large company? We asked that of employees and managers. We found an interesting and impor-tant paradox. On the one hand, we did find nearly everyone claiming that start-ups put more stress on an individual than do large corporations. On the other hand, we found several veterans of more than one start-up claiming they had no more stress in a start-up. How can it be that start-ups that people claim in-duce more stress also produce people claiming to experience no more stress? The paradox is explained as follows: Start-up stress is different—and to many better—than large-company stress. For instance, in a start-up there is:

- less back stabbing and big company politics, but more exposure to failure (or success)
- more creativity, but more chance of pet projects to be axed. For instance, in the case of a computer-aided design start-up, the company dumped a hard-working engineer's software project because of a last-minute board ultima-

tum to reduce the high cash burn rate. As a consequence, the CEO had to junk a promising, nearly finished new product suddenly, in spite of angry outcries from the demoralized engineering and marketing staffs. The tiny company could not afford to introduce the product that the engineer's software ran on. The start-up simply had too many products that cost too much to sell and support.

- more chance to finally show what you can do (and get promoted), but also more danger of being dismissed for really messing things up

**Terror.** For the CEO who has never been there, starting a company will be terrifying, with no one to share those fears. Most CEOs we spoke with believed their wives to be unable to cope with the reality of the chances of company bankruptcy. This meant that there was often no one at home with whom to share the inevitable troubles and problems. And no CEOs we met said they had an employee with whom they shared intimate feelings triggered by stress. Close friends also seemed to be missing. So the CEO was left alone with his troubled emotions.

This situation was vividly portrayed in a stunning story that has become a classic and has been reprinted several times. It first appeared in the February 1987 issue of *Inc.* magazine, and was entitled:

### Entrepreneurial TERROR

*Starting a company? Get ready for the most terrifying experience of your life.*

The article produced a flood of letters to the editor, most of them poignantly identifying with the author, Wilson Harrell, who had the guts to tell his story as he experienced it. He struck a lot of nerves. He and the *Inc.* editor should be congratulated for their courage and their contribution to the managerial literature on start-ups. The article has to be read in its entirety to be appreciated, but here are a few of the more stinging observations. Wilson opens with these lines:

> I would like to address a few words to a particular group of readers, to those of you, young and not so young, who are starting your first company. By that act, you have joined a very special organization. Admission is automatic; permission is neither needed nor sought; tenure is indefinite. Welcome to the Club of Terror.
>
> I myself have been a member of this club, and have known this terror, for close to 35 years. I can assure you that it is unlike anything you have ever experienced before. No longer do you have to be bothered with such ordinary feelings as concern, or frustration, or even fear; those gentle things are the least of your troubles now. You can put them away as a child puts away toys. From now on, you will be in the grip of a human emotion that the good Lord, or more likely his nemesis, created just for entrepreneurs.

Now, I realize that you didn't bargain on this when you started your company. Terror is something that entrepreneurs don't expect, can't escape, and have no way of preparing for.

Harrell goes on to explain the terror of which he speaks, both the positive and the negative terror. He goes on to give personal examples of how this terror occurred in his life and tells how he conquered it. At the end he shares a high point in his moments of positive terror (some call it the sweet smell of success, but not Harrell). He concludes with this:

> You will have your own highs to share once you have conquered your terror. In the meantime, you should at least be aware that you are not alone—far from it. There is a whole gang of us out here living with the same monster. And you can take some comfort in knowing that terror is an integral and necessary part of every new business started by anyone, anywhere, at any time. Which means that, for every company in existence, there is, or was, some poor soul who bore the cross of terror for all of the people who have benefited. Whether the name was Mr. Kraft, Mr. Pillsbury, Mr. Ford, or Joe Blow, they all shook hands with the devil and joined the club.
>
> My own belief is that the ability to handle terror, to live with it, is the single most important—and, yes, necessary—ingredient of entrepreneurial success. I also believe that it is the lonely entrepreneur living with his or her personal terror who breathed life and excitement into an otherwise dull and mundane world. From that perspective, the Club of Terror is a very exclusive one. Welcome.

The letters to the editor from readers of the article were just as soul-jerking. Here is one example, signed by a "Founder and Chief Executive Officer":

> My terror is not unlike that which I knew as a Vietnam soldier. I also know that while I have control of my entrepreneurial terror, my beautiful wife does not and knows more terror than I ever will. Will our precious sons have a home, a father, college if we get through it this time? It's no wonder that as I embark on another "terrorific"-filled joy ride, she wants out. Who can blame her?

We talked with "winners" and they told us of the same terror. Bill said it hit him hardest when he delivered his first semiconductors to distributors and then waited, and waited, and waited to see if they would move off the distributors' shelves, into the computers of customers. His road to glory at IPO time was filled with terror. Yet the public relations stories left all that out as they put his picture on the front page of the business section of the newspaper and talked about "focused strategy" and "leading-edge technology."

**The Workaholic.** The workaholic is the character type most likely to be damaged by failure in a start-up, or failure in his family because of his devotion to the new enterprise. The problem here is just like that of an alcoholic or sexaholic: How do you get the person you are concerned with to recognize that they are this type of personality?

There are a number of good books and web sites with practical tips and tests to assist the person dealing with this problem. If you are a driven person, we recommend checking out the tests in the books before you do a start-up (for the wrong reasons). A simple search on Amazon.com for "workaholism" will give you a list of sample books.

**Burnout.** Burnout is very common and dangerous to CEOs of start-ups and their key employees. The author has experienced near burnout personally in his first years while managing a software start-up and has assisted friends who were going through burnout in high-tech companies.

Since its "discovery" in the sixties by a New York psychoanalyst, Dr. Herbert J. Freudenberger, burnout has been accepted as a serious disorder among people who work hard. Dr. Freudenberger experienced it himself. Our friends in psychotherapy in Silicon Valley reported that burnout is a common and serious problem, often leading to executive dropout, divorce, drug use, and mental derangement that ruined lives.

The *San Jose Mercury News* featured several Silicon Valley therapists in an article in *West* magazine entitled, "Can Engineers Become Human?" It dealt with the special personal problems of people in the Valley. In the July 27, 1986, issue, *West* interviewed six counselors and therapists who talked about what they encountered and how they tried to help. It was clear that problems, including burnout, abound, whether the troubled individual's company has or has not been successful.

In its October 31, 1999, issue, *Silicon Valley* magazine published an article entitled "Surviving the Dot-com Boom. For the Sillicon Valley entrepreneur, the pressures are even greater than ever. Can anyone really run on Valley time forever?" Our research showed this to be a common topic among people close to employees of Internet and startups.

To assist you in the most practical terms, we recommend a quick trip to the bookstore for one of the practical books on the subject of burnout. In a recent search on Amazon.com, 149 books were listed dealing with the subject. Start-up people told us the recommended therapy works well and even better with the help of a good counselor. The books often include a simple test that has helped individuals detect burnout before it is too late. There are also tests on the Internet. Here is Freudenberger's definition of burnout:

BURNOUT: TO DEPLETE ONESELF. TO EXHAUST ONE'S PHYSICAL AND MENTAL RESOURCES. TO WEAR ONESELF OUT BY EXCESSIVELY STRIVING TO REACH SOME UNREALISTIC EXPECTATION IMPOSED BY ONE'S SELF OR BY THE VALUES OF SOCIETY.

Many men and women who come to me in pain report that life seems to have lost its meaning. Their enthusiasm is gone. They feel uninvolved, even in the midst of family and friends. Their jobs, which used to mean so much, have become drudgery with no associated feeling of reward.

All their lives, they have undertaken tough jobs and prided themselves on their ability to master situations . . . a difficult child, an exhausting job situation or economic reverses. They had enough determination and will power to lick anything. Now, however, no matter how great their efforts, the only result seems to be frustration. Some vital spark inside these men and women is burning out, leaving a terrible void.

Our advice is that no one should even attempt to do a start-up if he is on his way to burnout in the current job. And those already burned out because of a recent start-up, take heart: Dr. Freudenberger and many other therapists since then have treated the burnout problems of many people successfully. The author of this book is a good example of how professional help can lead to a complete cure of burnout.

# Fitness, Diet, and Health

How destructive is a start-up to a person's health? is a concern we often heard expressed by people considering a start-up. How you handle your well-being can have a profound impact on your ability to handle the pressures that inevitably confront entrepreneurs.

**Physical Exercise.** Demands on time are intense in a start-up, and that adds pressure to keep going without the "frills" such as exercise. Yet the facts about the behavior of small-company personnel show that such concerns are not warranted. By the 1990s exercise had become popular, even with busy start-up employees. In May 1987, *Venture* magazine published the results of a survey of 2,463 subscribers: "Not only do a panting three-quarters of respondents exercise regularly, two-thirds do so frequently—three times a week or more." The report went on to say, "According to the 1986 results of a Harris Poll commissioned by *Prevention* magazine, 77 percent of American adults get regular exercise."

*Venture* reported that "Steve Smith, president of Executive Fitness Center, New York, a health club that specializes in fitness training programs for executives, works with company founders and observes, 'They have high-pressure jobs, and exercise can be a time to be alone, in contrast to the teamwork required at the office.'"

Some managers have become innovative and disciplined about this problem. It is not uncommon to find a start-up manager riding a bike twenty miles each day instead of taking a long lunch hour. Silicon Valley is full of lunch-time runners, racquetball players, and swimmers. A CFO told about his daily discipline of prebreakfast runs no matter where he travels: in London parks, Paris shopping marts, beside Belgian canals, and along Munich's winding streets.

In the 1990s we found a vocal group of CEOs of new enterprises avidly claiming that their regular exercise program was a vital contributor to their excelling in business. Sharper minds, feeling better about oneself, and longer endurance while managing troubled start-ups were often cited as reasons for a start-up executive needing regular exercise more than other business people.

**Sleep.** We found sleep patterns and duration to be similar in start-ups and larger companies. Again, the difference appeared to be nil if any between the executives of new companies and established corporations. The *Venture* survey reinforced our findings:

> But it's hard to guess when some company founders find time for working out at all. Although a quarter spend a restful eight to nine hours sleeping, the majority (70 percent) catch only five to seven hours of sleep. Yet they typically put in a long day and work many weekends. Forty-six percent work 8 to 10 hours daily, while 38 percent work more than 10 hours. And on weekends, founders are often at the office: 54 percent give up more than two weekends a month for their companies, compared with only 31 percent for non-founders.

**Diet and Alcohol.** We found that alcohol was shunned at almost all the lunches we attended, starting with the CEO, who set a strict example regardless of the occasion. However, wine was popular for business dinners when customers and other VIPs were entertained. Yet, even over dinner, we found executives forgoing dessert and telling guests that they were watching their weight. *Venture* found that "diet was as important as exercise to the survey respondents. Sixty-nine percent supplement their meals with vitamins."

**Smoking.** As to smoking, a standard exists: "Don't!" There is a clear trend: Start-ups are starting from day one as 100 percent no-smoking companies. It is a strong factor in recruiting decisions. Interviews by *Venture* confirmed that "smoking is not a problem for most: Only a tenth of the respondents smoke cigarettes."

**Doctors.** With all the commitment to fitness, we were surprised to find that only a minority of start-up executives have annual physical examinations. Perhaps this is a consequence of the limited health benefits offered by some new enterprises—few insurance plans paid the costs of annual physical examinations. However, several individuals said they personally paid for annual exams. This finding was reinforced by the *Venture* survey report, which stated: "As for keeping an eye on their bodies, a wise 43 percent have had a physical checkup within a year and another third were examined in the last couple of years."

**Importance of Fitness**. Fitness businessman Steve Smith closed the *Venture* report with these words: "Only the fit survive [in business], and that not only means the smartest but also the most physically fit." We remind readers that Steve is selling fitness and may not be the experienced executive who can comment on years of experience with business survival. However, we did find that medical doctors and psychotherapists strongly recommend more exercise, no smoking, and care in diet for everyone, including the start-up executive. "Some of my patients need exercise as much as food," said one counselor. The trick is to juggle time commitments.

# Sudden Changes and Accompanying Problems

One poignant situation cited over and over again was the personal danger from violent changes in life-styles during the post-IPO period. After the IPO, people suddenly found their bank accounts and personal egos swollen by the success and publicity of their company. In reaction, many changed their lives dramatically, many for the worse. Sad personal stories ranged from the lonely bachelor who buys a huge estate in the mountains and quits work to live on cocaine, to the executive who suddenly decides the spouse is no longer right and gets a divorce. Soaring Internet stock valuations have contributed to this danger.

**Drug Abuse.** Drug abuse during the 1980s was believed to be common among some high-tech employees. But in the 1990s this appeared to have diminished. We could not find a quantified study that compared high-tech companies to other industries. Nor could we find a definitive study that showed to what degree this problem existed in start-ups and emerging-growth high-tech companies. Therapists talked about what their patients told them in the July 27, 1987, *West* magazine article in the *San Jose Mercury News*. Bill Hazle is a psychiatrist and the medical director of the Alcohol and Drug Treatment Program at Stanford University Hospital in Palo Alto, California. Here is how he described the drug situation that he must deal with daily:

"I have two populations of engineers," he comments. "The older group is over 40. These men are alcoholics. They've been working for the same company for over 25 years; they're dedicated, hard workers. Things haven't worked out quite like they'd expected. Over the years they've chemically isolated themselves from their families and the world. My challenge is to bring them back to reality, to help them feel.

The other group is mid-30s or younger. This guy moved to Silicon Valley five years ago; he's worked for four different companies and doubled his salary with each move. He's at the peak of his professional life, but there are 25-year-olds who know more than he does. His professional life expectancy isn't looking good. Coke is the perfect drug for him: It gives him high energy, euphoria. And he lives and works in a culture that makes coke available and acceptable. This is the guy who tells me he thought he'd arrived the first time he had coke delivered to his office. Six months later he's in my office.

About two-thirds of Hazle's clients are sent to therapy by their wives or employers. "Denial is the big word," he says. "Both age groups come in here wanting to be normal drinkers or drug takers. They want me to fix their stress so they can stop tooting up their BMW payments or learn to drink socially. But I hit them with the reality that everything has to change: what they do, who they do it with."

We found no one openly advocating the use of drugs. However, we did find private testimonials that the special form of stress in start-ups led a number of start-up executives and key employees to do drugs. Counselors in the 1990s told us of their experiences; for example, two psychiatrists were called into an emergency situation by the board of directors of a new software start-up. The company was holding up the worldwide introduction of one of America's top computer corporation's hottest new products. Upon arriving, they found the three-person project team doing cocaine in an attempt to meet the severe product delivery deadlines imposed by a management threatened with loss of their jobs and possible lawsuit, and by investors facing the company's bankruptcy.

And pot seemed to be an open joke in the 1980s among several of the leaders of well-known start-ups and IPO companies whom we got to know. Fortunately by the 1990s, the antidrug advocates seemed to be winning.

**Wives, Children, Family, and Divorce.** How likely is divorce for a start-up executive? Would you believe less than 26 percent?

Some insight is provided by a 1986 Heidrick & Struggles survey of high-tech CEOs of 350 independent, private, and public technology companies, all with annual sales of less than $450 million and at least fifteen employees. The survey's findings suggested that high-tech executives are more likely to be divorced than CEOs of America's bigger, lower-technology companies: "While 71 percent of high-tech CEOs said they're married to their first spouse, more than a quarter—26 percent—have been divorced or separated. More than 81 percent of Fortune 1000 chiefs say their first marriage is intact." As one start-up CEO veteran sadly put it, "You have to earn twice as much in a start-up because your ex-wife will get half after the IPO." Yet we also found happily married couples who had gone through start-ups and remained together.

In the 1990s, it was common for both parents to be working while the children were cared for by hired help in day care facilities. Some parents told us in wearied tones how difficult that was when one spouse worked in an intense start-up. By the end of the decade, we sensed a turn away from dual incomes and toward the mother raising the children full-time.

As for the impact of a start-up on raising children in recent years, we found no studies in this area, so we will comment from firsthand observation. CEOs seemed to us to be successful in raising their children and being loving parents, whether they are in larger, established corporations or in start-ups. The choice is there: a start-up does not automatically rule out the time or ability to be a responsible parent. We personally know of executives at famous high-tech start-ups who raised healthy families.

Wives told us that they had the same attitude toward a start-up or a big corporation, as long as the business took secondary priority to the wife and the family. This seems to be where the problems begin. Many CEOs and VPs of new companies have never before been responsible as executives. For a wife who has never before experienced the hours her husband must put into new job as CEO, the start-up looks like the culprit. The issue seems to us to be more of a measure of the normal demands on a top executive than of the special demands of a start-up.

However, people told us that they grew to find work all-consuming and one day just decided they did not want to be married any more. Again, to us the issue seemed to be one of choices, of personal values: What was personally more important, what got top priority when the going got rough—the company or the home?

One of the biggest single negative impacts on the wife of a start-up CEO can occur when the CEO decides to mortgage the house to get the cash to survive. This is not uncommon. The author was in that situation once and his wife was terrified for two years.

Security is not the stuff of which start-ups are made. But in this era of layoffs from even the largest high-tech companies around the world, there is no real security anywhere, only blind hope. That can be frightening to children as well as spouses. We have known kids who became bitter toward their father because they felt they lost out on material and psychological security when the start-up went sour, whereas other children got things the start-up CEO's kids wanted: more time from parents, assurances of no divorce for dad and mom, and deeper intimacy among the family members. These are the things that the counselors advise parents to provide when one of them is founding a high-tech company.

Fear of divorce tops the list of concerns of kids in the United States today, according to recent surveys. Stress from a start-up can trigger such an event or contribute to the cracks in a marriage.

And success can be as hard on a marriage as failure. One famous example of this is the divorce history of Apple cofounder Steve Wozniak, who, within seven years of Apple going public, was divorced from his second wife. Steve's wealth was estimated at that time to be in excess of $50 million.

# Right and Wrong, Morals and Ethics

Start-ups and emerging-growth high-tech companies get into special circumstances that challenge the integrity of employees. Here are some issues that we have encountered and that were often noted by start-up managers as especially difficult to cope with:

- *Intellectual-property theft.* Chapter 4 dealt with problems of this type. Managers find themselves under a spotlight these days, yet naïve but well-meaning engineers can and do take the wrong materials and ideas with them. Does a CEO of the company receiving the stolen property stop the start-up in its tracks upon learning of such a problem?
- *Promises to venture investors.* Hard selling to investors can distort the truth. We have experienced the selling of a business plan several times. How tempted would a CEO be to bias the facts in the company's favor during the due diligence sessions on competition?
- *Missed milestones.* As the inevitable occurs and early products fall behind their introduction schedules, there is a temptation to cover up all the bad news to the hostile VCs on the board of directors.
- *Capital shortfall.* Start-ups are always short of cash. The multiple rounds of fundraising will occur during times of varying success in a start-up. What should the CEO tell a prospective investor who has just asked how the latest sales backlog is developing, when the CEO knows that the top three customers just called to say sorry but they will not be buying after all, and when that investor is the last of twenty-three VC firms contacted to still be interested in making the necessary investment the company needs to avoid bankruptcy?
- *Missing payroll.* New companies are very likely to run out of funds and miss a

payroll or two. This happens with both good and bad managements when they encounter a period of bad times. What does the CEO tell employees when investors scheduled for visits call to cancel and decline to reschedule? How does an executive remain honest and yet keep the ship from sinking, still keep people working instead of dropping everything to start looking for new jobs?

- *Bad news for the board meeting.* The bad news comes as sure as winter follows summer: missed shipments of new products, overspending, bad publicity in the top newspaper, anger by a key employee who surreptitiously went to an investor, an archrival company that just eclipsed the company's core product line, and so on. How tempting is it to proclaim the good news and minimize the bad news (that kept the CEO from sleeping the past three nights)?

- *Recruiting stories.* Key personnel can be the difference between success and failure. The pressure is very intense to tell a lot of the dream without the negative side of the story. What should the CEO tell the only test engineer the company can attract (and who is vital to getting your first product to market before the window closes) when he inquires about how important it is to get this first product out on schedule? (The company is already five months behind and the board is furious with the CEO-founder for the company's poor results.)

- *Tales for the customers.* Marketing pressures mount as potential customers are lined up and first shipments begin. Engineers said they listened with dismay to promises of product performance that the company had no possibility of ever building with its technology. Should the vital customers be told that the promises by the VP of marketing are not likely to be kept?

- *Tales for the investors.* When it comes time to mark up the stock for the next round or to go public, there are enormous pressures to "make the books look good." Should the CEO deliberately postpone the next new product development project in order to get more short-term profit to the bottom line? Or create bookkeeping reserves to pad (boost) earnings for the next quarter?

These are categories of issues special to new enterprises that confront the CEO and his or her closest advisers. Board members also have to face such issues. There may be escape from big company politics, but there is no escape from the testing of character and integrity. Anyone scared by those issues should perhaps reconsider doing a start-up.

# Soul, Spirit, and Religion

Our findings in this section were gathered from personal observations over the past twenty years in Silicon Valley in an attempt to cover an important area in our lives that is rarely reported or researched. We have disguised names and circumstances when we were so requested to do so.

We don't read or hear much about the private lives of start-up CEOs or their top management teams. Most seem to prefer that the spotlight be confined to the business side of their lives. The public rarely gets a glimpse of the intimate side of their natures, their souls and emotions. It wasn't until Silicon Valley was booming that the *San Jose Mercury News* began a special section in its Saturday edition devoted to religion and ethics. But in spite of what appears to be a nonissue or one that many would prefer to avoid, religion, with its related issues about philosophy, morals, and value systems, does operate in centers of high-tech activity, including start-ups.

We met a number of men and women along the way who told us that they believed that their ability to survive the terror of a start-up was due entirely to their religious beliefs. They said that they had found peace in a storm by trusting the God of the Bible and Jesus Christ instead of just themselves. We also found people in high-tech companies that looked to Mohammed and Buddha, or to Hindu and Shinto beliefs for guidance through the minefields of start-ups. They felt strongly that there must be more to life than the fame and fortune of start-ups.

Individuals told us that the intensity of start-ups can produce problems of such a huge size and degree that even the most stalwart leaders are overwhelmed. Counselors confirmed that this was their experience with many of their patients who were embroiled in start-ups. Failing as a manager or losing all the money of investors is often too much for the self-worth held by many a man or woman. They quickly see themselves as abject failures and fall into clinical depression and worse. Escape via drugs or sex or thrills can set in. Burnouts abound. Marriages fall apart. Hearts are broken. It is in circumstances like these that we found people turning to religious teachings as the answer to finding personal peace, meaning, and purpose after experiencing failure in a start-up. And remember, getting rich and famous can spell failure for some people as well.

And then there is the ultimate price to pay for doing a start-up: your life. Heart attacks seem to be no more common in new companies than in larger, established ones. However, we found no studies to document this hypothesis. Veterans of Silicon Valley recall such tragedies as the terrible after-lunch ride in a hot red Ferrari that flipped and killed its two occupants, one the founder/CEO of the then-hot Eagle personal computer company. His successive replacements were never able to sustain the company through its later trials and tribulations, and today it is long gone and mostly forgotten.

Suicide is rare, but not absent. An electronic-game founder committed suicide after killing his family. Friends believe that business funding troubles got to him. The funding arrived the next day. One of Silicon Valley's most successful venture capitalists went for a cruise on his yacht in the Pacific and shot himself, reputedly after a reverred founder denied the venture capitalist a chance to invest in the founder's newest Internet start-up.

## Support Systems

We found numerous veterans of start-ups who implore individuals especially to consider the condition of their support systems before doing a start-up. Expectations that turn out to be different than what really transpires in a person's life are major contributors to burnout and personal anxiety, according to professional counselors and psychologists. For instance, if you expect to be part of a company that gets to IPO and becomes famous, but the company becomes much less than that, such defeated expectations can lead to personal problems and intense emotional troubles. Here are some constructive words of advice from people we interviewed:

*Get sanctions from your spouse and children.* It is unwise to attempt a start-up at a time when your marriage is in need of a lot of attention or when your children are in trouble in their lives. Get them to be honest about how they feel about your doing a start-up. Take their wishes seriously.

*Caring friends are worth a lot.* This is a vast understatement. Buddies to talk to are very important when the troubled times come and the fear sets in. You need caring listeners who will stick close to you through the tough times.

*Mentors are needed.* Solo leaders are very rare. CEOs said they sought advice regularly. You need a set of qualified mentors, people who can give personal time and professional advice.

*Don't drop all your avocations, hobbies, and friends just to have time to do a start-up.* Strong advice came to do the opposite. Adhere to and nurture those relations that are your current support system: your wife, children, and friends who will love you whether you are a failure or a success. Take time to garden, ski, read—whatever you are used to doing to make yourself feel better. Or if it is to try to save the whales or do nonprofit work, then continue. Don't stop. It is dangerous to cut out such activities under the guise of having no time to do them because you are doing a start-up. Figure out your sources of strengths and adhere to them. They will help you maintain stability. Balance your life. Work on that.

*Take vacations; make them short; take them often.* This was a pattern we detected in CEOs and their VPs. Seasoned start-up personnel said that is how they did it. It refreshes the mind and spirit, yet is short enough to not lose touch with the delicate situations underway at the start-up.

*Use consultants and counselors.* They can give you objective advice based on periodic observations of you and your behavior. Their suggestions can head off burnout. Think of them as personal coaches.

*Pick a trustworthy employer.* The dangers of losing your job are great enough without choosing employers randomly. Some bosses or boards of directors are going to be much less trustworthy than others. Personal stability is enhanced when you can seek to do your best while confident of the support of your employer.

*Keep an ace up your sleeve; stay in touch with the job market; and prepare a personal backup plan.* Be ready for the surprise that can result if you no longer have income from the start-up. Talk to a headhunter or two when they call. If nothing else, it helps you set wage guidelines for your employees. Plan any alternative lifestyle carefully with your spouse. Don't expect your partner to automatically go along with your plan to sell the house and live in an economical mobile home if the start-up goes bankrupt. Whatever you decide, create a well-thought-through plan for you and your family.

*If the kitchen is too hot, get out.* Life is indeed lonely at the top. Leaders are looked up to. Employees do not operate well when the boss expresses his anxiety to employees down the hierarchy. If you find yourself dumping on the company or talking often to people about your stress, consider moving to a less pressured means of earning a living.

*Get in touch with yourself.* That was repeated by many of the people we spoke with. Decide what motivates you: joy of work, love of wealth, the satisfaction of getting further than anyone expected, and so on. And decide what a failure means to you, as a person, as a company leader.

*Decide on your purpose in life.* Get this in place—before gloom and doom set in and lead to immobilization as a key decision maker and leader.

# Decision: To Do a Start-Up—That Is the Question

In this section we address the question: What can I do to test whether I am ready to do a start-up? We have gathered the opinions of CEOs, VCs, psychologists, and counselors. The findings are presented in two sections. The first is how to use professionals to get a perspective on the likelihood of sustaining the rigors of a start-up. The second section is a pragmatic how-to guide for screening each stage of a start-up and relating that to the choice to join at each stage.

**Professional Advice.** Seeking professional advice is an important option to consider when looking at one's own suitability to handle the stresses of the start-up environment. There is a modest cost that will be incurred, but it is not expensive and, compared with the high cost of a bad decision to join a start-up, the cost of professional advice is minimal. The field of psychology has developed an array of tests that can accurately and objectively assess your strengths and weaknesses. Such issues as personality, style, interpersonal effectiveness, vulnerability to stress, and intellectual ability are all important in such a venture. An objective opinion about these variables should prove to be well worth your effort.

In choosing the particular psychologist to provide this service, look for the following: The psychologist should be specialized in psychological testing and assessment. Either consulting or clinical psychologists can provide this service. Check with your local psychological association or family physician to find a psychologist. A thorough evaluation will include the following:

- Objective personality testing. Options include the Myers-Briggs Type Indicator® test or the formal Minnesota Multiphasic Personality Inventory (MMPI), Million Clinical Multiaxial Inventory (MCMI), and the 16-PF. Some are available in the Internet.
- Projective personality testing, often using the Rorschach Inkblot Test or the Thematic Apperception Test
- Tests of intellectual functioning. The standard test here is the Wechsler Adult Intelligence Scale-Revised (WAIS-R).
- Vocational interest and ability tests are also possibilities.

**Guide to Doing a Start-up.** Table 8-5 is a guide to help you consider the pros and cons of joining a start-up. It follows the format of the fourteen key stages noted in Chapter 3. The table summarizes advice from veterans of start-ups who were asked to comment on what to consider when deciding whether or not to join a start-up.

Under the right conditions, a start-up can be just the right next step in some people's career paths. Under the wrong conditions, a new enterprise can be very destructive to some others.

**TABLE 8-5. When to Join a Start-up**

| Stage | Join If: | Do Not Join If: |
|---|---|---|
| 1. Idea | + you have done a start-up before.<br>+ if you are highly motivated and very self-confident. | - bankruptcy and missing payrolls sound awful to you. |
| 2. Kitchen Table | + you have a close friend who will lead the start-up.<br>+ your know-how is vital to the success of the technology or marketing of the idea.<br>+ See (1) above. | - the leader is a stranger.<br>- See (1) above. |
| 3. Founders' Commitment | + your savings will carry you for nine months.<br>+ your family agrees.<br>+ the founders represent a powerful core to build a business around.<br>+ your lawyer says you are ethically clean and free to join a start-up. | - you need a job to pay the bills.<br>- your family thinks your doing a start-up is nuts.<br>- you need lots more experienced management talent in the company. |
| 4. Pullout | + your nerves are strong.<br>+ your lawyer has prepared a good plan to guide you in how to leave your employer without getting sued.<br>+ you are prepared to live on your savings only. | -you have not prepared a "pullout" plan with a good lawyer.<br>- your home budget does not exist.<br>- your family and you are not prepared to make home spending sacrifices. |
| 5. Business Plan | + you missed (4) above and are a great business plan writer and strategist. | - you never wrote a business plan before. |
| 6. Filling the Management Team | + you have read and analyzed the business plan.<br>+ you want a chance at a job in a strong leadership position. | - you just want more stock.<br>- the key VPs are not in place yet. |
| 7. Capital Raising | + you have missed the above stages. | - you could not stomach folding the tent because funds could not be raised. |
| 8. Capital Closing | + cash in the company's bank is important to you. | - you could not handle having to scramble for a job in nine to eighteen months because of disaster to the company, such as a layoff that bumps you off the payroll. |

| Stage | Join If: | Do Not Join If: |
|---|---|---|
| 9. Finding a Home | + the key VPs are in place.<br>+ See (8) above. | - you would be bothered by a "flameout" affecting your career. |
| 10. Start-up | + you are sure the cash is in the bank.<br>+ you are very excited about the company and its prospects. | - you want more assurance of being part of an initial public offering (IPO) soon. |
| 11. Secondary Rounds of Financing | + you like the progress that the company is making with prospects.<br>+ you need assurance of the staying power of the leadership and the investors.<br>+ you like the progress already made and plan for reaching the IPO goal. | - the IPO is too far away for you. |
| 12. Launch First Product | + you like riding a wave and are confident of the future of the successor products. | - you want to see how well customers receive the first product.<br>- you want to have several products succeed before joining. |
| 13. Working Capital | + you want to wade in and help build momentum.<br>+ the customers are good names and are reordering the products. | - the company is struggling to fund its growth.<br>- first products will not enable the company to get cash flow positive in a reasonable time period. |
| 14. Initial Public Offering | + you want to get in just before the IPO.<br>+ you want some of the experience of a start-up, but not much of the risk. | - you desire much more financial reward in your stock option and are willing to take more risk in earlier stages. |

*Source:* Saratoga Venture Finance

# 9

# Venture Capitalists

I n this chapter we will guide entrepreneurs seeking to build beneficial relationships with that strange, enigmatic breed of businessperson known as the
venture capitalist. Both experienced entrepreneurs and venture capitalists tell
us that many myths have been created about venture capitalists—myths that
mislead CEOs and contribute to start-up failures.

Venture capitalists, the men and women with the money, have learned to create large amounts of wealth—for their investors and themselves as individuals—
by following certain predictable and successful patterns of investment. By
investing time in learning how venture capitalists make money, the entrepreneur will be better prepared to negotiate with them and to operate a new company with realistic expectations.

We will start with the origin of venture capital money and show how VCs de-
rive their wealth and control the start-up companies they invest in. We will then
move on to suggestions from experienced start-up people on how to make good
presentations, and end with tips on closing deals.

## The Cost of a Venture Capitalist's Capital

The name of the game for the VC is return on investment (ROI). His money goes
in as preferred stock and comes out as common stock at the time of the initial
public offering (IPO) or sale of the company to a larger corporation. If the company is unsuccessful, its assets go on the auction block, including the technology; the preferred stock shareholders get all of the meager pickings, while
common stock shareholders get nothing.

**Figure 9-1 Stock Markets Drive Venture Capital Markets**

*Source:* Saratoga Venture Finance

The amount of ROI that a VC must earn on invested monies depends on the relative returns of alternative investments that the VC's limited partners could have put their money into.

Figure 9-1 shows how private venture funds are linked to the huge stock markets. There is a serial connection:

■ The IPO price for a company is set by a select group: powerful, famous portfolio managers assisted by their research analysts. This is an elite group, highly respected because of their investing successes, who have mountains of money to invest. Because their actions are eagerly mimicked by the vast number of other money managers, this select group is often referred to as the "lead steers," that is, the few leaders who are followed by the large number of less able investors who constitute the herd. Lead steers also set share prices of the Fortune 500 companies as well as those of stocks on NASDAQ and other

171

bourses around the world. They start with the ROI expected from investing in a "safe" security such as U.S. Government treasury bills, add their expected rate of inflation, and then add percentage points that represent premiums for taking on the risk of investing in a company. Each company must be expected to earn the resulting "hurdle" ROI or else the analysts will reduce the price of the stock of the company. If the company outperforms the hurdle ROI, they will increase the price of the company's stock.

- Venture capitalists start their valuation work by simulating the most likely IPO price for the start-up in which they are considering investing. VCs use simplified rules of thumb to approximate the IPO price per share.

- Having calculated the probable IPO value of a start-up, the VC then calculates the percentage of the company ownership needed at IPO time to get the high ROI target that has been set for the VC firm. The VC's target ROI or "hurdle rate" depends on several factors, including how well or badly the VC's investments in other start-up companies are doing. Our research shows that the range of ROI is wide at a given point in time, with many factors causing it to be greater or smaller. The key factors are discussed in Chapter 7 and elsewhere in this book.

- Each subsequent private round is priced this way, from seed to the last round just before IPO.

## Where the VCs Get Their Money

Giant pools of money called institutional funds dominate the world's money markets, especially in the United States. Research shows that individuals have been net disinvestors in stocks in America since 1945. Their decline in importance has been more than taken over by the pension plan and university trust pools of wealth ("endowments"). In 1962, individual investors owned about 82 percent of all the stock in American companies, according to the Securities Industry Association in New York. Today, individuals own less than 60 percent, according to estimates by Salomon Brothers in New York. And they account for less than 20 percent of the trading in the stocks. Individuals mostly invest via mutual funds managed by professional institutional investors who receive and pool 401k and other retirement savings. As Peter Drucker has put it, the pension plan money managers—and all of their "little people"—now own America's corporations. The Internet era further modified this trend somewhat by enabling high-risk-taking individuals to buy and sell stocks via electronic trading on the Internet. Intensely active in some stocks, these "day traders" have contributed to the "hot" nature of Internet IPO valuations. This has upset some institutional investors. Time will tell if this trend continues or is a passing fad.

With trillions of dollars needing to be invested each day, the trustees of those institutional pools of wealth have delegated the work to specialists. The trustees have put their funds in the hands of people called money managers. These money managers make a living by competing for the chance to be given some of those funds to invest. The goal is to earn the highest ROI possible in as short a time possible, for as many years as possible. They earn a fee for their efforts and in some cases share in the profits that may result. Venture capitalists are one variety of this type of professional money manager.

The goal of money managers like venture capitalists is to outperform the stock market. If they do, institutional pools of money will give them a chance to manage more money. VCs who do not perform will lose the second chance. It is a case of survival of the fittest.

# Venture Capitalist of Venture Capitalists

There has been a huge surge of money into venture capital since 1983. Figure 9-2 shows the wave of new firms entering the personal computer and biotech eras, their subsequent decline, and the effects of the Internet era. The annual rate of capital invested in start-ups ran about $1 billion in the 1980s. It grew to the $4.5 billion level, as shown in Figure 9-3, until the Internet era boosted it to double that and more. By 2000, this growth increased the pool of VC money by some measures above $100 billion, capable of creating over ten thousand new enterprises every seven years and affecting the lives of more than ten million people. Venture capital has arrived, becoming a significant economic factor in America. It has become the envy of countries around the world.

As successes mounted in the late 1970s, pension fund trustees increasingly were approached by very successful venture capitalists whose early track records produced very high ROIs, in excess of 50 percent per year. The trustees of a few pension funds began to dabble in venture capital by investing a tiny portion of their funds through the VCs, and others soon followed. This phenomenon still left many conservative money managers wondering (and having doubts about) how to make prudent investments consistently in what appeared to them to be the wild and woolly game of high-risk venture capital. By the 1990s it was commonplace to have funds in venture capital pools. Venture capital "had arrrived," at last.

How good are the VCs? The research says that during the 1980s the average long-term ROI was about 22 percent per year, compared with a 14 percent return for the Standard & Poor's index of public companies. However, by 1990 that rate had fallen off (due to excesses and poor VC decisions during the personal com-

**Figure 9-2. Number of Venture Funds Raised**

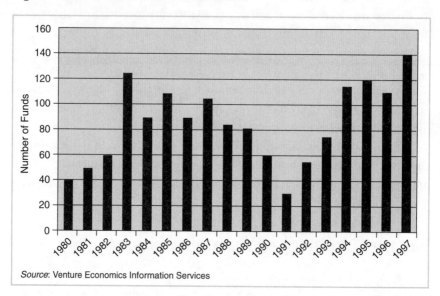

*Source*: Venture Economics Information Services

puter boom) and was struggling to stay in the teens. However, as the year 2000 arrived, *Venture Economics* reported that the soggy ROIs of many venture capital portfolios had turned upward, and many had returned to high-double-digit ROIs that once again made their institutional investors very happy. The wild successes of many Internet IPOs produced ROIs for several venture pools in excess of 60 percent per year! Like the boom years of the personal computer, these times created a lot of wealthy venture capitalists. Long term, venture capitalists around the world told us they are still very pleased when they can return in excess of 25 percent per annum over decades of investing.

But don't be fooled. That 25 percent per annum ROI is not what the VC will price his capital at for the investment in a start-up company. Instead, the VC must add in the cost of the losers, the investments in companies that will go bankrupt or do poorly. That is why the VC's calculations will show that the entrepreneur will end up with a small percentage of ownership at IPO time.

## The Life of a Venture Capitalist

For the start-up CEO the first contact at a venture capital firm is with one of several people who collectively will play key roles in the deal the entrepreneur wants to close. While there are still a few individuals who invest monies without help from other partners, the typical firm today consists of a couple of seasoned gen-

**Figure 9-3. Venture Capital Disbursements: 1989–the First Half of 1998**

Source: Venture Economics Information Services

eral partners who get along well and probably worked together in a prior company or venture capital firm, perhaps even in a successful start-up. These are the people who get the richest from profits on the investments made by the VC firm.

One or more other people, called associates, help the senior partners. These range from green business school graduates to more experienced associates working hard to become partners and share in more of the wealth. The larger firms have grades of partners and some employ executive recruiters and public relations experts.

The week for a VC begins with a Monday staff meeting where investments are reviewed and decisions made to proceed with or stop further investigation on various business plans. The rest of the week is a hectic scramble of early-morning breakfast meetings, shuffling through an impossibly large number of e-mails and voice mails, and flying or driving madly between companies in cities throughout the entire country, but especially in the metropolitan region in which the VC's offices are located. Lunches and dinners are consumed while investigating managers-to-be-hired and trading ideas with their vast network of contacts at universities, giant corporations, and the firms that service their beloved start-ups. Board meetings consume both emotional energy and several days per month.

Time in the VC office is used to interview potential start-up teams, view their presentations, and read their business plans. Meetings with partners of other VC firms are frequent and on-the-fly, usually on the phone, as the deal flow between the venture capital firms goes on by the hour. The most emotional times involve closings on precarious deals led by a partner of the firm. It is not uncommon when visiting a VC office to overhear earnest long-distance phone calls to round up the last of the critically needed money from British pension managers, Italian industrial giants, and Asian government funds.

The weekends and personal time of VCs often reflect the character of the companies that VCs invest in: fast-paced and risky. Only the rare few VCs who have become powerful icons of the VC community feel comfortable taking blocks of leisure time off from this hectic pace to enjoy life.

Fast communication is important to VCs. They always seem to be e-mailing or faxing something, and the Federal Express truck driver can find the way to the VC office with his eyes closed. Some observers think that VCs invented the cellular telephone—or at least the pressing need for one. Several of the partners in a VC firm carry their passports in their briefcases each day and keep a travel bag permanently packed for those unforeseeable emergency trips.

## How a VC Firm Makes Money

Venture capitalists can become very rich if they are successful. They are paid a percentage of the money they manage (the "carry") to pay themselves salaries and cover office and operating expenses, and they get a percentage of the profit of the money they invest; details are shown in Table 9-1.

The first source of income (the "carry") for the venture capitalist typically equals 1 percent times the gross amount of capital invested by limited partners in a pool called "limited partnership." The venture capitalists are the general partners. The top venture firms manage several of these pools at the same time, often exceeding $200 million. The pools vary in size, up to billions. Starting with $50 million, the management fee for that fund will be $500,000 a year. That is typically used to operate a three-partner office.

The second source of income—profit on successful investments—is where the real wealth can come from. Usually, 20 percent of the profit goes to the venture capitalist general partners. If they successfully invest and earn a 25 percent per annum return for five years (i.e., return to limited investors three times their money in five years), then there would be $152,587,880 of gross profit. After returning the $50 million of invested principal capital to limited partners, the remaining $102,587,880 is parceled out among the limited and general partners. At a 20 percent share, the three general partners of this fund would have $20,517,576 to divide among themselves, an average of $7,172,525 each, before any profit-sharing with other employees of the VC firm. The example in Table 9-1

**TABLE 9-1. Economics of a Single Partnership Managed by a Private Venture Capital Firm**

| | |
|---|---:|
| Amount of capital raised for investment ("Capital") | $50,000,000 |
| *Multiplied by* | |
| Profit on investments (25% per year for 5 years = 3.05) | 3.05 |
| *Equals* | |
| Gross profit | $152,587,880 |
| *Less* | |
| Investment capital | $50,000,000 |
| *Equals* | |
| Net profit | $102,587,880 |
| *Multiplied by* | |
| Percentage for general partners ("venture capitalists") | 20% |
| *Equals* | |
| Amount of investment income to general partners | $20,517,576 |
| *Plus* | |
| Cash compensation for general partners (included in the $500,000 of operating expenses) | $ |
| Operating expenses and benefits (e.g., cars, office) for general partners (= 1% × $50M Capital) | $500,000 |
| Net income to general partners before any profit sharing with others in venture firm | = $21,017,576 |

*Source:* Saratoga Venture Finance

is for a single partnership; larger VC firms manage several funds at once, multi-plying the financial return on the time they invest.

# The Risk/Reward Trade-offs: VC vs. Entrepreneur

According to Saratoga Venture Finance research, a CEO of a typical successful start-up can expect to earn about $6.5 million within five years. There are impor-tant exceptions during the boom phase of new eras. Huge Internet-era IPO suc-cesses often have increased that $ 6.5 million target by ten times or more! But over the long term the venture capitalist sharing one-third of a $21 million profit earned on a $50 million portfolio can earn about as much as the successful CEO: $7 million.

But the risk is higher for the CEO and employees of the company because the start-up personnel cannot spread their risk, whereas the venture capitalist can diversify his or her bets and come out a net winner. Saratoga Venture Finance estimates that the risk of a start-up CEO getting $6.5 million is more than six times greater than that of the venture capitalist earning 25 percent per annum on $50 million.

If the risk is six times greater, why isn't the reward six times greater? Our analysis strongly suggests that the reason is that the venture capital markets are not yet "efficient." Efficient is a technical term used by money market economists to describe a market in which competition keeps small numbers of individuals or institutions from gaining windfall or excessive profits.

In this case, the evidence suggests that the trend is toward increasing competition. More new venture capital firms were formed in the 1990s following the contraction (demise) of venture capital firms in the personal computer–era bust. The arrival of fresh funds with fresh money is better for start-ups. One consequence was a move toward closing the disproportionate risk-reward gap between the venture capitalists and the CEOs of the companies they finance and lead.

What that means for the start-up company's founders is that competition for their deal is the best negotiating tool they can find. It means that with competition there will be less dilution and more potential wealth to share with fellow pioneers and risk takers. It also means that such competition must be created and nurtured, because it won't occur naturally. As one founder CEO put it: "I learned the hard way that I had to get six top-tier VCs competing for funding my seed round in order to get the best deal I could!"

## What Motivates a Venture Capital Firm

Venture capitalists are expected by their investors to produce an ROI of at least 20 percent to 25 percent per annum, according to serious studies that have been made on portfolios invested over long periods of time. Table 9-2 shows the findings of six early pioneering studies that have reached the public. Figure 9-4 shows how the internal rates of return (IRR) on VC portfolios have rebounded in the Internet era as early IPOs soared to astronomical valuations. But after the bust of the personal computer and biotech eras, the venture industry took nearly ten years to climb back to averaging above the long-term-trend return of 25 percent.

That 25 percent ROI is excellent, compared with the performance of alternatives available to institutional investors. Figure 9-5 compares the VC's ROI with the ROI recorded over the same time period for leading indices of money market alternatives. If such 20 percent–plus ROIs can be maintained, fresh money will continue to flow to the VC pools. Institutional investors will be eager to invest.

**TABLE 9-2. Venture Capital Rates of Return**

| Source of Study | Year of Study | Period of Study (years) | Compound Annual Rate of Return (%) |
|---|---|---|---|
| Venture Economics | 1984 | 20 | 26 |
| Stanford | 1984 | 20 | 24 |
| Harvard | 1984 | 15 | 25 |
| CIGNA | 1985 | 14 | over 20 |
| Horsley Keogh | 1983 | 10 | 35 |
| First Chicago | 1985 | 9 | 24.5 |

*Sources:* Crossroads Capital, Pension & Investment Age, Venture, Venture Economics

This refueling of VC pools has continued each year to varying degrees through the 1990s, according to research from *Venture Economics Journal.*

Venture investors get their overall ROI from a mix of investments in start-ups. Table 9-3 shows the details of a typical portfolio of a venture capital partnership in a good year. It represents an agglomeration of actual data gathered by Saratoga Venture Finance from this very private VC world. The portfolio has earned a 20 percent p.a. ROI to date. Unless one or more of the last of the surviv-

**Figure 9-4. Venture Capital Performance: Annual Net IRRs (Venture Funds Formed 1969–1997)**

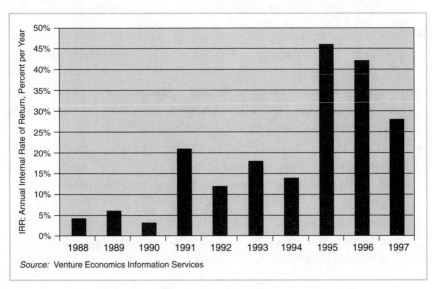

Source: Venture Economics Information Services

**Figure 9-5. Comparison of Venture Capital Annual Rates of Return**

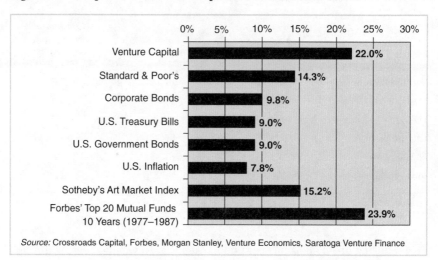

Source: Crossroads Capital, Forbes, Morgan Stanley, Venture Economics, Saratoga Venture Finance

ing portfolio companies—those that have neither gone public nor gone bankrupt—somehow turns out better than shown, that 20 percent ROI will be recorded as the final result. Table 9-3 suggests how sensitive the ROI is when just one more spectacular IPO occurs. It is very difficult to get actual data on specific venture portfolios. Most claims made by venture capitalists of their ROIs are hard to substantiate, particularly because the partnerships go on for twelve years or longer.

Looking closely at Table 9-3, we can learn some important lessons:

- About 60 percent of the companies that get funded eventually go bankrupt. Yet several VC partnerships investing today claim to have one-third to one-half fewer bankruptcies per portfolio company.
- Another 30 percent are sold off for pennies per dollar invested. "Zombies" become profitable but remain too small to go public. Others are sold for their technology. And some reach the auction block.
- "Wild Ones" like Apples and Compaqs and Ciscos and Yahoos are rare and seldom seen in VC portfolios. More common are "Winners" and "Solids," famous IPOs—companies that are still hot and in the news after their public offering.
- A large proportion of the companies never get to the IPO stage. Private buyouts are common, classically in the medical, biological, and genetic engineering industries and frequently in the Internet era. Investors still consider this an excellent channel to liquidity. The ROI to investors for such deals can

**Table 9-3. Venture Capital Partnership Portfolio Results**
(average investment in twenty-five start-ups = $4 million)

| | $ Invested $ M | $ Invested $ Mix (%) | Gross Results 5 Yr. ROI (% per year) | Gross Results 5 Yr. ROI (Multiple) | Net Return $M |
|---|---|---|---|---|---|
| Bankruptcies | $60 | 60% | -100% | 0.0 | ($60) |
| Breakeven | $12 | 12 | 0 | 1.0 | $12 |
| Fire Sales | $10 | 10 | 5 | 1.3 | $13 |
| Zombies | $8 | 8 | 10 | 1.6 | $13 |
| Solids (IPO) | $6 | 6 | 52 | 8.0 | $48 |
| Winners (IPO) | $4 | 4 | 109 | 40.0 | $160 |
| Wild Ones (IPO) | $– | 0 | 300 | 1,024.0 | $0 |
| Total Portfolio | $100 | 100% | 20% | 1.9 | $186 |

*Source:* Saratoga Venture Finance

equal that from a company that gets to an IPO, but seldom exceeds the IPO equivalent.

- Most employees of start-ups are working for companies that will not get into the limelight, will be denied the fame and the fortune that occupies most of the media's articles, or will go bankrupt. How the people in those companies handle the disappointment will shape their character.
- The winners subsidize the losers. This is very important for the CEO of the start-up to grasp. It explains part of the reason for the high dilutions to ownership that VCs consider a necessary requirement before they will invest the money that they manage.

# How to Price a Round of Funding for a Private Company

The title of this section could be rewritten "How to Convert Return on Investment to Percentage Sold to Investors in a Given Round of Financing." To price a share of stock in a private company the CEO must learn how to translate the VCs ROI investment rates into cost of capital (which determines the degree of dilution) and do the related calculations. When the CEO is finished he or she will be able to fill out a table looking like Figure 9-6. Use it as a guide. You will need a calculator

## Figure 9-6. Dilution of Founders

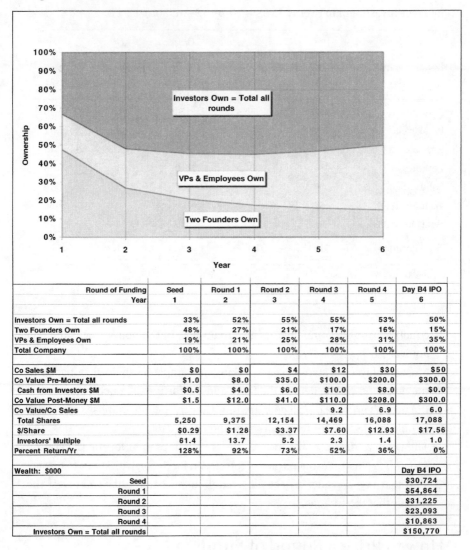

| Round of Funding | Seed | Round 1 | Round 2 | Round 3 | Round 4 | Day B4 IPO |
|---|---|---|---|---|---|---|
| Year | 1 | 2 | 3 | 4 | 5 | 6 |
| | | | | | | |
| Investors Own = Total all rounds | 33% | 52% | 55% | 55% | 53% | 50% |
| Two Founders Own | 48% | 27% | 21% | 17% | 16% | 15% |
| VPs & Employees Own | 19% | 21% | 25% | 28% | 31% | 35% |
| Total Company | 100% | 100% | 100% | 100% | 100% | 100% |
| | | | | | | |
| Co Sales $M | $0 | $0 | $4 | $12 | $30 | $50 |
| Co Value Pre-Money $M | $1.0 | $8.0 | $35.0 | $100.0 | $200.0 | $300.0 |
| Cash from Investors $M | $0.5 | $4.0 | $6.0 | $10.0 | $8.0 | $0.0 |
| Co Value Post-Money $M | $1.5 | $12.0 | $41.0 | $110.0 | $208.0 | $300.0 |
| Co Value/Co Sales | | | | 9.2 | 6.9 | 6.0 |
| Total Shares | 5,250 | 9,375 | 12,154 | 14,469 | 16,088 | 17,088 |
| $/Share | $0.29 | $1.28 | $3.37 | $7.60 | $12.93 | $17.56 |
| Investors' Multiple | 61.4 | 13.7 | 5.2 | 2.3 | 1.4 | 1.0 |
| Percent Return/Yr | 128% | 92% | 73% | 52% | 36% | 0% |
| | | | | | | |
| Wealth: $000 | | | | | | Day B4 IPO |
| Seed | | | | | | $30,724 |
| Round 1 | | | | | | $54,864 |
| Round 2 | | | | | | $31,225 |
| Round 3 | | | | | | $23,093 |
| Round 4 | | | | | | $10,863 |
| Investors Own = Total all rounds | | | | | | $150,770 |

in your spreadsheet (such as RATE in Excel) that does the percent per annum ROI calculations quickly.

- The secret trick is to do this *backward: Start at the IPO date* and *work back* to your seed round.
- Price each successive round to fit into its appropriate ROI range as noted in Figure 9-6.
- The end result will be a reasonable financing plan, complete with numbers of shares for each party.
- The result should be compared with those actual companies documented in the Saratoga Venture Tables.
- Also compare your numbers to recent IPOs. You can find the prospectuses (read the S-1 and 424B forms) housed in the EDGAR database at the Internet site of the Securities and Exchange Commission (http://www.sec.gov/cgibin/srch-edgar).
- A start-up coach or consultant can help CEOs do this important work and interpret the results, using your first numbers to refine the start-up's original business plan.
- Compare your proposed funding plan to real deals. Our research showed that other start-up CEOs are open and willing to sharing such sensitive data with other CEOs. Just ask.

There are some other tricks and tips we have learned that can help you price each round of funding:

- Start at the IPO date. Pick a year and work back to the seed round.
- Assume your company goes public at a value of $100 million. You have to be at least that large for Wall Street to accept your company as a public company. You can come back later and increase the IPO value if you wish.
- Figure out how much revenue your company needs to get to a $100 million valuation. An Internet company during boom times will be given about twenty dollars of stock market value for each dollar of revenue for the past year. Other industry sectors will be given a lower multiple: four is typical for many hardware companies. Slower growing companies get lower multiples in the same industry segment. The data is easy to get from stocks of public companies. It is well worth the effort. Do not bother with price-to-earnings ratios.
- Estimate a price per share each year. Even if you do not sell stock to investors, you will need a price each year to set the strike price for the common stock when granting options to employees. Ask your lawyer about the difference in pricing common stock (for options) and preferred stock (for sale to investors).

- Start the climb of the price per share by assuming the price per share doubles each year. That compounded ROI yields a 56 percent return, right in the ballpark of what VCs want to see. The 56 percent annual return is the same as investing one dollar on day one and getting back ten dollars in year five. That is what is meant by the phrase "VCs are looking for ten times their money by the time your start-up goes IPO." You can modify this later to suit your funding goals.

- Issue five million shares of stock to founders on day one. You can modify it as needed later (e.g., to boost or lower the IPO stock price per share to a desired range). The founders own 100 percent of the company on the first day it is incorporated (that is how they get to be "founders").

- Decide how much capital to raise from investors each year. Use the financial forecast of your balance sheet to do that. Either use software (such as QuickUp™ sold at www.startupweb.com) or build your own financial accounting model on a spreadsheet).

- Decide how much stock to grant as options to new employees. Create classes or layers of jobs. Predict the number and class fit of each new employee, attach shares to each, and add all the shares up for each year to IPO. (This daunting task can be eased by using an experienced human resources consultant. You can get current stock and pay compensation data by contacting the leading source of such compensation for high-tech start-ups, Advanced-HR, at http://www.advanced-hr.com

- Now you have all the shares and prices you need for each year. Finish your table by calculating the dollar value of the company each year, before funding ("Pre-Money") and after funding ("Post-Money"). Post-money equals pre-money plus the cash raised in that round of funding.

- Pre-money value is calculated by taking the total number of shares (common equivalents of preferred shares sold to investors plus all common shares reserved for eventual conversion by holders of stock options plus all shares sold to founders and others).

Remember: The VC money market is theoretically a free capital market, filled with competitors and risks. However, unlike the tight range of the price of a share of stock for IBM on a given day, there is a wider range around the price per share for a round of financing of a new enterprise. It is a market that delights the negotiator's heart but can be very frustrating to an engineer looking for more precision in pricing a round of funding!

Because of the uncertainty, the CEO is well advised to seek competitive bids for a round of funding. If the CEO finds a good VC firm that is more eager to invest in the CEO's excellent-sounding company—perhaps because the VC firm badly needs a few winners in its tarnished portfolio—then the founders have a better chance of retaining more of their company in the negotiations (reducing the cost of capital).

It is now possible to better understand why a VC firm does not want to miss the next hot deal. Putting an extra IPO into a portfolio does amazing things to boost the ROI to astronomical heights! But there are not many hot deals each year; one general partner of a top firm told us that he believes there are less than forty top-notch deals in the United States per year that are worth investing in. And that explains why being a part of the deal flow of the best VC firms is so important to the up-and-coming VC firms.

## Trends and Winds of Change

There are several shifts under way in venture capital portfolios. The marginally performing venture capital portfolios that were funded in 1982–1984 dropped out of the race. Money became cautious. Fewer start-up frenzies—such as the notorious disk drive start-ups—took place. That spelled the end of the personal computer–era boom. Then along came the Internet era. By the middle of the 1990s another boom had arrived. By the time the year 2000 approached, the initial phase of that boom had slowed and the huge valuations of Internet-intensive start-ups had been tested several times. Everyone wondered how long the boom would continue. Wall Street was making millionaires and even a few billionaires of a lot of employees and investors in Internet IPOs.

The trend most often noted as a boom cools down is a shift by VCs from trying to hit a home run on each investment to a strategy of hitting more singles, doubles, and triples. The overall results can be in the same range of 25 percent per annum ROI noted above, but the mix is different; there are proportionally fewer bankruptcies (more like 30 percent than 60 percent, say our sources), but there are fewer big-ticket Winners, and Wild Ones are rare.

We find this pattern encouraging. Theoretically, if there are fewer bankruptcies, the rewards are increased and the personal cost for the entrepreneur and family and supportive friends is decreased.

The pattern also suggests that more competition or fewer excesses can improve the risk-reward potential for the founders and employees. Most of all, it strongly suggests that everyone is making wiser, more prudent investment decisions. Entrepreneurs may be pitching less junk and more quality (although most VCs still lament the poor quality of the business plans they see).

And leading venture capitalists claim to be putting money into better deals more often.

Now if we all could learn to convert such wise initial decisions into higher ROI results, we would have a lot more wealth to share at a fraction of the current cost in terms of personal livelihoods.

**Other Motivating Factors.** Venture capitalists are people too. They have emotions like the rest of the human race and are subject to the same internal pulls and battles. The up-and-comers struggle like the CEOs of start-ups. The established VCs labor to retain their positions of supremacy against both other established firms and the newer firms. It is important for the CEO to understand the emotions that start-up work provokes.

Pride is a top motivator, especially in the powerful people who have gotten to the top. They are multimillionaires—Fred Adler was believed to be personally worth over $100 million before he left the VC race in the 1980s. He reemerged to dabble in billion-dollar deals in the 1990s. A second-tier general partner of a second-tier venture firm told us that his personal goal was to earn $20 million and then retire. VCs are not only financially successful, they are also noted as guiding lights to the successful companies that they backed. They are the men and women who are the leaders that made a significant difference to the success of the famous IPO companies. Anything that tarnishes that reputation of success will be dealt with harshly by wielders of power. Losing start-ups and floundering founders do not last long.

The feeling of belonging is another key motivator—the sense of belonging to that exclusive fraternity of winners, of venture capitalists who are revered by onlookers. Each wants to belong to the inside group, the first-tier club, the one that attracts the top deals, gets the accolades, does the best ROI, structures the most famous IPOs.

Feelings of worthiness are also important. If VCs do well, they feel good about themselves. If an investment does not perform, that reflects on them. They are very personally connected to the success or failure of the start-up's CEO and the company.

Feelings of competence are very intense for these people. They deal daily in a world of very high risk, like tightrope walkers over the Grand Canyon. To the newcomer it looks frightening, but to them it is just another day at the office. VC leaders like to associate with winners and shun those people and companies that sound like losers or flakes. Hollywood business society behaves similarly.

Emotions run high in VCs. The risks are high. Yet fear is not something the VCs talked about much in our interviews. They spoke more often about being angry at the incompetence of a CEO, or at the trouble an engineering group was having getting the first product working properly, or about trying to cope with a company on the ropes and nearly bankrupt. In spite of the track records of fired founders and bankruptcies, we found no one saying he felt guilty about his own behavior or his own treatment of start-up personnel. Love was never mentioned, except to describe a successful company. Greed also was never mentioned, but the degree of intensity of the negotiations for successive rounds of funding tells how vital maximum financial reward is to those who play this game in life.

The CEO-to-be should know that the venture capitalist is living a life of high risk and high reward. That high-stakes game is deadly serious—this individual is not investing money that he or she intends to lose.

The VC is also living life with a dilemma. Most VCs we have met stated over and over that they really intended to do more than just bring money to the party. They wanted to help the fledglings avoid the mistakes of the past by handing down their experience, which was learned in the school of hard knocks. One revered veteran put it this way: "Learning to be a winning VC requires you do an apprenticeship. There is no other school to go to to learn the trade."

However, when bad times come, VCs will switch instantly from backing the incumbent management team to doing whatever must be done to save their investment in the struggling company. If the CEO is in the way—viewed as a hindrance to survival and the success of the next round of venture capital—that can cost the CEO his or her job and unvested shares. The CEO will also live through the emotional struggle of seeing friendly, supportive VCs and board members turn into nasty antagonists. The CEO should be prepared to face this reality.

Finally, remember that each VC firm has a style and character unique to itself. The generalizations discussed here are no substitute for meeting the partners of the firm that wants to lead your start-up's investment syndicate. The venture capitalist community is filled with fine, ethical people with good intentions, many with special experience that can make the difference between a start-up being a successful or a poor investment. The CEO should take the time to pick wisely and carefully.

## How a VC Firm Controls Its Investment

Founders often talk about their plans to retain control and to avoid selling out to venture capitalists. Such intentions are strong, and founders often deliberately avoid VCs just to fulfill such a goal.

This attitude stems from the horror stories they have heard and perhaps from painful personal experience when venture capitalists exercised control to change a start-up and its management during times of duress or special significance, such as getting ready to go public. The more bitter people label the venture capitalists as "vulture capitalists" and "sharks." Their experiences or beliefs have led them to be eager to structure their next deal without any venture capital at all.

In the world of reality, few successful high-tech deals ("We went public!") are done without classic venture capital. There appear to be relatively more non-VC successes in the non-tech world, particularly in consumer goods.

The venture capitalist's degree of influence on a start-up can be reduced by attracting corporate venture capital and offshore money from Europe or Asia. Others have considered raising capital from the controversial Toronto exchange, while other founders have done deals on other non-U.S. stock exchanges, such as the new ones in Europe, and the local exchanges in Asia such as Taiwan, Singapore, Hong Kong, Korea, and India.

However, the most likely path for raising capital for a start-up will be to go through the doors of the venture firms. Entrepreneurs should prepare for the high likelihood of having at least some venture capitalists on their board of directors. A seat on the board of directors is the first level of control the VC uses. There the VC influences salaries, options of shares granted to employees, structures of deals with suppliers and customers, and the timing and pricing of the next addition of capital. The ultimate power is the hiring and firing of the CEO.

The next level of control is that of approval of the spending and cash burn rates (rate per month spent to grow the start-up). Approval of budgets and annual operating plans sets goals for the CEO. Missed goals are cause for termination of the CEO. Missed product development schedules and lower-than-forecast sales can cost the leader his or her job also, particularly if that trouble causes the company to run out of cash.

The next level of control is the exercise of the special covenants in the terms of the contract for the preferred stock that was sold to the VC. Those terms and conditions can include veto power over the next round of financing and can cause a major shift in the power in the start-up. Fights are common during conditions of duress. The goal is to stay cool and rational. But according to managers of some of the troubled start-ups that we spoke to in private, spite can cause powerful VCs and stubborn CEOs to act irrationally.

When the start-up needs more capital, the CEO will find the VCs on the board trying to stick together as much as possible. Because they do not want to be kept out of the next hot deals led by other VC firms, the VCs on the board will exercise a powerful influence on the choices of the next sources of money. This is common behavior mentioned to us in strictest privacy by several CEOs whose start-ups found their VC board members exercising their power to interfere with the CEO in the process of raising multiple rounds of capital.

**A Positive Side of Control.** Other CEOs told us they appreciated the controls put on them by their VCs. We found a strong correlation between the degree of success and the degree of praise for a VC's positive contribution. The more successful the company was, the more was the praise of the VCs (and vice versa).

For instance, John Warnock, president of the highly successful Adobe Systems now of San Jose, California, had this to say about one of the VCs that invested in his company:

> We were fortunate to have experienced venture capitalists from successful start-ups on our board from the inception. They have an immense range of experience, with excellent insight into when a company is running well or not. They acted as our parachute and safety net.

Other CEOs noted their deliberate choices of VCs having personal track records in operations and industries that could be directly applied to increase the start-up company's chances of success. Jerry Crowley of Gazelle Microcircuits of Santa Clara, California, handpicked leaders of Gazelle, including the board and the advisers to the board, who were world-class veterans from the semiconductor industry, executives from National Semiconductor, Signetics, and Texas Instruments. One Internet company founder said, "I had to learn that a lot came along with the money besides money."

"Success breeds success" is a common phrase in venture circles. This seems to have some degree of truth to it. In application, we suggest that the founders pick their VCs as carefully as they pick their key employees. It will greatly influence the degree of success the company can have.

**Opening Doors and Other Assistance.** Finally, VCs gladly will go out on a limb for the start-up CEO when necessary. They will give a lot of their time to interview key personnel, get world-class companies' presidents to consider becoming early customers, and much more. VCs are fighters; they also are going to try to help their investment do well through the tough times. Many have a lot of operational experience and almost instinctively know what to do when the alligators are neck high and the cash flow is getting very negative.

When it comes time to do the IPO, the VC firm will help plan and carry out the tactics that attract a top Wall Street banker to do the underwriting. Muscle and power plays often are going on behind the scenes, invisible to the CEO. It is one explanation of why the VCs hang on so long to the job of a chief financial officer, particularly the treasury function and setting financial policy.

# The Process of Raising Venture Capital

Chapter 7 dealt in detail with the techniques and methods of raising venture capital and suggested a model of the process the start-up will go through. We will concentrate here on the aspects closely linked to the individual venture firm.

**Finding Venture Capitalists.** Venture capitalists now exist within easy reach of virtually any corner of the United States. Increasing numbers operate in Europe and Asia. It has been estimated that in the United States there are more than two thousand actively venturing individuals working in over five hundred VC investment firms. We found many start-up Internet web sites with links to homepages of venture capital firms. Remember to get introductions from your lawyer, accountant, and angels.

An entrepreneur should start with those firms in his geographical region and look carefully at the types of investments each firm says it is interested in. For instance, it is a waste of time to contact a firm that does later-round deals when the start-up is looking for seed money. The tactics suggested in Chapter 7 will help avoid mistakes and wasted time.

**Choosing a Venture Capital Firm.** CEOs should pick a VC firm as carefully as they pick the start-up's most important employee. Here are some reasons for making a careful choice of your VC:

- The VC will be with the company a long time, and the founders want the best they can find for the long haul.
- Each VC firm has its own character; compatibility with the CEO is important.
- A VC's references must be checked. The VC firm should provide three or more names of CEOs of companies in their portfolios. And the entrepreneur must insist on talking to at least one that got into serious trouble or went bankrupt. Character comes out best under duress, so ask the tough questions.
- The entrepreneur must review the VC's portfolios—all of the companies, including the turkeys. It is important to discuss the losers as well as the winners with the VC who will be the lead.
- What do competing VCs think of the firm? Other VCs should be asked what their experiences have been with the firm. Check with out-of-town VC firms as well.
- The investigation should conclude with an evaluation of the VC firm that is as thorough as the VC firm will do on the start-up's potential as an investment or as the CEO would do on a vital key employee. It is important to check for integrity, ethics, and honesty.

**Other Sources of Information.** Venture Economics publishes a helpful monthly journal, *Venture Capital Journal.* It is now in many libraries and most venture firms have it handy. Each issue tells of deals done recently and analyzes trends.

Many firms provide a carefully prepared written description of the character of their firm and the kinds of investments they are looking for. We have reprinted some of them in the appendix.

**How Venture Capitalists Differ from One Another.** Until the fledgling CEO has dealt with several venture firms it is hard to grasp just how different each one is from the other. Some opinions on how they differ are shown in Table 9-4. The observations presented were collected from interviews with managers with start-up companies, CPAs, and lawyers.

The firms in Table 9-4 were selected to show contrasts, not to recommend those firms over others. They will give the start-up CEO a taste of how unique each venture firm is, according to the opinions of managers who have dealt often with the venture capital community. Actual experiences with each firm differed among the people we interviewed. Only personal meetings and careful research should be used to reach conclusions on this important aspect of raising capital for a start-up.

**Presenting to Venture Capitalists.** Like a job hunter, the CEO's primary goal is to get the invitation for the first interview. This is a golden opportunity that requires careful preparation. It should be treated like the presentation of the annual plan to the board of directors at one's former employer. The CEO should be just as thoroughly prepared to field tough questions and should practice beforehand. Homework is vital.

The VCs' attitudes at presentations will be deceptively simple, casual, and informal. This is partially because the partners want to see the person behind the presentation and at the same time make the CEO comfortable with them. They also realize that good managers are very hard to find and that competing VC firms will be eager to contact the qualified CEO.

The presentation must be done well. Desktop publishing and PowerPoint are used to make presentations look very slick and convincing. Handouts should be kept to a minimum, talk to the maximum. And the CEO must never leave any proprietary material on the first visit, if ever. VCs do not sign nondisclosure agreements.

The degree of teamwork used to make the presentation will also tell the VC that the start-up is likely to be an organization that will work together effectively and smoothly.

**TABLE 9-4. Comparisons of Some Venture Capital Firms**

| *Venture Firm* | |
| --- | --- |
| Arthur Rock<br>San Francisco, California | Considered by many to be the "father" of modern venture capital. Operates quietly from small office in San Francisco. Often invests in referred business deals. |
| Sequoia Capital<br>Menlo Park, California | One of the icons of venture investing. Does wide range of technologies. Seed to later stage deals. Extensive Internet start-ups. Prefers being lead investor. |
| Kleiner Perkins<br>Caufield & Byers<br>Menlo Park, California | One of the older, most experienced firms. Distinguished by its operational involvement in start-ups, often acting as CEO until launch is successfully achieved. Likes being lead investor. |
| Benchmark<br>Menlo Park, California | New fund by veteran VCs and others. First hit was eBay. Focus is on Internet-centric start-ups at early stage. Known for creativity. |
| Brentwood Associates<br>Los Angeles and<br>Menlo Park, California | Manages large fund. Takes strong lead position. Invests in companies in California and other cities in United States. Very experienced partners, well connected in venture community. |
| TA Associates<br>Boston, Massachusetts<br>Palo Alto, California | Operating one of the largest pools of capital. Focus is on later stage and established enterprises. TA usually takes the lead role. It makes multimillion-dollar investments in a wide variety of technologies. |
| Phillips-Smith<br>Dallas, Texas | An experienced investor in retail start-ups at seed and later stages. Recent investments in electronic commerce. Prefers hands-on involvement with management. |
| AsiaTech Ventures<br>San Bruno, California<br>Hong Kong<br>Taiwan<br>Singapore | Experienced venture fund investing across Pacific in a range of technology and Internet start-ups. Looks at seed and later stage deals. |

*Source:* Saratoga Venture Finance

**What VCs Look For.** Table 9-5 shows selected issues that VCs told us they especially look for. It should be used as a checklist well before the presentation at the VC's office.

Some day the start-up will go public—at least this is the plan of both founders and venture capitalists. Here is what one influential group looks for in a company ready for IPO. These criteria can be compared to a start-up company's condition and plans in three to five years. By the end of the 1980s the foundations for IPOs that made the U.S. NASDAQ the envy of the world were in place. Their principles

**TABLE 9-5. Issues Venture Capitalists Are Sensitive To**

---

*Management*

CEO's credentials as a successful businessperson

Caliber of the founders

Completeness of the management team

Degree of drive of the core team

*Market*

Size of the market, intensity of competition, and revenue potential over the next five years

How revolutionary the idea or technology is, its breakthrough qualities

Does the company just have a nifty product, or is this a business?

Names and phone numbers of potential customers who will tell investors of their intent to buy the product

*Unfair Advantage*

Why is the competitive advantage going to be sustainable?

What is the distinctive competence of the company?

How workable is the business model?

How early or late will the company be?

*Financial and Legal*

Size of the company in five years, likelihood of the company going public within three to five years

Pricing of the financing round (percent owned after financing)

Seats on the board of directors

---

*Source:* Saratoga Venture Finance

have been used successfully ever since. Following are good examples of the fundamentals:

Hambrecht & Quist's head of research, Bill Welty, was quoted in *Business-Week's* April 20, 1987, issue that his firm looks for these factors to guide its decisions to buy, sell, or hold emerging growth stocks (these have now become classical in the IPO business):

■ *New Products:* "The company must have on stream new products that will help change the future of the industry it's in. In the case of Genentech and Apple, he said, we identified such new products early."

■ *Leadership:* "The company must be a leader in its particular niche business and face little competition."

- *Price Targets:* "As long as we believe the stock has the potential for a 50 percent climb, we stay with it."
- *Unique Knowledge:* When H & Q feels that it no longer has more information about a particular stock than is circulating on Wall Street, it sells the stock.

The CEO can gain further insights about what goals to set for an IPO by reflecting on history. In May 1986, *BusinessWeek* ran a story entitled, "Now High-Tech Moneymen are Picky, Picky, Picky." Its point related to the degree of interest in investing in start-up computer companies. Here are a few quotes worth applying to a start-up in any industry:

> The difference now is that everyone's a lot more cautious. . . . Whatever the start-up, it is more important than ever to have seasoned management that won't lose sight of what the market needs. People don't want more technology—they want solutions to their problems, says Clifford Higgerson, a partner in Hambrecht & Quist Communication Ventures.
>
> Whatever the product, having the right leader is crucial. In the heady days of 1983, eager investors often overlooked management weaknesses when backing start-ups in hot technology markets. Now stable, seasoned management is prized as highly as innovative products. Investors are willing to pay a premium for an industry veteran launching a second or third new venture.

Our research during the Internet-era boom shows those are the same things investors are especially looking for in today's start-ups: seasoned management that understands what the (hopefully huge, exploding) markets (customers) are eager for. The only problem: There continues to be a global shortage of seasoned start-up management!

**Closing Deals.** Closing deals is tough work. Many CEOs have celebrated before the cash arrived and later learned that it never would. How does a CEO avoid that? For one thing, by pressing on to the close as if the CEO were the only person doing the work to get to the close. Another is to recall what motivates the VC and to use that knowledge in the negotiations.

If the CEO is a "techie" and hates to negotiate, he should get a consultant or lawyer who likes to rough and tumble with VCs, someone who is familiar with the notorious "creeping close" phenomenon, someone who can coach the CEO on how to close a deal. It is well worth their fees to use such a advisers to get the best deal possible. Once the deal is done there is no getting back the excess stock that was needlessly given away.

The CEO must brush up on negotiating skills, just as professional ballplayers brush up on their basic skills. He will never regret doing the best job ever in this phase of the company's life.

As for secondary rounds of capital, a CEO should plan well in advance, start earlier than he thinks is necessary, and plan for fundraising to take a lot longer than it seems it should take. There is nothing less dependable than a venture capitalist's assurances that "we'll get the money, don't worry." What can be done if the VC chooses to string things out until the company starts missing payroll? It takes weeks and months to get alternative VCs interested and to get them to complete their due diligence on the struggling start-up. The best negotiating lever is getting several VCs into competition and to retain plenty of cash in the bank. Meeting key milestones is a strong foundation on which to raise more money. Success attracts success.

**Points to Remember.** Here are some key points for CEOs to remember as they go searching for capital:

- The CEO is competing with more than one thousand business plans that the venture firm receives in a given year.
- The VC is looking for a few key things in a CEO and a business plan. Chapter 5 is the guide to follow. Table 9-5 provides a quick checklist.
- After a large, growing, open market, management is worth the most to an investor in today's market, or at least as much as the technology. Without a top leader, a start-up will have to be very special to get seed money.
- The CEO will have to be an excellent negotiator (or very lucky) to end up with more than 3 percent of the company at IPO time. The CEO can use all the help he can get in this once-in-a-lifetime negotiating event.
- VCs have to make a living too. They take large risks. It is important to respect their need for high ROIs.
- Many VCs have learned a lot and earned a lot. The CEO will benefit by listening.
- The CEO must be deliberate and not rush. In picking the VC firm to lead the financing, the CEO must make the best possible decisions.
- The character of the VC partners is important. The CEO will be dealing with his board member for the next five years. They will be the CEO's new bosses and control the CEO in the rough days ahead.

Chih-Chao Lam, founder of ShoppingList.com an Internet start-up, said, "Founder CEOs have to plan from day one to do multiple rounds of funding for their start-ups. Plan three rounds and the IPO. Expect to do most of the fundraising yourself, while also running the company. It takes a lot more time and effort than anyone expects!"

Examples follow of CEOs who experienced the process of raising funds for their start-ups. The first case study follows Hans, a determined founder of a software start-up, New Software, Inc. This case study is—unfortunately—rather typical.

---

# Case Study: New Software, Inc.

New Software, Inc., was founded by Hans, a scientist with a breakthrough technology in Internet database software. The prototype worked well in the laboratory and had been funded all with his own money. Hans decided it was time to get the real stuff, venture capital, to hire some engineers to convert the lab product into a viable commercial success.

He called up a few VCs he had read about in the newspaper and got quick invitations to visit. Hans did so, clad in his usual tieless attire, equipped with just himself and his ideas.

The VCs listened and were interested. Hans had distinguished himself in past years as a senior engineer of an emerging growth company. They told him, however, that they needed to see a business plan. Could he get started writing one soon? And would he be open to recruiting a strong CEO?

Hans said he would get started right away and drove back to his home, where he worked at night and on weekends on his business plan. The more he worked on it, the more he realized that he needed lots of help, from a general manager to a strong marketing manager and top sales manager. The hardest part was explaining how Hans's database technology would be so much better that people would stop purchasing Oracle versions and start buying his product.

The more Hans tried to work on the business plan, the more frustrated he became. He did not want to hire a CEO. He really wanted to lead this effort himself and not give up leadership to someone he didn't know. He decided to seek corporate venture funds instead.

After nine months of work, the interest of corporate venture capital managers remained low, so Hans finally gave in to an offer for the seed round from an angel he had run into on the opposite coast. No one in his region would back Hans without an experienced CEO in place.

That seed cash lasted eight months before the company realized it was in trouble. By then, Hans and his skeleton engineering crew were behind schedule, had less than half the software written, and were not close to the speed of performance that they had promised from Hans's technology.

Suddenly aware that he was going to miss the next payroll, Hans dropped all development work, got everyone to help create a nifty demo piece of software, and personally started trying to get corporate venture capital to save his company.

After four nightmarish months of constant worry and eight payroll advances from the seed investor in the form of a loan secured on all rights to the technology, Hans successfully got verbal agreement for $4 million of capital from a Fortune 500 company that wanted full access to Hans's technology. Hans agreed.

But the seed investor vetoed the deal three times until Hans dropped the price per share to a point where the VC suddenly announced he would be investing in 25 percent of that round. The Fortune 500 company refused to go along with such a deal. Meanwhile, the corporate giant had suddenly been shocked to find that its bread-and-butter business had gone flat. All spending was suddenly frozen, including the commitment to invest in Hans's start-up.

As it turned out, Hans's engineers quit after missing two payrolls. The seed investor ended up with half-finished technology worth nothing. And Hans's dreams went down the drain. Had Hans instead started by recruiting a strong CEO and together creating a well-thought-out business plan, the company might have succeeded. Instead, Hans had to settle on a VC investor and suffered severe consequences. Hans never prepared a capital-raising plan; rather he just shot from the hip and hoped for the best. The result was failure.

---

Some CEOs have better results than Hans. Angels and corporate investors can help produce great results. In the next case study (using disguised names), the real-life CEO not only got started in better condition than Hans, but has gone on to become the leader of one of America's five hundred fastest-growing companies, according to a survey by *Inc.* magazine.

---

## Case Study: Devices Corp.

Devices Corp. was founded by two top technologists, Dick and Arthur, with less than ten years of successful experience in business. College friends, they joined a giant, IC Corp., after graduation from engineering school, and later quit to join the R & D group of an exciting new start-up, Oak Micro Technology. Its chairman, the chief scientist, and the CEO were wrangling from the first day the company got started, and after three years of mediocre progress, Dick and Arthur quit to start their own company.

They got $500,000 of venture money from Carl, a businessman who had started a venture capital firm. He was a respected personality in the semiconductor industry. He understood their technology and believed that a large market existed for products that could be built with Dick and Arthur's new ideas.

However, as a condition to investing, Carl had insisted that a top-flight CEO be found well before the $500,000 of seed money ran out. Dick and Arthur agreed, willingly.

By January of the following year, the three-man board and the two founders had recruited Jim, one of the best marketing and sales leaders in the industry. Jim was just finishing his last year at the start-up he had founded seven years earlier and had let Carl know that he was looking for a good start-up to lead as CEO.

Jim negotiated a tough package with the venture capitalists, including repricing the seed round because Jim felt the dilution to the founders and employees was excessive. Carl would be board chairman. Jim joined Devices Corp. and immediately launched into upgrading the company's business plan, particularly the strategy and market positioning of the company and its products. Using word processing and color laser printers, the new plan was completed in very professional style in five weeks. Jim then sat down with the company's experienced lawyer and the start-up consultant Jim had hired. Together they began to plan the strategy and tactics for the next round of capital.

Two weeks later, the search for the second round was started. The goal of the core team was to get $5 million in the bank in three months, including funding from four VCs, the seed round firm and three new ones, one of which must come from the opposite coast.

The deal closed in seventy-one days. Instead of $5 million, there were offers for $11 million from nine firms. The core team and board of directors decided to accept offers for $6 million from five firms, picking the firms according to their character, experience as operating managers in the company's industry, and their track records as investors.

While the capital was being raised, Dick and Arthur remained focused on product development. As a result, before the second round closed, the engineers had met their key milestones. On the day of closing on the financing, everyone celebrated at dinner.

A careful funding plan was built upon a carefully prepared business plan. A team drew up the plan, lead by a CEO savvy in marketing and strategy. The two founders turned leadership over to a stranger whose efforts contributed to a very successful funding effort. Needless to say, the employees finished this stage of the company's life with smiles on every face.

There is an old saying, "Experience is cheapest second-hand." So why not apply that to your capital-raising campaign? Sure, owning 100 percent of your own company sounds great, but having enough capital to achieve the fullest potential of your company sounds even better to most CEOs.

We recommend that you read the material in the appendix, which includes the written descriptions provided by leading VC firms. A careful review of these descriptions will allow you to compare typical differences in what VCs are looking for.

So now that you understand—better than most—how the VC investor thinks and acts, you can plan and negotiate a fair deal, fairer than you would without good preparation.

Now let's go on to look at a popular source of alternative capital, venture leasing.

## 10

# Leasing as a Source of Capital

Smart entrepreneurs quickly learn to protect their precious equity capital. In other words, they soon realize that almost any source of money other than equity is less expensive capital. Leasing is an important source for the high-tech start-up. In this chapter, we will discuss important additional sources of venture capital, in particular how to raise equity capital in the form of venture leasing.

Entrepreneurs also catch on to how important it is to have financial flexibility—the time and room to maneuver, particularly when the sharks are circling. Sustainable competitive advantages are built on lower costs of capital and quicker speed in responding to freshly perceived opportunities and problems in the marketplace. Leasing can make a valuable contribution to the creation of competitive advantage.

Leasing money is not only cheaper funding—it also has proved reliable. Our research shows that it is found in many balance sheets of IPOs since 1980, providing a valuable source of specialized growth capital for start-ups and emerging high-tech companies.

However, our research also revealed that most CEOs are inexperienced with lease money, and that they consequently often overlooked lease capital, incorrectly priced leasing company offers, and generally underused this significant source of capital. Interviews showed that the CEO needs to know where to look for lease capital, how to price it, and how to negotiate a lease deal.

The two primary sources most commonly found participating in lease deals are the landlord and the equipment lessor; we will discuss their roles in detail, and we will also analyze the terms and conditions of a typical leasing term sheet.

Three case studies illustrate the role of leasing capital in start-ups. The case study of Chips and Technologies shows how the landlord became a key partner at just the right moment—when the chips were down, one could say. It was a win-win situation, and history showed that both parties made out handsomely, particularly in financial terms.

The case study of Tophill Systems is based on an actual start-up that successfully negotiated a leaseline that added 23 percent to its capital base immediately after closing its round-one venture deal. It is a classic case of a winning CEO who was unfamiliar with sophisticated leasing salespeople, but who learned and ended up in the driver's seat with a fine deal.

The case study of Range Semiconductor is another classic case, that of the start-up that had to downsize. It all happened in the Great Electronics Winter of 1983–1986. Faced with a severe shortfall of revenue well below its business plan, this start-up company decided to try to buy more time by converting fixed leasing costs to more flexible, stretched-out, monthly payments.

These three case studies provide examples and lessons learned that will help CEOs better plan their financial flexibility.

# The Landlord as a Source of Venture Capital

"Rent, don't buy!" was the consistent advice of the CEOs and venture capitalists we talked to. That advice was applied universally to decisions on leasing or buying real estate. Yet that is the opposite of what some of the grand giants of Silicon Valley like National Semiconductor and Intel did. They began to buy land as soon as they could. National bought parcels at below $90,000 an acre in the 1960s and 1970s—land that is now worth millions of dollars an acre. Intel began buying out its existing leases as soon as the good times began to flow in the late 1970s. Yet giants still lease a great deal of space. Why? For the same reason that start-ups rent: to get a lower cost of capital and to retain more strategic flexibility. Many observers of the early 1980s assert that high-tech start-ups should not be in the business of investing in real estate. Considering the 30 million square feet of newly constructed, empty R&D space in Silicon Valley from 1985 to 1990, those counselors proved right.

Landlords thus become venture capitalists. They size up the start-up's chances of success, check it out with the venture capitalists, and sign the CEO to a five-year lease.

As the lease document begins to be negotiated, landlords quickly separate into two camps: paper people and deal makers. Paper people want to put the lease documents in a vault and collect the monthly check without interruption, except for an occasional "How's it all going?" on the phone during periods of slack business. These landlords constitute about 80 percent of those in real estate in Silicon Valley.

The deal-makers are people like John Arrillaga of Peery-Arrillaga Santa Clara, California. That firm strongly prefers to negotiate without an expensive middleman (a real estate broker). A broker gets about 6 percent of a five-year lease, adding a cost of about $40,000 to $150,000; such brokers or developers have been known to bend corners to get a desirable start-up into one of the many local buildings that they personally built and financed.

Freed of the constraints of a middleman, these deal makers will give a period of free rent and add needed special leasehold improvements in exchange for warrants to buy the start-up company's stock. The deal then turns into more of a horse-trading session than the staid negotiation of a boring lease.

For capital-intensive start-up companies in businesses like semiconductor manufacturing, cooperation on leasehold improvements can be worth millions of dollars of capital supplied through the facility lease instead of from expensive venture capital. Semiconductor companies are now among the most capital intensive of the electronics start-ups; some have even gone into a business partnership with deal makers in order to extract cash from the vaults of landlords. The following case study is an all-time classic in how effective leasing can be for a start-up.

## Case Study: Chips and Technologies

Chips and Technologies was founded on December 5, 1984, with personal capital from Gordon Campbell, who was soon joined by Gary Martin as CFO. Campbell found to his shock that at that time classic venture funds were nearly impossible to obtain at any price, so he decided to turn to alternative sources. Bill Marocco, principal of W.L. Marocco Development Company, was already his choice as landlord, based on the rates charged start-ups at that time and his prior knowledge that Marocco understood start-ups. Campbell started his search for alternative funding with Marocco, who was to play an important role in the life of Chips.

Marocco, a well-known independent industrial real estate developer in Silicon Valley, welcomed Campbell's interest in talking over a deal in person. Campbell was known to Marocco, who had done some discreet checks on Campbell's new business prior to both parties signing the office lease. Marocco's decision was based largely on character references: He sized up Campbell and decided he was a manager worth the risk.

They met in Marocco's office to talk business. Campbell chose to focus Marocco's attention on one single point: getting him to understand Chips's sustainable competitive advantage. He was well prepared from arduous (and unproductive) presentations to more than forty classic venture capital firms; he kept to a simple agenda and avoided elaborate slides and overhead foils or handouts. Instead, he talked about the vast, untapped market—in the millions of units per month—that awaited the first company to ship the most obviously needed product in the personal computer industry. He patiently presented the skills of Chips's management, the technical team's talent, and the cash flows that could result from a success.

Then he gave Marocco the bottom line: "Bill, I want you to invest $1 million in the next round of financing of Chips."

Most people would blanch at that request. However, deal makers respond with, "For how much of the company?" Shortly thereafter, in October 1985, round one closed for $1,705,000. The shares went for $0.65 each. Marocco was elected to the Chips board of directors, where he continued to serve for several years. Chips shipped its first products in the fourth quarter, ending December 1985.

Based on the business's successes, round two quickly followed, adding $1,528,000 by January 1986. Those shares were sold for $1, mainly to four Japanese companies that had contracted with Chips to provide it with manufacturing facilities and services. That further leveraged the seed capital. Thus, Campbell and his team were able to turn near disaster into sweet victory. By IPO time the Chips stock sold for $5 per share. Campbell, his fellow founders, key managers, and all employees with options collectively owned 63 percent of the company. In contrast, Cypress Semiconductor personnel owned 25 percent of their company.

## Equipment Lessors

A second important source of funding is the lessors who invest in start-ups by leasing equipment to new enterprises. Companies that provide lease capital to start-ups are a special breed of capitalist. They come in several forms and make their money in several ways. The entrepreneur who understands the differences will be much more likely to attract lease capital at competitive rates successfully.

**Who They Are.** Because of the complexity of an equipment lease, there are several types of leasing companies. A leasing deal looks deceptively simple, but it can be a complex collection of elements: parties that provide capital in the form of tax breaks; other parties that collect interest and principal payments;

providers of the portion of the lease that is equity; and suppliers of debt in several maturities. There is nothing simple behind the scenes about leasing. However, the Internet has brought many new leasing companies into existence and there is no shortage of alternative sources.

One source of computer equipment is the vendors themselves. Compaq and Dell have competed aggressively at times and are known to supply a lot of equipment to start-ups. Gateway and MP3.com were allies, and MP3.com used a lot of Gateway equipment.

Commercial bankers focused on start-ups also lease equipment. Those banks are discussed in the next chapter.

Another source is the dedicated venture leasing firm. There the lessor is either a broker or an institutional investor. Brokers bring together the complex parties—as do institutional sources of funds—but brokers typically do not put their capital at risk in the start-up. Examples in northern California include Western Technology Investment of San Jose and Costella Kirsch of Menlo Park. They are experienced at arranging warrant-based high-tech equipment leasing for venture-backed start-ups in the United States.

Here is how Costella Kirsch describes itself:

Costella Kirsch began financing start-up companies in 1985. Typical deals involve leases for capital equipment which allow young companies to conserve and leverage their equity dollars. Our leases are generally for amounts ranging from $250,000 to $2,500,000 and include a warrant position. We can structure a broad range of financing alternatives, including subordinated debt, unsecured loans, and equity investments.

We have used our own capital to provide in excess of $150,000,000 of financing for new and emerging companies located in the Silicon Valley. Because we do not involve outside investors, we are able to act quickly to provide flexible financing.

We are more concerned with the quality of management and other investors than with the quality of the assets financed.

To the entrepreneur, the differences among lessors are important if they represent an opportunity to reduce the cost of funds and increase the flexibility of the funding.

First, the start-up CEO must be sure the lease money actually comes in. That turns out to be quite important. Some firms take their offer to you and then find money to fit the offer. Finding capital takes a great deal of time and emotional energy, two resources a start-up company lacks. Our research revealed that a high proportion of lease deals are not completed. The lessor often turned out to be unable to get all the parties behind the scenes to sign up to take on the risks of (in essence) loaning long-term money to a shaky, unproven company. The CEO is also sometimes subjected to the dangers of bait-and-switch tactics from the lesser-quality leasing salespeople.

Second, there is a correlation between the higher quality of firms and a lower cost of capital for a lease. Professional, experienced firms often are found in the final Silicon Valley runoffs, after elimination of other, less experienced bidders.

Finally, each lease deal has terms and conditions that are customized to fit the particular needs of the start-up. Experienced players are much more inclined to give and take significantly in their negotiations, and this is true even of the leading electronic lending banks that sometimes enter this market. The large institutional investors tend to avoid the riskier deals and are more likely to be entering start-up financing at later stages than the brokers. Recent entries have, however, tended to be aggressive in their negotiations but short on valuable venture leasing experience.

Equipment lessors have differing motivations for being in this high-risk financing market. The astute CFO should attempt to uncover the lessor's priorities. Some want to maximize their gain ("upside") through warrants and will take more risk for more warrants. Some are just looking for financing opportunities for their funds and attempt to minimize risk via additional security and shorter maturities.

**How They Make Their Money.** Equipment lessors make their money by owning equipment used by start-up companies that pay monthly for its use. At the end of a preset term, the start-up must either stop using the equipment or purchase it, typically at fair market value, or sign up for a new lease.

Meanwhile, the lessor typically has sold the tax benefits, such as depreciation, which the start-up would have had to wait to use until it became profitable several years later. And the lessor also has arranged to restructure and sell packages of the incoming cash flows to be safer to debt participants and riskier to equity participants.

In exchange for the greater risk, the equity partner then asks for warrants from the start-up. We found that the broker sometimes takes them all, while at other times deals were made that split the warrants into complex pools of capital.

**Cost of Leasing: Cash and Equity.** The combinations of cash flow, tax benefits, equity, warrants, and debt, plus the security deposits and fees, all boil down to an offer called "the term sheet." An example of one is contained in Table 10-1. It is a composite of the actual terms of start-up equipment lease deals revealed to Saratoga Venture Finance for deals done in Silicon Valley .

## Table 10-1. Typical Term Sheet of Equipment Lease Financing for a Start-up Company

---

*Parties to the Transaction:*

1. Lessee    XYZ Company ("XYZ")
2. Lessor    To be arranged by Lease Broker

*Equipment*

1. **Equipment Description:** The equipment to be leased will include test equipment, computer equipment, and furniture and fixtures.
2. **Total Cost:** Not to exceed $_____
3. **Deliveries:** The equipment is expected to be delivered prior to December 31, 200_.

*Transaction Structure:*

On or before December 31, 200_, the Lessor will purchase the equipment from the vendor and/or the Lessee and simultaneously lease the equipment to the Lessee. The Lessor will provide 100 percent of the funds necessary to purchase the equipment.

A true lease document will evidence the agreement between the Lessor and Lessee. It is anticipated that the lease will be a Master Lease with schedules evidencing periodic takedowns.

*Lease Information*

1. **Delivery and Acceptance:** All equipment delivered and placed in service will be acknowledged and accepted by the Lessee per a written Delivery and Acceptance Certificate.
2. **Base Lease Term Commencement Date:** There will be a Base Lease Term Commencement Date for the equipment subject to each funding by the Lessor.
3. **Lease Rate Factors:**

   __monthly payments each in advance equal to ____% of equipment cost.
4. **End of Lease Purchase:** At lease expiration the Lessee will have the option of buying the equipment at its then fair market value or renewing the lease at the equipment's then fair rental value.
5. **Casualty Values (Stipulated Loss Value):** In the event the equipment is destroyed or otherwise rendered permanently unfit for service, the Lessee will pay a Casualty Value. The Casualty Value will be calculated at the outset of the transaction and will dictate the amount of the Lessee's casualty insurance coverage.

---

- The after-tax internal rate of return (IRR) for the monthly cash payment is typically between 16 percent and 30 percent per annum.
- The cost of warrants almost tripled the total cost of capital of the typical start-up equipment lease financing, raising the ROI or internal rate of return to a range of 36 percent to 46 percent per annum after taxes.

## Table 10-1, continued.

*Other Considerations*

1. **Federal Income Tax:** The Lease Rate Factors quoted herein are based upon the following assumptions:

   a. **Investment Tax Credit:** It is assumed that no investment tax credit (ITC) is available to the Lessor.

   b. **Depreciable Life:** The equipment is expected to be depreciated over five (5) years using the "200 percent double declining balance switching to straight line" schedule as outlined in the Tax Reform Act of 1986.

2. **Tax Indemnification:** The Lessee will indemnify Lessor for any loss of tax benefits as listed above caused by acts, omissions, or misrepresentations by Lessee.

3. **Net Lease:** The Lease will be net to the Lessor. Lessee will be responsible for all expenses in connection with the equipment, including taxes (except taxes based on the income of the Lessor), franchise taxes, charges in lieu of taxes, assessments, insurance premiums, all costs of operation, repair, maintenance, and rebuilding, and all the charges related to the equipment or its operation.

4. **Expenses:** Any expenses incurred by the parties, including fees and expenses of counsel and/or accountants, are for the account of those parties. Appraisal fees will be for the account of the Lessee.

5. **Stock Warrants:** As an inducement to lease equipment to the Lessee, the Lessor will be granted the option to purchase _____ shares of the Lessee's series X preferred stock at $_____ per share. This represents a __% coverage ratio. The warrants have an exercise period of ___ years from the final Base Lease Term Commencement Date. The warrants will contain piggyback registration rights similar to those granted to the holders of this series of preferred stock.

6. **Commitment Fee:** A Commitment Fee of $____ is required by the Lessor to initiate its due diligence review process. The entire Commitment Fee is refundable if the transaction is declined by the Lessor. Should the transaction be approved and the lease line instituted, the fee will be applicable on a pro rata basis to the first period's rental as the line is drawn down. Should the transaction be approved and the Lessee choose not to utilize the lease line, the fee will be retained by the Lessor and treated as compensation for time and effort expended.

*Source:* Saratoga Venture Finance

## More Than Leasing Money

CEOs should know that so-called leasing companies are also sources of start-up capital in special forms. Be aware of this as you open discussions with a leasing company. For instance, Western Technology tells start-ups to look at them in the role of "filling the gap between equity financing and traditional bank lending and leasing. These services are offered nationally to companies representing all areas of venture capital investments." Knowing that, the CEO can talk about a long-term relationship from the first moment, set up for the day when later stage funding is ripe, and be ready to go back to the leasing company as a source of midround venture funding.

## Case Study: Tophill Systems

Jim, the CEO of Tophill, had just finished round one for $7 million. The venture capital participants were first class and he was now ready to commit to a three- to five-year lease for a more permanent home for his team, which had been squeezed into rented quarters for the six months between the seed round and round one. The furniture rental fees were eating the cash supply and the engineers were eager to get their hands on leading-edge computer-aided engineering systems.

Good publicity in the *San Jose Mercury News* "Business Monday" section had alerted the leasing community. The phone had been ringing with salespeople seeking a visit to check out Tophill. Jim had also been given a couple of names of lessors by two of his lead venture capitalists. He called an old CFO friend to check out the quality of those he had been considering. Although he was a superb negotiator, Jim had no prior contact with leasing people and was not sure of his ability to analyze and make a wise decision. Moreover, some members of his board of directors were strongly in favor of purchasing everything to avoid the cost of paying interest.

Jim also had decided to scrimp on new hires and had been using part-time help hired at a deep discount from a top accounting firm, the blue-chip CPA firm. He planned to add a strong CFO at a later date. For now, he would get along with a smart administrative assistant, and he would use Bob, his CFO acquaintance, as a consultant on this project.

After exploring eight proposals, Bob and Jim cut the number of offers to a total of five firms and then put in personal phone calls to each finalist, requesting final written offers. The five selected firms responded in four working days. But the eliminated firms rebid aggressively anyway!

By Friday of the first week, nine proposals were facing Tophill. Each had different cash flows, terms, warrants, and special conditions. Jim was disappointed that there was no clear-cut winner. (He didn't know that lessors do not go for approval within their own firms until after the lessor is awarded the deal; that is why it is important to have multiple bidders.) When Bob and Jim reviewed the proposals, here's what they found:

- It was deceiving to use the lowest lease rate factor because the up-front deposit and fee arrangements differed so much.
- The warrants were at different costs and lengths of term, with different IPO conditions.
- Each lessor had different reputations for certainty of getting a deal done.
- The cheapest cash flow IRR lessor required the largest security deposit.
- The second lowest IRR lessor would not finance software for more than 25 percent of the $1.5 million lease line.
- A third would not fund more than $65,000 worth of furniture.
- A fifth insisted on attending all board meetings and getting all materials and minutes of the board.

Jim made his final deal with Bluebird Leasing, based on these decision factors:

- No leasing companies in board meetings. Informal meetings were welcome, but not formal sessions with the board.
- He requested written assurance from the lessor's ultimate source of money that the deal had been prescreened. Jim wanted no surprises.
- Two rounds of counteroffers had gotten a top lessor to be the lowest in both the after-tax cash flow IRR and the all-in IRR, although by only the narrowest of margins over the number-two lessor.
- The number-one lessor, Bluebird Leasing, had expressed an early desire to continue funding Tophill through and beyond the IPO.

Bluebird Leasing got the deal, on terms along the lines of those shown in the term sheet in Table 10-1.

# Case Study: Range Semiconductor

Mike, the new CEO of Range Semiconductor, had just finished looking at the CFO's latest business plan projections. If layoffs could be done as his VPs had agreed, the variable costs would be cut low enough to give Range a chance at survival.

After two years of revenue, this four-year-old start-up was going through the pain of massive restructuring, including a new president. The new president, brought in by the venture capitalists on the board, was given one goal: Save Range.

To keep the technology team in place and to give the marketing leader a chance to build some revenue-building new products, Mike decided he needed more room to maneuver. The only costs left to attack were the fixed ones—the building and equipment leases.

Mike told his CFO to figure out some way to cut the lease cash flow drain and to do so in 90 days. The goal was to get an extra year of cash flow out of the concessions of the leasing participants, including the landlord.

Tim, the CFO, had been with Range since the early days; he was employee number sixteen. He personally had arranged the company's four lease lines and its five-year facilities lease. The $8 million of equipment and the facility lease represented about 68 percent of the company's fixed costs.

Eager to get started, Tim launched into action. He called for a gathering, an "all-hands meeting," to start the ball rolling. He expected an uphill battle but was confident that much of the $2.5 million in deposits could be freed up and some concessions in monthly payments could be negotiated. After all, he reasoned, "Isn't it in everyone's best interests to keep Range alive?"

Over the next seven months Tim struggled in vain to get his concessions completed. In the end, he was unable to succeed for reasons of "good news": the semiconductor industry began to rebound in 1987, and under Mike's leadership Range's revenues began at last to climb. However, Tim learned the hard way some important lessons on leases:

- Stick to just one simple source of equipment lease money. Tim had arranged so many, in such complex deals with multiple parties headquartered around the country, that he was never actually able to get all of them around the table for a unified negotiating session. In this case, the quest to get the lowest cost funds ended up being high cost when the going got rough.
- The landlord was indeed willing to negotiate revised terms. But only if he "was not the patsy." The equipment lessors had to give just as much.
- The easiest landlord to negotiate with is one who owns the property. All others must act "as a prudent man" on behalf of the remote, uncaring pension fund whose money has purchased the building.
- Don't believe that security deposits are "free"—that is, that they cost nothing. This becomes clear as soon as the start-up gets into trouble. Cash spells life to the start-up that is missing payroll.
- Commercial banks are more likely to renegotiate terms in times of trouble than other sources of lease money. Tim believes that there are two reasons for this: Banks have much more skill at working out troubled loans, and their goal is to have a long-term relationship with those start-ups they choose to support with loans and leases.

■ Range's sole negotiating lever was the danger of bankruptcy. Private talks with people familiar with restructured high-tech companies showed this to be true. The winners had engaged special bankruptcy legal counsel—rugged, determined types who spearheaded the gathering of all related parties. Postscript: As of 1991, Range (a disguised name) turned around and went IPO.

---

**The Lessons of Leasing.** The alert CFO should realize that equipment lessors have different investment objectives from venture capital investors, and in distress situations their interests may be different from those of the company's investors. These differences will become even more apparent as we examine the role for commercial bankers in the next chapter. As for obtaining cash from landlords and venture equipment lessors, the CEO who uses the lessons learned in this chapter's case studies will incur less dilution, obtain greater flexibility, and get closer to achieving the capital-raising plan needed for his or her company to succeed.

## 11

# Bankers and Bootstraps as Funding Sources

The old hands, experienced at starting new enterprises, have found many ways to get the most benefit from a long-term relationship with a banker, even if the bank grants them not a penny to get the company started. In this chapter we will look at what commercial bankers and other funding sources can—and can't—do for a start-up.

## The Role of Bankers

We will first explore the conventions and practices that prevail currently, indicating what can be expected realistically from a friendly banker. Next we will look at how loans can be used for a start-up. We will also suggest other sources of capital, such as government money and funds from family and friends, with the goal of relating these alternative sources of capital to venture capital sources. We will consider whether the entrepreneur is wise to mix them, and under what circumstances they might be mixed.

Finally, we have provided insight from our interviews with start-up veterans about how they pick and work with a top banker.

**Conventions and Practices.** Because of the business economics of today's commercial banker in the United States, the CEO of a start-up must be prepared to work with a bank in a very different way than is appropriate with venture capital equity investors.

A commercial bank earns most of its money by making loans at interest rates higher than the cost of money it buys to make such loans. It counts on 97 percent to 100 percent of the loaned monies to return as principal, whereas a venture capital firm expects that 30 percent to 60 percent of its invested capital will never return anything. For the commercial banker, interest payments must cover the loan losses—typically under 1 percent of the principal at risk—as well as provide the gross margin needed to pay for operating expenses and profit. The banker considers it a good piece of business when a loan earns at least a 3 percent spread between interest income from the loan and interest expense on the supporting deposits.

Because of this low-risk profile, the commercial banker is not in the business of providing venture capital to start-ups, many of which may never see success. Furthermore, the bank usually is constrained by U.S. law from taking much in the form of shares as compensation. Therefore, the banker generally is precluded from sharing in the high potential rewards open to the venture capitalist. As a result, banks do not provide equity capital of any kind. The bank expects the entrepreneur to get high-risk capital from other sources.

Some of those sources, however, are often related cousins to the commercial bank. The larger banks are owned by holding companies that can go into other businesses, some of which can help provide start-up capital. Banks have subsidiaries that lease equipment. A few have successful venture capital subsidiaries, while others have groups dedicated to making loans to private, emerging growth companies. And small as well as large banks will lend money to a small business if it qualifies for one of the several U.S. government-backed loan guarantee programs. But these are money businesses that are separate from the familiar commercial bank.

Since banks are not a source of start-up funding, what good is a commercial banker to a start-up?

**The Long-term Partner.** A start-up represents the dream customer to bankers with a long-term view. They have visions of a long relationship, of growing huge along with the next Amazon.com. Accordingly, if the start-up passes the banker's screening and due diligence, he or she is willing to begin working with it from the first day of business. The banker will start cautiously, getting to know the CEO, the company, and its investors. He will read your business plan carefully. Because of the banker's long-term importance to the start-up, the CEO should cooperate from the beginning and plan each step of the relationship as it progresses. The CEO and CFO should invest time in growing the relationship. It is worth the time. The commercial banker can help add millions of dollars of value to a company.

**Business Adviser.** A banker should be chosen as carefully as a CPA firm. The advice given in Chapter 5 for selecting a CPA firm can be applied as well to choosing a banker. The banker should be a competent business person, someone familiar with the larger emerging growth companies in high-technology businesses. The banker's experience will be valuable for many reasons, including these:

- The banker will spot soft areas in the business plan. He has advance knowledge of upcoming capital shortages. The banker can also correct unrealistic assumptions about inventory and accounts payable and receivable, and can explain the magic ratios that bankers' credit analysts will use later to evaluate granting the first request for a working capital loan.
- The banker's experience can head off unrealistic expectations, such as an unrealistic rate of projected sales growth, or profit margins much larger than any that have been sustainable by other clients over many years in your industry.
- Some of the banker's customers may be good customer candidates for the start-up. The banker can provide personal introductions to busy executives who are hard to reach yet are important to the start-up.
- The banker knows the best venture capitalists in the area and will help get the CEO in to see them, a very valuable introduction. A CEO will be identified by the venture capitalist according to the company that he keeps.

**Credit References.** The business plan probably has assumed that the company will be able to get its suppliers to grant credit so the start-up can pay its bills in thirty days or so. That is a reasonable assumption and a good goal, but is much harder to achieve than might be expected. Some suppliers are wary of a new company, one that does not yet have a track record at anything except spending a dwindling pot of money (and that has not yet shipped its first product).

A loyal banker can help bridge the time period until sales get started and the company earns its Dun and Bradstreet credit rating. By being informed about a company from the beginning a banker is in a position to be a credit reference, talking with the suppliers who call the bank and telling them why he has confidence in your company.

This will help the start-up get needed credit from key suppliers, and get the suppliers started on the right foot and in the habit of granting the company good credit terms. The payoff is that later, when the start-up is a large, fast-growing company, the suppliers' credit will add up to millions of dollars of financing that the start-up did not have to use precious equity for.

**Lease Lines.** The banker may have an equipment leasing subsidiary or good relations with an independent firm. If so, this is one way to start an early credit relationship with the affiliated bank. Chapter 10 supplies leasing details. A banking relationship should be included in any leasing plans and in the decision of which leasing company to do business with.

**Loans.** Bankers call loans by various names, depending on their purpose, security, and risk. The type that a start-up company will be eligible for first is called a working capital loan. It comes in the form of a line of credit and, in the case of a start-up, will be intended to finance the cash flow delay between the time the company ships the product and the time it finally collects all the cash from the customer. It is a loan whose amount is limited to some percentage of the total of the accounts receivable (United States only) that are outstanding from reliable customers at the end of each month. As the receivables go up and down, so does the principal amount of the loan. The banker can explain the details, and the CEO and CFO should review the business plan with the banker to fit such financing into the start-up's long-term plan.

The important thing for the CEO to know is when a company can qualify for such loans. They are a lot cheaper than venture capital. Bankers all use different criteria to test the creditworthiness of a young company, but a banker familiar with high-tech start-ups will begin by looking for the date the first receivables are booked. That will be the first test. Next, the banker will look at when the start-up plans to begin being profitable. Then the banker will look at the start-up's ability to repay the loan—from what source the needed repayment cash will be coming. The banker must understand all of this in case the start-up experiences adversity that raises the risk level and causes the bank to disqualify temporarily it as a credit worthy customer.

All of this quantified analysis is done on computer models built by the bank. They digest a business plan and produce new data and facts that a banker needs to do his homework. (In fact, the output of the banker's credit analyst is put into a spreadsheet, which is where the concept for VisiCalc and Lotus started.) By getting the business plan at the beginning of the company's life, the loan officer can determine quickly the degree of realism in the CEO's goal of attaining the working capital loans. For instance, the banker will tell the CEO whether a planned debt-to-worth ratio of 1.75 to 1.1 is acceptable in the current business climate. The banker also will demonstrate how financial statements are viewed from a banker's conservative perspective.

And behind all of the numbers, the banker will be looking to the CEO as the leader, to be responsible to repay the bank's precious principal, even in the bad times. The more confident the banker is in the CEO and the start-up's team of managers, the more likely the company is to get the loan sooner than its competitors. And even more important, the banker will support the start-up when it runs into trouble, through the hard times, when capital and business counsel are needed the most. So get the banker in to meet the whole team, on the company's premises. The more the banker knows, the more likely he or she is to provide support through thick and thin.

**Payroll and Other Services.** As soon as the start-up is incorporated it will need a bank account, and the need for a payroll account will follow quickly. The banks are very competitive in services to do payroll and related tax bookkeeping, starting with even the smallest of businesses. These are areas where a business wants the best quality service and the most "free" accounting help it can get. The changing payroll tax legislation is a headache to keep up with, especially when a sales force will be operating in many of the fifty states. And the required reports are a burden on a company's administrative staff. Such services often are provided best by the banker. The bank's references in this area should be compared with the payroll service alternatives such as ADP, but the future and the long-term relationship should be kept in mind when a decision is being made.

**Growing Together.** A CEO must pick a banker as carefully as the company's investors and treat the relationship as very long term. As the company succeeds, the commercial banker will help more and more. International subsidiaries will need a local banker, and customs departments of governments and overseas suppliers will require letters of credit. The business between the company and its bank will grow accordingly. It will need services such as trustee and transfer agent when it goes public, and here again the banker will want to help. It is important that the banker and the CEO get to know each other early, and that the banker is kept informed as the company grows.

How does one choose a banker for an emerging company? We found the most interesting answer coming from one of high-technology's great veterans, Don Cvietusa, now-retired senior vice president of Silicon Valley Bank:

> Choose a banker for a start-up very carefully. Take some time to select an experienced technology banker who is knowledgeable about emerging companies, one who has excellent venture capital relationships. Approach with a deposit in hand, thereby providing the banker with his "raw material." Build "depositor leverage" and be "bankable" well before you become bankable in a credit sense.

That advice has been taken by many technology start-ups over the years. By 2000, Silicon Valley Bank had spread out across the United States, having followed start-ups and their founders to many states and having thus become America's premier start-up bank for such enterprises.

## Personal Loans

If the CEO is determined to start the company with his or her own equity capital and does not want classic venture capitalists in the company, the personal loan can be important at the beginning. We found it common for careful founders to self-fund the seed round themselves, get the first product finished, and then go after venture capital. Software start-ups and Internet portals were typical. But venture capitalists told us that for purposes of flexibility and control, VC firms generally do not want the clutter and complication of commercial loans to the entrepreneur in the capital structure of a company after the VCs have entered the picture.

The entrepreneur who has decided to go on without venture capital backing will find the personal loan to be a limited source of funds for starting a company. In our research we found that loans from commercial banks to individuals were made primarily to the sole proprietorships and closely held companies, but rarely to the high-tech start-up. And a track record was preferred strongly, with an active, healthy business in operation, and with good customers and their receivables on the books. Home equity loans were mentioned often by the entrepreneurs, who told us how they had done it. Bankers always want some security to fall back on to repay their loan in case of trouble.

**The Personal Cost.** The entrepreneur must be sure to count the cost before doing any personal borrowing, especially if the family home is put up as security for a bank loan. A spouse may not be able to stand the strain of waiting to see whether you will lose or keep the house and, if you do forfeit the house, the kids would have to relocate in the middle of their school year. This adds to the stress of the already hard job of launching a complex company successfully, and an entrepreneur may not want to add such problems to an already full bag. More than 60 percent of the funded companies go bankrupt, and Dun & Bradstreet says that, according to its extensive records on nearly every business in the United States, small businesses are seldom successful.

## Government-Backed Loans

In many countries, governments have several active small-business loan programs. Any commercial banker can provide details about them. They are intended to reduce the risk to the banker in loaning money to a company. There is, however, a big gap between the intent and the practice. To get such a loan one must go through an ocean of paperwork, forms, and time-consuming work, and the outcome is far from guaranteed.

Because of these conditions, one should be careful about counting on government-backed loans in a financing plan. Venture capital has worked successfully for many good reasons. The commercial banker will have good advice about the trade-offs in the alternative sources of capital for a company.

**Small Business Administration (SBA).** There is a bureaucracy in Washington, D.C., that was created to promote good things for small businesses. We could not find a single use of it in famous start-ups or in the interviews of companies we have dealt with over the years since this research started. However, we did find examples in several Asian countries.

Anyone determined to start on his own should seek all the help available. We did find that the commercial banker was the source most familiar with what help might be obtained from government assisted funding sources.

*Inc.* and *Asian Entrepreneur* magazines are full of examples of start-ups that got going without classic venture capital sources. Every issue makes suggestions on where to go for alternative sources of funds. Such reading is probably much more beneficial than government-generated documents.

**SBICs and MESBICs.** These are abbreviations for two American organizations that operate under federal legislation to encourage equity capital investments in small companies. The SBA licenses SBICs under state laws. The SBA adds capital to that raised by the owners of the SBIC, which makes equity and loan investments in small companies. It all started in 1958, intended to fill a shortage of capital for small companies. A MESBIC is a cousin to the SBIC.

Some early venture capitalists got started as SBICs and some still exist and are active. We found that most SBICs are affiliated with a commercial bank holding company, so the friendly commercial banker is again the best information source. Several of the guides to venture capital firms list SBICs next to the venture capital firms.

# Mom and Dad and Other Friendly Bankers

Many start-ups got going with cash from Mom and Dad or from relatives; some say that is what really got Microsoft started. After we did some checking, we found that it was the start-up classified as a "bootstrap" that used this source of funds most often.

Classic venture capitalists and their lawyers are wary of having to get permission from investors that they view as unsophisticated. The phrase "sophisticated investor" is intended to classify the type of investor who knows what he is doing, has a large net worth, won't go bankrupt if a start-up goes bankrupt, and has invested often in a wide variety of companies. In the course of getting a company off the ground it may be neccessary to make big changes and obtain refinancing, and the small investors who put their money in because of a personal relationship may have trouble dealing with these changes. The laws of each state are restrictive about what the big "sophisticated" investor can do to the so-called widows and children who invested their life savings in the first round of financing; for example, they are prevented from writing down all investors' stock to near zero value and reinvesting fresh cash in the hope of turning the company around at last. And VCs do not relish having to kick the CEO out in case of trouble and then face the wrath of a few small investors that are the CEO's friends and relatives.

We asked the successful and unsuccessful company CEOs what their advice was in these cases. The consensus was that the entrepreneur should stick to seeking funds from only those investors who can afford to lose all the money invested in the company. In fact, some high-tech attorneys insist that such a warning be sent in writing to each potential investor. The entrepreneur must listen to and follow the advice of his attorney in all these cases. Just mentioning an investment possibility to an individual starts to invoke many state small-investor protection laws. In order to stay out of trouble, the entrepreneur must know what can be said to whom and how often.

It is also important to count the cost realistically: What kind of damage would be done to family relationships if all the savings of one's family and parents were lost because the entrepreneur's company failed? How would a spouse feel? And what about the kids' college expenses?

# Bootstraps

A word on bootstraps. These are companies started by a few founders who decided to fund the whole company with their (or other individuals') personal money. They are famous in the folklore of the high-tech start-up business because they smack of the cowboy in all of us and have the romance (and revenge) of the rebel who showed the world that the founders could indeed succeed in spite of everyone else's lack of faith in their wild and wonderful idea and themselves.

Bootstraps that make it big in the high-tech world are rare. Yet they are yet another case of the great American dream and should not be ruled out as impractical.

---

## Case Study: Dell Computer

As a word of realistic hope to bootstraps, remember Dell Computer of Austin, Texas. According to *Business Week,* Michael Dell "launched his business at age 19 from a University of Texas dorm room. His strategy—selling IBM-compatible computers through the mail to customers who were reluctant to pay computer-store prices—was an instant success."

Dell got started in 1984 as a bootstrap. Only when growth exploded did he sell a portion of his company to later-stage venture sources so that he could grow the company to IPO size. IPO was in 1988.

In 1991 Dell Computer was an international operation, employing 2,100 people and generating 40 percent of its sales overseas. Chairman Dell's 35 percent ownership of the stock of the company, which had $500 million in annual sales, was worth $200 million. This is a classic bootstrap, a true example of how a smart CEO saw an opportunity in the market and self-funded his bootstrap to success. The rest is history.

For further bootstrap ideas, get your hands on a classic article: the September 1991 copy of *Inc.* magazine. It features an article titled: "Great Companies That Were Started with $1,000 or Less: The Secrets of Bootstrapping."

---

## Personal Savings

Without realizing it, most start-up founders use a lot of their personal savings to get their company started, even if they do not self-fund a single round of capital themselves.

The founder must first be prepared to finance the time between leaving an employer and getting the first paycheck from the funded start-up. And he must be prepared to absorb the cost of a cut in pay, particularly if the founder is an upper-level executive of a large corporation. Finally, those first legal expenses and marketing reports often come out of the founder's bank accounts.

And if the founder decides to gamble his savings on the seed round (or more) of the start-up, it is necessary to plan on how to deal with the adverse effects of the company's getting into trouble, such as missing payroll for a month or two.

The founder must be prepared to lose it all—that's the nature of risk in a start-up, no matter how well he or she plans and believes in it.

In the next chapter we will further discuss the role for corporations as venture capitalists and how to raise funds from wealthy individuals. As the next century began, large amounts of fresh venture funds were arriving in venture pools around the world. And there was a clear resurgence of funding from wealthy individuals, angel funding was booming. These funding sources and alternative, "small" stock exchanges will be reviewed to show the advantages and pitfalls of using such alternatives to fund your start-up.

## 12

# Angels and Other Sources of Venture Capital

W e spoke with a lot of founders whose initial plan was to "get a big company or a few rich guys to finance us, at least for the start." Their goal was
to avoid the more sophisticated venture capitalists and thereby retain a higher
proportion of ownership of their company. Such alternative investors include a
type that are dubbed "angels" in the jargon of Silicon Valley. Other examples include corporate funding of start-ups.

Our research revealed that there were benefits and costs associated with such
funding, many of which were surprises to the founder/CEO.

The first good news is that many technology start-ups get funding from angels and alternatives to regular venture capital. The Internet–era start-ups have
many such examples.

The first trouble with the plan to avoid traditional venture capital is that it has
proven very hard to attract such funds predictably in amounts large enough to
fund adequately all the needs of a start-up that reaches IPO. Even worse, according to a few of the CEOs who had to live with these investors, they often proved
very sharp, and the percentage the founders gave up was often larger than what
other conventionally funded, comparably sized companies gave up.

Raising funds from individuals is not simpler than raising it from venture
capitalists. The process of getting the money must be done according to strict
rules laid down in each state by the government body that controls the issuing of

securities. Their purpose is to protect the naïve founder or investor. A good attorney is necessary for anyone who decides to go this route.

Let's take a look at various nontraditional sources of funding.

# Angels: "Old 49ers" Who Struck It Rich

There is one type of individual investor, dubbed an "angel," who some start-ups have found can be an acceptable source of funds. These are people who have made it big in another start-up and are searching actively for a similar company—or one they believe they can understand—in which to invest their earnings. They are financially independent, do not have to work for a living, but want to "stay in the game," and thus invest some of their money in the (smaller) seed rounds of new start-ups.

The good connotation in the name "angel" comes from their reputation as a positive influence behind the funding. Rightly or wrongly, founders told us they expected angels to be less ruthless and more patient than some venture capitalists.

Three to six such investors can usually fund the seed round (under $1 million); they are often people who have known each other over several years. The trick is to find these people. They are typically free spirits, found in very private circles, not regularly in offices or at venture capital firms. They are found by asking the people who are in contact with such business successes—a friendly banker, their accounting firm, a start-up consultant, and CEOs of other companies. Some of these angels have formed local groups to review investments and diversify their risks. One of the most well known is the Band of Angels led by Hans Severins, with an office in Menlo Park, California, the heart of venture funding in Silicon Valley.

If this type of private investor investigates the start-up and chooses not to invest, the angel often can lead you to a favorite venture capital firm, where your work with the individual will accelerate the due diligence process.

Start-up veterans tell us they believe such people make good board members, but that they drive just as hard a bargain as the venture capitalists.

# Angels: Sophisticated Pools of Money

The pioneer high-tech toy company, Worlds of Wonder, got started with capital from a large pool of private funds not run by an investor specializing in high-tech deals. Family fortunes made in wood products, oil, and paper have funded several new enterprises. Ross Perot is an example who started with a high-tech business. We found numerous other examples of such mega-buck investors seeking out high-tech start-ups in order to get higher returns on their capital. An Internet-era example is Jim Barksdale, who left Netscape after it was acquired by America Online and formed a venture fund.

Unlike the 49ers, these pools of funds are run by full-time professional staffs. Their investigation processes are similar to that of venture capitalists. The track record for these investors is not public, so we could not determine how likely they will be to stick with a start-up as a long-term investor in high-tech start-ups. We suggest that the entrepreneur look for them at the same time they search for classic venture capital. Try to get a bit of competition working, and then choose from the best of the lot.

## Asian and European Sources

Since the early 1980s, foreign capital has entered the U.S. venture money markets in huge quantities. The venture capital industry saw a regular increase in funds from Europe and Japan, as well as from the Middle East, particularly Israel, and Southeast Asia, particularly Hong Kong, Taiwan, and Singapore. By 2000, funding was also coming from Korea and India. Some venture funds were opening two offices: one in the home country and the second in Silicon Valley. Some countries were experiencing direct government investing in high-risk start-ups.

These funds mainly are entering one of two channels of investment. The first channel is that of joining the limited partnerships of the established venture capital firms. Some VCs spend time enjoying Europe and Asia as part of their treks to raise more capital.

The second channel is direct investment in start-ups, especially by the larger foreign corporations. Fortune 500 companies in Europe and Asia have started and continue to make diverse equity investments in U.S. start-ups. One of the most famous pioneering examples of the 1980s was Chips and Technologies. Investors from Southeast Asia funded Pericom, a successful semiconductor company that went IPO in the 1990s. In the Internet era, the venture capital arm of the Japanese firm Softbank (www.sbvc.com ) made many investments in start-ups that became famous (Yahoo, E*Trade). By 2000 the trend was frequent enough to become a regular pattern in starting Silicon Valley companies.

Foreign investors can be found mainly through personal contacts working with expatriates or foreign business people. Personal trust is required to an even greater degree than when working with American businesses—the trust that comes from working together over long periods of time. Personal introductions help, but we were told in our interviews to warn start-up companies to expect little enthusiasm for an unknown American seeking capital for an untested idea unless the founder has some connection with a trusted local in the home country.

Foreign corporations are more active in merger and acquisition activity. If, for example, a small start-up needs capital to launch a second product family, and the company has already established its position as a producer of high-tech products, the CEO will be better able to attract foreign sources of capital than at the seed round. According to the people with whom we spoke, the prices to be paid were fair and the negotiators used U.S. measures of valuation.

With the good comes the bad. One case study that we found sobering was that of Tony LaPine. In a *Forbes* article (August 10, 1987) on how LaPine was "lured by the siren song of strategic alliances," the story is told of how corporate investors in the form of Kyocera Corporation and other Japanese firms put up $2 million and built an $8.4 million plant in Japan to make LaPine's disk drives. The strategic alliance was arranged by the lead investor, Prudential-Bache. It started with good intentions, but new product deliveries and investors' payments went sour and so did the deal. It then took an even worse turn when LaPine and all but a handful of his hundred employees were dismissed, leaving the technology in the hands of investors.

Other deals have been very successful, including many quietly acquired companies that did not get up enough steam to get to the IPO stage. Softbank of Japan has funded start-ups that became worth billions.

We recommend that any decision to go after foreign capital be tempered with the reality that it is just like other venture capital; it has its own special costs. For instance, American venture capitalists prefer investing with local VCs so that quick decisions can be made, preferably in person, by investors with similar business practices. That is why off-shore start-ups rarely are funded from Silicon Valley. Furthermore, according to skeptics, foreign investors can in fact be at least as dangerous to work with as the nearby venture capitalists. However, other experienced CEOs highly endorse the use of foreign capital and have had excellent results with it. We suggest that the CEO be cautious and not assume that non-American investors are a way of avoiding the trials of finding a good local venture capitalist.

# Corporate Venture Capital: Fortune 500 Companies

Many start-up CEOs feel strongly that an alliance cemented with funding from a strong corporate giant will help them get ahead of the pack and into a leadership position, and that their start-up will be more likely to succeed.

We found many examples of this in the Internet dot coms, the genetic engineering industry and in a number of deals done within the electronics sector. During the Internet boom it became an everyday occurrence. Almost every genetic engineering company has some corporate partner. In electronics, investment deals between high-tech start-ups and domestic giants like IBM, General Motors, Raytheon, and Kodak—as well as foreign companies like Siemens and Olivetti and Nixdorf—became common in the 1980s. More recently, Internet deals have been cut with the gorillas of the day: Cisco, Yahoo, Amazon, Intel, Microsoft, and many more.

Our sources told us that they have learned a number of lessons over the past years, based on the results from start-ups that worked with corporate investors. This advice can help the CEO plan a wise strategy for raising capital:

- *Corporations make good operating partners.* They are operations and technology biased; they are not focused on maximizing the ROI of their investment in your company. Their experience at running similar high-tech businesses may be of considerable advisory assistance when a start-up runs into trouble.
- *Corporate pricing of deals is less expensive.* People interviewed said they believed that corporate venture capitalists often set shares at price levels somewhat below those of the typical venture capitalist. Corporate investors have less pressure to get rich on the start-up company because they have more interest in the start-up's technology than in its potential wealth.
- *Corporate deals can be dangerous.* Several founders told us they lost their jobs, their technology, and their companies when the corporate investors' bread-and-butter businesses got into trouble and the investors put a freeze on all funds, including the promised next round for the starving start-up.
- *Venture capitalists prefer to invest early without corporate venture capital.* VCs prefer to keep corporations out until nearly IPO time or unless a big sales or Internet deal can be done between the start-up and the corporate investor as part of an investment transaction. Part of the reasoning for this is similar to the VCs' bias against working with the CEO's relatives as investors—their goals are too different. VCs also tend to believe that corporate investors generally underprice a deal.
- *Corporate investors take longer to decide.* Venture capitalists can act much faster because they do not have to wait for the next quarterly board meeting or public shareholders' meeting to call for a vote on the investment.
- *Corporate deals can be very complex.* A sales deal for a thousand systems or to license a company's next technology can sound great, but the legal work may cost months of precious time before the deal is concluded. Contingent deals and deals linking equity pricing to units that may—or may not—be purchased

by the corporate investor are sophisticated contracts, requiring skilled lawyers who often must travel halfway around the globe in order to get the deal documented and ready to sign.

- *Corporate partners can greatly increase credibility.* For example, Sun Microsystems learned this lesson quickly when Kodak became a committed buyer and later an equity investor. Another example is Inktomi, which was formed in May 1996 and in August announced a corporate-linked deal, with NTT, the first in a string of blue chip links that boosted credibility and made headlines all the way to the IPO in October 1998. The business models of Internet-era start-ups make corporate deals virtually inevitable.

- *Corporate board members are more patient than VCs.* Several CEOs held this opinion strongly. Their contention was that corporate representatives are more humane or patient than the VCs are. They translated this to mean that the CEO probably would be allowed to stay on the job longer with corporate investors on the board than when VCs are the sole source of funding.

This advice represents the consensus of those we talked to. Each corporate investor has its own character, just as each VC firm does. The deans of the venture firms are sought after eagerly by experienced start-up CEOs. Each investor should be reviewed carefully. The corporate investor must be evaluated as carefully as the VC—don't blindly assume that our advice will hold in every specific corporate situation. The priorities of the corporate investor candidates must be determined so that the CEO can find a good fit with the start-up's capital-raising plan. There are pros and cons, but corporate investors may have an important role to play in a start-up's capital formation plan. Such a generalization is difficult to substantiate and was denied by several successful CEOs. Whatever the case, be forewarned.

## Securities Registration and Legal Limitations

We strongly advise entrepreneurs not to raise a penny of investment capital from another party until legal counsel experienced in such matters has been consulted. There are carefully created laws governing the process of raising money, because the public has so often been cheated in the past by unscrupulous people.

A good securities attorney will be able to steer the entrepreneur clear of the land mines. It's impossible even to call a few friends up on the phone to solicit their money without falling under some aspect of securities law. Well-intended founders often have created a bag of snakes for a professional attorney and for sophisticated investors by hustling a lot of people for funds, leaving a trail of green investors eager for their "first killing" and a wide-ranging collection of warrants and other contingent securities behind for the attorneys to clean up. That kind of behavior has killed deals with top VC firms.

**Stock Exchanges as Sources of Venture Capital.** Over the past years interest has been expressed in how to use small public stock exchanges to raise funds for start-ups instead of getting venture capital. According to our research, there are several reasons for this:

- Capital raised in a public offering is believed to be cheaper than private capital.
- Larger amounts of capital can be raised from the public than from private pools of capital.
- Members of the board of directors can be selected without including venture capitalists.
- Entrepreneurs have succeeded in using public stock exchanges to raise venture capital.
- Investors seem to remain willing to invest in private deals floated over the exchanges.

The large NASDAQ stock exchange of America is the world's giant for IPOs by start-ups from not only America, but from countries around the world. It has been used by blue chip venture firms and their genetic engineering and Internet start-ups to raise capital for companies that have not yet become profitable or who have nothing to sell but R&D contracts and licenses. But there are other public stock exchanges that are mentioned as alternatives to venture capital: Denver, Vancouver, London, Taiwan, Korea and lately the Neuer Markt in Frankfurt, Germany. Hong Kong created yet another late in 1999.

**Denver Stock Exchange.** Stocks with a very low price per share, called "penny stocks," have been sold on the NASDAQ as IPOs from time to time, but the Denver Stock Exchange is the clear leader in this category. However, the brokers on the Denver exchange are notorious for flouting of SEC rules and for the many hucksters who have landed in jail and returned to the same business (selling penny stocks) shortly after serving their sentence. *Forbes* magazine regularly warns investors of the scams, as do other watchers of the securities industries. The title of an article in the June 29, 1987, issue of *Forbes* was:

### Crime Wave

*Yes, the SEC is nailing fat-cat insider traders. But meanwhile, outright crooks, big and small, prey on the investing public almost with impunity. Are the laws inadequate? Or the cops?*

The article speaks for itself. In our research, we found no famous start-ups that used this source of venture capital. We advise you to avoid it.

**Vancouver Stock Exchange.** Over the years there has been an occasional rise of interest in the Vancouver, Canada, stock exchange, and investment activity there has grown in such times. A number of stories about the Vancouver Stock Exchange have appeared in popular publications.

Vancouver is an exchange where a start-up company can sell shares while it is still in the development stages of life and have middlemen tout the company's business plan until it gets to the selling stages and beyond. It acts as a kind of stock market for private deals, actively trading on the basis of the uncertainty of a company's realizing some, all, or more of the goals in its five-year plan.

Small companies have raised millions per issue, and some, including a few high-tech start-ups, have become successful.

However, CEOs are strongly advised to get the best help possible to protect them from running afoul of the law and securities regulations. And it will consume a lot of the CEO's time to answer the new investors' questions on how the start-up is coming along.

Most people we spoke to consider Vancouver to be just a step less controversial than the Denver Stock Exchange. Media articles are sobering in their reviews of the speculation, manipulation, and dangers of Vancouver. We advise alternatives. Anyone who insists on taking a look must proceed with caution, including consultation with one of the better CPA firms and a reputable law firm.

**Non-American Stock Exchanges.** During the personal computer boom of the 1980s, the entrepreneurial fever in America spread to Europe and then to Asia. Here are a few examples:

- London was the first to become the European stock exchange of choice for IPOs in the 1980s. Learning about the much more lucrative fees charged by Wall Street firms, European exchanges began to act less like closed clubs, with the attendant inefficiencies, and started to try to compete with Wall Street as a source of world-class capital, including capital for start-ups. European investment bankers began looking for IPO deals as an additional source of income. During the 1980s this resulted in several U.S. start-ups going public in London before they had their U.S. IPO.

- Meanwhile, Asia was heating up and, by 1990, the Taiwan stock exchange was booming and many companies used it to go IPO. However, the exchange claimed few world-class high-tech IPO success stories that might have taken attention away from NASDAQ. Korea also set up a successful small company stock exchange, as did Singapore and other Asian countries.

- For a while, the Tel Aviv stock exchange learned to play a "pre-IPO role" in high-tech start-ups founded in Israel. Those local start-ups quickly set up U.S. located offices to sell in the American market with a plan to eventually go IPO on the NASDAQ. However, that role has now largely passed away, supplemented by classical venture funding, often in the United States. Such Israeli companies have prospered. By 1999, over 120 had gone public on NASDAQ!

- The arrival of the German Neuer Markt opened a floodgate of new stock offerings by German companies. Valuations soared and companies came out of nowhere to go public. Plans for similar exchanges appeared in press releases from France and other countries. Asians scrambled to do the same in Malaysia and Hong Kong, in spite of lackluster results and lower valuations with Singapore's and Korea's "second exchanges" designed especially for start-ups.

Opinions about the rationale for the roles for non-NASDAQ stock exchanges varied a great deal among the observers with whom we have spoken. One venture capitalist who supported the strategy of using non-U.S. sources for IPOs argued that investors had learned of the U.S. successes of IPOs and that demand exceeded the supply; ergo, doing a non-U.S. IPO would fetch better prices than in the States. All our findings indicate the contrary to that hypothesis.

One respected Wall Street firm said that the founders of the U.S. company he took public in London were greatly afraid of robbers and kidnappers in America, believing that an offshore offering that made them wealthy would attract less attention than a U.S. IPO.

Other reasons for non-U.S. IPOs included: the start-up had large investors headquartered in the region; the start-up did considerable business in related countries; or the founders were born and raised in neighboring countries where investors would possibly be more likely to identify with the founders' original country of birth.

We concluded that an IPO offering on some of these non-American exchanges would be a good choice under special conditions. However, law firms did warn us that certain restrictions on IPOs might be required that could be avoided in a U.S. offering. Taiwan and Neuer Markt often have been a hotbed of speculative investing with post-IPO run-ups in valuations that make even the wildest Internet stocks on NASDAQ look conservative and bring doubt to their long-term viability.

# Potential Problems and Pitfalls

The personal lust to do the dream start-up with clever financing can become both the energy that pulls it off and the cause of doing something very unwise to raise funding. Desperation to succeed can create demands on individuals that result in actions that border on the foolish or even the illegal.

When problems occur between founders and potential investors, we often find that the idea behind the start-up was not realistic relative to other start-up alternatives that investors had. Competition for money pools exists every day. As every ballplayer has learned, some days it is best to head for the showers and get ready for the next game rather than continue a clearly losing cause.

When there are too many private investors the situation can become unmanageable for a small company. The entrepreneur may find himself spending large amounts of time talking with (investing) relatives. It may greatly exceed what he imagined when he first thought of asking for their money.

Mixtures of other types of investors may prove unwieldy. We have found that successful investment deals are usually marked by simplicity and we urge the entrepreneur to try for the least complex deal structures possible. Based on the experiences of those we interviewed, we doubt that more than two of the alternative sources of capital we have described here can be mixed successfully.

# 13

# Wall Street and the Initial Public Offering

When it's time for your initial public offering, you—the successful entrepreneur who has made it through all stages of start-up funding and of getting your product to market—must now look to Wall Street. In this chapter we will look at how investment bankers are ranked for high-tech companies, their role in the IPO, what and who motivates them, and how rich they can get from an IPO. You will learn how to choose the best investment banker for your company.

The IPO is explained in detail, particularly how to time it, how to conform to securities laws, and how to price it, including how to apply some financial technology. We'll also look at the question, "What should we do after the IPO?"

The chapter includes lessons from the IPO trenches, specifically from details about the actual Microsoft IPO. Microsoft faced all the key issues that a start-up's CEO and CFO must deal with at IPO time.

## New Issues and IPOs

"New issue" is the term applied to the first offering of stock of a new company, while IPO stands for "initial public offering." They are two terms from the jargon used in the special investment world that high-tech industry observers talk about so often. This world is filled with glamour, glory, and a great deal of work for participants, who plan to make a ton of money when the IPO is completed.

This is the stage at which investment bankers enter the world of the start-up.

The investment banker is in charge of the process that results in a single transaction that causes a flurry of activity in a start-up. The most significant change for the CEO and the start-up is being in the public limelight. Now the media are interested in the company and its leadership, and they request many time-consuming interviews, which takes up the time of the CEO and his or her staff.

The Wall Street security analysts enter the picture, taking up even more time for interviews than the media.

All this activity has a single objective: to attract and retain the institutional investors who will buy and hold the newly issued shares of the company. The analysts forecast the financial outcomes, the investors listen to their prognostications, place their bets, and wait for the company's results.

Institutional investors are looking for new issues that will get them a higher return than they can get by trading stocks on one of the major stock exchanges: National Association of Securities Dealers Automated Quotations (NASDAQ), or the New York Stock Exchange (NYSE). The risk to investors in new issues is high, because the investment jungle is filled with hot speculators and rapidly moving stock prices. The number of shares available for purchase in a company already on the stock exchange is a tiny fraction compared to the number of shares that can be purchased in a new issue of a start-up, which means that the liquidity risk is much higher for an IPO investor. The business risk is also higher, and therefore a higher return is required to attract investors.

*Forbes, BusinessWeek, Inc.,* other business magazines and web-based 'zines, and the *Wall Street Journal*—as well as a lot of newsletters for investors who specialize in IPOs—also cover the new issues market, and their articles make for instructive, sobering reading. In the long run, the IPO investing world is not a bed of roses and sure wealth creation. Annual reviews and regular IPO articles appear regularly in the media, including these headlines from our collection of classic clippings over the years:

### Stellar performances of companies in

### Venture's Fast-Track 100 chart have Wall Street under a spell

### When the going gets good, the good go public
*But even in a hot IPO market, there are precautions entrepreneurs and investors must take.*

### Wall Street Goes Public
*Last year, we told you investors were looking for proven management and a history of solid performance. Well, they changed their minds.*

### From Harleys to Teddy Bears, everybody's going public
*The explosion of new stocks is astounding—and investors keep snapping them up.*

**Smart Money**

**IPOs: It can pay to have second thoughts first.**

*Hot, hot, plop. Investment bankers set records in the new-issue market. Investors did not do as well.*

**Stacked Odds**

*Here's a tip on playing the stocks in the steaming new-issue market boom.*

*But with the investment tip come important caveats.*

Over the years we have found that the new-issues market takes on fads and fancies, just like other investment markets. There is an enduring interest in high-tech companies because of the belief that they have an above average chance of growing much more rapidly than other corporations. This means that the investors in such companies will become richer than if they had invested in low-tech companies. Is an Internet dot com a high-tech company? The wisdom of investment strategy is debated daily in the investment circles of Wall Street institutional investors, who range from endowment managers at universities to pension and mutual fund managers. IPOs are hot topics on the chat sites frequented by Internet traders looking for the lastest "buzz" on an upcoming public offering.

All this interest in an IPO puts the pricing of one share of stock into a new zone of financial estimation, scrutiny, techniques, and limits. Publicly traded stocks are compared with recent companies that went IPO, in order to get relative pricing comparisons. Techniques for placing a price on a share of the IPO company's stock range from very crude to very sophisticated, and all this methodology receives the cold test of reality in the real world of stocks that are bought and sold every minute. This is a far cry from the much more private world of the start-up.

At times investors lose most of their money and become angry, believing they were misled by the company and its IPO helpers. The result is a lawsuit. Some companies associated with these legal actions are well known to media readers. Such lawsuits began to become all too familiar in the 1980s and continued in the 1990s in spite of legislation intended to curtail related abuses. For instance, in the August 10, 1987, issue of *Business Monday,* the *San Jose Mercury News* reported on fourteen Silicon Valley companies whose shareholders hit them with lawsuits alleging that investors were misled during stock offerings in the 1982–1983 bull stock market. Four of the defendants made settlements that totaled $50.3 million. In early 1990 several very successful high-tech darlings "hit the wall," slowed their growth unexpectedly, and their stock prices crashed. Oracle and a half dozen others were quickly sued by lawyers specializing in such lawsuits. Most of these legal actions were against established companies, ones that had gone public long ago. But the message is clear: Do not try to get public money if bad news is just around the corner. It is dangerous to try to raise money just before bad news becomes public. The underlying, fundamental problem is the danger of investing in a "shooting star"—a company that gets going well, goes public, but has no staying power and sinks into mediocre financial performance shortly after IPO. It is no wonder that veterans of IPOs with whom we spoke talked a lot about "juryproof prospectuses" and "D&O" (directors and officers) insurance.

Now let's turn to the process of going public, starting with the investment bankers.

# The Role of the Investment Banker

The investment banker will take the central leadership role at the time a company decides to do its first public offering of stock. It is the investment banker and his firm that will gather the lawyers, the analysts, and the many others who are needed to do the work for the IPO. The documents must comply with sophisticated securities laws. The behind-the-scenes workload is enormous and very time-consuming, requiring intense amounts of effort from a lot of people inside and outside the company. The process is complicated and must be done well. The investment banker is hired and paid a very large sum of money as a fee to ensure that the deal is done successfully by all the individuals involved. This job is akin to that of a shepherd herding a flock of sheep into the fold.

**How Investment Bankers Are Organized.** Whether you are interested in a large investment banker, like Goldman Sachs, or a specialist firm like Hambrecht & Quist, an examination of their organization demonstrates what the investment banker really does. The organization consists roughly of the following kinds of people:

- *A pool of new business employees* who call on private companies to screen them and discuss their interest in taking the company public. These specialized sales people ("new business" managers) are usually the CEO's first contacts with the investment banking firm.
- *The corporate finance staff of the investment banker.* This group stands prepared to arrive at the start-up to do the work required after the CEO chooses their firm to do the IPO.
- *The research staff,* people who investigate the start-up once the firm is chosen. They give an independent opinion of the company's quality and the risk and potential of good financial results over the next year or so.

- *The syndication staff,* which assembles a group of other Wall Street firms to insure (underwrite) the IPO so that the risk of the deal can be diversified. Each member signs up to share in supplying capital to back the deal. That group is called the "underwriters."

- *The sales department,* which consists of stockbrokers who offer the new stock to investors, mainly institutional investors. These people are called "institutional sales people."

- *The traders* are those who make a market for the stock by trading it, buying and selling shares in various quantities each minute of the day.

All together, the people mentioned above make up the organization called an investment banking firm. They are also known as stockbrokers and Wall Street firms.

There are many variations of this organizational structure, depending on the various securities that a firm decides to try to make a profit on. For instance, some investment bankers have their own venture capital business that invests along with the classic venture capitalists. Other firms have merger and acquisition departments or departments that make markets in stocks of much larger companies. The giants of Wall Street, such as Goldman Sachs, are full-service organizations that offer virtually any security-related service to investors. Internet investment bankers are the latest version.

Investment banking firms make money in various ways, including charging fees equal to a percentage of the money raised for an IPO. In a good year the owners of these firms make many millions of dollars per person and exceed even the league of riches that venture capitalists range in.

This is a service industry, and the competition is fierce and intense. There is much drama in the behind-the-scenes power plays and politics among Wall Street firms, venture capitalists, and members of the boards of directors of start-up companies. On the other hand, investment bankers try never to miss a chance to do an attractive deal and are therefore rarely confrontational. As one observer told us, "They are always trying to be very polite to everybody."

**Differentiating Investment Banking Firms.** Investment bankers are like venture capitalists: Each person has a distinctive character, and collectively these people make up a firm's unique approach to the business. There are several distinctions that are important to you and your company. The most important is the firm's track record with new issues, as distinct from its experience in raising capital for much larger, more mature companies. We have assembled a list of investment bankers based on those we found most often mentioned as participating in IPO stock offerings of high-tech companies. Table 13-1 lists those firms that have done IPO business in 1998. The top dozen are the giants in the field of high-tech

**Table 13-1. Ranking of Investment Bankers for 1998 IPOs**

| Rank | Managers | $m | Market Share (%) | Number of Issues |
|------|----------|-----|------------------|------------------|
| 1. | Goldman Sachs | $802 | 21.2 | 13 |
| 2. | Bankers Trust/Alex Brown | $420 | 11.1 | 8 |
| 3. | Hambrecht & Quist | $317 | 8.4 | 6 |
| 4. | BankBoston Robertson Stevens | $263 | 7.0 | 8 |
| 5. | Morgan Stanley Dean Witter | $240 | 6.4 | 5 |
| 6. | Bear, Stearns | $226 | 6.0 | 2 |
| 7. | Deutsche Bank | $204 | 5.4 | 5 |
| 8. | Salomon Smith Barney | $183 | 4.9 | 2 |
| 9. | Merrill Lynch | $147 | 3.9 | 2 |
| 10. | Lehman Brothers | $145 | 3.9 | 1 |
| 11. | Bank of America (Montgomery) | $137 | 3.6 | 5 |
| 12. | Credit Suisse First Boston | $131 | 3.5 | 3 |

*Source:* Venture Economics Information Services

start-up IPOs. The remainder are much smaller firms that often focus on limited markets in regional portions of the country. While smaller, these firms often do IPOs that perform well for investors in the post-IPO market. Research by *Forbes* magazine reports that frequently regional firms have done IPOs that outperformed those done by the bigger firms.

Some distinctions are worth noting:

■ *Rising stock prices do not necessarily mean a good investment banker did the deal.* How well an IPO did is a controversial issue. In the Internet era a lot of "dot com" stocks went IPO followed by an immediate huge spike upward in the price of the stock. At first that sounds like a good thing. But a big rise in the publicly traded stock price after the IPO was finished does not necessarily mean the offering was a success. If the rise is too large, the underwriter misjudged the market badly and cost the company millions of dollars. The value represented by the run-up in the stock price went to the pockets of the investment bankers' favored investors at the expense of the start-up's employees and private-round investors. Often such favored investors quickly sell the stock and reap a quick, usually large, windfall profit. This is the often criticized phenomena known as "flipping." And if the stock price sinks back to near the offering price, many investors will be "under water," holding stock worth a lot less than they paid for it.

- *Smaller, regional firms should not be ruled out.* They often have better track records than the larger high-tech specialists or the giants of Wall Street.
- *Competition and the movement of professionals from one firm to another have caused changes in the leadership of the firms that do a lot of IPOs.* In the 1970s, the most often mentioned IPO firms for high-tech companies consisted of the venerable Hambrecht & Quist, Alex Brown, Robertson Colman & Stephens, Montgomery, and L. F. Rothschild, Unterberg and Tobin. The arrival in the early 1980s of Goldman Sachs, Morgan Stanley, and other big names from Wall Street increased the competition for IPOs, and the rankings shifted considerably. And then during the 1990s consolidation set in. For instance, Bank of America bought Robertson Stevens (and through a merger with another bank ended up with Montgomery for a time). Bankers Trust bought Alex Brown (and then Deutsche Bank bought Bankers Trust). And in 1999, Chase Manhattan owned Hambrecht & Quist.
- *By the time the year 2000 arrived, fresh competition in the form of Internet-centric investment bankers arose.* Wit Capital was a successful Internet pioneer and Goldman Sachs later invested in them. Bill Hambrecht resigned from Hambrecht & Quist and formed W. R. Hambrecht & Co. to deliver a fresh way of eliminating IPO stock flipping. Sandy Robertson resigned from Robertson Stevens and later announced he would work with E*Trade to form an Internet-driven IPO firm E*OFFERING. The new arrivals promised companies doing IPOs lower costs without losing quality (and the Securities and Exchange Commission announced in 1999 an investigation into possible price fixing by traditional investment bankers). This fresh form of competition excited the investment community. The related controversy will be interesting to watch as the new century unfolds.
- *Choosing the best research analyst to write about the IPO company is very important.* Choosing an investment banker for a firm should be done carefully, using several criteria, only one of which is the rankings shown in Table 13-1. Veteran CEOs most often said their first and most important selection criterion was which investment banker had the best research analyst. Investment bankers will not do IPOs for direct competitors and thus CEOs had to often settle for their second choices in research analysts.

# How Investment Bankers Make Money

A CEO can do a better job of negotiating and managing the investment bankers if he or she understands how the investment banking firm makes its money on taking a company public. The "fee" that is charged by the investment banking firm is actually not one fee, but a collection of fees granted to various members of the syndicate that team up to take a company public. The name or names on the front cover of the prospectus share the "management fee" for what is called "running the books." This is more than a policeman or accountant type of duty. Those investment bankers have worked hard to get accepted as the lead underwriters and have agreed to be held responsible for the degree of success of the offering. They grant the rest of the syndicate the privilege of participating in sharing the fee.

The number-one position is granted to the firm whose name appears on the left side of the prospectus cover. Although the management fee often is shared equally by the two or three firms on the cover that choose to co-manage the deal, the left-hand position gains reputation and prestige for that firm, particularly for influencing the next IPO candidate company's CEO with respect to how capable the firm is. The research community uses this positioning to create lists such as Table 13-1.

The underwriting fee, which typically is about 7 percent of the capital raised, is shared by the long list of firms that have put up a portion of their firm's capital as a sort of guarantee to back the deal. The fee is split in proportion to the amount of capital the firm agrees to put up to back the deal. This is the least profitable of the investment banking activities, because it is used to cover expenses and is involved in stabilizing the price of the stock in its first days of very risky trading. Bankers regularly spend more than this fee covers. Academic research (such as that done by Roni Michaely of Cornell University's Johnson Graduate School of Management) supports our findings.

The best way for the syndicate to make a great deal of money is to sell as much of the stock as possible. Aggression is extreme among the sales staffs of the firms. The goal is to outsell everyone, regardless of size, and to capture as much of the selling fee—which equals about 60 percent of the whole fee—as is possible. The bankers we interviewed told us that some pretty wild dealing takes place when shares allocated to one firm that cannot sell all of its shares are offered to other firms that have obtained orders for more than their allotments.

**Green Shoe.** Green Shoe is an overallotment option (to buy stock at a fixed price), which is given by the IPO company to the investment bankers doing the IPO. For instance, Sun Microsystems granted a thirty-day option to their investment bankers, co-led by Robertson Stephens & Company, to purchase up to 600,000 shares at the IPO price.

The over allotment shares are used to supply extra shares needed when an IPO is "hot" and (in oversimplified terms) more investors want shares than are available. This is part of a complex process, what is known as "making an orderly market for the stock," and is an important responsibility of the lead underwriter.

Unlike the underwriting contract for the IPO shares, which obligates the underwriters to buy all the IPO shares at the IPO price, there is no obligation to the investment bankers to purchase any of these additional shares.

In effect, this appears to be a "bonus" to the underwriters, because if the aftermarket price rises to above the IPO price within thirty days, then the underwriters may purchase the extra shares at the lower IPO price, sell them to investors at the higher market price, and pocket the difference as a profit. For instance, the Sun shares were offered at $16 each. A 20 percent increase in thirty days to $19.25 would mean $1.95 million in additional profit for the underwriters, in addition to their fee of $3.92 million—a 50 percent boost! While that sounds like a windfall, research by Michaels and others shows it is most often used up (at no profit to the underwriter) as a cost of supporting the market for trading the stock after the IPO!

# The Cost of Doing an IPO

Investment bankers first sign a company to an exclusive contract to do the IPO. The contract includes charging the company for certain of the expenses they incur in doing the deal, plus a percentage of the total capital raised. The CPA and legal expenses can easily be $500,000 for even a small $25 million offering. The "underwriters' commission" or "investment banker's fee" is in the vicinity of 6 percent to 12 percent (mostly 7 percent) of the total offering, including any capital sold in the IPO by selling shareholders.

These expenses are probably the most costly a start-up ever incurs because, under U.S. federal and state tax laws, none of them are tax-deductible. Thus, if the combined tax rate were 42 percent for a company, a 7 percent fee (including expenses) would be the equivalent of 12 percent pretax cost of IPO money!

The fee is negotiated between the company and the investment banking firm. It includes many subsets of fees, each composing a pool for many participants doing many tasks. They are broken down into two main groups: the fee of the investment banker, and all the other expenses. These are discussed in detail below.

**Details of IPO Expenses.** To start with, assume a start-up chooses to raise $10 million in a very small IPO, with all the capital going to the company and no selling shareholders. The costs for such an offering would be about 9 percent to 12 percent of the $10 million raised. The exact amount of expenses depends on three factors:

**Table 13-2. The Cost of a $10 Million IPO**

| | |
|---|---|
| *Underwriter's commission* | $850,000 (8.5%) |
| *Other Expenses:* | |
|     Legal fees | $120,000 |
|     Printing the prospectus | $90,000 |
|     Accounting firm's fee | $80,000 |
|     State registration (Blue Sky) expense | $20,000 |
|     Stock transfer agent | $4,000 |
|     SEC registration fee | $2,000 |
|     National Association of Securities Dealers fee | $1,000 |
|     All other expenses | $15,000 |
|     Total Other Expenses | $332,000 (3.3%) |
|     Total All Expenses | $1,182,000 (11.8%) |
| Total Capital Raised | $10,000,000 (100%) |

*Source:* Grant Thornton, Capital Markets Group

1. The *size of the deal.* The larger deals have the lower percentage costs, but the absolute dollars of expenses get very substantial.
2. The *degree of work* that lawyers and auditors must go through to clean up the books and records of the company and to convert them into a satisfactory prospectus.
3. The *amount of competition* between the investment bankers desiring to do an IPO and degree of difficulty they anticipate in selling investors on buying the stock offered by the company.

Table 13-2 contains a list of expenses for a small new issue. It was compiled by an investment industry group that sought to issue a list of "typical costs" of going public. It is for a very small underwriting, $10 million.

IPO costs—as a percentage of the value of all the shares sold in the IPO—rise rapidly as the deal gets smaller. This occurs because the amount of work to raise $10 million is about the same as the amount of work to raise $25 million. The top investment bankers will strongly advise a start-up to raise as much as possible, at least in the region of $25 million. Of course, this also increases the absolute dollars of fee or "commission" for the investment banker and syndicate.

The percentage represented by "Other Expenses" shown in Table 13-2 is larger than in most of the actual IPOs that we have analyzed; this is largely because the IPOs we examined were mostly in the region of $25 million or more. It was not unusual for other expenses in the Internet dot com prospectuses we reviewed to total nearly $1 million or more, or about 2 percent of the capital raised. This percentage was more consistent than we anticipated. We had hypothesized that these expenses were rather fixed and not dependent on the amount of capital raised. But while our sample was small, our findings suggest that the participants—especially lawyers and accountants—may incur and bill their fees as some implicit percentage of the capital offered, just as the investment bankers do.

CEOs who have done IPOs recommend that a first-time CEO should set and adhere to a budget for each item on the Other Expenses list, using the same level of judgment as for any other service supplied to a company. The amount of cash expenses that could be saved by the company appears to be considerable, perhaps lowering the costs by as much as 20 percent.

**Microsoft IPO.** Table 13-3 contains our estimates of the details of what made up the fee charged in one of the most famous IPOs in history, the Microsoft offering of March 13, 1986. IPOs since then, including those in the 1990s, show that very similar results prevail today. The Microsoft deal shows the magnitude of a large IPO offering. In terms of percentages it is therefore a good measure of the efficiency of the costs charged to a company going public. CEOs told us they would expect that a less famous company will probably incur somewhat greater expenses.

Table 13-3 uses the Microsoft IPO as a basis for estimating the approximate fees received by each member of the investment banking group. Because the actual details are private, the data in the table is an estimate of the approximate compensation earned by one of the co-lead bankers, Goldman Sachs. Goldman is considered by most to be number one in the world in doing equity deals of various sizes and types, and a firm of unequaled high character. The estimate is based on discussions with underwriters who were not in that deal but who compete with Goldman and others for IPOs. The exact numbers are less important than the reader's appreciation for what motivates the investment banking group to behave as it does to earn the larger portion of the overall fee.

An analysis of the costs charged Microsoft reveal the following:

- The $58.7 million offering in this IPO is about double the size of many offerings of other highly successful companies that go public. This suggests that the efficiency of the cash cost per dollar raised by an IPO company will go up as the size of the deal rises (if one uses percentages to measure efficiency).
- The fee of 6.24 percent was consistent with the range of fees charged in simi-

## Table 13-3. Economics of an Initial Public Offering: The Microsoft IPO

| | | | |
|---|---|---|---|
| Size of Microsoft IPO | $58,695,000 | | |
| × | | | |
| Total fee of whole investment banking group | × 6.24% | | |
| Total financing fee = | $3,661,450 | | |

| | | | |
|---|---|---|---|
| Total financing fee | $3,661,450 | | |
| × | | | |
| Proportion for the managers who are "running the books"; "Names on the front cover of the prospectus" | × 20% | = | 1.248% |
| Management fee (often split equally between the managers) = | $732,290/2 | = | $366,145/mgr. |

| | | | |
|---|---|---|---|
| Total financing fee | $ 3,661,450 | | |
| × | | | |
| Underwriting fee for syndicate of underwriters | × 20% | = | 1.248% |
| Underwriters fee | $732,290 | | |
| × | | | |
| Proportion for each underwriter set by number of shares underwritten; share for lead firm = | × 15.76% | = | 440,500 shares |
| | | | 2,795,000 all shares |
| Lead firm's share of underwriters' fee | $115,409 | | |

| | | | |
|---|---|---|---|
| Total financing fee | $3,661,450 | | |
| × | | | |
| Fee for selling stock | × 60% | = | 3.744% |
| Selling commission = | $2,196,870 | | |
| × | | | |
| Proportion for lead firm: Assume they sold 20% of the Microsoft IPO shares | × 20% | | |
| Selling commission for lead firm = | $439,374 | | |

### SUMMARY

| Total Fee | | Lead Firm's Share (Estimated) |
|---|---|---|
| *Managers* | | |
| $732,290 | 1.25% | $366,145 |
| *Underwriters* | | |
| $732,290 | 1.25% | $115,409 |
| *Sales* | | |
| $2,196,870 | 3.74% | $439,374 |
| *Total financing fee* | | |
| $ 3,661,450 | 6.24% | $920,928 |

*Source:* Saratoga Venture Finance

lar-size offerings. The split of the Microsoft fee shown in Table 13-3 is esti-mated. Actual fees, splits, and amounts are uniquely negotiated by partici-pants in each deal, depending on several factors, mainly size of the IPO capital to be raised. A fee closer to 7 percent or higher would be more typical for a $25 million IPO.

- Fees can be negotiated downward some distance below any so-called normal range. Some CEOs believe competition works in such negotiating situations. The CEO should try to set the target lower than 7 percent and get agreement to it before signing the underwriting contract. Some of the new Internet-centric investment bankers are charging less, in the range of 4 percent. In fact, some CEOs think it may be desirable to make the fee a primary determinant in choosing an investment banker.

- Not shown in Table 13-3 is a category called Other Expenses, which are in ad-dition to the investment bankers' fee. For Microsoft, the total Other Expenses (for CPA firm, lawyers, and special prospectus printer) were $541,000, or 0.92 percent of capital raised. These expenses are first revealed on the cover of the prospectus. They can be as high as 2% of the IPO.

- In the case of the Microsoft deal, we do not know exactly what the final fee was for each participant. But we believe we are pretty close in estimating that Goldman Sachs made at least $1 million on that offering. At the end of the day, everyone we spoke to said that they could appreciate how hard Goldman Sachs worked to earn its share of the fee.

- As for profit, it is much less than the calculated $3,661,450. Usually all of the portion called the underwriters' fee is used to pay expenses of doing the deal, supporting the post-IPO trading in the stock, and the end is often a small loss on this portion of the deal. The selling commission requires paying for the costs of the personnel doing the work as well as their related overheads, as does the fee for running the books. The pretax bottom line for the deal was probably about $2 million, about half the gross fee of $3.7 million.

For more recent IPOs, CEOs can analyze the prospectuses of comparible IPOs and look at examples in the Saratoga Venture Tables™ at the end of this book.

## The Role of Institutional Investors

The power brokers in the world of publicly traded securities are institutional in-vestors. That is also true for the IPO deals. Wealthy individuals are somewhat of a factor. In the Internet era, "day traders" became a significant factor. (They are in-dividuals who actively buy and sell IPO stocks, particularly speculative Internet stocks. They hold the investments for short periods of time, days or hours. They use "chat rooms" to exchange information about stock trading. They trade via their personal computers connected to discount brokerage firms communicating over the Internet.) However, the giant institutional investors who favor long-term investing remain dominant in IPO trading as in the other stocks traded over the NASDAQ and New York stock exchanges.

Investment bankers work hard to be the firm that gets to place the purchase orders for the institutions that buy shares in a new issue. Salespeople told us that the competition for sales and trading commissions is fierce. Investment bankers are eager for the buying customer to make a gain on the IPO stock. Several individuals said they believed this desire causes a strong bias against overpricing the opening trading price of the stock of a new issue. The necessary role of the investment banker is to delicately balance a nice increase in the price of the stock of the new issue on the one hand against the danger of being embarrassed because of an unexpectedly wild up and down ride in the stock's price in the after market. In the pre-Internet era, too much run-up and the selling company would be upset because it had to sell too many shares to get the funds it wanted; too little rise in the price and the buying institutions would be upset because they want to count on a solid price increase. By 2000, it seemed everything had reversed: an IPO whose stock price did not triple or more was considered a dud!

Although the company is paying the fee and expenses, the investment bankers are not really working for the company doing the IPO. Over the years they have changed to become oriented more to very short-term transactions and less to long-term relationships. Many decades ago the investment banker sat on a company's board forever and advised it on financing strategies. Today the economic forces at work cause these bankers to race from deal to deal, concerned about how to make as much money as possible for their customers—the institutional investors who have billions to invest every day. Although the bankers try to retain and nurture long-term relationships, one can really expect most investment bankers' interest in a company to be limited to the next deal that they can do for it. The competition in their business is fierce, and they must be on their way, chasing the next deal as soon as the current one is done. They have a short attention span. Some venture capitalists compared such behavior to that of used-car salespeople and real estate brokers. We consider this remark unfair to the quality investment banker. Start-ups need strong Wall Street firms. This controversial situation presents additional problems in post-IPO relations with Wall Street, which we will discuss later in this chapter.

Together, the investment banker and the institutional investors are very powerful, and they can make a lot of money. *Financial World* magazine estimates that the ten most highly paid Wall Street professionals—investment bankers or institutional money managers—earned an average of $68.8 million per person in 1986, and in research about the 1990s showed many Wall Street partners earning in excess of $20 million per year. The IPO hot year of 1999 made many Wall Street people very rich. Such powerful, wealthy people represent a group that must be respected, one that must be incorporated into plans for a company's capital formation.

## Choosing an Investment Banker

Choosing an investment banker is exciting. The choice involves making selections that are not black and white, but the right choice is important. The consensus of start-up CEOs is that a good choice can make a large positive difference, while a poor choice can compromise a company's future well-being.

While a company is still private, the CEO will receive a few phone calls from new business professionals of investment banking firms. They are checking to see whether the company should be on their list of target accounts.

Once a company is on an investment banker's list, the CEO can expect to receive a lot of flattering attention, as will the members of its board of directors. The goal of the banker is to lock up the lead position, to become the designated manager who runs the books and thus earns a nice IPO fee. Because there is intense competition between firms for the handful of top IPOs each year, a CEO of a promising start-up has an excellent starting point from which to begin the selection process.

For the company ready for an IPO, any of the top twenty Wall Street firms could get the job done. But just getting the money in the bank is not enough. After the IPO, someone has to help make a good market for the stock. The degree of attention by Wall Street investors is a direct function of the amount and quality of research reports written about a company by the underwriting firm's analysts. Furthermore, some firms have business reputations that a CEO would prefer to associate with or avoid. And board members, particularly venture capitalists, will also have various, often strong, opinions about which firm to choose.

Here is the advice of experienced high-tech CEOs on choosing an investment banking firm:

■ *Start by finding the best research analyst, one who understands the industry and technology.* This is the person who will interpret a technology and its business applications for the salespeople pushing the stock. It is also the person who will go on the "road show" with the CEO, when the CEO stands up before institutional investors to tout the company's good future. It is the analyst who will take precious time to write long reports about the company's chances of success and its products. A company's customers and employees will read those reports. Never pick an investment banker who lacks a top research analyst—one who is familiar with and respected as an analyst of the company's technology and who favors that industry. A CEO can identify the top analysts easily by conferring with an experienced CFO of a large public company in the same industry.

- *Pick a firm known for its integrity.* This is very important because of the abuses and poor service that some technologically astute but financially naïve companies have had over the past years. Most well-known firms have retained high reputations, but some have grown tarnished over the past years. Presidents of some IPO companies have told us in strictest confidence of shockingly unethical misdeeds of the bankers who led their underwriting. The CEOs complained that their companies had suffered from the misuse of information and that post-IPO support dwindled to near zero. They also complained of questionable stock trades by bankers that they soon grew to mistrust. We concluded that the best check on investment bankers is to talk privately with the CEOs and CFOs who have done IPOs in bad times as well as good times. One can learn as much from the reasons a firm was not picked—or would not be picked for the next offering—as from the reasons it was chosen. Such work should be treated as seriously as a reference check of a key candidate for a vice presidency in the company.

- *Look for managers who are businesslike, people whom it would be desirable to work and be associated with.* As with picking an accounting or law firm, the CEO should be looking for character as well as competence. It is important to be methodical and thoughtful and to avoid being distracted by flattery. You want the best the company can attract. CEOs unfamiliar with the Wall Street crowd should start with the person who will manage the deal. It is important to look for characteristics that indicate the presence of a good business person, someone that can negotiate well on the founders' behalf, someone who can be trusted. One good way to find this person is to attend the many meetings and investor conferences put on by investment bankers to expose the newest in high-tech companies to institutional investors. Dinners and lunches over a period of a year or so are also advised. This is an important decision and should not be made in haste.

- *Compare statistics on IPO successes and failures.* The post-IPO facts are important, as well as how many and how much capital was raised. The CEO should look for the bias of the banker; some have stronger retail and mutual fund customers than wholesale or institutional. The bankers themselves will each supply data, and the CEO can compare the facts presented by each firm. *Forbes* magazine and other publications also closely scrutinize IPO and investment banking firms' performance.

■ *Be sure to check out how thoroughly the banker's research analyst followed and wrote about the IPOs that the firm took public.* Some CEOs told us of poor post-IPO service and were bitter about the "greediness" and "grab and run" attitudes of their bankers. CEOs with recent IPO experience can be helpful. The start-up CEO should talk to them about their experiences with (or without) the finalists on the list for investment banker. Note that analysts quite often move between firms. The analyst who did a good job for banker A may now work for banker B.

The importance of the analyst in selection of an investment banker is noted in this classic piece by Raymond Moran, then the director of research of Cowen and Company, a strong investment research and banking player in the personal-computer era (his message applies just as well today). Moran's comment reflects our findings as we spoke with CEOs who went through the IPO process:

A research analyst with superior understanding of a client's business and needs improves the ability to better position the company and communicate its long-term value in a highly credible manner.

And here is the suggestion of one of the grand veterans of high-tech IPOs, Sandy Robertson, founder of Robertson Stevens in San Francisco:

I recommend that CEOs looking for an IPO investment banker should seek a firm where everyone in the organization understands the company's industry and business. This is especially important because an IPO is a chain of events—each critical to the success of the delicate IPO. Each person in the investment banking firm—corporate finance, research analyst, syndicate, sales, trading, and 144 stock administration—has to be successful when it is their time to carry the ball. To have a single expert in your high-tech industry just won't get the job done. An IPO is too important to be left up to generalists or an individual. Everyone must be competent, experienced with high-tech IPOs, able to team up and do their part, and do it well for the IPO to be a success. That is what to look for when picking your investment banker.

And finally, here is the advice of Goldman Sachs to a CEO selecting an investment banker:

The selection of an investment banker involves both near-term and long-term criteria. For the purposes of executing a successful IPO, the investment bank should be actively involved in leading a significant number of equity offerings of high-quality technology companies. The investment bank should have a strong research presence in technology in general and in the company's business in particular, and should provide active trading markets and significant distribution capabilities. Since the choice of an investment banker represents a commitment to a longer term relationship as well, the banker's capabilities should also be able to accommodate a company's anticipated growing and changing needs. The firm should project a global presence that provides its clients with access to capital markets and other opportunities throughout the world. The investment bank should have capabilities, experience, and dedicated resources in the areas of mergers, acquisitions, joint ventures, and strategic alliances. In addition, the bank should be able to provide advice and expertise in areas that will likely become important over time, such as real estate/headquarters financing and foreign exchange. Finally, but very important, a CEO should feel comfortable with the members of the prospective investment banking team and its firm's long-standing commitment to technology and its clients.

# The Initial Public Offering—The Holy Grail

A CEO will be better equipped to run a company while it is private if he or she understands how important the IPO event is to each participant in the IPO process. This perspective helps the CEO get the company tuned up and in good shape as it approaches the magic IPO date. This is an important part of planning, because the CEO may have to halt R&D expansion for a while or put on an extra heavy sales staff to boost revenues. The toughest decisions for the CEO will be to consider doing something that would be good in the short term for the IPO but could be bad for the success of the company three years or so later.

**Employees.** Psychological research reveals that every one of us wants to belong to a group, preferably a successful one. The IPO creates just that situation, as well as creating a pool of wealth that employees can share in. In reality, only a few people make a financial killing as an employee, except in unusual conditions such as with Yahoo and the early years of the Internet revolution. In fact, behavioral scientists note that, rather than actual wealth, the primary stimulant to people on payroll is the association of belonging to a company that is an observable winner.

These people want to believe in themselves, in their leaders, and in the whole company as winners. This success orientation was borne out by our talks with doctors, psychologists, and family counselors at hospitals and clinics in Silicon Valley.

When a company finally goes public, the CEO is fully exposed and must live in the spotlight, explaining disappointments as well as achievements to a vast audience that tends to be highly critical of the company and its leadership. "The press seem to be looking for the negative more than the good results," lamented one CEO.

The management of employees goes a lot better when the stock price continues to rise; no one sells his or her stock then. But eventually the price will drop. Then the party comes to an end, and the reality of hard work returns. CEOs warned: "Too much IPO fever is like too much alcohol—it produces hangovers." When Microsoft got to IPO, Bill Gates was concerned that having the company's stock public would adversely distract employees. Similar comments have been heard from CEOs of Internet-era companies whose stock prices rocketed upward after the IPO. And remember: sky-high stock prices make stock options less attractive to prospective employees.

Finally, the CEO should keep in mind that missing an IPO window can be very demoralizing to employees. It is hard to avoid building up expectations, but keeping the IPO dreams farther away than nearer is better than having to deal with a tired crew that has just had its balloon pop.

**Founders.** To the original core team, the IPO means a lot—especially as the reality sinks in and the bank account begins to grow in riches. Lives change. Families change. People change.

Some told us that the reward is having recognition and fame at last. To others it was the arrival at a peer level with some role model in the high-tech world. Some people frankly said that it was pleasant to get revenge of sorts on the venture firms and business colleagues that turned them down or said that they would never succeed.

In cases we have observed firsthand, founders exhibited an enormous zeal to get to IPO time, some willing to pay almost any price—to their friends or their families. This appeared especially evident as the company came within a year or so of the first IPO date. Loyalties appeared to shift to the faction that favored an earlier IPO date. Pressure mounted to "get public while we can." And we also detected a tendency for founders to believe that "after the IPO, things will get back to normal."

**Investors.** Venture capitalists view the IPO as the date to get liquid. They told us that they work hard to get this far, enduring great risks, disappointments, and hard times. At last the day comes when they can begin to distribute shares to limited partners, rack up another high ROI in their portfolios, and seek out fresh money to manage, based on the latest successes.

The pressure on a VC to get his companies public is enormous. The VC does not run the operation of the start-ups; that must be left to much less experienced people, often with questionable track records. The possibility of a rising star turning into a fading star is always there, as history shows. Markets can turn against the start-up while it is still private. Microsoft or some other giant can make (and more than once has made) a surprise move that ruins the tiny company's bright prospects.

Stock markets cannot be counted on. They move up and down, with little the CEO can do but watch. IPO stocks move in and out of fashion. When the new-issues market is dull or dead, the VC must risk more capital and invest to keep the private company alive, further draining funds intended for investment in other new enterprises. When the new-issues market is hot, the VC can sleep better at night because the windows of liquidation opportunity are wide open and unlikely to close in a day or so. Dave Anderson of venture capital firm Sutter Hill noted that the venture community is excited when IPO conditions are excellent, but that as soon as the stock market's success flattens or turns down, the venture capital community gets much less euphoric. This happened after the great stock market crash on Wall Street on October 19, 1987. But by early February 1988 the first IPOs appeared with more rumored to be coming soon. The long-running IPO window that opened in 1990 was very good to start-ups, especially the Internet-intensive ones. Good days in the post-IPO stock market make for great prices per share in each IPO. More IPO successes mean more fresh money for VCs, and they too are happy. This positive trend was still going as 2000 arrived.

Because of these factors, the VC is not friendly to anyone who would hinder one of his private companies from going public. This includes founders who logically argue for waiting because the changes to the company plan might reduce its long-term potential.

## The Process of Going Public

Vast numbers of books and articles have been written to educate the CEO on the process of going public. There are many other fine publications available from the top accounting firms and from the specialized printers of prospectuses. They are updated often, and most are free—just call one of their local offices for a copy or look them up on the Internet.

The value in these documents is that they serve as discussion pieces for planning sessions with the company's staff, lawyers, and accountants prior to going public. The real education comes in actually doing an IPO. When searching for the right VP of finance, the CEO should look for someone who has some experience with an IPO.

**Timing Is Everything.** Nothing is so disheartening as missing the boat. "Get the IPO done when it can be done," said several veteran board members of start-ups. Some famous misses include Internet pioneers *Wired* magazine and PointCast.

A close second to missing the IPO (for another year or so) is selling a new issue into a softening market, going out at $6 a share instead of $16—only to see the market rebound and the price explode up to $19 per share shortly thereafter.

Treasurers are specialists in timing successful financings, but few have yet to become CFOs of high-tech companies. Occasionally the original CFO is very experienced at picking the timing of the IPO, but that is not common, and the necessary judgment and wisdom is commonly defaulted to the VCs on the board of the company.

Investment bankers are skilled at sensing the opportunity for good timing of a new issue. They are eager to do deals and will sense even the tightest window available to squeeze the deal through. They do not want a slow-selling deal because that means they get stuck with "inventory," stock that remains unsold because not enough buyers could be found on the day the IPO was sold. The underwriting firms can lose millions on a bad day if the stock market plunges and the new issue price follows the drop. Thus the banker does not want to overprice a deal and will instead underprice the stock a bit to cover the risk. The banker would prefer to sell into a rising stock market than into a flat or declining one. The banker will also know when the road show has produced enough oversubscription and will call it off and close the deal while it is hot. The short-term timing of an IPO should be left up to the lead investment banker. CEO thinking should be concentrated on getting into a financial condition that will give the company the flexibility and luxury of choosing the best date to go public. Financial flexibility is worth a lot. Table 13-4 lists six ranked reasons most often cited by the participants for going public. Another factor that sometimes plays a part is the number of stockholders. Securities and Exchange Commission regulations require the shares of a private company to be registered when the number of shareholders reaches five hundred. For example, Microsoft went public just as the number of shareholders was approaching five hundred.

**Participants, Practices, and Principles.** The group that is assembled to do the company's IPO will work together very closely over a short, intense period of weeks. Their first focus will be to get the prospectus written, along with the related SEC registration documents. Here is what IPO veterans say about the participants in an IPO:

- *Lawyers.* There will be two law firms, one representing the company, the other the investment banker. They should send partners to do the work; no one else can make the necessary on-the-spot decisions that are needed to keep the work progressing quickly over the inevitable hurdles.

   The job of the legal people is to keep their client from getting too exposed

**Table 13-4. Factors Triggering the Timing of Going Public**

1. **Capital Needed:** Start-up needs capital in such a large amount that a private placement would be difficult.

2. **Cheaper Cost:** IPO costs less than another round of venture capital.

3. **Cash In Chips:** Everyone wants to get liquid, particularly the venture capitalists.

4. **Large Enough:** Start-up is now large enough and profitable enough to take public.

5. **Hot Stock Market:** Stock market is "hot" and hungry for IPOs of new high-tech companies.

6. **Prestige:** Management, employees, board of directors, and venture capitalists want the fame and glory of being associated with a "successful high-tech company."

7. **Number of Stockholders:** Securities and Exchange Commission regulations require the shares of a private company to be registered when the number of shareholders reaches five hundred.

*Source:* Saratoga Venture Finance

in the written documents. They will fight each other over trade-offs between who should be more or less exposed, the company or the underwriters. Both law firms are trying to write a document that fully complies with securities law, tells an exciting story about the company, and, in case of lawsuit, is easily defensible, or "juryproof."

These high-tech-experienced lawyers are very expensive and scarce. Picking carefully can save expenses. The rules of thumb are: the farther from New York City the better; the farther from major cities the cheaper. Many smaller law firms familiar with high-tech start-ups are very experienced in public securities law. They are familiar with the start-up company and can do an excellent job. The investment banker's counsel should be from a firm as close to the company's location as possible and familiar with high-tech deals; the CEO should insist on this. The costs are likely to be lower because the hourly rate will be cheaper. Understanding of the business, industry, and technology will be there in depth.

- *Accountants.* The CPA firms will be trying to get the company's books to balance for all of the past five years and to comply 100 percent with GAAP (Generally Accepted Accounting Principles). If the books have been kept up to date from the beginning, the accountants will be preparing the company for the IPO date and there should be no surprises. Using personal computer–based accounting systems for even the earliest stages of a start-up is also helpful in getting the books ready for public offering time without as much cleanup work as in the past. The partners of accounting firms are very aware of the many lawsuits that arose from the 1982–1983 IPO boom (unfortunately they continued as 2000 arrived), such as the precedent-setting Osborne Computer lawsuit against auditor Arthur Young by venture capitalists. Before the partner signs the formal CPA firm's opinion that a company's books are clean, it is the partner's job to be sure that all the numbers have been checked many times over.

The accounting fee for the IPO is expensive, but it is not as large as it seems because the IPO-related work carries over to the annual audit, which uses much of the IPO accounting work. The IPO does, however, begin a new era of life for the company. The lower rates charged by the auditor for a fledgling start-up company no longer apply. The company will also be required to file SEC documents each year and will be charged additional auditing fees for the new SEC filings such as 10-Qs and 10-Ks.

- *Investment Bankers.* The lead investment bankers' teams must include the top high-tech partner in at least a couple of the meetings, and a senior corporate finance veteran in all the sessions. The firms will be sure to have several very young people doing a lot of the detailed, grubby work, chasing down facts and figures, fetching the needed materials from the company's accounting and other staffs. The bankers must make the prospectus sound at least interesting, if not a bit exciting, without increasing the risk of lawsuits. The partners will be extremely busy, typically simultaneously doing several other deals. One sign of this is that they constantly leave the work room to make phone calls during the drafting of your prospectus.

  Most of all, the lead investment banker wants the SEC papers prepared and filed as soon as possible to avoid missing any window of opportunity to get the deal out and finished.

- *Printers.* There are specialist printing companies whose sole job is to print, in strictest confidence, 100-percent accurate securities documents such as prospectuses in large quantities, at any time of day or night, and distribute them in hours to virtually any location of the world.

  These printers are very expensive as printers go, and charge for every edit and change. Their bills are usually far over the budget they submitted in their bid for the job. They will be able to document every charge to the penny, attributing every change to instructions from the prospectus team. The key to keeping the bills lower is to submit only the final—or nearly final—draft to the printer and to use all the electronic tools possible to cut down manual labor in these mostly union shops.

**Practices and Principles.** The lead investor is the controller of the IPO working group, and is held responsible for adhering to the agreed-upon schedule.

The attorneys will be expected to compromise along the way and still produce a juryproof prospectus. The attorneys will try to eliminate any exaggerated claims made by the company's marketing staff in its aggressive efforts to sell to customers and to the industry media.

The due diligence work is the double-checking done by the underwriters and the CPA firm. They will carefully check the facts claimed in the prospectus by the company. The investment banker has the freedom to challenge any figure or claim made.

"Get it done" is the slogan of the whole IPO team, especially as the second week of work proceeds. Life can get pretty agonizing as draft after draft follows change after change. To quote an investment banker who was one of the Microsoft IPO working group; "As usual, it was like the Bataan death march."

**Writing the Prospectus.** The key to understanding a prospectus is to know that it is never used to sell the company's stock. That is the job of the investment banker's sales staff and is the reason the road show is so important.

The prospectus is a foundation document that marks a point in the life of the company. It is like a written business plan—its importance diminishes quickly as time passes.

As a result, things said by management to potential investors become more important than things written. At this point, practices that were acceptable for a private company must begin to be more disciplined. This applies particularly to statements by company officers about forecasts of sales or profits. Officers used to telling customers or employees about the company's planned results must be trained to restrain themselves after the IPO date, because such projections have fueled lawsuits.

## Pricing the Shares

When leading Alex Brown's corporate finance group, Dick Franyo said, "I let the market tell us the price of each IPO." He feels that his firm's job is to fairly present the company to potential buyers and let them make up their minds on the price at which to sell the shares.

That is the reason the research analyst's opinion is so important and the road show is taken so seriously. The road show is a trip organized by the investment banker. It takes the CEO and the company's top management to the big money market cities. Over a week or more of whirlwind meetings, the CEO's team endures countless breakfasts, lunches, and dinners; then, in the mornings and afternoons, it endures making presentations to selected institutional investors who have expressed interest in buying shares of the company.

The IPO share prices are determined by the market makers in much the same way that they set prices for the stocks of larger companies with longer track records. The most obvious difference is in the strong emphasis on the future—especially the growth in earnings and magnitude of return on invested capital of the new company, which is less than five years old. Special attention is given to the likelihood that the company will have excellent results over the next twelve months. In addition, the "uniqueness" of the company is examined closely. Managers are looked squarely in the eyes so that investors can decide whether the (usually) young management can continue to keep the company on the road to success.

Institutional salespeople from investment bankers are looking for "a good story"—their term for the company that has the best prospects for explosive success but that has not yet been discovered by the larger investment community. They try to find good stories, get their customers into the stock, and then turn their find over to the "herd," hopefully to get the demand for the limited supply of stock to drive the price up. Weekly meetings with the research and corporate staffs of investment bankers focus on the details of the outlook for companies that the investment banker is close to, including the IPOs. The salespeople grill their counterparts to test the suggestions and investment opinions presented, then proceed to their phones and round up orders from clients around the globe, from Tokyo and Singapore to London and Paris, as well as throughout the United States.

While all of this activity is going on, the traders in the syndicate are testing the market with their colleagues in the firm. They must decide how to handle oversubscriptions if the stock gets hot and demand exceeds supply (that is the role for the extra shares waiting on standby in the form of the underwriter's option). Similarly, they must be prepared to act if interest in the stock dwindles and the inventory of shares that the underwriters bought from the company is in danger of remaining unsold. If the expectations for preliminary demand for the stock are not met, the company may change its mind on the number of new shares to be offered, as well as on any amounts of shares to be sold by selling shareholders. This in turn will influence the price.

By the time the IPO is ready to go public, the whole focus is on setting the "strike price," or the exact price at which shares will be sold to the investment banker (who will immediately sell them to waiting investors). The size of the order book and the ratio of orders to available stock will influence the final decision to increase or decrease the number of shares offered, or to change the intended price. In the end, the judgment of the investment banker will be relied upon to set the exact price. The agreed-upon price is then fixed, checks are exchanged, and the shares become the property of the underwriters. They, of course, hope to hold the shares for only a few minutes, selling the whole lot and the Green Shoe as quickly as possible.

**Comparables.** Investment bankers rely heavily upon comparables to price an IPO. They prefer to look for companies in the same or a related business and use those companies as a guide to pricing the new issue. The more unusual the company, the more the bankers run into difficulty using this technique. The start-up's bankers will prepare such data for its deal and the CEO will be able to see and review the data with them. The CEO can also request that the investment banker prepare similar data on any company with which the CEO wants to compare his company.

**Ratios.** Comparables still do not answer the question, "What numbers do the investors look at to make a pricing decision?" That is the subject of hot debate among investors worldwide, but it has been well researched over the past twenty-five years. The truth is that a few leaders set the prices and the herd follows. The numbers that the leaders look at most are future expectations (not history) of cash flow (not profits) and operating earnings tax adjusted (not net income), and return on invested capital (not earnings per share). The more important figures and ratios used are shown in Table 13-5. These primary factors are then converted into traditional financial statements in projected form and translated to price per share and multiples of revenue.

The CEO can forecast the numbers for his own company and apply the ratios used by research analysts, thereby reaching a decision on what the stock price should be. This will help in dissecting the reasoning the investment banker uses in setting the stock offering price. It will also help the CEO decide whether to hold off and wait for a better stock market or go now for a sure deal but at a lower price.

# What Constitutes a Successful IPO?

Deciding what constitutes success in an IPO is worth thinking about, because the difference between a good and a bad IPO is worth millions in value to the company.

**Potential Problems and Pitfalls.** The central problem is picking the timing of the IPO. Waiting can be risky if business slips away from the company, but waiting can mean higher sales and greater value per share. There are also legal pitfalls linked to the post-IPO business performance of the company. The dangers of a

**Table 13-5. Quantitative Factors Used By Leaders to Set Stock Prices**

- **Multiple of Revenue.** This is the price of the stock market value of the company divided by the total annual sales of the company. Sometimes revenue per customer is used.

- **Cash Flow from Operations.** This is the sum of the cash in and out of the business—before considering the effect of cash from sources of financing.

- **Growth Rate of Business Profits.** This is the rate of growth of the operating profit, not the "bottom line," which is distorted by interest income (surplus cash) and expenses (capital structure).

- **Return on Invested Capital:** This measures return as the operating profit adjusted for taxes divided by capital. Capital equals the total of all capital (interest-bearing plus equity) already invested in the company. The higher the return, the higher the worth of the company (per share).

- **Likely ROI from Capital That Has Yet to Be Put to Work:** This measures the possible return over extended future periods from the company's investing fresh money in new projects such as R&D on new technology and new products.

- **Requirement for Fresh Capital Needed to Run the Business.** This determines the "cash flow" requirement of the company, measuring the amount of fresh capital needed each year to support the company's planned growth.

- **Financial Structure:** This measures the proportion of total capital that will be in the form of interest-bearing capital the company intends to use. This is then converted to a measure of risk. More and more debt per dollar of total capital will increase risk and reduce the worth of the company (per share). However, debt is cheaper than equity because of the tax deductibility of interest expenses. Thus, more debt reduces the company's cost of capital. This increases the worth of the company (per share).

*Source:* Saratoga Venture Finance

lawsuit are quite real. In one classic case, founder Gene Amdahl personally had to pay $2.4 million in one lawsuit. Legal actions are daily pending on many more millions of dollars for companies whose stock prices plunged after their IPO.

On the other hand, missing the window can be very costly. There is an old treasurers' saying: Take your money while you can get it. There are companies that have been waiting for a good part of a decade because they missed their chance while an industry boom was on.

IPO investors are very picky about the companies in which they choose to invest. Investment bankers familiar with IPOs said this about what their people look for: "Comparables are less important. We look at the uniqueness of their concept, barriers to entry, size of their market, management quality, and the downside risks."

The post-IPO price of the stock is of intense concern to everyone. The consensus is that the price per share should rise a lot, quickly; to most commentators that spells success. But if the rise is too sharp, it means the selling company has lost: It has sold more shares and its investors sold a larger percentage of the company than was necessary. A better solution would have been to sell at the price where the shares do not move in price after the IPO until an increase is due to a change in the perceived performance of the company's future or to improved actual results that pleased investors.

It is very costly to pick an investment banker who does a poor job. This can and does happen when an IPO gets second-class attention or when the investment bankers are inept at IPOs. This is most likely in hot markets, when alternative deals are vying for the attention of overworked corporate finance staffs at the banks. The solution is for the CEO to manage and oversee the IPO, relying heavily on the CFO to ensure that the deal gets its "unfair share of attention." Close scrutiny will also pressure sales staffs of the investment bankers to control information leaks better and to more carefully manage trading in the shares.

The company is put into a very dangerous situation when there are no Wall Street security analysts following and writing about the company after the IPO. This possibility is very real. Jerry Anderson, a cofounder and former chairman of the computer-aided engineering company Valid Logic of San Jose, California, lamented that one of his two lead bankers promised but never wrote more than a short introductory piece on Valid within the two years after the banking firm got its fee for the IPO. The *Wall Street Journal* wrote a lead article about that kind of problem in the August 12, 1987, issue of the newspaper. The headline read as follows:

**Feeling Neglected**
*High-tech companies say Wall Street firms are abandoning them*
*after initial stock offerings,*
*some entrepreneurs say, bankers' attention wanes*
*paying for the prestige factor*

How to address and correct this post-IPO problem is discussed in the next section.

# After the IPO

A successful conclusion to the IPO does not end when the IPO deal closes. It continues to the point at which the company is understood with reasonable accuracy by the investment community, and the company's strategy, competitive advantage, and future prospects are being reasonably re-communicated by the Wall Street research community.

How do you achieve this desired result in a multitrillion-dollar global stock market that trades trillions of shares daily, has tens of thousands of stocks of companies to invest in—not to mention bonds, government bills, mortgages, real estate, gold, paintings, and so on? A fledgling company with less than two million shares sold to the public is not of much interest to most of the giant investors. Furthermore, each high-tech company must compete with other hot IPOs that are much more easily understood, such as consumer products companies that have huge upside potential in the large consumer markets. Getting regular attention is difficult and requires a lot of planning, strategy, and hard work, day after day after day.

The following sections reflect the advice of high-tech company CEOs and CFOs whom we have interviewed. We're providing a summary of their comments, but their opinions about what to do were wide-ranging.

**Managing Shareholder Relations.** Shareholder management, or "investor relations," is the process of controlling information released to the public while remaining in compliance with the law, so that expectations about the company's future are kept in line with reality.

This process must be managed actively, because experience has shown that, left on their own, the investment community and general public media will gradually create distorted stories about a company, its products, its financial health, and its managerial competence. Such distortions increase the difficulty of managing the business, especially when large Fortune 500 customers begin to believe that the tiny company is in serious financial difficulty.

To do the job properly, the company must create a careful investor relations plan that is designed with the same thoroughness as a marketing plan for a product line. This requires skill and experience, such as that of a CFO who has done it before, a PR firm that offers such services, or an investor relations consultant who specializes in this area.

The company will need one person whose primary daily task is to disseminate and control the release of information to Wall Street research analysts and institutional investors. This person must be intimate with the policies and strategies of top management; in other words, he or she must know what is going on behind the closed doors of the CEO's office. Surprises are unforgivable by Wall Street. Trust and discretion are two of the working skills of the investor relations manager.

Fire-fighting is a regular task of the investor relations manager. It occurs all too frequently: All companies hit a quarter when business suddenly is going to be shockingly below last week's forecast; or the industry starts to sink and everyone starts layoffs; or a company's newest, highly touted wonder product suddenly cannot be finished on schedule by its engineering department; or when a company's latest product release turns out to be full of software bugs and customers are screaming murder!

The nature of investor relations is that of ferocious intensity. When trouble sets in, the CEO and his staff must drop all tasks until a tactical plan is created to deal with the latest rumors, good or bad, on Wall Street. The phones start ringing madly and will not stop until management provides satisfying answers to questions from the local business-news editors, irate investors, and worried research analysts.

Honesty and integrity are very important. Once burned, analysts are like elephants: They do not forget. "Burning an analyst" consists of surprising him or her, and a good surprise is as undesirable as a bad surprise. Any surprise prevents the analyst from being able to get the story—good or bad—out to favored institutional investors, complete with advice on what to do about it. Analysts are burned often, and therefore are experienced doubters, capable of detecting—from tone changes and intimations on the phone—any deliberate withholding of information about significant current or upcoming events—good or bad.

Consistency is important. Once a CEO starts to give out numbers, he must not stop during the embarrassing times. For instance, some companies openly talk about order backlog when it is strongly rising but stop when it gets bad. Good analysts have learned to read the situation exactly that way, and no one is fooled. Inconsistency makes the research analyst's job more difficult. The analyst has built a spreadsheet model to forecast the financial statements of your company, using the parameters that the CEO has been giving out. If the CEO stops giving out the information, more uncertainty will be introduced into the analyst's forecast; the CEO may then read of negative reports by the formerly favorable analyst, who is now explaining to his investing clientele why the new forecast and report on a company have changed so much.

**Potential Problems and Pitfalls.** Investor relations must be managed deliberately—as actively and deliberately as any other aspect of a business. Here are some of the problems the fledgling public company may face:

- *Time Consumption.* A CEO should count on the same percentage of time needed for managing investor relations as was required while the company was private. During Intel's earliest years after its IPO, PR and marketing pioneer Regis McKenna got Intel's top management committed to spending at least 10 percent and sometimes 20 percent of their time on each business trip with the media and Wall Street analysts.

- *What Is Said.* There is a large difference between what one says to insiders such as employees and venture capitalists and what one says to outsiders such as the top research analysts of the Wall Street firms. Some CEOs have found this hard to learn, particularly those who have been heads of divisions of large corporations and have become CEO of a company for the first time in their lives. Inability to adjust has cost several CEOs their jobs, according to some we spoke to who have experienced this problem firsthand.

- *Control.* Frustration of CEOs rises as they learn how independent the outside media reporters and research analysts are. It is difficult to adjust to the reality that those people can say whatever they want about a company—and do. Trying to "fix" and "correct" their opinions is often a time- and emotion-consuming effort that is wasted.

- *Consistency.* A company's Wall Street positioning must be consistent with its business marketing positioning. Its customers will seek out and read the written Wall Street reports about its successes, failures, and expected future. Such reports must be considered an important part of a company's marketing communications program. Wall Street will not regurgitate an exciting story about your company if that company's marketing positioning statement is not defined crisply and in place. Analysts are very astute at poking holes in strategies, and uncovering "me-too" plans, and they are good at detecting lack of sustainable competitive advantage and distinctive competence.

A company can get special help from veterans of such investor relations activities by attending local chapter meetings of the National Investor Relations Institute. Here is a short list of the key principles that investor relations veteran Carol Abrahamson presented to members of the National Investor Relations Institute:

- Stocks are sold, not bought.
- Financial markets are influenced strongly by supply and demand factors.
- Information moves Wall Street as it builds expectations leading to assessment of the value of the stock of a company.
- Investors come in many types, some more appropriate for a company than others.
- Every company has unique investor relations needs that change over time.
- Every different type of investor has different information needs.
- Companies must compete fiercely to be noticed by investors.

Investor relations specialists can help a CEO build an investor relations program that is customized for a company's special needs, whether it went public a year ago and is now frustrated at dwindling interest by Wall Street, is recently public, or has an IPO coming up in a few months and wants to plan ahead of time. The consultants feel their work will help a company reap appropriate benefits: consistent demand for its shares, fair valuing of its stock, and orderly trading of its shares.

**Participants and the Role of the Securities Analyst.** There is a collection of people who will team up regularly in the investor relations program for a company. Experts can get a company started quickly and methodically. In addition, there are special roles for each of the other participants:

- *Lead Spokesperson.* This is the person designated to answer directly the numerous daily phone calls from investors and others inquiring about the company's stock and prospects. New IPO companies usually designate the CFO for this job. Others choose the CEO. It is a time-consuming assignment and is rarely delegated to the investor relations manager.
- *Investor Relations Manager.* This person must handle the administration and details of the newly public company. This includes taking the first calls from Wall Street analysts who will be requesting personal telephone interviews with the CEO and CFO, as well as visits to the company. This manager will be very influential in how well Wall Street regards the quality of communication with the investment community. It is a demanding job, one for people who are very good at being discreet, who are absolutely trustworthy, and who are skilled at articulating the company's positioning statement and strategy.
- *The CFO.* The investor relations manager is usually responsible to the chief financial officer. This arrangement is a consequence of the need to comply with SEC regulations and the CFO's familiarity with the financial community. The VP of marketing usually cooperates with the CFO, but focuses more time on communicating with customers than with investors. The CFO is considered a close second in importance to the CEO as far as communicating with research analysts is concerned. That responsibility can be daunting to a financial leader who has come up the ladder as a controller or auditor. This is one reason so many VCs hesitate to automatically grant CFO status to VPs of finance in companies about to go public. This is evidenced by the frequent number of times a start-up adds a CFO "heavy" shortly before it goes public.
- *Lawyer.* The chief counsel to the company, usually an outsider in a private law firm that helped the company go public, assists in several ways. He or she reviews and advises on 10-Qs and other SEC submissions read by analysts. This attorney counsels on press releases affecting investors, especially those involving responses to wild trading in the company's stock, bad news such as

layoffs, or unexpectedly bad financial results. The attorney provides practical advice on what to tell analysts in difficult circumstances, based on firsthand experience. In the end, however, the CEO, not the chief counsel, is responsible for what is said. The objective is to give the law firm an opportunity to review special news intended to be sent to Wall Street and the press, so that the company can benefit from a legal professional's advice and avoid unnecessary legal mistakes in communications with analysts and reporters.

- *Board Members.* Especially important news is almost always previewed in confidence with those members of the board of directors who are active in the company. Quarterly earnings and bad news are most often discussed before release, typically on the phone or after the nearly final draft of the related press release is faxed in confidence to the secretary of the board member. This enables the CEO to keep everyone together, keeps communication consistent, and enables the CEO to benefit from the experience and judgment of board members, who often have been through similar situations in the past. The spate of shareholder suits in the twenty years up to 2000 demonstrates the importance of this practice.

- *Public Relations Firm.* The company's public relations firm often helps implement the investor relations program. Even if it does not, it must be kept informed of important events so it can keep up with the company's media communications, in which it is closely involved. The most common mistake made, according to veterans we spoke to, is to tell the PR firm after the fact. Close cooperation between investor relations and public relations will keep the two programs consistent.

- *National Investor Relations Institute.* This and local clubs of investor relations people are where the tactics and skills of investor relations are learned and new ideas are discussed openly.

- *Research Analysts.* These are the people employed by the investment community to investigate and report on companies. They differ in their role and relations with a company. Analysts work for one of the two sides on Wall Street: the sell side, consisting of the famous brokerage and investment banking firms on Wall Street such as Goldman Sachs and Morgan Stanley, as well as the specialized high-tech firms such as Hambrecht & Quist and Alex Brown; or the buy side, consisting of the institutional investors such as the diversified financial services firm of The Capital Group of Los Angeles, managers of mutual funds such as T. Rowe Price of Baltimore, and hired money managers such as Rosenberg Capital Management of San Francisco. They specialize in technologies and industries. Sell-side analysts can earn in the hundreds of million dollars in compensation in a hot year. The top ones can exceed a million dollars in a great year. It is rare to see reports written by buy-side analysts, but that does not make the buy-side analyst any less important to spend time with than the sell-side analyst.

The toughest job is to keep the analyst's expectations in line with reality without forecasting a company's financial results for the next quarter or year. This requires experience and very careful communication in order to avoid legal trouble in dealing with "whisper numbers" and other secrets of the trade.

**The Speaking Forums.** There is a regular circuit of meetings at which officers of a new issue can speak. These are arranged by high-tech business firms so that institutional investors can hear CEOs present their companies. There is a plethora of forums to present the company each year on the west and east coasts of the United States as well as a few in Europe. Each of the high-tech investment banking firms such as Hambrecht & Quist and Alex Brown put together specialized investor meetings that focus on technologies such as life sciences or information sciences. Participation is by invitation, but invitations are not too difficult to obtain. The lead investment banking firm should help the company plan its year of meetings.

Investors come to these meetings as one method of efficiently looking at live managers of the exciting new companies they have heard about. Both analysts and portfolio managers attend. They sit in on the daily meetings where the CEO tells the company's story; they also spend dinners and lunches talking in small groups with a company's representatives. Both public and private (soon to go IPO) companies present.

---

# Case Studies: Critical Path, E-Loan and Microsoft Go Public

In closing, we wish to suggest that you spend time reading articles about the inside details of going public. One is "Diary of an Internet IPO: How Critical Path took the money and ran" in the July 1999 issue of *Red Herring*. Another is "Inside an Internet IPO," in the September 6, 1999 issue of *BusinessWeek*, which gives the story of the IPO of E-Loan. The other is an IPO classic: the unusually well written case study of a real IPO—Bro Uttal's "fly-on-the-wall" inside look at the Microsoft IPO process, published in a 1986 *Fortune* magazine.

These are worth studying because it is rare that such detail is documented so well. The articles accurately apply to other IPOs in other times and other industries. They convey the reality of the IPO event in accord with our interviews and personal experiences in the recent past.

It is also worthwhile studying the prospectuses of recent IPO offerings, and to calculate one's own forecast of the offering price of your own start-up at the time of IPO. This is especially important in boom times when the stock prices shoot up so strongly after the public offering. Take the position of the CEO at IPO time: Think about your strong desires and goals for the IPO and compare your imagined pre-IPO desires to what actually happened with the IPOs you chose to study. Practice standing in the CEO's IPO shoes and decide on the timing, pricing, and management of the pre- and post-offering events and then adjust plans to get your own start-up public.

# 14

# Mergers, Spinouts, and Corporate Venture Capital

There are good funding and exit alternatives in addition to the IPO. In this chapter we will describe the pros and cons of each approach. The Internet era produced many investments in start-ups by VPs of business development of large corporations. There are increasing uses of other creative funding techniques such as creation of an internal start-up, spinouts (leaving a company to start a new one), and joint ventures (two companies form a new third company). The most frequent exit alternative to the IPO is merger or acquisition by another company. Each funding and exit source has unique requirements and considerations for the CEO of the high-tech start-up, and each has proved successful as a viable source of funds for a new enterprise.

## Mergers, Acquisitions, and Corporate Investing

Venture capitalists of the pre-1970 era used to look to mergers and acquisitions (M&A) as the most likely means by which to cash in their investments. Today, the emphasis is on getting to an initial public offering. However, more companies are still acquired than go public.

In 1987, the *San Jose Mercury News* researched the fates of forty-three selected companies that had received venture capital funding during the previous five years in Silicon Valley. Of the forty-three, only nine made it to a public offering.

The thirty four others included bankruptcies as well as several that were acquired, such as American Cardiovascular.

Since the venture boom days of the early 1980s, mergers have been taking place at a faster pace as consolidation of start-ups becomes a reality. The Internet era increased the pace, according to Venture Capital Economic Services: The number of VC-backed companies that were sold (merged) in 1993 was 78; by 1998 the number had risen steadily to 186. All types of companies are involved: Internet, electronics, hardware, software, telecommunications, life sciences, and environmental. Data suggest life sciences is most likely to have the largest portion of start-ups sold. There also have been private purchases of U.S. start-ups by Asian, European, and other non-U.S. corporations of considerably larger size. That is how the Japanese headquartered Softbank became a venture backer of companies like Yahoo.

After the VC bust of the personal computer era, the number of venture-backed IPOs began to rise, from 39 in 1989 to a record 276 in 1996. Then a cooling began, with a decline to 134 in 1997 and 77 in 1998. Meanwhile, the number of venture-backed companies sold rose from 101 in 1996 to 160 the next year and to 186 in 1998. Clearly the trend is for sales of companies to rise when IPOs wane.

Some of the mergers take a start-up to instant IPO, via getting shares of a public company. Other start-ups get cash on the way to the independent IPO. We will now examine the process and give tips about such investing.

**Corporate Investment—How and Where to Start.** Let's help you, the founder/ CEO, look at this from the viewpoint of advising the corporate executive, typically the vice president of business development of a large public corporation, who would like to acquire or invest in your start-up or access its technology. When asked how the merger and acquisition teams of Fortune 500 corporations should approach a high-tech start-up, the VCs uniformly responded by saying, "Start with a board member who can be quietly approached to test the waters."

Investors suggested that corporations approach a member of a venture firm first because such contacts often can lead to additional opportunities for acquisition of technology and businesses. When the large-company executive has a specific start-up in mind, early discussions with the venture capitalist who funded the start-up can help the suitor. Specifically, the goal is to better understand the degree of sensitivity that the managers of the start-up may have to being approached by a corporate buyer. If the suitor is acceptable, the proper introductions will be made and the talks can get off on the right foot. VCs noted that few high-tech founder/CEOs have firsthand experience with an acquisition or investment from a large corporation, whereas the VCs are most likely to have such know-how and to be more astute in handling the more sophisticated aspects of acquiring a high-tech corporation without causing the core team to turn down the opportunity to talk with the large corporation.

**Pricing.** Pricing an acquisition of a private start-up will follow the same techniques and methodology described in earlier chapters. A number of independent consulting firms offer services that include valuing private companies. It is important to understand the tools used by venture capitalists. Learn their motivations, techniques for pricing, target ROIs, and current portfolio condition. The last item is especially important to know about each VC investor. The VC firm whose other portfolio companies are in trouble will be more likely to support and urge the sale of one of its start-ups because the resulting ROI will increase the overall performance of a sagging portfolio.

**Management Thinness.** One should be especially careful of the thinness of management in any start-up. Even the most experienced CEO has little support or backup, and rarely enough to get all of the job done every day. The corporate buyer may be dismayed to find that a large part of the expected profits went to just adding badly overdue managerial support to the struggling start-up. In fact, the start-up may be for sale because the current management does not have the ability to build enough success out of the start-up to satisfy its investors.

**Business or Just Technology?** One should be especially thorough in separating a start-up's exciting technology from any problems it may have in sustaining a viable business. The methods for detecting and analyzing this problem are discussed in detail in Chapter 5, following practices familiar to large public corporations and the research and guidelines of consultants such as Peter Drucker and McKinsey & Company. Investors in one-product companies are eager to sell the company.

**Learn the Venture Capital Formation Process.** It is important to respect the process of capital formation in the high-tech start-up. Chapter 3 uncovers the phases and jargon of the process, step by step. This process is described from the viewpoint of the start-up's CEO, but it includes the important issues that the potential acquirer will encounter along the way in considering the acquisition. It will keep the acquirer from stepping out of line and from bumbling along like a newcomer trying to get along in the very private, very strange world of high-tech start-ups. Large corporations that skipped studying the start-up process have ended up losing a lot of money.

**Respect the Soul and Spirit of the Start-up.** High-tech companies have an intense soul and spirit in their cultures that the acquirer must respect. To win over the core group of employees who are strongly leading the culture of the company is a must. The technology team will be especially skittish about any outsider taking over control. Even in a troubled company, the high-tech artists are an independent lot. Anything the newcomer does that puts water on the flame of a company's spirit is very dangerous. Ben Rosen, who backed Lotus and Compaq, was asked how he rekindled the flame of a start-up once it was extinguished, and he replied, "I really do not know of a formula for doing that; it is extremely difficult to accomplish." Winning over the entrepreneurial hearts of the employees is critical to the successful acquisition of a start-up. If not, the buyer will see the new enterprise dwindle to a fraction of its promised potential.

## Case Studies

Our first case study is an M&A classic: It is about the psychology and culture of a high-tech company. It is a real story about how the president of National Semiconductor (at the time a young, rapidly growing high-tech company that had gone public) reacted to the painful situation of vulnerability to takeover. The study of this case can help the business development executive of a large corporation who is looking for a way of investing in start-ups to access strategic technology or increase revenue and profits. It is also a good example of how jealous a high-tech CEO can feel about his company, particularly about an unwanted outside corporation coming in to take away a position of authority in the company he has founded.

The second case study, American Cardiovascular, illustrates the acquisition of a start-up that was a success for both the acquiring company and its investors as well as the start-up.

---

## *Case Study: National Semiconductor*

In 1976, Charles E. "Charlie" Sporck, president of National Semiconductor Corporation of Santa Clara, California, was faced with a serious problem. The stock of his company had skyrocketed ever since he had left Fairchild to lead the creation of what had become National, the wonderchild of the semiconductor industry in the decade of the seventies. But after setting record after record for financial performance, Sporck saw the dream turn into a nightmare as sudden internal problems caused earnings to first slow and then sharply reverse their former upward path. The stock plunged from highs in the mid-fifties to the low teens in 1976. Wall

Street rumors spread like wildfire, and soon there were stories of raiders looking at National. The stock market value of the company hit a low of $62 million.

Sporck was angry that anyone even mentioned a possible merger with another company. He got even angrier at the mention of a possible raider buying the company. He had seen firsthand at Fairchild Camera and Instrument Corp. what an established eastern-based management had done to the western-based fledgling transistor and integrated circuit operations of Fairchild. "They never understood the business," he would comment frequently. "They didn't know what they were doing." It was that concern—of an outsider coming in and wrecking National because strangers didn't understand the semiconductor business— that disturbed him so much.

Sporck also had a very heavy emotional attachment to National. He recalled the years of loyalty of employees. Longtime employees told of the end of one quarter when Spork's wife and children showed up at the factory in Santa Clara to help employees box semiconductors for shipment to customers—so that the company would have enough cash flow from collecting the receivables to meet the next quarter's payroll. Employees fondly retold such stories to visitors; the company had a very intimate character to its culture. In 1976, as the takeover rumors continued, the employees grew openly angry at the idea of someone other than "Charlie" running National. They rallied to support him and his leadership.

Sporck listened to the wide-ranging advice people offered on what to do in the threatening situation. While Sporck's people were working around the clock from Connecticut to Bangkok to Santa Clara to fix the internal problems, world-famous law firms and Wall Street investment bankers flew to headquarters to meet Sporck, each proposing some tactical plan designed to ward off a raider or exact the highest price if the raid were successful. The fees for attorneys and Wall Street bankers would represent a substantial payoff in either scenario. They would get their fees if National won against a raider, but would also get their fees if National lost against the raider. It was the latter scenario that made Sporck furious.

Finally Sporck made his decision: "Tell the press that National will leave a 'scorched earth' if any raider tries to make a pass at us," were Sporck's instructions to his staff. After considering the myriad of possible solutions, Charlie, as he was affectionately known, decided that there was only one worthwhile way of dealing with the problem: He would personally resign from National if a raider tried to take control of even a portion of the stock of the company. Even a single seat for the suitor on the board of directors of National was too much. Sporck could leave and be employed instantly by a competitor of National's. Sporck did not manage under a noncompete contract; in fact, he hated management contracts and refused to use them in his company. And people in large numbers pledged that they would follow him from National—especially key top and middle managers who deeply respected Sporck—as well as the intensely loyal R&D staff and hourly employees. A raider would be left with an empty shell: Not only the brains and know-how would be gone, but the company's soul as well.

As it turned out, Sporck retained control of his company, solved the internal problems, and later went on to acquire several businesses for National in friendly transactions. These were merged into the National culture, some becoming the foundation for what became the Systems Division of National, which represented over half the revenue and even proportionally more of the profits when the semiconductor industry was in the depths of a major recession in 1985 to 1986.

The final irony came in 1987: National acquired Fairchild from its parent, Schlumberger. This was made possible by circumstances as well as by management. After the 1976 National takeover rumors had died out, new ones arose of several other possible unfriendly takeovers. Eventually Gould came after Fairchild. Wilfred Corrigan and his managers at Fairchild fought back with lawyers and investment bankers, but eventually had to give up by selling out to a "white knight," the French oil equipment supplier Schlumberger. A highly successful company, Schlumberger was expected by many analysts in the Wall Street community to turn Fairchild around quickly in a display of management brilliance that would dazzle the homegrown methods of the current crop of high-tech managers of Silicon Valley companies.

Rebuffed but undaunted, Gould made a second attempt, this time at the much smaller but technology-rich Texas company, Mostek. Feisty L. J. Sevin and his loyal Texan management fought back, but they too ended up in the arms of a white knight, United Technology.

Less than three years after those acquisitions, the companies' leaders left and so did their key technologists. Corrigan left to found LSI Logic, a gate array ASIC (application-specific integrated circuits) start-up company that went public successfully. Sevin left and teamed up with Ben Rosen to start their own venture capital firm that later was the lead investor in Lotus and Compaq. The Fairchild and Mostek technologists landed in semiconductor companies all over the United States, including many new enterprises.

United later shut down Mostek and sold off its assets.

Schlumberger finally put Fairchild up for sale in 1987 after losing vast sums of money in the operation. The final buyer was Charlie Sporck, who had been the general manager of Fairchild's semiconductor operations just before he left to lead National.

## Case Study: American Cardiovascular

This is a real story about how a giant acquired a successful start-up. The new enterprise was funded by a team of venture investors led by Ray Williams, a very quiet, successful, hands-on investor in high-tech early-stage companies, and eventually sold to Eli Lilly in 1986.

Williams says he often prefers to sell to large corporations after a successful start-up finds it is ready to cash in the chips. In this case, the customers of American Cardiovascular were in the medical profession, where the channels of distribution are dominated by the selling staffs of the large pharmaceutical companies. The American products were a natural fit in the strategy of the buyer. The selling founders and employees exchanged private stock for instantly registered public shares, without the hassle of having to fight for post-IPO attention in crowded Wall Street.

Williams noted that he strongly prefers to begin without corporate venture capital, however. He feels corporations involved in the earliest stages hinder management from realizing the fullest potential of the technology, and can often slow the company's reaction to the market and to overcoming the many troubles that a start-up encounters. After the birth pangs are over, however, Williams believes that acquisition by a large public corporation makes a very attractive way for the start-up to get public while adding further strength to the new company.

This friendly acquisition has been considered a successful marriage by both parties. The change of leadership was done in an orderly fashion. Williams had been CEO for a long time and had increasingly turned over daily management tasks to operating managers; he quietly bowed out. The American Cardiovascular company remained intact, and the buyer, Lilly, gained entry into the new business it was seeking. Employees got career paths in a well-run corporation, some with the opportunity to become technology "fellows" of a corporation where R&D is a revered discipline with vast sums of money and resources at its disposal.

During the Internet boom, large corporations—often recent IPOs themselves—went on acquisition sprees. The huge multiples given Internet stocks "made money free," according to one wag. Cisco and Yahoo and Amazon created departments called business development, staffed them with energy-filled people, and started purchasing technology, entering new markets, and doing the buying side of the "make-or-buy" decision. Intel and Softbank formed similar departments, as did most large public companies. Lucent went public as a spinout from AT&T and quickly formed a business development department, led by Tom Uhlman, to make the most of the ideas streaming from the revered Bell Labs. These corporations appeared in articles in the media about the latest investments by angels and venture firms. This formed a trend that continued into the next century.

# Internal Start-Ups

By 2000, another form creating and financing a high-tech company has become more popular. We call it an "internal start-up." It is a novel approach—an evolution of the lessons learned by independent and successful new enterprises—and it has advantages over a merger or acquisition. We provide two case studies that illustrate successful internal start-ups.

The internal start-up (sometimes dubbed a "start-in") is a separate business entity of an operating high-tech company. It may or may not be a subsidiary (a separate—daughter—corporation wholly or partially owned by the larger—parent—corporation). The parent company wants to keep the management and employees of the parent company focused on its bread-and-butter business while simultaneously creating and entering a related business run by carefully chosen personnel. The personnel in the internal start-up are motivated like start-up entrepreneurs and receive founders' shares, which eventually are bought out by the parent corporation in accordance with some prearranged valuation method.

**Potential Problems and Pitfalls.** As with new children, there are a number of special things to watch out for when doing an internal start-up. Our research reveals the number-one enemy of this type of start-up is jealousy by employees who do not get to be a part of the new internal enterprise. One should have the patience to study such phenomena and work them out, because we found that there is a very high success rate for internal start-ups, according to our research. It is an area of pioneering, and it offers the entrepreneurs a large degree of creativity. It also requires substantial work to construct the legal and financial elements of the new enterprise and to put in place a workable process in a large public corporation.

**Incentive Compensation.** The internal start-up pays competitive wages and adds an equity incentive package. The wages often include a cash bonus program in addition to base wages. Large cash bonuses are less common in start-ups where equity is the big payoff. The modification in compensation for the internal start-up reflects the reality of the start-up market. The equity incentive is in the form of options to buy stock, usually in the form of a standard incentive stock option package with four-year vesting. If the internal start-up is not a subsidiary, phantom stock is used. The rest of the option structure can get quite creative; some alternatives are discussed below.

**Tax Benefits.** The parent company can reduce the cash cost of its investment in the internal start-up if it can qualify for a write-off of the capital invested in the start-up. To do so, several companies have purchased at least 80 percent of the start-up at the beginning of its existence. Thus, a $4 million capital investment would be reduced by the approximate combined U.S. federal and state tax rate (about 40 percent). Other structures in the past have included starting with an R&D partnership that gained the benefits of tax write-off of the first expenses of the start-up.

**Accounting.** One of the greatest problems of an internal start-up is that of accounting for a buyout by the parent of the minority shareholders (who are the founders, management, and employees) of the internal start-up. This issue seems to be continually in flux. We will reflect on the current accounting issues and watch as the future unfolds. The American Institute of Certified Public Accountants (AICPA) and its theoreticians have forced its member CPA firms to require that under certain conditions (ask your independent accounting firm for a lesson) buyout of minority shareholders must be recorded as an acquired asset that must be depreciated over the economic life of the asset. Translated into business terms, this means that a $4 million investment that creates a new enterprise that is owned 80 percent by the parent and that becomes worth $50 million in five years requires the buyer of the remaining 20 percent, worth $10 million, to write off the high-tech asset against the combined earnings of the acquiring parent. Since the life of the technology at the moment of acquisition could be argued by the CPA firm to be short, a five-year life or $2 million of non-tax-reduced paper expense would be charged against earnings for five or fewer years. That is enough to wipe out the profit from the consolidated internal start-up in many cases. Obviously, this is controversial and calls for care in dealing with the strategic issues.

CFOs and CEOs we spoke with feel this is irrelevant nonsense created by accounting theoreticians. The combined entity has no less or greater cash flow than on the day before the two were combined. A company doing an IPO does not record its increased worth and charge it against its own earnings. In fact, the buyer of the internal start-up adds value by consolidating 100 percent of the start-up for tax purposes.

We found some creative efforts under way to circumvent the accounting problem. One was to use "phantom shares" that are like a special stock option granted to the employees of the start-up and are cashed in for stock in the parent corporation.

Another method is to aim from the beginning at letting the internal start-up do an IPO, to be set free at some time from the parent. Claris Corp., a subsidiary of Apple Computer, is one example. The proponents of such a start-up argue that this kind of internal start-up was created because of an "incompatibility" problem within the parent company, and an IPO is a fine way for the parent to reap the rewards of its investment and hard work. Yet Claris was "reacquired" by Apple after all the dust settled.

Another creative method is for the eventual cashing in of the chips to take place immediately. This structure has the parent immediately putting a future value on the shares owned by management and employees, buying 100 percent of the start-up from day one, and vesting the shares over four years, contingent on reaching revenue and profit goals of the business plan.

Some corporations have used R&D equity partnerships. Classical in form, they allow special tax benefits to be created and thus reduce the cost of the start-up to the investor. The buyout accounting issues remain, but not if the start-up does an IPO and goes off to operate independently of the parent.

**Valuation.** Valuing an internal start-up is no more difficult than valuing a company going public or one selling shares in a private round of financing (review Chapter 9). Several companies used a combination of hired help—a consultant, an investment banker, a CPA firm—and their own financial staffs to reach a value for the buyout of the company. Fear of the valuation issues should not prohibit anyone from considering an internal start-up.

**Expert Help.** The same caliber of professional help is needed for this new variety of start-up as for the classical kind. An internal entrepreneur can benefit from the experience of a good start-up consultant, start-up lawyer, or high-tech CPA firm, as well as the professional investment banker familiar with high-tech start-ups. Such help will be needed because of the pioneering nature of an internal start-up.

# Case Studies

The following are two classic studies of internal start-ups. The first is considered the pioneer of it all, Quantum and Plus Development. The second is about Lucent and Bell Labs and its outstanding program to mine the gold in the creativity of the laboratories run by Ph.D.s in Bell Laboratories. The lessons can be applied and modified to suit the needs of other large public corporations.

# Case Study: Quantum and Plus

Quantum Corporation, a pioneering disk drive manufacturer in Milpitas, California, started what became a trend when it successfully used an internal start-up to solve a business dilemma that prosperity had created for the company. The company had reached IPO as an original equipment supplier of large disk drives to systems corporations. Quantum's technology then enabled them to create a skinny disk drive that fit a slot in personal computers. Market tests showed that the potential was very large. But management—ranked one of the top 10 percent of well managed companies by several electronic publishers' polls—was concerned that the retail computer store focus of the new business opportunity would confuse the parent company, distracting from the heart of the company's success as an OEM supplier.

Management decided to solve their problem by creating an internal start-up. Its name was Plus. A separate corporate structure was created, complete with a separate building, its own business plan, and dedicated personnel. Compensation was arranged in a confidential manner, with an incentive package of stock for the risk-taking employees that was competitive with other start-ups.

Plus quickly leaped to the head of its served market, becoming the industry standard. Revenue and profits rolled in. Plus and Quantum won. So did the risk-taking employees of Plus.

Since this success, other companies have taken this idea and have advanced it further.

# Case Study: Lucent and Bell Laboratories

Created as a spinout of the AT&T breakup in 1996, Lucent Technologies included Bell Laboratories, filled with scientists and engineers. An immediate goal of the Lucent leader, Henry Schacht, was to use Bell Labs to increase the growth of Lucent. Tom Uhlman, a twelve-year Silicon Valley veteran and former leader of business development at Hewlett-Packard, took on fresh challenges as president of Bell Labs' New Ventures Group. After two years of work, nine new ventures were created in a wide range of high-technologies based on work pioneered by researchers inside Bell Labs. Any Lucent employee can propose internal funding of an idea, and if it passes screenings like those done by VCs on Sand Hill Road, the cash is committed to the new enterprise. Employees get phantom shares in the new enterprise at the cost of stopping their cash bonuses. There are over four hundred people working with the New Ventures Group, some located inside Lucent, others in quarters outside the parent company. Ventures have the right to consider spinning out of Lucent, and Lucent has the right to buy them back again. A good example was reported in the February 20, 1999, issue of *The Economist:* "Veridicom, which sells a finger-printing identification system for data networks, is located in Santa Clara, California. It has recently made it into the big leagues, with financing from Intel as well as San Francisco's top venture-capital firm Hambrecht & Quist, and is expected to go public later this year."

---

The Internet-era examples are many and involve strategic moves by many giant corporations. The "dot-com" start-ups seem to be the most intensive, involving large corporations as partners. Here are some examples of several types of corporate involvement:

- *TiVo* was created in 1998 as a start-up producing a new television replay system. Its trail of funding reveals how intensive corporate involvement by strategic partners can get. The partners contributed a wide range of investments, from cash to distribution channels. The string of partners included Quantum Corp., Philips Electronics, DIRECTV, Vulcan Ventures, Showtime Networks, ZDTV, Weather Channel, HBO, General Motors, and NBC. In July 1999 a press release announced additional equity partners: CBS, Comcast Interactive Capital, Cox Communications, Discovery Communications, the Walt Disney Company, Liberty Digital, Advance/Newhouse, and TV Guide Interactive.

- *Conexant* was created on December 31, 1998, via a spinout to shareholders of the parent, Rockwell International Corporation. Its focus is on delivering semiconductors for communications. The stock climbed after the IPO and the company attracted many talented engineers.

- *Savi Technologies* announced its birth via a buyout of the business from Raytheon in August 1999. Vector Capital was the lead investor and there were four other organizations backing the company and management.

- *Cisco Systems* agreed in August 1999 to put $50 million in Akamai Technologies a deal the valued that Internet company investors at $1.2 billion, according to a report in the *Wall Street Journal.* Akamai was led by George H. Conrades, a high-tech veteran and former IBM executive who had also run BBN, a leading Internet provider that was acquired by GTE. Cisco previously had acquired many start-ups since Cisco itself went public.

# Corporate Venture Capital

The larger public companies are active in the venture capital business. Pools of big-company money are invested in start-ups. This presents a number of opportunities for the entrepreneur, and many have proved successful. We will focus here on the mechanics of dealing with such sources of capital.

**Finding Corporate Venture Capital.** Some Fortune 500 companies have created subsidiaries to enter the venture capital market. Others simply invest as part of the strategy of their business development units. Usually run by a corporate officer of the parent, these operations are chartered to seek out and recommend areas for new investment. One choice their leaders have is to fund new enterprises that are in fields of technology and business to which the large corporation is eager to gain access. A founder/CEO can locate such personnel via introduction or simply by contacting the large company's CEO's or CFO's office and ask whether they might be interested in what the start-up company has to offer. Start-up CEOs told us that they found that their cold calls were answered, as were calls that followed carefully arranged personal introductions. CEOs needing more discretion found their lawyers or accounting firms were quick to make the desired connection.

**ROI Versus Technology.** Corporate venture capitalists are less interested in turning a high ROI on their portfolio of company investments than they are in helping the parent company gain access to the desired strategic technology or business. Amazon's acquisitions are good examples of this, as are Cisco's. As giants begin to fall behind in technology or markets, the urge to merge rises, and we see companies such as Microsoft beginning to make investments in a wide array of private ventures. The strategic—rather than financial—emphasis is very clear in many of the prospectuses of IPOs that describe the extensive arrangements between the start-up and the investing corporate giant (often referred to as a "strategic partner").

**Pricing.** The cost of capital from corporate sources usually has been lower than when a classical venture capitalist is the investor. This is for a combination of reasons, mainly because there is less competitive pressure to perform as a portfolio manager. Other CEOs told us that the greed factor was much lower, and there was a refreshingly lower drive for financial success at all costs. In other cases we found corporations charging the same cost of capital as VCs. We found it very difficult to get sufficient data on this pricing, especially on the magnitude of the reduced cost of capital. However, the patterns in our data suggested that corporations grant a modest percent reduction below the cost of classical corporate venture capital, perhaps 10 percent to 20 percent less, depending heavily upon the technology contract between the start-up and big corporation. No CEO of a start-up told us he had to pay more for capital from corporate venture capitalists than from classical venture capitalists.

**Business Deals and Documentation.** Corporate venture deals are almost always accompanied by some form of additional legal documentation that formalizes the related business deal that accompanies the investment. The deals range from large-quantity purchases by Kodak of workstations supplied by Sun Microsystems to technology licenses linked to software and hardware purchases, such as an OEM deal between a big company that is a hardware reseller and a start-up that is a supplier of advanced technology hardware. Internet deals involve suppliers of content with web portals that distribute it. The degree of creativity is almost unlimited.

It is mandatory that the entrepreneur use experienced legal help in structuring and documenting such deals. International deals are especially complex and tricky.

**View of Classical Venture Capitalists.** There are differing and often conflicting objectives and goals when corporate and classical venture capitalists are compared. Both claim to be long-term in their thinking, yet both have certain motivations to act in the shorter term. The corporate investor seeks more than the maximum ROI, whereas that is the fixation of the classical VC. Corporate investors are slower, some say more deliberate and methodical, whereas fast decisions and immediate reaction to changes in events mark the habits of the classical venture investor. CEOs of start-ups seem to believe that the corporate investor is less likely to fire the founders than are the classical venture capitalists.

As a result, classical venture capitalists are sometimes reluctant to invest on the same terms as corporate venture capitalists. And in extreme cases, some VC firms will not invest at all in private companies that already have been funded by corporate venture capital. We did not, however, find that the top VC firms are reluctant to join a deal with corporate venture capitalists. Instead, they seem to be simply wanting to be extra careful that the corporate investor and any related business deals made good business sense for the start-up.

# Foreign Corporate Capital

We must especially address the issue of foreign venture capital in U.S. start-ups. The trend for foreign investment in start-ups began to grow in the 1980s along with the cheaper dollar, and continued in the 1990s.

- The French and Germans initially began to be active in the 1982–1985 years, forming later-stage venture funds and doing deals as large corporations funding some start-ups. By 2000, more American-style venture funds had formed in Europe and were spreading slowly around Europe.

■ The Japanese entered in the late 1980s, to become a major player whose corporate investors often acquired troubled start-ups and thus gained full access to all their technology. By 2000, Softbank had become the gigantic start-up investor from Japan. Meanwhile, Taiwan start-ups were forming, backed by rich angels and local corporations. Later the Koreans became very visible. Singapore and Korea experimented with modest amounts of government funds backing both direct investment in start-ups as well as in small local venture capital firms, and Malaysia announced large government programs designed to leapfrog other Asian start-up efforts. Intensive competition had begun by 2000, with large sums of capital available throughout Asia, especially Taiwan, Hong Kong, Korea, and Singapore. A few more venture funds operated offices in cities in Asia as well as Silicon Valley. Private funds also were experimenting with direct investment in high-tech start-ups in China.

■ Israel meanwhile had created the envy of the non-U.S. countries: By 1999, that tiny country had more than 120 start-ups go IPO on NASDAQ! Clearly, the lessons of Israeli high-tech start-ups are worth emulating.

It should also be noted that off-shore venture funds arose and are now active in both the United States and in their home countries. These funds help bridge the oceans and fill a role for start-ups outside the United States to begin on a solid footing and later come to compete in the larger U.S. market with dreams of an IPO on the NASDAQ.

We expect these trends to continue. They represent another alternative for the start-up CEO to go to for capital and another way to increase competition for a funding deal. To date, the pricing of deals with foreign sources of capital has appeared to follow the pricing of the American corporate venture capitalist, but there are signs that the entrepreneur offshore pays more for venture capital than in the United States due to the lack of competition between the few local venture funds.

One special characteristic of offshore corporate funding, however, is the degree of accompanying business dealing; foreign investors virtually insist that any investment include both full access to all the start-up's technology and some form of commitment to manufacture in the country supplying the capital. Most of the corporate money goes to later-stage deals, rarely to seed start-ups.

# Corporate Opportunities

Corporate deals (buyouts, spinouts, spin-ins, and joint ventures) as well as corporate venture funds are available and actively looking for good start-ups and their technologies. The sources are from very large companies in North America, Europe, and Asia. Every deal looks for access to the start-up's technology. The cost of capital is equal to or slightly less than what a classical VC would charge. Internal start-ups continue to proliferate in creative companies. They require buyout formulas and special management techniques. CEOs of start-ups should not look for seed-round money from corporations, but rather for mid- and later-round funding. If all goes well, the CEO should also expect to be considered for buyout (instead of an IPO) by the big corporate partner.

*Appendix A*

---

*Saratoga Venture Tables*

---

# SARATOGA VENTURE FINANCE EQUITY TABLE™
WAGES AND STOCK OWNERSHIP AT INITIAL PUBLIC OFFERING (IPO)

This is a portion of a Table

| TITLE | (4) COMPENSATION | MGT & EMPS OWNERSHIP (3),(6),(7) |
|---|---|---|
| f = Founder | | |
| f  Chair,CEO,Pres | $121,000 | 3.1% |
| f  VP Engineering | $82,000 | 4.6% |
| VP Mktg & Sls | | 0.0% |
| VP Mfg | $72,450 | 0.0% |
| f  VP R&D-Left | $73,886 | 0.5% |
| OTHER | Avg. = $63,667 | 1.4% |
| OFFICERS & EXECUTIVES | | 9.6% |
| ALL OTHER | | 15.1% |
| TOTAL COMMON BEFORE OPTIONS | | 24.7% |
| OPTIONS-Outstanding | | 1.4% |
| OPTIONS-Available | | 7.9% |
| OPTIONS-Total | | 9.3% |
| COMMON-Total | | 34.0% |
| Major Venture Capital | | 32.9% |
| OTHER | | 21.3% |
| VENTURE Total | | 54.2% |
| PRE-IPO: sum of all stock | | 88.2% |
| IPO shares | | 11.8% |
| TOTAL OUTSTANDING | | 100.0% |

## ABBREVIATIONS OF JOB TITLES

| | |
|---|---|
| CEO | Chief Executive Officer |
| COO | Chief Operating Officer |
| EVP | Executive Vice President |
| SVP | Senior Vice President |
| VP | Vice President |
| CFO | Chief Financial Officer |
| CSO | Chief Scientific Officer |
| Pres | President |
| BisDev | Business Development |
| EUR | Europe |
| F&A or FIN | Finance and Administration |
| HR | Human Resources |
| HW | Hardware |
| INT | International |
| MFG | Manufacturing |
| MKT | Marketing |
| MS | Marketing and Sales |
| NA | North American or Not Available |
| OPS | Operations |
| PROD DEVEL | Product Development |
| QR | Quality and Reliability |
| SLS | Sales |
| SW | Software |
| TECH | Technology |

## LABELS & EXPLANATIONS

The Tables contain summaries and approximations. For actual data, see the prospectus.

| | | |
|---|---|---|
| # | = | See list below for footnote explanations |
| MGT & EMPS | = | Management and employees |

Blank compensation occurs when data is not available.

| | | |
|---|---|---|
| # | = | Zeros for shares occur when data is not available (see averages for approximations). |
| Left | = | Shows executive left company before IPO. |
| Avg. | = | Arithmetic average is used for data given for a group. |
| ALL OTHER | = | Usually shares purchased by exercising granted options. |
| Major Ven. Cap. | = | Includes largest venture investors |
| OTHER | = | All investors, including strategic partners |
| VENTURE Total | = | May include some cash of founders. |
| p | | |

## FOOTNOTES TO HEADERS

(1) As reported to SEC in prospectus, including Option Plan grants net of repurchases.

(2) Equals (1) plus all option plan shares: granted plus available, net of options exercised for common.

(3) Original shares purchased by executives, net of repurchases from resigned employees, and other private transactions.

(3B) Includes some granted options as well as purchased stock.

(4) As reported to Securities and Exchange Commission in prospectus for recent fiscal year.

(5) Shows average for earnings of executives for periods subsequent to the last 12 months.

(6) Uses entire option pool: outstanding plus available shares.

**SARATOGA VENTURE FINANCE EQUITY TABLE**
WAGES AND STOCK OWNERSHIP AT INITIAL PUBLIC OFFERING

**Amazon.com Inc**

| | | |
|---|---|---|
| Internet book retailer | | State of Incorporation: Delaware |
| Seattle, WA | Initial Public Offering (IPO) date: May 15, 1997 | Date of Inception: July 1994 |
| Price per Share $18.00 | Company value $631,956,636 | Years from inception to IPO: 2.9 |
| Stock symbol: AMZN | Internet URL: www.amazon.com | |

f = Founder
D=Director

| f=D | | (4) Comp | (3B) Officers' Ownership | (3),(6),(7) Mgt & Emps Ownership | (1) Pre IPO Ownership | (2) Post IPO Ownership | (3B) Officers' Ownership | (3),(6),(7) Mgt & Emps Ownership | (1) Pre IPO Ownership | (2) Post IPO Ownership | IPO Value $18.00 Per Share |
|---|---|---|---|---|---|---|---|---|---|---|---|
| fD Pres., CEO, Chairman | Jeffrey P. Bezos | $64,333 | 100.0% | 35.4% | 31.2% | 28.2% | 9,885,000 | 9,885,000 | 9,885,000 | 9,885,000 | $177,930,000 |
| VP, Exec. Editor | Rick R. Ayre | - | | | | | | | | | - |
| VP of Mktg | Mark L. Breier | - | | | | | | | | | - |
| CFO, VP of Fin. & Admin | Joy D. Covey | - | | | | | | | | | - |
| VP of Operations | Oswaldo F Duenas | - | | | | | | | | | - |
| VP of Publisher Affairs | Mary E. Engstrom | - | | | | | | | | | - |
| VP, CTO | Sheldon K. Kaphan | - | | | | | | | | | - |
| VP of Business Expansio | Scott E. Lipsky | - | | | | | | | | | - |
| VP of Product Developm | John D. Risher | - | | | | | | | | | - |
| VP of Engineering | Joel R. Spiegel | - | | | | | | | | | - |
| OFFICERS & EXECUTIVES | | | 100.0% | 35.4% | 31.2% | 28.2% | 9,885,000 | 9,885,000 | 9,885,000 | 9,885,000 | $177,930,000 |
| ALL OTHER COMMON | | | | 25.9% | 22.8% | 20.6% | | 7,227,326 | 7,227,326 | 7,227,326 | $130,091,868 |
| TOTAL COMMON BEFORE OPTIONS | | | | 61.3% | 54.1% | 48.7% | | 17,112,326 | 17,112,326 | 17,112,326 | $308,021,868 |
| OPTIONS-Outstanding | | | | 12.7% | 11.2% | 10.1% | | 3,543,849 | 3,543,849 | 3,543,849 | $63,789,282 |
| OPTIONS-Available | | | | 26.0% | 22.9% | 20.7% | | 7,256,151 | 7,256,151 | 7,256,151 | $130,610,718 |
| OPTIONS-Total | | | | 38.7% | 34.1% | 30.8% | | 10,800,000 | 10,800,000 | 10,800,000 | $194,400,000 |
| TOTAL-Executives and employees | | | | 100.0% | 88.2% | 79.5% | | 27,912,326 | 27,912,326 | 27,912,326 | $502,421,868 |
| Investors (includes major venture capital; excludes management as investors) | | | | | 11.8% | 10.7% | | | 3,746,376 | 3,746,376 | $67,434,768 |
| Other Investors | | | | | 0.0% | 0.0% | | | 0 | 0 | $0 |
| TOTAL-Investors Preferred & Other (shares, options & warrants) | | | | | 11.8% | 10.7% | | | 3,746,376 | 3,746,376 | $67,434,768 |
| PRE-IPO: sum of all stock | | | | | 100.0% | 90.2% | | | 31,658,702 | 31,658,702 | $569,856,636 |
| Initial Public Offering-New shares sold | | | | | | 8.5% | | | | 3,000,000 | $54,000,000 |
| Option to underwriters | | | | | | 1.3% | | | | 450,000 | $8,100,000 |
| TOTAL OUTSTANDING including Options & warrants | | | | | | 100.0% | | | | 35,108,702 | $631,956,636 |

| IPO Total cash raised before fees and expenses | | $54,000,000 | 100% |
|---|---|---|---|
| | Paid to underwriters | Less: | $3,780,000 | 7.0% |
| CPA and other related expenses | Less: | $850,000 | 1.6% |
| | Net: | $49,370,000 | 91.4% |
| Shares sold by company | 3,000,000 | 100% |
| Shares sold by selling shareholders | 0 | 0% |
| Total shares sold in this offering | 3,000,000 | 100% |
| Option to underwriters | 450,000 | 15% |

Vesting for Incentive Stock Option Plans is usually over five years.

| CPA firm | Lead Underwriters |
|---|---|
| Ernst & Young | Deutsche Morgan Grenfell |
| | Alex. Brown & Sons |
| | Hambrecht & Quist |
| Counsel for Company | Counsel for Underwriters |
| Perkins Coie | Wilson Sonsini Goodrich & Rosati |
| Outside Directors | Madrona Investment Group, Tom A. Alberg; Intuit, Scott D. Cook; Kleiner Perkins Caufield & Byers, L. John Doerr; Patricia Q. Stonesifer |

| | REVENUE $ | REVENUE $ |
|---|---|---|
| | 1996 | 1995 |
| | $15,746 | $511 |
| | Growth/Year | Growth/Year |
| | NM | NM |
| | Nr employees: 256 | |

SARATOGA VENTURE FINANCE EQUITY TABLE
WAGES AND STOCK OWNERSHIP AT INITIAL PUBLIC OFFERING

| | | Internet advertising services<br>New York, NY<br>Price per Share $17.00<br>Stock symbol: DCLK | DoubleClick Inc.<br>Initial Public Offering (IPO) date: February 20, 1998<br>Company value $329,607,152<br>Internet URL: www.doubleclick.com | State of Incorporation: Delaware<br>Date of Inception: January 1996<br>Years from inception to IPO: 2.1 |
|---|---|---|---|---|

| f = Founder<br>D=Director | (4)<br>Comp | (3B)<br>Officers'<br>Ownership | (3),(6),(7)<br>Mgt & Emps<br>Ownership | (1)<br>Pre IPO<br>Ownership | (2)<br>Post IPO<br>Ownership | (3B)<br>Officers'<br>Ownership | (3),(6),(7)<br>Mgt & Emps<br>Ownership | (1)<br>Pre IPO<br>Ownership | (2)<br>Post IPO<br>Ownership | IPO Value<br>$17.00<br>Per Share |
|---|---|---|---|---|---|---|---|---|---|---|
| fD CEO, Chairman — Kevin J. O'Connor | $126,250 | 57.2% | 37.7% | 16.3% | 12.9% | 2,508,286 | 2,508,286 | 2,508,286 | 2,508,286 | $42,640,862 |
| President & CFO — Kevin P. Ryan | $152,500 | 6.8% | 4.5% | 2.0% | 1.5% | 300,000 | 300,000 | 300,000 | 300,000 | $5,100,000 |
| fD CTO — Dwight A. Merriman | | 29.2% | 19.2% | 8.3% | 6.6% | 1,278,901 | 1,278,901 | 1,278,901 | 1,278,901 | $21,741,317 |
| EVP Marketing & Sales — Wenda Harris Millard | $180,000 | 2.7% | 1.8% | 0.8% | 0.6% | 120,000 | 120,000 | 120,000 | 120,000 | $2,040,000 |
| Controller & Asst. Sec. — Stephen R. Collins | | | | | | | | | | |
| VP Engineering — John L. Heider | $101,280 | 1.7% | 1.1% | 0.5% | 0.4% | 75,000 | 75,000 | 75,000 | 75,000 | $1,275,000 |
| VP International — Barry M. Salzman | $105,136 | 0.0% | 0.0% | 0.0% | 0.0% | 100,000 | 100,000 | 100,000 | 100,000 | $1,700,000 |
| OFFICERS & EXECUTIVES | | 100.0% | 65.8% | 28.5% | 22.6% | 4,382,187 | 4,382,187 | 4,382,187 | 4,382,187 | $74,497,179 |
| ALL OTHER COMMON | | 0.0% | 0.0% | 0.0% | 0.0% | | 0 | 0 | | $0 |
| TOTAL COMMON BEFORE OPTIONS | | | 65.8% | 28.5% | 22.6% | | 4,382,187 | 4,382,187 | 4,382,187 | $74,497,179 |
| OPTIONS-Outstanding | | | 19.4% | 8.4% | 6.7% | | 1,293,066 | 1,293,066 | 1,293,066 | $21,982,122 |
| OPTIONS-Available | | | 14.7% | 6.4% | 5.1% | | 979,833 | 979,833 | 979,833 | $16,657,161 |
| OPTIONS-Total | | | 34.2% | 14.8% | 11.7% | | 2,272,899 | 2,272,899 | 2,272,899 | $38,639,283 |
| TOTAL-Executives and employees | | | 100.0% | 43.3% | 34.3% | | 6,655,086 | 6,655,086 | 6,655,086 | $113,136,462 |
| Investors (includes major venture capital; excludes management as investors) | | | | 40.6% | 32.2% | | | 6,234,434 | 6,234,434 | $105,985,378 |
| Other Investors | | | | 16.1% | 12.8% | | | 2,474,136 | 2,474,136 | $42,060,312 |
| TOTAL-Investors Preferred & Other (shares, options & warrants) | | | | 56.7% | 44.9% | | | 8,708,570 | 8,708,570 | $148,045,690 |
| PRE-IPO: sum of all stock | | | | 100.0% | 79.2% | | | 15,363,656 | 15,363,656 | $261,182,152 |
| Initial Public Offering-New shares sold | | | | | 18.1% | | | | 3,500,000 | $59,500,000 |
| Option to underwriters | | | | | 2.7% | | | | 525,000 | $8,925,000 |
| TOTAL OUTSTANDING including Options & warrants | | | | | 100.0% | | | | 19,388,656 | $329,607,152 |

| | | |
|---|---|---|
| IPO Total cash raised before fees and expenses | $59,500,000 | |
| Less: Paid to underwriters | $4,165,000 | 7.0% |
| Less: CPA and other related expenses | $750,000 | 1.3% |
| Net: | $54,585,000 | 91.7% |
| Shares sold by company | 3,500,000 | 100% |
| Shares sold by selling shareholders | 0 | 0% |
| Total shares sold in this offering | 3,500,000 | 100% |
| Option to underwriters | 525,000 | 15% |

| | |
|---|---|
| REVENUE $ FY1997 | $30,597 |
| REVENUE $ FY1996 | $6,514 |
| Growth/Year | 370% |
| Growth/Year | NM |
| Nr employees: | 185 |

Vesting for Incentive Stock Option Plans is usually over 3 years by quarter

| | |
|---|---|
| CPA firm | Price Waterhouse |
| Lead Underwriters | Goldman, Sachs & Co. / BT Alex Brown |
| Counsel for Company | Cowen & Company / Brobeck, Phleger & Harrison |
| Counsel for Underwriters | |
| Outside Directors | Hale & Dorr |

Greylock, David Strohm; Bain, Mark Nunnelley; Hoenemeyer, Grant Gregory; Marketing 1:1, Donald Peppers

Source: Saratoga Venture Finance © All rights reserved. See prospecutus for data. The above contain certain estimates.

**SARATOGA VENTURE FINANCE EQUITY TABLE**
WAGES AND STOCK OWNERSHIP AT INITIAL PUBLIC OFFERING

Internet auction site
San Jose, California
Price per Share $18.00
Stock symbol: EBAY

**Ebay Inc.**
Initial Public Offering (IPO) date: 23-Sep-1998
Company value $914,667,318
Internet URL: www.ebay.com

State of Incorporation: California, Delaware
Date of Inception: May 1996
Years from inception to IPO: 2.4

| f = Founder D=Director | (4) Comp | (3B) Officers' Ownership | (3),(6),(7) Mgt & Emps Ownership | (1) Pre IPO Ownership | (2) Post IPO Ownership | (3B) Officers' Ownership | (3),(6),(7) Mgt & Emps Ownership | (1) Pre IPO Ownership | (2) Post IPO Ownership | IPO Value $18.00 Per Share |
|---|---|---|---|---|---|---|---|---|---|---|
| fD Chairman | Pierre M. Omidyar | $65,446 | 49.2% | 40.7% | 32.5% | 30.0% | 15,229,425 | 15,229,425 | 15,229,425 | 15,229,425 | $274,129,650 |
| D Pres, CEO | Margaret C Whitman | $175,000 | 7.7% | 6.4% | 5.1% | 4.7% | 2,400,000 | 2,400,000 | 2,400,000 | 2,400,000 | $43,200,000 |
| SVP Marketing | Brian Swette | $150,000 | 1.9% | 1.6% | 1.3% | 1.2% | 600,000 | 600,000 | 600,000 | 600,000 | $10,800,000 |
| VP Strategic Planning | Jeffrey S. Skoll | $30,000 | 32.9% | 27.3% | 21.8% | 20.1% | 10,200,000 | 10,200,000 | 10,200,000 | 10,200,000 | $183,600,000 |
| VP Prod. Dev | Michael K Wilson | $78,000 | 2.9% | 2.4% | 1.9% | 1.8% | 900,000 | 900,000 | 900,000 | 900,000 | $16,200,000 |
| VP Marketing, Bus Dev | Stephen P Westly | $120,000 | 2.8% | 2.3% | 1.8% | 1.7% | 864,000 | 864,000 | 864,000 | 864,000 | $15,552,000 |
| CFO, VP ops | Gary F Bengier | $125,000 | 1.7% | 1.4% | 1.1% | 1.0% | 525,000 | 525,000 | 525,000 | 525,000 | $9,450,000 |
| VP Legal, Secretary | Michael R. Jacobson | $150,000 | 0.8% | 0.7% | 0.5% | 0.5% | 250,002 | 250,002 | 250,002 | 250,002 | $4,500,036 |
| OFFICERS & EXECUTIVES | | | 100.0% | 82.8% | 66.2% | 60.9% | 30,968,427 | 30,968,427 | 30,968,427 | 30,968,427 | $557,431,686 |
| ALL OTHER COMMON | | | 0.0% | 0.0% | 0.0% | 0.0% | | 0 | 0 | 0 | $0 |
| TOTAL COMMON BEFORE OPTIONS | | | 82.8% | 66.2% | 60.9% | 30,968,427 | 30,968,427 | 30,968,427 | $557,431,686 |
| OPTIONS-Outstanding | | | | 3.8% | 3.0% | 2.8% | 1,410,315 | 1,410,315 | 1,410,315 | $25,385,670 |
| OPTIONS-Available | | | | 13.4% | 10.7% | 9.9% | 5,007,748 | 5,007,748 | 5,007,748 | $90,139,464 |
| OPTIONS-Total | | | | 17.2% | 13.7% | 12.6% | 6,418,063 | 6,418,063 | 6,418,063 | $115,525,134 |
| TOTAL-Executives and employees | | | 100.0% | 79.9% | 73.6% | 37,386,490 | 37,386,490 | 37,386,490 | $672,956,820 |
| Investors (includes major venture capital; excludes management as investors) | | | | 18.8% | 17.3% | | | 8,791,836 | 8,791,836 | $158,253,048 |
| Other Investors | | | | 1.3% | 1.2% | | | 622,250 | 622,250 | $11,200,500 |
| TOTAL-Investors Preferred & Other (shares, options & warrants) | | | | 20.1% | 18.5% | | | 9,414,086 | 9,414,086 | $169,453,548 |
| PRE-IPO: sum of all stock | | | | 100.0% | 92.1% | | | 46,800,576 | 46,800,576 | $842,410,368 |
| Initial Public Offering-New shares sold | | | | | 6.9% | | | | 3,489,275 | $62,806,950 |
| Option to underwriters | | | | | 1.0% | | | | 525,000 | $9,450,000 |
| TOTAL OUTSTANDING including Options & warrants | | | | | 100.0% | | | | 50,814,851 | $914,667,318 |

IPO Total cash raised before fees and expenses $63,000,000 100%
Paid to underwriters — Less: $4,410,000 7.0%
CPA and other related expenses — Less: $975,000 1.5%
Net: $57,615,000 91.5%

Shares sold by company 3,489,275 100%
Shares sold by selling shareholders 10,725 0%
Total shares sold in this offering 3,500,000 100%
Option to underwriters 525,000 15%

| Vesting for Incentive Stock Option Plans is usually over four years. | Lead Underwriters |
|---|---|
| CPA firm *Price Waterhouse* | Goldman Sachs |
| | Donaldson Lufkin |
| | BancBoston Robertson Stevens |
| | BT Alex. Brown |
| Counsel for Company *Fenwick & West* | Counsel for Underwriters *Sherman & Sterling* |
| Outside Directors | Intuit, Scott Cook, Benchmark Capital, Robert Kagle, Starbucks, Howard Schultz |

| | REVENUE $M 6 Months 1998 | REVENUE $M 6 Months 1997 |
|---|---|---|
| REVENUE $M | $14.9 | $1.7 |
| | Growth/Year | Growth/Year |
| | 800% | NM |
| | Nr employees: 76 | |

**SARATOGA VENTURE FINANCE EQUITY TABLE**
WAGES AND STOCK OWNERSHIP AT INITIAL PUBLIC OFFERING

**eToys Inc.**

Internet retail
Santa Monica, CA
Price per Share $20.00
Stock symbol: ETYS

Initial Public Offering (IPO) date: May 19, 1999
Company value $2,529,878,600
Internet URL: www.etoys.com

State of Incorporation: Delaware
Date of Inception: Nov 1996
Years from inception to IPO: 2.5

| f = Founder D=Director | | (4) Comp | (3B) Officers' Ownership | (3),(6),(7) Mgt & Emps Ownership | (1) Pre IPO Ownership | (2) Post IPO Ownership | (3B) Officers' Ownership | (3),(6),(7) Mgt & Emps Ownership | (1) Pre IPO Ownership | (2) Post IPO Ownership | IPO Value $20.00 Per Share |
|---|---|---|---|---|---|---|---|---|---|---|---|
| fD | Pres,CEO,UncleOfBord Edward C. Lenk | $105,000 | 63.7% | 19.0% | 9.0% | 8.3% | 10,500,000 | 10,500,000 | 10,500,000 | 10,500,000 | $210,000,000 |
| | SVP, Product Dev. Frank C. Han | $103,750 | 20.2% | 6.0% | 2.8% | 2.6% | 3,325,002 | 3,325,002 | 3,325,002 | 3,325,002 | $66,500,040 |
| | Senior VP, Operations Louis V. Zambello III | $315,000 | 5.0% | 1.5% | 0.7% | 0.7% | 825,000 | 825,000 | 825,000 | 825,000 | $16,500,000 |
| | Senior VP, CFO Steven J. Schoch | $150,000 | 4.6% | 1.4% | 0.6% | 0.6% | 750,000 | 750,000 | 750,000 | 750,000 | $15,000,000 |
| | Senior VP, CIO John R. Hnanicek | $210,000 | 3.6% | 1.1% | 0.5% | 0.5% | 600,000 | 600,000 | 600,000 | 600,000 | $12,000,000 |
| | Senior VP, Marketing Janine Bousquette | $213,462 | 2.9% | 0.9% | 0.4% | 0.4% | 480,000 | 480,000 | 480,000 | 480,000 | $9,600,000 |
| OFFICERS & EXECUTIVES | | | 100.0% | 29.9% | 14.1% | 13.0% | 16,480,002 | 16,480,002 | 16,480,002 | 16,480,002 | $329,600,040 |
| ALL OTHER COMMON | | | | 3.0% | 1.4% | 1.3% | | 1,628,646 | 1,628,646 | 1,628,646 | $32,572,920 |
| TOTAL COMMON BEFORE OPTIONS | | | | 32.8% | 15.5% | 14.3% | | 18,108,648 | 18,108,648 | 18,108,648 | $362,172,960 |
| OPTIONS-Outstanding | | | | 20.8% | 9.8% | 9.0% | | 11,447,676 | 11,447,676 | 11,447,676 | $228,953,520 |
| OPTIONS-Available | | | | 46.4% | 21.9% | 20.2% | | 25,572,324 | 25,572,324 | 25,572,324 | $511,446,480 |
| OPTIONS-Total | | | | 67.2% | 31.7% | 29.3% | | 37,020,000 | 37,020,000 | 37,020,000 | $740,400,000 |
| TOTAL-Executives and employees | | | | 100.0% | 47.1% | 43.6% | | 55,128,648 | 55,128,648 | 55,128,648 | $1,102,572,960 |
| Investors (includes major venture capital; excludes management as investors) | | | | | 52.7% | 48.7% | | | 61,587,483 | 61,587,483 | $1,231,749,660 |
| Other Investors | | | | | 0.2% | 0.2% | | | 209,799 | 209,799 | $4,195,980 |
| TOTAL-Investors Preferred & Other (shares, options & warrants) | | | | | 52.9% | 48.9% | | | 61,797,282 | 61,797,282 | $1,235,945,640 |
| PRE-IPO: sum of all stock | | | | | 100.0% | 92.4% | | | 116,925,930 | 116,925,930 | $2,338,518,600 |
| Initial Public Offering-New shares sold | | | | | | 6.6% | | | | 8,320,000 | $166,400,000 |
| Option to underwriters | | | | | | 1.0% | | | | 1,248,000 | $24,960,000 |
| TOTAL OUTSTANDING including Options & warrants | | | | | | 100.0% | | | | 126,493,930 | $2,529,878,600 |

Vesting for Incentive Stock Option Plans is usually over four years.

| IPO Total cash raised before fees and expenses | | $166,400,000 | 100% |
|---|---|---|---|
| | Paid to underwriters Less: | $11,232,000 | 6.8% |
| CPA and other related expenses Less: | | $1,700,000 | 1.0% |
| | Net: | $153,468,000 | 92.2% |
| Shares sold by company | | 8,320,000 | 100% |
| Shares sold by selling shareholders | | 0 | 0% |
| Total shares sold in this offering | | 8,320,000 | 100% |
| Option to underwriters | | 1,248,000 | 15% |

| REVENUE $K | REVENUE $K |
|---|---|
| FY 1999 | FY 1998 |
| $34,727 | $687 |
| Growth/Year | Growth/Year |
| NM | NM |
| Nr employees: 306 | |

| CPA firm | Ernst & Young |
|---|---|
| Lead Underwriters | Goldman, Sachs & Co. |
| | BancBoston Robertson Stevens |
| | Donaldson. Lufkin & Jenrette |
| | Merrill Lynch & Co. |
| Counsel for Company | Venture Law Group |
| Counsel for Underwriters | Gunderson, Dettmer, Stough, Villeneuve, Franklin & Hachigian |
| Outside Directors | Wildkin, Peter Hart; Dynafund Ventures, Tony Hung; Sequoia Capital, Michael Moritz; Highland Capital, Daniel Nova |

**SARATOGA VENTURE FINANCE EQUITY TABLE**
WAGES AND STOCK OWNERSHIP AT INITIAL PUBLIC OFFERING

Internet Data Centers
Santa Clara, CA
Price per Share $15.00
Stock symbol: EXDS

## Exodus Communications Inc.

Initial Public Offering (IPO) date: March 18, 1998
Company value $269,094,360
Internet URL: www.exodus.com

State of Incorporation: Delaware
Date of Inception: February 1995
Years from inception to IPO: 3.1

| f = Founder / D = Director | | (4) Comp | (3B) Officers' Ownership | (3),(6),(7) Mgt & Emps Ownership | (1) Pre IPO Ownership | (2) Post IPO Ownership | (3B) Officers' Ownership | (3),(6),(7) Mgt & Emps Ownership | (1) Pre IPO Ownership | (2) Post IPO Ownership | IPO Value $15.00 Per Share |
|---|---|---|---|---|---|---|---|---|---|---|---|
| fD CEO, Chairman | K.B. Chandrasekhar | $240,373 | 34.8% | 15.0% | 7.9% | 5.7% | 1,014,998 | 1,014,998 | 1,014,998 | 1,014,998 | $15,224,970 |
| President | Ellen M. Hancock | $300,000 | 27.1% | 11.7% | 6.2% | 4.4% | 791,981 | 791,981 | 791,981 | 791,981 | $11,879,715 |
| COO, CFO | Richard S. Stoltz | $187,500 | 10.6% | 4.6% | 2.4% | 1.7% | 309,667 | 309,667 | 309,667 | 309,667 | $4,645,005 |
| VP, Marketing | Mark Bonham | | | | - | | | | | | |
| f VP, Engineering | B.V. Jagadeesh | $175,000 | 18.6% | 8.0% | 4.2% | 3.0% | 542,999 | 542,999 | 542,999 | 542,999 | $8,144,985 |
| VP, Worldwide Sales | Sam S. Mohamad | $343,626 | 5.7% | 2.5% | 1.3% | 0.9% | 166,668 | 166,668 | 166,668 | 166,668 | $2,500,020 |
| VP, Customer Support | Louis J. Muggeo | | | | - | | | | | | |
| VP, Operations | Robert V. Sanford III | $136,250 | 0.0% | 0.0% | 0.0% | 0.5% | 91,667 | 91,667 | 91,667 | 91,667 | $1,375,005 |
| OFFICERS & EXECUTIVES | | | 100.0% | 43.1% | 22.8% | 16.3% | 2,917,980 | 2,917,980 | 2,917,980 | 2,917,980 | $43,769,700 |
| ALL OTHER COMMON | | | | 0.0% | 0.0% | 0.0% | | | | 0 | $0 |
| TOTAL COMMON BEFORE OPTIONS | | | | 43.1% | 22.8% | 16.3% | | 2,917,980 | 2,917,980 | 2,917,980 | $43,769,700 |
| OPTIONS-Outstanding | | | | 25.2% | 13.3% | 9.5% | | 1,709,286 | 1,709,286 | 1,709,286 | $25,639,290 |
| OPTIONS-Available | | | | 31.6% | 16.7% | 11.9% | | 2,142,440 | 2,142,440 | 2,142,440 | $32,136,600 |
| OPTIONS-Total | | | | 56.9% | 30.1% | 21.5% | | 3,851,726 | 3,851,726 | 3,851,726 | $57,775,890 |
| TOTAL-Executives and employees | | | | 100.0% | 52.8% | 37.7% | | 6,769,706 | 6,769,706 | 6,769,706 | $101,545,590 |
| Investors (includes major venture capital; excludes management as investors) | | | | | 43.2% | 30.8% | | | 5,530,469 | 5,530,469 | $82,957,035 |
| Other Investors | | | | | 4.0% | 2.9% | | | 514,449 | 514,449 | $7,716,735 |
| TOTAL-Investors Preferred & Other (shares, options & warrants) | | | | | 47.2% | 33.7% | | | 6,044,918 | 6,044,918 | $90,673,770 |
| PRE-IPO: sum of all stock | | | | | 100.0% | 71.4% | | | 12,814,624 | 12,814,624 | $192,219,360 |
| Initial Public Offering-New shares sold | | | | | | 25.1% | | | | 4,500,000 | $67,500,000 |
| Option to underwriters | | | | | | 3.5% | | | | 625,000 | $9,375,000 |
| TOTAL OUTSTANDING including Options & warrants | | | | | | 100.0% | | | | 17,939,624 | $269,094,360 |

| IPO Total cash raised before fees and expenses | | $67,500,000 | 100% |
|---|---|---|---|
| Paid to underwriters | Less: | $4,725,000 | 7.0% |
| CPA and other related expenses | Less: | $1,400,000 | 2.1% |
| | Net: | $61,375,000 | 90.9% |
| Shares sold by company | | 4,500,000 | 100% |
| Shares sold by selling shareholders | | 0 | 0% |
| Total shares sold in this offering | | 4,500,000 | 100% |
| Option to underwriters | | 625,000 | 14% |

| REVENUE $ FY1997 | REVENUE $ FY1996 |
|---|---|
| $12,408,000 | $3,130,000 |
| Growth/Year | Growth/Year |
| 122% | 294% |
| Nr employees: 220 | |

Vesting for Incentive Stock Option Plans is usually over fifty months.

| CPA firm | KPMG Peat Marwick |
|---|---|
| Lead Underwriters | Goldman, Sachs & Co. |
| | BT Alex. Brown |
| | Nationsbanc Montgomery Securities |
| Counsel for Company | Fenwick & West |
| Counsel for Underwriters | Wilson Sonsini Goodrich & Rosati |
| Outside Directors | |

8 outside Directors: 6 venture capitalists and 2 independents

**SARATOGA VENTURE FINANCE EQUITY TABLE**
WAGES AND STOCK OWNERSHIP AT INITIAL PUBLIC OFFERING

Network Systems
Sunnyvale, California
Price per Share $25.00
Stock symbol: FDRY

# Foundry Networks Inc.

Initial Public Offering (IPO) date: Sep 27, 1999
Company value $1,563,390,850
Internet URL: www.foundrynetworks.com

State of Incorporation: Delaware
Date of Inception: May 1996
Years from inception to IPO: 3.4

| f = Founder / D = Director | Name | (4) Comp | (3B) Officers' Ownership | (3),(6),(7) Mgt & Emps Ownership | (1) Pre IPO Ownership | (2) Post IPO Ownership | (3B) Officers' Ownership | (3),(6),(7) Mgt & Emps Ownership | (1) Pre IPO Ownership | (2) Post IPO Ownership | IPO Value $25.00 Per Share |
|---|---|---|---|---|---|---|---|---|---|---|---|
| fD Pres., CEO, Chairman | Bobby R. Johnson, Jr. | $139,560 | 66.8% | 33.4% | 21.3% | 19.3% | 12,075,000 | 12,075,000 | 12,075,000 | 12,075,000 | $301,875,000 |
| f VP HW Engineering | H. Earl Ferguson | | 13.2% | 6.6% | 4.2% | 3.8% | 2,392,500 | 2,392,500 | 2,392,500 | 2,392,500 | $59,812,500 |
| VP Marketing | Drusilla W. Demopoulos | $122,747 | 5.0% | 2.5% | 1.6% | 1.4% | 900,000 | 900,000 | 900,000 | 900,000 | $22,500,000 |
| VP Finance, CFO | Timothy D. Heffner | | - | - | - | - | | | | | |
| VP Product Mgt | Ken K. Cheng | | 3.4% | 1.7% | 1.1% | 1.0% | 622,500 | 622,500 | 622,500 | 622,500 | $15,562,500 |
| VP Mfg | Wilburn W. McGill | $149,850 | 4.0% | 2.0% | 1.3% | 1.2% | 727,500 | 727,500 | 727,500 | 727,500 | $18,187,500 |
| VP N.Amer. Sales | Robert W. Shackleton | $188,706 | 4.1% | 2.0% | 1.3% | 1.2% | 738,750 | 738,750 | 738,750 | 738,750 | $18,468,750 |
| VP Int'l Sales | William S. Kallaos | $145,281 | 3.4% | 1.7% | 1.1% | 1.0% | 607,500 | 607,500 | 607,500 | 607,500 | $15,187,500 |
| OFFICERS & EXECUTIVES | | | 100.0% | 49.9% | 31.8% | 28.9% | 18,063,750 | 18,063,750 | 18,063,750 | 18,063,750 | $451,593,750 |
| ALL OTHER COMMON | | | | 1.1% | 0.7% | 0.6% | | 403,648 | 403,648 | 403,648 | $10,091,200 |
| TOTAL COMMON BEFORE OPTIONS | | | | 51.1% | 32.5% | 29.5% | | 18,467,398 | 18,467,398 | 18,467,398 | $461,684,950 |
| OPTIONS-Outstanding | | | | 2.0% | 1.2% | 1.1% | | 707,203 | 707,203 | 707,203 | $17,680,075 |
| OPTIONS-Available | | | | 47.0% | 29.9% | 27.2% | | 16,992,047 | 16,992,047 | 16,992,047 | $424,801,175 |
| OPTIONS-Total | | | | 48.9% | 31.2% | 28.3% | | 17,699,250 | 17,699,250 | 17,699,250 | $442,481,250 |
| TOTAL-Executives and employees | | | | 100.0% | 63.7% | 57.8% | | 36,166,648 | 36,166,648 | 36,166,648 | $904,166,200 |
| Investors (includes major venture capital; excludes management as investors) | | | | | 35.3% | 32.1% | | | 20,044,486 | 20,044,486 | $501,112,150 |
| Other Investors | | | | | 1.0% | 0.9% | | | 574,500 | 574,500 | $14,362,500 |
| TOTAL-Investors Preferred & Other (shares, options & warrants) | | | | | 36.3% | 33.0% | | | 20,618,986 | 20,618,986 | $515,474,650 |
| PRE-IPO: sum of all stock | | | | | 100.0% | 90.8% | | | 56,785,634 | 56,785,634 | $1,419,640,850 |
| Initial Public Offering-New shares sold | | | | | | 8.0% | | | | 5,000,000 | $125,000,000 |
| Option to underwriters | | | | | | 1.2% | | | | 750,000 | $18,750,000 |
| TOTAL OUTSTANDING including Options & warrants | | | | | | 100.0% | | | | 62,535,634 | $1,563,390,850 |

| | | | |
|---|---|---|---|
| IPO Total cash raised before fees and expenses | | | $125,000,000 |
| Paid to underwriters | Less: | $8,750,000 | 7.0% |
| CPA and other related expenses | Less: | $850,000 | 0.7% |
| | Net: | $115,400,000 | 92.3% |
| Shares sold by company | | 5,000,000 | 100% |
| Shares sold by selling shareholders | | 0 | 0% |
| Total shares sold in this offering | | 5,000,000 | 100% |
| Option to underwriters | | 750,000 | 15% |

| REVENUE $K FY 1998 | REVENUE $K FY 1997 |
|---|---|
| $17,039 | $3,381 |
| Growth/Year 404% | Growth/Year NM |
| Nr employees: 131 | |

Vesting for Incentive Stock Option Plans is usually over five years.

| | |
|---|---|
| CPA firm | Arthur Andersen |
| Lead Underwriters | Deutsche Banc Alex. Brown |
| | Merrill Lynch |
| | J. P. Morgan |
| Counsel for Company | Venture Law Group |
| Counsel for Underwriters | Pillsbury Madison & Sutro |
| Outside Directors | Crosspoint Ventures, Seth D. Neiman; Andrew K. Ludwick, Independent |

**SARATOGA VENTURE FINANCE EQUITY TABLE**
WAGES AND STOCK OWNERSHIP AT INITIAL PUBLIC OFFERING

## Juniper Networks, Inc.

| | | Internet routers | Mountain View, CA |
|---|---|---|---|
| Price per Share $34.00 | Stock symbol: JNPR | | |

Initial Public Offering (IPO) date: June 24, 1999
Company value $2,342,993,934
Internet URL: www.juniper.net
State of Incorporation: Delaware
Date of Inception: February 1996
Years from inception to IPO: 3.4

| f = Founder / D=Director | | (4) Comp | (3B) Officers' Ownership | (3),(6),(7) Mgt & Emps Ownership | (1) Pre IPO Ownership | (2) Post IPO Ownership | (3B) Officers' Ownership | (3),(6),(7) Mgt & Emps Ownership | (1) Pre IPO Ownership | (2) Post IPO Ownership | IPO Value $34.00 Per Share |
|---|---|---|---|---|---|---|---|---|---|---|---|
| D CEO, Pres., Chairman | Scott Kriens | $170,000 | 41.3% | 9.2% | 4.8% | 4.6% | 3,153,485 | 3,153,485 | 3,153,485 | 3,153,485 | $107,218,490 |
| fD CTO, Vice Chairman | Pradeep Sindhu | $165,225 | 29.5% | 6.6% | 3.4% | 3.3% | 2,251,785 | 2,251,785 | 2,251,785 | 2,251,785 | $76,560,690 |
| VP Marketing | Joe Furgerson | | 5.9% | 1.3% | 0.7% | 0.7% | 450,000 | 450,000 | 450,000 | 450,000 | $15,300,000 |
| CFO | Marcel Gani | $150,000 | 5.5% | 1.2% | 0.6% | 0.6% | 417,165 | 417,165 | 417,165 | 417,165 | $14,183,610 |
| VP Sales & Service | Steven Haley | $219,039 | 4.9% | 1.1% | 0.6% | 0.5% | 375,630 | 375,630 | 375,630 | 375,630 | $12,771,420 |
| VP Operations | Gary Heidenreich | | 4.0% | 0.9% | 0.5% | 0.4% | 305,445 | 305,445 | 305,445 | 305,445 | $10,385,130 |
| VP Engineering | Peter L. Wexler | $150,000 | 8.9% | 2.0% | 1.0% | 1.0% | 676,020 | 676,020 | 676,020 | 676,020 | $22,984,680 |
| OFFICERS & EXECUTIVES | | | 100.0% | 22.2% | 11.5% | 11.1% | 7,629,530 | 7,629,530 | 7,629,530 | 7,629,530 | $259,404,020 |
| ALL OTHER COMMON | | | | 20.4% | 10.6% | 10.2% | | 7,022,246 | 7,022,246 | 7,022,246 | $238,756,364 |
| TOTAL COMMON BEFORE OPTIONS | | | | 42.7% | 22.1% | 21.3% | | 14,651,776 | 14,651,776 | 14,651,776 | $498,160,384 |
| OPTIONS-Outstanding | | | | 14.1% | 7.3% | 7.0% | | 4,830,084 | 4,830,084 | 4,830,084 | $164,222,856 |
| OPTIONS-Available | | | | 43.3% | 22.4% | 21.6% | | 14,857,416 | 14,857,416 | 14,857,416 | $505,152,144 |
| OPTIONS-Total | | | | 57.3% | 29.7% | 28.6% | | 19,687,500 | 19,687,500 | 19,687,500 | $669,375,000 |
| TOTAL-Executives and employees | | | | 100.0% | 51.9% | 49.8% | | 34,339,276 | 34,339,276 | 34,339,276 | $1,167,535,384 |
| Investors (includes major venture capital; excludes management as investors) | | | | | 23.6% | 22.7% | | | 15,613,836 | 15,613,836 | $530,870,424 |
| Other Investors (various warrants) | | | | | 24.5% | 23.6% | | | 16,238,474 | 16,238,474 | $552,108,126 |
| TOTAL-Investors Preferred & Other (shares, options & warrants) | | | | | 48.1% | 46.2% | | | 31,852,310 | 31,852,310 | $1,082,978,550 |
| PRE-IPO: sum of all stock | | | | | 100.0% | 96.1% | | | 66,191,586 | 66,191,586 | $2,250,513,934 |
| Initial Public Offering-New shares sold | | | | | | 2.9% | | | | 2,000,000 | $68,000,000 |
| Option to underwriters | | | | | | 1.0% | | | | 720,000 | $24,480,000 |
| TOTAL OUTSTANDING including Options & warrants | | | | | | 100.0% | | | | 68,911,586 | $2,342,993,934 |

| | | | |
|---|---|---|---|
| IPO Total cash raised before fees and expenses | | $163,200,000 | 100% |
| Paid to underwriters | Less: | $11,440,000 | 7.0% |
| CPA and other related expenses | Less: | $1,025,000 | 0.6% |
| | Net: | $150,735,000 | 92.4% |
| Shares sold by company | | 2,000,000 | 42% |
| Shares sold by selling shareholders | | 2,800,000 | 58% |
| Total shares sold in this offering | | 4,800,000 | 100% |
| Option to underwriters | | 720,000 | 36% |

| REVENUE $ | | REVENUE $ | |
|---|---|---|---|
| Qtr Mar 99 | $10,044 | Year 1998 | $3,807 |
| Growth/Year | NM | Growth/Year | NM |
| | | Nr employees: 190 | |

Vesting for Incentive Stock Option Plans is usually over four years.

| CPA firm | Ernst & Young |
|---|---|
| Lead Underwriters | Goldman, Sachs & Co. |
| | Credit Suisse First Boston |
| | BancBoston Robertson Stephens |
| | Dain Rauscher Wessels |
| Counsel for Company | Wilson Sonsini Goodrich |
| Counsel for Underwriters | Brobeck Phleger & Harrison |
| Outside Directors | Kleiner Perkins Caulfield & Byers, William R. Hearst III and Vinod Kosla: New enterprise Associates, C. Richard Kramlich; Enterprise Partners, William Stensrud |

*Source: Saratoga Venture Finance © All rights reserved. See prospectus for data. The above contain certain estimates.*

**SARATOGA VENTURE FINANCE EQUITY TABLE**
WAGES AND STOCK OWNERSHIP AT INITIAL PUBLIC OFFERING

| | | | | | |
|---|---|---|---|---|---|
| | Internet music retail | | **MP3.com Inc.** | | State of Incorporation: California |
| | San Diego, CA | | Initial Public Offering (IPO) date: July 21, 1999 | | Date of Inception: March 1998 |
| | Price per Share $28.00 | | Company value $1,865,853,444 | | Years from inception to IPO: 1.3 |
| | Stock symbol: MPPP | | Internet URL: www.mp3.com | | |

f = Founder
D=Director

| | | (4) Comp | (3B) Officers' Ownership | (3),(6),(7) Mgt & Emps Ownership | (1) Pre IPO Ownership | (2) Post IPO Ownership | (3B) Officers' Ownership | (3),(6),(7) Mgt & Emps Ownership | (1) Pre IPO Ownership | (2) Post IPO Ownership | IPO Value $28.00 Per Share |
|---|---|---|---|---|---|---|---|---|---|---|---|
| fD CEO, Chairman | Michael Robertson | $150,000 | 85.8% | 64.6% | 45.0% | 38.0% | 25,337,010 | 25,337,010 | 25,337,010 | 25,337,010 | $709,436,280 |
| D President, COO | Robin Richards | $240,000 | 8.3% | 6.2% | 4.3% | 3.7% | 2,437,500 | 2,437,500 | 2,437,500 | 2,437,500 | $68,250,000 |
| CFO, Exec. VP | Paul Ouyang | $150,000 | 2.1% | 1.6% | 1.1% | 0.9% | 630,000 | 630,000 | 630,000 | 630,000 | $17,640,000 |
| Exec. VP. Sales & Mktg | Steven Sheiner | $200,000 | 1.7% | 1.2% | 0.9% | 0.7% | 487,500 | 487,500 | 487,500 | 487,500 | $13,650,000 |
| Pres. Strategic Bis. | Paul Alofs | $200,000 | 1.7% | 1.3% | 0.9% | 0.7% | 495,000 | 495,000 | 495,000 | 495,000 | $13,860,000 |
| Exec. VP. Technology | Ronald Dotson | $140,000 | 0.5% | 0.4% | 0.3% | 0.2% | 150,000 | 150,000 | 150,000 | 150,000 | $4,200,000 |
| OFFICERS & EXECUTIVES | | | 100.0% | 75.3% | 52.5% | 44.3% | 29,537,010 | 29,537,010 | 29,537,010 | 29,537,010 | $827,036,280 |
| ALL OTHER COMMON | | | | 7.9% | 5.5% | 4.6% | | 3,083,485 | 3,083,485 | 3,083,485 | $86,337,580 |
| TOTAL COMMON BEFORE OPTIONS | | | | 83.2% | 58.0% | 49.0% | | 32,620,495 | 32,620,495 | 32,620,495 | $913,373,860 |
| OPTIONS-Outstanding | | | | 7.0% | 4.9% | 4.1% | | 2,757,750 | 2,757,750 | 2,757,750 | $77,217,000 |
| OPTIONS-Available | | | | 9.8% | 6.8% | 5.7% | | 3,823,500 | 3,823,500 | 3,823,500 | $107,058,000 |
| OPTIONS-Total | | | | 16.8% | 11.7% | 9.9% | | 6,581,250 | 6,581,250 | 6,581,250 | $184,275,000 |
| TOTAL-Executives and employees | | | | 100.0% | 69.6% | 58.8% | | 39,201,745 | 39,201,745 | 39,201,745 | $1,097,648,860 |
| Investors (includes major venture capital; excludes management as investors) | | | | | 28.3% | 23.9% | | | 15,910,878 | 15,910,878 | $445,504,584 |
| Other Investors | | | | | 2.1% | 1.8% | | | 1,175,000 | 1,175,000 | $32,900,000 |
| TOTAL-Investors Preferred & Other (shares, options & warrants) | | | | | 30.4% | 25.6% | | | 17,085,878 | 17,085,878 | $478,404,584 |
| PRE-IPO: sum of all stock | | | | | 100.0% | 84.5% | | | 56,287,623 | 56,287,623 | $1,576,053,444 |
| Initial Public Offering-New shares sold | | | | | | 13.5% | | | | 9,000,000 | $252,000,000 |
| Option to underwriters | | | | | | 2.0% | | | | 1,350,000 | $37,800,000 |
| TOTAL OUTSTANDING including Options & warrants | | | | | | 100.0% | | | | 66,637,623 | $1,865,853,444 |

| | | | | | |
|---|---|---|---|---|---|
| IPO Total cash raised before fees and expenses | | | $252,000,000 | | 100% |
| Paid to underwriters | Less: | | $17,640,000 | | 7.0% |
| CPA and other related expenses | Less: | | $1,600,000 | | 0.6% |
| | Net: | | $232,760,000 | | 92.4% |
| Shares sold by selling shareholders | | | 0 | | 0% |
| Total shares sold in this offering | | | 9,000,000 | | 100% |
| Option to underwriters | | | 1,350,000 | | 15% |

| | | |
|---|---|---|
| | REVENUE $ | REVENUE $ |
| | Qtr Mar 99 | 8 Mos Dec 99 |
| | $665,785 | $1,162,438 |
| | Growth/Year | Growth/Year |
| | NM | NM |
| | | Nr employees: 142 |

Vesting for Incentive Stock Option Plans is usually over four years.

| | |
|---|---|
| CPA firm | Lead Underwriters |
| Ernst & Young | Credit Suisse First Boston |
| | Hambrecht & Quist |
| | Bancboston Robertson Stevens |
| Counsel for Company | Charles Schwab & Co. |
| Cooley Godward | Counsel for Underwriters |
| Outside Directors | O'Melveny & Myers |

Cox Enterprises, David Esterly; Electronic Arts, Lawrence Probst; Sequoia Capital, Mark Stevens; Gateway 2000, Theodore Waitt. *The above contain certain estimates.*

**SARATOGA VENTURE FINANCE EQUITY TABLE**
WAGES AND STOCK OWNERSHIP AT INITIAL PUBLIC OFFERING

**Net2Phone Inc.**

| | |
|---|---|
| Internet telephone services | Initial Public Offering (IPO) date: July 29, 1999 |
| Hackensack, NJ | Company value $940,659,555 |
| Price per Share $15.00 | Internet URL: www.Net2Phone.com |
| Stock symbol: NTOP | |

State of Incorporation: Delaware
Date of Inception: January 1996
Years from inception to IPO: 3.6

| f = Founder / D=Director | Name | (4) Comp | (3B) Officers' Ownership | (3),(6),(7) Mgt & Emps Ownership | (1) Pre IPO Ownership | (2) Post IPO Ownership | (3B) Officers' Ownership | (3),(6),(7) Mgt & Emps Ownership | (1) Pre IPO Ownership | (2) Post IPO Ownership | IPO Value $15.00 Per Share |
|---|---|---|---|---|---|---|---|---|---|---|---|
| D Chairman | Clifford M. Sobel | $100,000 | 40.0% | 22.2% | 5.9% | 5.3% | 3,338,018 | 3,338,018 | 3,338,018 | 3,338,018 | $50,070,270 |
| D CEO, Vice Chairman | Howard S. Balter | | 22.5% | 12.5% | 3.3% | 3.0% | 1,874,499 | 1,874,499 | 1,874,499 | 1,874,499 | $28,117,485 |
| President | Jonathan Fram | | 12.2% | 6.8% | 1.8% | 1.6% | 1,020,000 | 1,020,000 | 1,020,000 | 1,020,000 | $15,300,000 |
| COO | David Greenblatt | $104,238 | 5.8% | 3.2% | 0.8% | 0.8% | 480,000 | 480,000 | 480,000 | 480,000 | $7,200,000 |
| CTO | Ilan M. Slasky | | 4.3% | 2.4% | 0.6% | 0.6% | 360,000 | 360,000 | 360,000 | 360,000 | $5,400,000 |
| | H. Jeff Goldberg | | 6.1% | 3.4% | 0.9% | 0.8% | 510,000 | 510,000 | 510,000 | 510,000 | $7,650,000 |
| EVP Mktg & Corp Dev | Jonathan Reich | $209,447 | 3.3% | 1.8% | 0.5% | 0.4% | 275,000 | 275,000 | 275,000 | 275,000 | $4,125,000 |
| EVP Strategic Sales | Martin Rothberg | | 4.3% | 2.4% | 0.6% | 0.6% | 360,000 | 360,000 | 360,000 | 360,000 | $5,400,000 |
| EVP Int'l Sales, Treas. | Jonathan Rand | | 1.4% | 0.8% | 0.2% | 0.2% | 120,000 | 120,000 | 120,000 | 120,000 | $1,800,000 |
| OFFICERS & EXECUTIVES | | | 100.0% | 55.5% | 14.8% | 13.3% | 8,337,517 | 8,337,517 | 8,337,517 | 8,337,517 | $125,062,755 |
| ALL OTHER COMMON | | | | 4.2% | 1.1% | 1.0% | | 637,137 | 637,137 | 637,137 | $9,557,055 |
| TOTAL COMMON BEFORE OPTIONS | | | | 59.8% | 15.9% | 14.3% | | 8,974,654 | 8,974,654 | 8,974,654 | $134,619,810 |
| OPTIONS-Outstanding | | | | 33.6% | 8.9% | 8.0% | | 5,040,000 | 5,040,000 | 5,040,000 | $75,600,000 |
| OPTIONS-Available | | | | 6.7% | 1.8% | 1.6% | | 1,000,501 | 1,000,501 | 1,000,501 | $15,007,515 |
| OPTIONS-Total | | | | 40.2% | 10.7% | 9.6% | | 6,040,501 | 6,040,501 | 6,040,501 | $90,607,515 |
| TOTAL-Executives and employees | | | | 100.0% | 26.6% | 23.9% | | 15,015,155 | 15,015,155 | 15,015,155 | $225,227,325 |
| Investors (includes major venture capital; excludes management as investors) | | | | | 73.4% | 66.2% | | | 41,485,482 | 41,485,482 | $622,282,230 |
| Other Investors | | | | | 0.0% | 0.0% | | | 0 | 0 | $0 |
| TOTAL-Investors Preferred & Other (shares, options & warrants) | | | | | 73.4% | 66.2% | | | 41,485,482 | 41,485,482 | $622,282,230 |
| PRE-IPO: sum of all stock | | | | | 100.0% | 90.1% | | | 56,500,637 | 56,500,637 | $847,509,555 |
| Initial Public Offering-New shares sold | | | | | | 8.6% | | | | 5,400,000 | $81,000,000 |
| Option to underwriters | | | | | | 1.3% | | | | 810,000 | $12,150,000 |
| TOTAL OUTSTANDING including Options & warrants | | | | | | 100.0% | | | | 62,710,637 | $940,659,555 |

| | | | | |
|---|---|---|---|---|
| IPO Total cash raised before fees and expenses | | $81,000,000 | | 100% |
| Paid to underwriters | Less: | $5,040,000 | | 6.2% |
| CPA and other related expenses | Less: | NA | | NA |
| | Net: | $5,040,000 | | 6.2% |
| Shares sold by company | $81,000,000 | 5,040,000 | | 100% |
| Shares sold by selling shareholders | | 0 | | 0% |
| Total shares sold in this offering | $5,400,000 | 5,400,000 | | 100% |
| Option to underwriters | | 810,000 | | 15% |

| REVENUE $K FY 1998 | REVENUE $K FY 1997 |
|---|---|
| $22,203 | $7,954 |
| Growth/Year 179% | Growth/Year NM |
| Nr employees: 171 | |

Vesting for Incentive Stock Option Plans is usually over four years.

| | |
|---|---|
| CPA firm *Ernst & Young* | Lead Underwriters *Hambrecht & Quist*, *BT Alex Brown*, *Bear, Stearns & Co.* |
| Counsel for Company *Morrison & Foerster* | Counsel for Underwriters *Brobeck, Phleger & Harrison* |
| Outside Directors *Softbank, Gary E. Rieschel; Rockefeller Foundation, Jesse King; Deutsche Bank Securities, James R. Mellor; IDT: Howard S. Jonas, James A. Courter, James R. Mellor* | |

**SARATOGA VENTURE FINANCE EQUITY TABLE**
WAGES AND STOCK OWNERSHIP AT INITIAL PUBLIC OFFERING

Internet software
Mountain View, California
Price per Share $28.00
Stock symbol NSCP

## Netscape Communications Corporation

Initial Public Offering (IPO) date: August 5, 1995
Company Value: $1,068,520,432
Internet URL: http://home.netscape.com

State of Incorporation: Delaware
Date of Inception: April 1994
Years from inception to IPO: 1.3

| f = Founder / D=Director | Name | (4) Est 12 Mos Comp | (3B) Officers' Ownership | (3),(6),(7) Mgt & Emps Ownership | (1) Pre IPO Ownership | (2) Post IPO Ownership | (3B) Officers' Ownership | (3),(6),(7) Mgt & Emps Ownership | (1) Pre IPO Ownership | (2) Post IPO Ownership | IPO Value $28.00 Per Share |
|---|---|---|---|---|---|---|---|---|---|---|---|
| fD Chairman | James H. Clark | | 56.1% | 41.2% | 30.0% | 25.5% | 9,720,000 | 9,720,000 | 9,720,000 | 9,720,000 | $272,160,000 |
| D Pres, CEO | James L. Barksdale | | 23.1% | 17.0% | 12.3% | 10.5% | 4,000,000 | 4,000,000 | 4,000,000 | 4,000,000 | $112,000,000 |
| fD VP Technology | Marc L. Andreessen | $80,000 | 5.8% | 4.2% | 3.1% | 2.6% | 1,000,000 | 1,000,000 | 1,000,000 | 1,000,000 | $28,000,000 |
| VP Engineering | Richard M. Schell | $215,000 | 2.3% | 1.7% | 1.2% | 1.0% | 400,000 | 400,000 | 400,000 | 400,000 | $11,200,000 |
| VP Marketing | Michael J. Homer | | 1.7% | 1.3% | 0.9% | 0.8% | 300,000 | 300,000 | 300,000 | 300,000 | $8,400,000 |
| VP Sales & Field Ops | Conway Rulon-Miller | $225,000 | 2.3% | 1.7% | 1.2% | 1.0% | 400,000 | 400,000 | 400,000 | 400,000 | $11,200,000 |
| VP GM Integrated Apps | James C.J. Sha | $200,000 | 3.5% | 2.5% | 1.9% | 1.6% | 600,000 | 600,000 | 600,000 | 600,000 | $16,800,000 |
| VP CFO | Peter L. S. Currie | | 1.7% | 1.3% | 0.9% | 0.8% | 300,000 | 300,000 | 300,000 | 300,000 | $8,400,000 |
| VP Gen Counsel & Sec | Roberta R. Katz | | 1.7% | 1.3% | 0.9% | 0.8% | 300,000 | 300,000 | 300,000 | 300,000 | $8,400,000 |
| VP Human Resources | Kandis Malefyt | | 1.7% | 1.3% | 0.9% | 0.8% | 300,000 | 300,000 | 300,000 | 300,000 | $8,400,000 |
| OFFICERS & EXECUTIVES | | | 100.0% | 73.4% | 53.4% | 45.4% | 17,320,000 | 17,320,000 | 17,320,000 | 17,320,000 | $484,960,000 |
| ALL OTHER COMMON | | | | 21.1% | 15.4% | 13.0% | | 4,976,328 | 4,976,328 | 4,976,328 | $139,337,184 |
| TOTAL COMMON BEFORE OPTIONS | | | | 94.5% | 68.8% | 58.4% | | 22,296,328 | 22,296,328 | 22,296,328 | $624,297,184 |
| OPTIONS-Outstanding | | | | 3.6% | 2.6% | 2.2% | | 855,000 | 855,000 | 855,000 | $23,940,000 |
| OPTIONS-Available | | | | 1.9% | 1.4% | 1.2% | | 443,672 | 443,672 | 443,672 | $12,422,816 |
| OPTIONS-Total | | | | 5.5% | 4.0% | 3.4% | | 1,298,672 | 1,298,672 | 1,298,672 | $36,362,816 |
| TOTAL-Executives and employees | | | | 100.0% | 72.8% | 61.8% | | 23,595,000 | 23,595,000 | 23,595,000 | $660,660,000 |
| Investors (includes major venture capital; excludes management as investors) | | | | | 27.2% | 23.1% | | | 8,816,444 | 8,816,444 | $246,860,432 |
| Other Investors | | | | | 0.0% | 0.0% | | | 0 | 0 | $0 |
| TOTAL-Investors Preferred & Other (shares, options & warrants) | | | | | 27.2% | 23.1% | | | 8,816,444 | 8,816,444 | $246,860,432 |
| PRE-IPO: sum of all stock | | | | | 100.0% | 84.9% | | | 32,411,444 | 32,411,444 | $907,520,432 |
| Initial Public Offering-New shares sold | | | | | | 13.1% | | | | 5,000,000 | $140,000,000 |
| Option to underwriters | | | | | | 2.0% | | | | 750,000 | $21,000,000 |
| TOTAL OUTSTANDING including Options & warrants | | | | | | 100.0% | | | | 38,161,444 | $1,068,520,432 |

| IPO Total cash raised before fees and expenses | | $140,000,000 | 100% |
|---|---|---|---|
| Paid to underwriters | Less: | $9,800,000 | 7.0% |
| CPA and other related expenses | Less: | $900,000 | 0.6% |
| | Net: | $129,300,000 | 92.4% |
| Shares sold by company | | 5,000,000 | 100% |
| Shares sold by selling shareholders | | 0 | 0% |
| Total shares sold in this offering | | 5,000,000 | 100% |
| Option to underwriters | | 750,000 | 15% |

| REVENUE $M 6 Mos 1995 | REVENUE $M Q2 FY95 |
|---|---|
| $16.6 | $11.9 |
| Growth/Year NM | Growth/Year NM |
| Nr employees: 257 | |

Vesting for Incentive Stock Option Plans is usually over 50 months after 10 month wait period.

| CPA firm | Lead Underwriters |
|---|---|
| Ernst & Young | Morgan Stanley |
| | Hambrecht & Quist |
| Counsel for Company | Counsel for Underwriters |
| Wilson Sonsini | Morrison & Foerster |
| Outside Directors | |
| Kleiner Perkins - John Doerr; Adobe - John E. Warnock | |

**Source:** *Saratoga Venture Finance © All rights reserved. See prospectus for data. The above contain certain estimates.*

**SARATOGA VENTURE FINANCE EQUITY TABLE**
WAGES AND STOCK OWNERSHIP AT INITIAL PUBLIC OFFERING

**Red Hat Inc**

Computer Software
Durham, NC
Price per Share $14.00
Stock symbol: RHAT

Initial Public Offering (IPO) date: July 31, 1999
Company value $1,174,189,128
Internet URL: www.redhat.com

State of Incorporation: Delaware
Date of Inception: March 1993
Years from inception to IPO: 6.4

| f = Founder D=Director | | (4) Comp | (3B) Officers' Ownership | (3),(6),(7) Mgt & Emps Ownership | (1) Pre IPO Ownership | (2) Post IPO Ownership | (3B) Officers' Ownership | (3),(6),(7) Mgt & Emps Ownership | (1) Pre IPO Ownership | (2) Post IPO Ownership | IPO Value $14.00 Per Share |
|---|---|---|---|---|---|---|---|---|---|---|---|
| fD | CEO, Chairman Robert F. Young | $227,599 | 38.6% | 22.1% | 12.3% | 10.8% | 9,081,826 | 9,081,826 | 9,081,826 | 9,081,826 | $127,145,564 |
| D | President Matthew J. Szulik | $185,000 | 11.6% | 6.7% | 3.7% | 3.3% | 2,736,248 | 2,736,248 | 2,736,248 | 2,736,248 | $38,307,472 |
| fD | Exec. VP, CTO Marc Ewing | $165,125 | 38.6% | 22.1% | 12.3% | 10.8% | 9,088,476 | 9,088,476 | 9,088,476 | 9,088,476 | $127,238,664 |
| | Sr. VP, COO Timothy J. Buckley | $155,000 | 10.2% | 5.8% | 3.2% | 2.9% | 2,393,972 | 2,393,972 | 2,393,972 | 2,393,972 | $33,515,608 |
| D | CFO, Dir, Admin, Treas, Manoj K. George | | | | | | | | | 240,000 | $3,360,000 |
| | Chief Mktg. Officer Tom Butta | | 1.0% | 0.6% | 0.3% | 0.3% | 240,000 | 240,000 | 240,000 | | |
| | OFFICERS & EXECUTIVES | | 100.0% | 57.3% | 31.9% | 28.1% | 23,540,522 | 23,540,522 | 23,540,522 | 23,540,522 | $329,567,308 |
| | ALL OTHER COMMON | | | 19.7% | 10.9% | 9.6% | | 8,075,606 | 8,075,606 | 8,075,606 | $113,058,484 |
| | TOTAL COMMON BEFORE OPTIONS | | | 77.0% | 42.9% | 37.7% | | 31,616,128 | 31,616,128 | 31,616,128 | $442,625,792 |
| | OPTIONS-Outstanding | | | 10.4% | 5.8% | 5.1% | | 4,259,996 | 4,259,996 | 4,259,996 | $59,639,944 |
| | OPTIONS-Available | | | 12.6% | 7.0% | 6.2% | | 5,174,804 | 5,174,804 | 5,174,804 | $72,447,256 |
| | OPTIONS-Total | | | 23.0% | 12.8% | 15.1% | | 9,434,800 | 9,434,800 | 12,632,250 | $176,851,500 |
| | TOTAL-Executives and employees | | | 100.0% | 55.6% | 52.8% | | 41,050,928 | 41,050,928 | 44,248,378 | $619,477,292 |
| | Investors (includes major venture capital; excludes management as investors) | | | | 19.9% | 17.5% | | | 14,711,328 | 14,711,328 | $205,958,592 |
| | Other Investors | | | | 24.4% | 21.5% | | | 18,010,946 | 18,010,946 | $252,153,244 |
| | TOTAL-Investors Preferred & Other (shares, options & warrants) | | | | 44.4% | 39.0% | | | 32,722,274 | 32,722,274 | $458,111,836 |
| | PRE-IPO: sum of all stock | | | | 100.0% | 91.8% | | | 73,773,202 | 76,970,652 | $1,077,589,128 |
| | Initial Public Offering-New shares sold | | | | | 7.2% | | | | 6,000,000 | $84,000,000 |
| | Option to underwriters | | | | | 1.1% | | | | 900,000 | $12,600,000 |
| | TOTAL OUTSTANDING including Options & warrants | | | | | 100.0% | | | | 83,870,652 | $1,174,189,128 |

| | | | | |
|---|---|---|---|---|
| IPO Total cash raised before fees and expenses | | | | $84,000,000 |
| Paid to underwriters | | | Less: | $5,880,000 |
| CPA and other related expenses | | | Less: | $1,250,000 |
| | | | Net: | $76,870,000 |
| Shares sold by company | | | | 6,000,000 |
| Shares sold by selling shareholders | | | | 0 |
| Total shares sold in this offering | | | | 6,000,000 |
| Option to underwriters | | | | 900,000 |

Vesting for Incentive Stock Option Plans is usually over 3 years by quarter

| CPA firm | Price Waterhouse-Coopers |
|---|---|
| Lead Underwriters | Goldman, Sachs & Co. Thomas Weisel Partners Hambrecht & Quist |
| Counsel for Company | Testa, Hurwitz & Thibeault E*Offering |
| Counsel for Underwriters | Hale & Dorr |
| Outside Directors | Landmark Communications, Frank Batten, Jr.; Greylock Mgmt., William S. Kaiser; Inventures Group, Eric Hahn |

| REVENUE $ FY1999 | REVENUE $ FY1998 |
|---|---|
| $10,790 | $5,156 |
| Growth/Year 109% | Growth/Year 98% |
| Nr employees: 140 | |

*Source: Saratoga Venture Finance © All rights reserved. See prospectus for data. The above contain certain estimates.*

**SARATOGA VENTURE FINANCE EQUITY TABLE**
WAGES AND STOCK OWNERSHIP AT INITIAL PUBLIC OFFERING

**Redback Networks Inc**

| High Speed Internet Systems | | State of Incorporation: Delaware |
|---|---|---|
| Sunnyvale, CA | Initial Public Offering (IPO) date: May 17, 1999 | Date of Inception: August 1996 |
| Price per Share $23.00 | Company value $663,740,440 | Years from inception to IPO: 2.8 |
| Stock symbol: RBAK | Internet URL: www.redback.net | |

f = Founder
D = Director

| | | (4) Comp | (3B) Officers' Ownership | (3),(6),(7) Mgt & Emps Ownership | (1) Pre IPO Ownership | (2) Post IPO Ownership | (3B) Officers' Ownership | (3),(6),(7) Mgt & Emps Ownership | (1) Pre IPO Ownership | (2) Post IPO Ownership | IPO Value $23.00 Per Share |
|---|---|---|---|---|---|---|---|---|---|---|---|
| D President, CEO | Dennis L. Barsema | $270,000 | 34.8% | 6.2% | 3.7% | 3.3% | 953,480 | 953,480 | 953,480 | 953,480 | $21,930,040 |
| VP Worldwide Sales | Randall J. Kruep | $225,422 | 13.7% | 2.4% | 1.4% | 1.3% | 375,000 | 375,000 | 375,000 | 375,000 | $8,625,000 |
| VP Engineering | William E. Miskovetz | $108,750 | 11.6% | 2.1% | 1.2% | 1.1% | 317,500 | 317,500 | 317,500 | 317,500 | $7,302,500 |
| VP Finance, CFO | Geoffrey C. Darby | $79,000 | 8.2% | 1.5% | 0.9% | 0.8% | 225,000 | 225,000 | 225,000 | 225,000 | $5,175,000 |
| VP Marketing | Larry D. Blair | | - | - | - | - | - | - | - | - | - |
| f CTO | Edward S. Harriman | | - | - | - | - | - | - | - | - | - |
| f VP Business Dev. | Gilles G. Concordel | | - | - | - | - | - | - | - | - | - |
| f VP BizDev & StratPlan | Gaurav Garg | | 31.8% | 5.7% | 3.4% | 3.0% | 872,550 | 872,550 | 872,550 | 872,550 | $20,068,650 |
| f Dir. of Software Dev. | William M. Salkewicz | | - | - | - | - | - | - | - | - | - |
| OFFICERS & EXECUTIVES | | | 100.0% | 17.9% | 10.6% | 9.5% | 2,743,530 | 2,743,530 | 2,743,530 | 2,743,530 | $63,101,190 |
| ALL OTHER COMMON | | | | 33.5% | 19.8% | 17.8% | | 5,139,576 | 5,139,576 | 5,139,576 | $118,210,248 |
| TOTAL COMMON BEFORE OPTIONS | | | | 51.4% | 30.3% | 27.3% | | 7,883,106 | 7,883,106 | 7,883,106 | $181,311,438 |
| OPTIONS-Outstanding | | | | 18.7% | 11.0% | 9.9% | | 2,866,411 | 2,866,411 | 2,866,411 | $65,927,453 |
| OPTIONS-Available | | | | 29.9% | 17.6% | 15.9% | | 4,582,750 | 4,582,750 | 4,582,750 | $105,403,250 |
| OPTIONS-Total | | | | 48.6% | 28.7% | 25.8% | | 7,449,161 | 7,449,161 | 7,449,161 | $171,330,703 |
| TOTAL-Executives and employees | | | | 100.0% | 59.0% | 53.1% | | 15,332,267 | 15,332,267 | 15,332,267 | $352,642,141 |
| Investors (includes major venture capital; excludes management as investors) | | | | | 41.0% | 36.9% | | | 10,651,013 | 10,651,013 | $244,973,299 |
| Other Investors | | | | | 0.0% | 0.0% | | | 0 | 0 | $0 |
| TOTAL-Investors Preferred & Other (shares, options & warrants) | | | | | 41.0% | 36.9% | | | 10,651,013 | 10,651,013 | $244,973,299 |
| PRE-IPO: sum of all stock | | | | | 100.0% | 90.0% | | | 25,983,280 | 25,983,280 | $597,615,440 |
| Initial Public Offering-New shares sold | | | | | | 8.7% | | | | 2,500,000 | $57,500,000 |
| Option to underwriters | | | | | | 1.3% | | | | 375,000 | $8,625,000 |
| TOTAL OUTSTANDING including Options & warrants | | | | | | 100.0% | | | | 28,858,280 | $663,740,440 |

| | | | |
|---|---|---|---|
| IPO Total cash raised before fees and expenses | | $57,500,000 | 100% |
| Paid to underwriters | Less: | $4,025,000 | 7.0% |
| CPA and other related expenses | Less: | $1,000,000 | 1.7% |
| | Net: | $52,475,000 | 91.3% |
| Shares sold by company | | 2,500,000 | 100% |
| Shares sold by selling shareholders | | 0 | 0% |
| Total shares sold in this offering | | 2,500,000 | 100% |
| Option to underwriters | | 375,000 | 15% |

| REVENUE $ | REVENUE $ |
|---|---|
| Qtr Mar 99 | Qtr Dec 98 |
| $6,517 | $4,501 |
| Growth/Year | Growth/Year |
| NM | NM |
| Nr employees: 127 | |

Vesting for Incentive Stock Option Plans is usually over four years.

| CPA Firm | Lead Underwriters |
|---|---|
| PricewaterhouseCoopers | Morgan Stanley Dean Witter |
| | BancBoston Robertson Stevens |
| Counsel for Company | Dain Rauscher Wessels |
| Wilson Sonsini Goodrich & Rosati | Counsel for Underwriters |
| Outside Directors | Gunderson Dettmer Stough Villeneuve Franklin & Hachigian |

Accel Partners, James R. Flach; Sequoia Capital, Pierre R. Lamond; Network Appliance, Daniel J. Warmenhoven

**SARATOGA VENTURE FINANCE EQUITY TABLE**
WAGES AND STOCK OWNERSHIP AT INITIAL PUBLIC OFFERING

Internet software
Sunnyvale, California
Price per Share **$13.00**
Stock symbol: YHOO

**Yahoo! Inc.**

Initial Public Offering (IPO) date: April 12, 1996
Company value $481,458,874
Internet URL: www.yahoo.com

State of Incorporation: California
Date of Inception: March 1995
Years from inception to IPO: 1:1

| f = Founder<br>D=Director | | (4)<br>Comp | (3B)<br>Officers'<br>Ownership | (3),(6),(7)<br>Mgt & Emps<br>Ownership | (1)<br>Pre IPO<br>Ownership | (2)<br>Post IPO<br>Ownership | (3B)<br>Officers'<br>Ownership | (3),(6),(7)<br>Mgt & Emps<br>Ownership | (1)<br>Pre IPO<br>Ownership | (2)<br>Post IPO<br>Ownership | IPO Value<br>$13.00<br>Per Share |
|---|---|---|---|---|---|---|---|---|---|---|---|
| D | Pres, CEO | Timothy Koogle | $68,750 | 11.4% | 5.5% | 3.0% | 2.8% | 1,025,510 | 1,025,510 | 1,025,510 | 1,025,510 | $13,331,630 |
| fD | Chief Yahoo | Jerry Yang | $65,000 | 44.3% | 21.3% | 11.8% | 10.8% | 4,003,750 | 4,003,750 | 4,003,750 | 4,003,750 | $52,048,750 |
| f | Chief Yahoo | David Filo | $65,000 | 44.3% | 21.3% | 11.8% | 10.8% | 4,003,750 | 4,003,750 | 4,003,750 | 4,003,750 | $52,048,750 |
| | Sr VP Business Ops | Jeff Mallett | | | | | | | | | | - |
| | Sr VP, CFO | Gary Valenzuela | | | | | | | | | | - |
| | Sr VP Product Devel | Farzad Nazem | | | | | | | | | | - |
| OFFICERS & EXECUTIVES | | | | 100.0% | 48.1% | 26.5% | 24.4% | 9,033,010 | 9,033,010 | 9,033,010 | 9,033,010 | $117,429,130 |
| ALL OTHER COMMON | | | | | 6.6% | 3.6% | 3.3% | | 1,231,716 | 1,231,716 | 1,231,716 | $16,012,308 |
| TOTAL COMMON BEFORE OPTIONS | | | | | 54.7% | 30.2% | 27.7% | | 10,264,726 | 10,264,726 | 10,264,726 | $133,441,438 |
| OPTIONS-Outstanding | | | | | 25.8% | 14.2% | 13.1% | | 4,834,868 | 4,834,868 | 4,834,868 | $62,853,284 |
| OPTIONS-Available | | | | | 19.5% | 10.8% | 9.9% | | 3,665,132 | 3,665,132 | 3,665,132 | $47,646,716 |
| OPTIONS-Total | | | | | 45.3% | 25.0% | 23.0% | | 8,500,000 | 8,500,000 | 8,500,000 | $110,500,000 |
| TOTAL-Executives and employees | | | | 100.0% | | 55.1% | 50.7% | | 18,764,726 | 18,764,726 | 18,764,726 | $243,941,438 |
| Investors (includes major venture capital; excludes management as investors) | | | | | 15.9% | 14.6% | | 5,415,344 | 5,415,344 | | $70,399,472 |
| Other Investors | | | | | 29.0% | 26.6% | | 9,865,228 | 9,865,228 | | $128,247,964 |
| TOTAL-Investors Preferred & Other (shares, options & warrants) | | | | | 44.9% | 41.3% | | 15,280,572 | 15,280,572 | | $198,647,436 |
| PRE-IPO: sum of all stock | | | | 100.0% | | 91.9% | | 34,045,298 | 34,045,298 | | $442,588,874 |
| Initial Public Offering-New shares sold | | | | | | 7.0% | | | 2,600,000 | | $33,800,000 |
| Option to underwriters | | | | | | 1.1% | | | 390,000 | | $5,070,000 |
| TOTAL OUTSTANDING including Options & warrants | | | | | | 100.0% | | | 37,035,298 | | $481,458,874 |

IPO Total cash raised before fees and expenses $33,800,000 100%
Paid to underwriters Less: $2,366,000 7.0%
CPA and other related expenses Less: $700,000 2.1%
Net: $30,734,000 90.9%
Shares sold by company 2,600,000 100%
Shares sold by selling shareholders 0 0%
Total shares sold in this offering 2,600,000 100%
Option to underwriters 390,000 15%

Vesting for Incentive Stock Option Plans is usually over four years.

| CPA firm | Lead Underwriters |
|---|---|
| *Price Waterhouse* | Goldman Sachs |
| | Donaldson Luftkin |
| | Montgomery |
| Counsel for Company | Counsel for Underwriters |
| Venture Law Group | Wilson Sonsini |
| Outside Directors | |

Sequoia Capital, Michael Moritz; Ziff-Davis, Eric Hippeau; American Media, Arthur Kern

| REVENUE $M<br>6 Mos 1995 | REVENUE $M<br>Qtr Dec31 1995 |
|---|---|
| $1.4 | $1.1 |
| Growth/Year<br>NM | Growth/Year<br>NM |
| Nr employees: 49 | |

**Source: *Saratoga Venture Finance* © All rights reserved. See prospectus for data. The above contain certain estimates.**

**SARATOGA VENTURE FINANCE EQUITY TABLE™**
WAGES AND STOCK OWNERSHIP AT INITIAL PUBLIC OFFERING (IPO)

# Apple Computer, Inc.

IPO DATE: 12 December 1980
$22.00  Price per Share

Microcomputers
Inception: 3 January 1977
Cupertino, California

| TITLE<br>f = Founder | (4)<br>COMPENSATION | (3B)<br>OFFICERS<br>OWNERSHIP | (3),(6),(7)<br>MGT & EMPS<br>OWNERSHIP | (1)<br>PRE IPO<br>OWNERSHIP | (2)<br>POST IPO<br>OWNERSHIP | (3B)<br>OFFICERS<br>OWNERSHIP | (3),(6),(7)<br>MGT & EMPS<br>OWNERSHIP | (1)<br>PRE IPO<br>OWNERSHIP | (2)<br>POST IPO<br>OWNERSHIP | IPO VALUE<br>$22.00<br>Per Share |
|---|---|---|---|---|---|---|---|---|---|---|
| Chairman,EVP | $135,182 | 25.8% | 15.4% | 12.6% | 11.2% | 7,029,448 | 7,029,448 | 7,029,448 | 7,029,448 | $154,647,856 |
| f V.Chairman,VP | | 27.7% | 16.5% | 13.5% | 12.0% | 7,542,448 | 7,542,448 | 7,542,448 | 7,542,448 | $165,933,856 |
| President,CEO | | 14.0% | 8.3% | 6.8% | 6.1% | 2,810,232 | 2,810,232 | 2,810,232 | 2,810,232 | $61,825,104 |
| f VP | | 14.7% | 8.7% | 7.1% | 6.4% | 3,989,231 | 3,989,231 | 3,989,231 | 3,989,231 | $87,763,082 |
| All Others = 7 | | 21.5% | 12.8% | 10.5% | 9.3% | 5,853,312 | 5,853,312 | 5,853,312 | 5,853,312 | $128,772,864 |
| OFFICERS & EXECUTIVES | | 100.0% | 59.5% | 48.7% | 43.4% | 27,224,671 | 27,224,671 | 27,224,671 | 27,224,671 | $598,942,762 |
| ALL OTHER | | | 28.1% | 23.0% | 20.5% | | 12,860,963 | 12,860,963 | 12,860,963 | $282,941,186 |
| TOTAL COMMON BEFORE OPTIONS | | | 87.6% | 71.8% | 63.9% | | 40,085,634 | 40,085,634 | 40,085,634 | $881,883,948 |
| OPTIONS-Outstanding | | | 12.4% | 10.1% | 9.0% | | | 5,652,600 | 5,652,600 | $124,357,200 |
| OPTIONS-Available | | | 0.0% | 0.0% | 4.5% | | | 0 | 2,852,600 | $62,757,200 |
| OPTIONS-Total | | | 12.4% | 10.1% | 13.6% | | | 5,652,600 | 8,505,200 | $187,114,400 |
| COMMON-Total | | | 100.0% | 81.9% | 77.5% | | | 45,738,234 | 48,590,834 | $1,068,998,348 |
| Major Venture Capital | | | | 7.8% | 7.0% | | | 4,375,816 | 4,375,816 | $96,267,952 |
| OTHER | | | | 10.3% | 9.2% | | | 5,753,882 | 5,753,882 | $126,585,404 |
| VENTURE-Total | | | | 18.1% | 16.2% | | | 10,129,698 | 10,129,698 | $222,853,356 |
| PRE-IPO: sum of all stock | | | | 100.0% | 93.6% | | | 55,867,932 | 58,720,532 | $1,291,851,704 |
| IPO-shares | | | | | 6.4% | | | | 4,000,000 | $88,000,000 |
| TOTAL-OUTSTANDING | | | | | 100.0% | | | | 62,720,532 | $1,379,851,704 |

Average $1.8M

| REVENUE $M | REVENUE $M |
|---|---|
| *Last 12 mos* | *Last Qtr* |
| $117.9 | $41.5 |
| *Growth/Year* | *Growth/Year* |
| 146.0% | 109.0% |

Nr. employees: 1,015

(7) Vesting for Stock Option Plans is usually 4 years, with six month waiting period, 1/48 per mo thereafter and FMV at time of grant.

Lead Underwriters: Morgan Stanley + Hambrecht & Quist

| | | |
|---|---|---|
| $101,200,000 | | IPO TOTAL CASH RAISED BEFORE FEES AND EXPENSES |
| $5,980,000 | 5.91% | IPO fee for underwriters |
| $661,600 | 0.65% | Estimated expenses of IPO |
| $94,558,400 | 93.44% | NET TO COMPANY |

4,000,000  shares sold by company
600,000  is sold by selling shareholders

**SOURCE:** *Saratoga Venture Finance © All rights reserved. See prospectus for data. The above contain certain estimates.*

**SARATOGA VENTURE FINANCE EQUITY TABLE ™**
WAGES AND STOCK OWNERSHIP AT INITIAL PUBLIC OFFERING (IPO)

## Business Land

IPO DATE: 14 December, 1983
$10.00  Price per Share

Chain of retail microcomputer stores
Inception: 30 March 1982
San Jose, California

| TITLE f = Founder | (4) COMPENSATION | (3B) OFFICERS OWNERSHIP | (3),(6),(7) MGT & EMPS OWNERSHIP | (1) PRE IPO OWNERSHIP | (2) POST IPO OWNERSHIP | (3B) OFFICERS OWNERSHIP | (3),(6),(7) MGT & EMPS OWNERSHIP | (1) PRE IPO OWNERSHIP | (2) POST IPO OWNERSHIP | IPO VALUE $10.00 Per Share |
|---|---|---|---|---|---|---|---|---|---|---|
| f CEO | $75,000 | 43.1% | 34.7% | 12.0% | 9.1% | 2,153,336 | 2,153,336 | 2,153,336 | 2,153,336 | $21,533,360 |
| f VP-MKTG | $75,000 | 14.0% | 11.3% | 3.9% | 3.0% | 700,000 | 700,000 | 700,000 | 700,000 | $7,000,000 |
| VP-OPS | $70,000 | 0.0% | 0.0% | 0.0% | 0.0% | 0 | 0 | 0 | 0 | $0 * |
| VP-STORES | * | 0.0% | 0.0% | 0.0% | 0.0% | 0 | 0 | 0 | 0 | $0 * |
| VP-BIS DEVL | * | 0.0% | 0.0% | 0.0% | 0.0% | 0 | 0 | 0 | 0 | $0 * |
| VP-FINANCE | * | 0.0% | 0.0% | 0.0% | 0.0% | 0 | 0 | 0 | 0 | $0 * |
| OTHER = 4 | *Avg. = $31,667 | 42.9% | 23.3% | 8.1% | 6.1% | 2,143,088 | 1,443,088 | 1,443,088 | 1,443,088 | $14,430,880 * |
| OFFICERS & EXECUTIVES | | 100.0% | 69.3% | 24.0% | 18.2% | 4,996,424 | 4,296,424 | 4,296,424 | 4,296,424 | $42,964,240 |
| ALL OTHER | | | 13.2% | 4.6% | 3.5% | | 818,756 | 818,756 | 818,756 | $8,187,560 |
| TOTAL COMMON BEFORE OPTIONS | | | 82.5% | 28.6% | 21.7% | | 5,115,180 | 5,115,180 | 5,115,180 | $51,151,800 |
| OPTIONS-Outstanding | | | 17.5% | 6.1% | 4.6% | | 1,088,650 | 1,088,650 | 1,088,650 | $10,886,500 |
| OPTIONS-Available | | | 0.0% | 0.0% | 3.0% | | 0 | 0 | 701,350 | $7,013,500 |
| OPTIONS-Total | | | 17.5% | 6.1% | 7.6% | | 1,088,650 | 1,088,650 | 1,790,000 | $17,900,000 |
| COMMON-Total | | | 100.0% | 34.7% | 29.3% | | 6,203,830 | 6,203,830 | 6,905,180 | $69,051,800 |
| Major Venture Capital | | | | 30.1% | 22.8% | | | 5,392,476 | 5,392,476 | $53,924,760 |
| OTHER | | | | 35.2% | 26.7% | | | 6,304,848 | 6,304,848 | $63,048,480 |
| VENTURE Total | | | | 65.3% | 49.6% | | | 11,697,324 | 11,697,324 | $116,973,240 |
| PRE-IPO: sum of all stock | | | | 100.0% | 78.8% | | | 17,901,154 | 18,602,504 | $186,025,040 |
| IPO shares | | | | | 21.2% | | | | 5,000,000 | $50,000,000 |
| TOTAL OUTSTANDING | | | | | 100.0% | | | | 23,602,504 | $236,025,040 |

Average $3.6M *

(7) Vesting for Stock Option Plans is usually 4 years, with six month waiting period, 1/48 per mo thereafter and fair market value at time of grant.
Lead Underwriters: Rothschild + Lehman

| | | | |
|---|---|---|---|
| 5,000,000 nr shares sold by company | $50,000,000 | | IPO TOTAL CASH RAISED BEFORE FEES AND EXPENSES |
| 0 nr shares sold by selling shareholders | $2,900,000 | 5.80% | IPO fee for underwriters |
| | $475,000 | 0.95% | Estimated expenses of IPO |
| 5,000,000 IPO TOTAL | $46,625,000 | 93.25% | NET TO COMPANY |

| REVENUE $M | REVENUE $M |
|---|---|
| Last 12 mos | Prior Quarter |
| $10.1 | $13.6 |
| Growth/Year | Growth/Year |
| Not meaningful | Not meaningful |

Nr of employes: 341

**SARATOGA VENTURE FINANCE EQUITY TABLE ™**
WAGES AND STOCK OWNERSHIP AT INITIAL PUBLIC OFFERING (IPO)

## Cirrus Logic

IPO DATE: 8 June 1989
$10.00  Price per Share

Semiconductors
Inception: November 1984
Milpitas, California

| TITLE<br>f = Founder | (4)<br>COMPENSATION | (3B)<br>OFFICERS<br>OWNERSHIP | (3),(6),(7)<br>MGT & EMPS<br>OWNERSHIP | (1)<br>PRE IPO<br>OWNERSHIP | (2)<br>POST IPO<br>OWNERSHIP | (3B)<br>OFFICERS<br>OWNERSHIP | (3),(6),(7)<br>MGT & EMPS<br>OWNERSHIP | (1)<br>PRE IPO<br>OWNERSHIP | (2)<br>POST IPO<br>OWNERSHIP | IPO VALUE<br>$10.00<br>Per Share |
|---|---|---|---|---|---|---|---|---|---|---|
| f CEO | $213,087 | 24.8% | 13.5% | 2.6% | 2.1% | 328,857 | 328,857 | 328,857 | 328,857 | $3,288,570 |
| f VP-R&D | $127,131 | 36.4% | 19.8% | 3.8% | 3.1% | 483,554 | 483,554 | 483,554 | 483,554 | $4,835,540 |
| f Employee | | 8.8% | 4.8% | 0.9% | 0.8% | 117,000 | 117,000 | 117,000 | 117,000 | $1,170,000 |
| f Employee | $134,083 | 8.4% | 4.5% | 0.9% | 0.7% | 111,000 | 111,000 | 111,000 | 111,000 | $1,110,000 |
| VP-Mfg | $132,830 | 6.8% | 3.7% | 0.7% | 0.6% | 90,000 | 90,000 | 90,000 | 90,000 | $900,000 |
| VP-Eng. | $123,904 | 0.0% | 0.0% | 0.0% | 0.0% | 0 | 0 | 0 | 0 | $0 * |
| VP-Mktg | | 0.0% | 0.0% | 0.0% | 0.0% | 0 | 0 | 0 | 0 | $0 * |
| f Employee | | 0.0% | 0.0% | 0.0% | 0.0% | 0 | 0 | 0 | 0 | $0 * |
| f VP-Strategic Development-Left | | 0.0% | 0.0% | 0.0% | 0.0% | 0 | 0 | 0 | 0 | $0 * |
| OTHER  Avg. of 5 = $94,649 | | 14.9% | 8.1% | 1.5% | 1.3% | 198,000 | 198,000 | 198,000 | 198,000 | $1,980,000 |
| OFFICERS & EXECUTIVES | | 100.0% | 54.3% | 10.3% | 8.6% | 1,328,411 | 1,328,411 | 1,328,411 | 1,328,411 | $13,284,110 |
| ALL OTHER | | | 14.0% | 2.7% | 2.2% | | 343,342 | 343,342 | 343,342 | $3,433,420 |
| TOTAL COMMON BEFORE OPTIONS | | | 68.4% | 13.0% | 10.8% | | 1,671,753 | 1,671,753 | 1,671,753 | $16,717,530 |
| OPTIONS-Outstanding | | | 31.6% | 6.0% | 5.0% | | 772,990 | 772,990 | 772,990 | $7,729,900 |
| OPTIONS-Available | | | 0.0% | 0.0% | 3.0% | | 0 | 0 | 470,882 | $4,708,820 |
| OPTIONS-Total | | | 31.6% | 6.0% | 8.0% | | 772,990 | 772,990 | 1,243,872 | $12,438,720 |
| COMMON-Total | | | 100.0% | 19.0% | 18.8% | | 2,444,743 | 2,444,743 | 2,915,625 | $29,156,250 |
| Major Venture Capital | | | | 64.8% | 53.9% | | | 8,340,200 | 8,340,200 | $83,402,000 |
| OTHER | | | | 16.1% | 13.4% | | | 2,076,236 | 2,076,236 | $20,762,360 |
| VENTURE Total | | | | 81.0% | 67.3% | | | 10,416,436 | 10,416,436 | $104,164,360 |
| PRE-IPO: sum of all stock | | | | 100.0% | 86.1% | | | 12,861,179 | 13,332,061 | $133,320,610 |
| IPO shares | | | | | 13.9% | | | | 2,150,000 | $21,500,000 |
| TOTAL OUTSTANDING | | | | | 100.0% | | | | 15,482,061 | $154,820,610 |

Avg. of 4=$495K

| REVENUE$M | REVENUE$M |
|---|---|
| Last 12 mos | Prior Quarter |
| $36.9 | $12.1 |
| Growth/Year | Growth/Year |
| 299.5% | NA |
| Nr of employes: 178 | |

(7) Vesting for Stock Option Plans is usually 4 years, with 25% at end of a one year waiting period, 1/48th per month thereafter and fair market value at time of grant.

Lead Underwriters: Goldman Sachs + Alex. Brown + Robertson

| | | |
|---|---|---|
| 2,150,000 nr shares sold by company | $33,400,000 | IPO TOTAL CASH RAISED BEFORE FEES AND EXPENSES |
| | $2,338,000 | 7.00% IPO fee for underwriters |
| 1,190,000 nr shares sold by selling shareholders | $660,000 | 1.98% Estimated expenses of IPO |
| 3,340,000 IPO TOTAL | $30,402,000 | 91.02% NET TO COMPANY |

**SARATOGA VENTURE FINANCE EQUITY TABLE ™**
WAGES AND STOCK OWNERSHIP AT INITIAL PUBLIC OFFERING (IPO)

# Conner Peripherals, Inc.

IPO DATE: 12 April 1988
$8.00   Price per Share

Disk drives
Inception: 18 June 1985
San Jose, California

| TITLE f = Founder | (4) COMPENSATION | (3B) OFFICERS OWNERSHIP | (3),(6),(7) MGT & EMPS OWNERSHIP | (1) PRE IPO OWNERSHIP | (2) POST IPO OWNERSHIP | (3B) OFFICERS OWNERSHIP | (3),(6),(7) MGT & EMPS OWNERSHIP | (1) PRE IPO OWNERSHIP | (2) POST IPO OWNERSHIP | IPO VALUE $8.00 Per Share |
|---|---|---|---|---|---|---|---|---|---|---|
| f Chair,CEO | $189,518 | 40.0% | 24.4% | 9.2% | 8.0% | 3,000,000 | 3,000,000 | 3,000,000 | 3,000,000 | $24,000,000 |
| Pres,COO | $160,396 | 2.5% | 1.5% | 0.6% | 0.5% | 187,500 | 187,500 | 187,500 | 187,500 | $1,500,000 |
| EVP R&D | $148,857 | 26.6% | 16.3% | 6.2% | 5.3% | 2,000,000 | 2,000,000 | 2,000,000 | 2,000,000 | $16,000,000 |
| EVP Sls&Mktg | $130,190 | 0.0% | 0.0% | 0.0% | 0.0% | 0 | 0 | 0 | 0 | $0 * |
| SVP, CFO | | 0.0% | 0.0% | 0.0% | 0.0% | 0 | 0 | 0 | 0 | $0 * |
| VP Sales | $109,611 | 0.0% | 0.0% | 0.0% | 0.0% | 0 | 0 | 0 | 0 | $0 * |
| OTHER=3 | $99,427 | 4.1% | 2.5% | 1.0% | 0.8% | 310,627 | 310,627 | 310,627 | 310,627 | $2,485,016 * |
| Not an exec   Left company | | 26.8% | 16.3% | 6.2% | 5.4% | 2,009,020 | 2,009,020 | 2,009,020 | 2,009,020 | $16,072,160 |
| OFFICERS & EXECUTIVES | | 100.0% | 61.1% | 23.1% | 20.0% | 7,507,147 | 7,507,147 | 7,507,147 | 7,507,147 | 60,057,176 |
| ALL OTHER | | | 6.3% | 2.4% | 2.1% | | 770,110 | 770,110 | 770,110 | $6,160,880 |
| TOTAL COMMON BEFORE OPTIONS | | | 67.4% | 25.5% | 22.1% | | 8,277,257 | 8,277,257 | 8,277,257 | $66,218,056 |
| OPTIONS-Outstanding | | | 20.2% | 7.7% | 6.6% | | 2,486,939 | 2,486,939 | 2,486,939 | $19,895,512 |
| OPTIONS-Available | | | 12.4% | 4.7% | 4.1% | | 1,523,834 | 1,523,834 | 1,523,834 | $12,190,672 |
| OPTIONS-Total | | | 32.6% | 12.4% | 10.7% | | 4,010,773 | 4,010,773 | 4,010,773 | $32,086,184 |
| COMMON-Total | | | 100.0% | 37.8% | 32.8% | | 12,288,030 | 12,288,030 | 12,288,030 | $98,304,240 |
| Major Venture Capital | | | | 19.5% | 16.9% | | | 6,330,070 | 6,330,070 | $50,640,560 |
| Other: Compaq Computer Corporation | | | | 42.7% | 37.0% | | | 13,854,524 | 13,854,524 | $110,836,192 |
| INVESTORS-Total Holdings | | | | 62.2% | 53.9% | | | 20,184,594 | 20,184,594 | $161,476,752 |
| PRE-IPO: sum of all stock | | | | 100.0% | 86.7% | | | 32,472,624 | 32,472,624 | $259,780,992 |
| IPO shares | | | | | 13.3% | | | | 5,000,000 | $40,000,000 |
| TOTAL OUTSTANDING | | | | | 100.0% | | | | 37,472,624 | $299,780,992 |

| REVENUE $M | REVENUE $M |
|---|---|
| Last 12 mos | Recent Qtr |
| $113.2 | $51.2 |
| Growth/Year Not meaningful | Growth/Year Not meaningful |
| Nr of employes: 1,286 | |

Average $414K *

(7) Vesting for Incentive Stock Option Plans is usually over 4 years, vesting at 1/48th per month.
Lead Underwriters: Sherson + Montgomery

| | |
|---|---|
| 5,000,000 | Shares sold by company |
| 0 | Shares sold by selling shareholders |

| | | |
|---|---|---|
| $40,000,000 | | IPO TOTAL CASH RAISED BEFORE FEES AND EXPENSES |
| $2,800,000 | 7.00% | IPO fee for underwriters |
| $685,000 | 1.71% | Estimated expenses of IPO |
| $36,515,000 | 91.29% | NET TO COMPANY |

**SOURCE: *Saratoga Venture Finance © All rights reserved. See prospectus for data. The above contain certain estimates.***

**SARATOGA VENTURE FINANCE EQUITY TABLE ™**
WAGES AND STOCK OWNERSHIP AT INITIAL PUBLIC OFFERING (IPO)

## Convex

IPO DATE: 17 October 1986
$7.50  Price per Share

Minisupercomputers
Inception: 8 September 1982
Richardson, Texas

| TITLE f = Founder | (4) COMPENSATION | (3B) OFFICERS OWNERSHIP | (3),(6),(7) MGT & EMPS OWNERSHIP | (1) PRE IPO OWNERSHIP | (2) POST IPO OWNERSHIP | (3B) OFFICERS OWNERSHIP | (3),(6),(7) MGT & EMPS OWNERSHIP | (1) PRE IPO OWNERSHIP | (2) POST IPO OWNERSHIP | IPO VALUE $7.50 Per Share |
|---|---|---|---|---|---|---|---|---|---|---|
| f CEO | $86,500 | 28.8% | 19.1% | 5.5% | 4.3% | 750,000 | 750,000 | 750,000 | 750,000 | $5,625,000 |
| f VP-TECH | $86,500 | 28.8% | 19.1% | 5.5% | 4.3% | 750,000 | 750,000 | 750,000 | 750,000 | $5,625,000 |
| VP-DEVEL | $82,308 | 10.7% | 7.1% | 2.1% | 1.6% | 280,000 | 280,000 | 280,000 | 280,000 | $2,100,000 |
| VP-INT OPS | $77,846 | 9.6% | 6.4% | 1.8% | 1.4% | 250,000 | 250,000 | 250,000 | 250,000 | $1,875,000 |
| VP-FINANCE | $77,846 | 0.0% | 0.0% | 0.0% | 0.0% | 0 | 0 | 0 | 0 | $0 * |
| VP-SALES | * | 0.0% | 0.0% | 0.0% | 0.0% | 0 | 0 | 0 | 0 | $0 * |
| VP-OPS | | 0.0% | 0.0% | 0.0% | 0.0% | 0 | 0 | 0 | 0 | $0 * |
| VP-HR | | 0.0% | 0.0% | 0.0% | 0.0% | 0 | 0 | 0 | 0 | $0 * |
| VP-SW | * | 0.0% | 0.0% | 0.0% | 0.0% | 0 | 0 | 0 | 0 | $0 * |
| CONTROLLER | * | 0.0% | 0.0% | 0.0% | 0.0% | 0 | 0 | 0 | 0 | $0 * |
| OTHER=Avg* | $69,552 | 0.0% | 14.7% | 4.3% | 3.3% | 577,000 | 577,000 | 577,000 | 577,000 | $4,327,500 |
| OFFICERS & EXECUTIVES | | 100.0% | 66.4% | 19.3% | 14.9% | 2,607,000 | 2,607,000 | 2,607,000 | 2,607,000 | $19,552,500 |
| ALL OTHER | | | 30.9% | 9.0% | 7.0% | | 1,213,735 | 1,213,735 | 1,213,735 | $9,103,013 |
| TOTAL COMMON BEFORE OPTIONS | | | 97.4% | 28.2% | 21.9% | | 3,820,735 | 3,820,735 | 3,820,735 | $28,655,513 |
| OPTIONS-Outstanding | | | 2.6% | 0.8% | 0.6% | | 103,024 | 103,024 | 103,024 | $772,680 |
| OPTIONS-Available | | | 0.0% | 0.0% | 5.2% | | 0 | 0 | 913,162 | $6,848,715 |
| OPTIONS-Total | | | 2.6% | 0.8% | 5.8% | | 103,024 | 103,024 | 1,016,186 | $7,621,395 |
| COMMON-Total | | | 100.0% | 29.0% | 27.7% | | 3,923,759 | 3,923,759 | 4,836,921 | $36,276,908 |
| Major Venture Capital | | | | 52.0% | 40.4% | | | 7,039,942 | 7,039,942 | $52,799,565 |
| OTHER | | | | 19.0% | 14.7% | | | 2,565,508 | 2,565,508 | $19,241,310 |
| VENTURE Total | | | | 71.0% | 55.1% | | | 9,605,450 | 9,605,450 | $72,040,875 |
| PRE-IPO: sum of all stock | | | | 100.0% | 82.8% | | | 13,529,209 | 14,442,371 | $108,317,783 |
| IPO shares | | | | | 17.2% | | | | 3,000,000 | $22,500,000 |
| TOTAL OUTSTANDING | | | | | 100.0% | | | | 17,442,371 | $130,817,783 |

Average $721K *

(7) Vesting for Stock Option Plans is usually 4 years, with 1/4 at the end of each of the first two years, 1/48 per mo thereafter; fair market value at time of grant.

Lead Underwriters: Goldman Sachs + Robertson

| | | | | |
|---|---|---|---|---|
| 3,000,000 | nr shares sold by company | $23,512,500 | IPO TOTAL CASH RAISED BEFORE FEES AND EXPENSES | |
| 135,000 | nr shares sold by selling shareholders | $1,504,800 | IPO fee for underwriters | 6.40% |
| 3,135,000 | | $479,400 | Estimated expenses of IPO | 2.04% |
| | | $21,528,300 | NET TO COMPANY | 91.56% |

| REVENUE $M | REVENUE $M |
|---|---|
| Last 12 mos | Recent Qtr |
| $13.5 | $9.1 |
| Growth/Year | Growth/Year |
| Not meaningful | 356.3% |
| | Nr of employees: 272 |

**SARATOGA VENTURE FINANCE EQUITY TABLE ™**
WAGES AND STOCK OWNERSHIP AT INITIAL PUBLIC OFFERING (IPO)

## Cygnus Therapeutic Systems

IPO DATE: 31 January 1991
$9.00  Price per Share

Transdermal drug delivery systems
Inception: April 1985
Redwood City, California

| TITLE f = Founder | (4) COMPENSATION | (3B) OFFICERS OWNERSHIP | (3),(6),(7) MGT & EMPS OWNERSHIP | (1) PRE IPO OWNERSHIP | (2) POST IPO OWNERSHIP | (3B) OFFICERS OWNERSHIP | (3),(6),(7) MGT & EMPS OWNERSHIP | (1) PRE IPO OWNERSHIP | (2) POST IPO OWNERSHIP | IPO VALUE $9.00 Per Share |
|---|---|---|---|---|---|---|---|---|---|---|
| f Chair.,SVP-R&D | $135,519 | 55.5% | 35.8% | 22.9% | 16.6% | 2,042,115 | 2,042,115 | 2,042,115 | 2,042,115 | $18,379,035 |
| Pres., CEO | $136,519 | 9.8% | 6.3% | 4.0% | 2.9% | 359,580 | 359,580 | 359,580 | 359,580 | $3,236,220 |
| VP-Mktg | $115,315 | 0.0% | 0.0% | 0.0% | 0.0% | 0 | 0 | 0 | 0 | $0 |
| VP-Ops | $88,062 | 0.0% | 0.0% | 0.0% | 0.0% | 0 | 0 | 0 | 0 | $0 |
| OTHER | Avg. of 2 = $89,875 | 34.7% | 22.4% | 14.3% | 10.4% | 1,277,196 | 1,277,196 | 1,277,196 | 1,277,196 | $11,494,764 * |
| OFFICERS & EXECUTIVES | | 100.0% | 64.5% | 41.3% | 30.0% | 3,678,891 | 3,678,891 | 3,678,891 | 3,678,891 | $33,110,019 |
| ALL OTHER | | | 13.5% | 8.6% | 6.3% | | 771,188 | 771,188 | 771,188 | $6,940,692 |
| TOTAL COMMON BEFORE OPTIONS | | | 78.0% | 49.9% | 36.2% | | 4,450,079 | 4,450,079 | 4,450,079 | $40,050,711 |
| OPTIONS-Outstanding | | | 22.0% | 14.1% | 10.2% | | 1,255,788 | 1,255,788 | 1,255,788 | $11,302,092 |
| OPTIONS-Available | | | 0.0% | 0.0% | 2.9% | | 0 | 0 | 360,597 | $3,245,373 |
| OPTIONS-Total | | | 22.0% | 14.1% | 13.2% | | 1,255,788 | 1,255,788 | 1,616,385 | $14,547,465 |
| COMMON-Total | | | 100.0% | 64.0% | 49.4% | | 5,705,867 | 5,705,867 | 6,066,464 | $54,598,176 |
| Major Venture Capital | | | | 24.2% | 17.6% | | | 2,155,560 | 2,155,560 | $19,400,040 |
| OTHER | | | | 11.8% | 8.6% | | | 1,055,748 | 1,055,748 | $9,501,732 |
| VENTURE Total | | | | 36.0% | 26.2% | | | 3,211,308 | 3,211,308 | $28,901,772 |
| PRE-IPO: sum of all stock | | | | 100.0% | 75.6% | | | 8,917,175 | 9,277,772 | $83,499,948 |
| IPO shares | | | | | 24.4% | | | | 3,000,000 | $27,000,000 |
| TOTAL OUTSTANDING | | | | | 100.0% | | | | 12,277,772 | $110,499,948 |

Avg. of 3=$3.8M *

(7) Vesting for Stock Option Plans is usually 4 years, with 25% at end of a one year waiting period, 1/48th per month thereafter and fair market value at time of grant.

Lead Underwriters: Hambrecht & Quist + Robertson

| | | | |
|---|---|---|---|
| 3,000,000 nr shares sold by company | $27,000,000 | | IPO TOTAL CASH RAISED BEFORE FEES AND EXPENSES |
| 0 nr shares sold by selling shareholders | $1,890,000 | 7.00% | IPO fee for underwriters |
| | $500,000 | 1.85% | Estimated expenses of IPO |
| 3,000,000 IPO TOTAL | $24,610,000 | 91.15% | NET TO COMPANY |

| REVENUE $M | REVENUE $M |
|---|---|
| Last 12 mos | Prior Quarter |
| $3.2 | NA |
| Growth/Year | Growth/Year |
| 26.8% | NA |
| Nr of employees: 58 | |

SOURCE: *Saratoga Venture Finance* © *All rights reserved.  See prospectus for data.  The above contain certain estimates.*

**SARATOGA VENTURE FINANCE EQUITY TABLE ™**
WAGES AND STOCK OWNERSHIP AT INITIAL PUBLIC OFFERING (IPO)

## Cypress Semiconductor

IPO DATE: 29 May 1986
$9.00 Price per Share

Semiconductors
Inception: December 1982
San Jose, California

| TITLE (f = Founder) | (5) COMPENSATION | (3B) OFFICERS OWNERSHIP | (3),(6),(7) MGT & EMPS OWNERSHIP | (1) PRE IPO OWNERSHIP | (2) POST IPO OWNERSHIP | (3B) OFFICERS OWNERSHIP | (3),(6),(7) MGT & EMPS OWNERSHIP | (1) PRE IPO OWNERSHIP | (2) POST IPO OWNERSHIP | IPO VALUE $9.00 Per Share |
|---|---|---|---|---|---|---|---|---|---|---|
| f President, CEO | $150,000 | 27.9% | 11.3% | 2.9% | 2.1% | | 754,666 | 754,666 | 754,666 | $6,791,994 |
| f VP-Mktg&Sales | $106,866 | 11.1% | 4.5% | 1.1% | 0.9% | | 300,000 | 300,000 | 300,000 | $2,700,000 |
| f VP-Mfg | $105,918 | 11.1% | 4.5% | 1.1% | 0.9% | | 300,000 | 300,000 | 300,000 | $2,700,000 |
| f VP-Fabrication | $101,909 | 11.1% | 4.5% | 1.1% | 0.9% | | 300,000 | 300,000 | 300,000 | $2,700,000 |
| f VP-R&D | $103,553 | 11.1% | 4.5% | 1.1% | 0.9% | | 300,000 | 300,000 | 300,000 | $2,700,000 |
| f VP-Engineering | | 11.1% | 4.5% | 1.1% | 0.9% | | 300,000 | 300,000 | 300,000 | $2,700,000 |
| VP-F&A, CFO | | 5.8% | 2.3% | 0.6% | 0.4% | | 155,625 | 155,625 | 155,625 | $1,400,625 |
| Others | | 10.7% | 4.3% | 1.1% | 0.8% | | 290,132 | 290,132 | 290,132 | $2,611,188 |
| OFFICERS & EXECUTIVES | | 100.0% | 40.3% | 10.3% | 7.7% | 2,700,423 | 2,700,423 | 2,700,423 | 2,700,423 | $24,303,807 |
| ALL OTHER | | | 26.5% | 6.7% | 5.0% | | 1,774,992 | 1,774,992 | 1,774,992 | $15,974,928 |
| TOTAL COMPANY BEFORE OPTIONS | | | 66.8% | 17.0% | 12.7% | | 4,475,415 | 4,475,415 | 4,475,415 | $40,278,735 |
| Options-Granted | | | 33.2% | 8.5% | 6.3% | | 2,225,415 | 2,225,415 | 2,225,415 | $20,028,735 |
| Options-Available | | | 0.0% | 0.0% | 4.2% | | 0 | 0 | 1,474,585 | $13,271,265 |
| OPTIONS-Total | | | 33.2% | 8.5% | 10.5% | | 2,225,415 | 2,225,415 | 3,700,000 | $33,300,000 |
| COMMON-Total | | | 100.0% | 25.5% | 23.2% | | 6,700,830 | 6,700,830 | 8,175,415 | $73,578,735 |
| Major Venture Capitalists | | | | 54.2% | 40.4% | | | 14,265,444 | 14,265,444 | $128,388,996 |
| Monolithic Memories, Inc. | | | | 2.9% | 2.1% | | | 750,000 | 750,000 | $6,750,000 |
| Other Preferred Investors | | | | 17.4% | 13.0% | | | 4,590,067 | 4,590,067 | $41,310,603 |
| Preferred-Total | | | | 74.5% | 55.6% | | | 19,605,511 | 19,605,511 | $176,449,599 |
| PRE-IPO: sum of all stock | | | | 100.0% | 78.7% | | | 26,306,341 | 27,780,926 | $250,028,334 |
| IPO-shares | | | | | 21.3% | | | | 7,500,000 | $67,500,000 |
| TOTAL OUTSTANDING | | | | | 100.0% | | | | 35,280,926 | $317,528,334 |

(7) Vesting for Stock Option Plans is usually 4 years, with a one year waiting period, 1/48 per mo thereafter and fair market value at time of grant.

Lead Underwriters: Morgan Stanley + Robertson

| | | | |
|---|---|---|---|
| 7,500,000 nr shares sold by company | $67,500,000 | | IPO TOTAL CASH RAISED BEFORE FEES AND EXPENSES |
| 0 nr shares sold by selling shareholders | $4,200,000 | 6.22% | IPO fee for underwriters |
| | $500,000 | 0.74% | Estimated expenses of IPO |
| | $62,800,000 | 93.04% | NET TO COMPANY |

| REVENUE $M | REVENUE $M |
|---|---|
| Last 12 mos | Prior Quarter |
| $16.6 | $8.9 |
| Growth/Year | Growth/Year |
| 412.9% | 218.2% |
| Nr of employes: 340 | |

SARATOGA VENTURE FINANCE EQUITY TABLE ™
WAGES AND STOCK OWNERSHIP AT INITIAL PUBLIC OFFERING (IPO)

# Linear Technology Corporation

IPO DATE: 28 May 1986
$8.00 Price per Share

Analog semiconductors
Inception: 10 September 1981
Milpitas, California

| TITLE f = Founder | (4) COMPENSATION | (3B) OFFICERS OWNERSHIP | (3),(6),(7) MGT & EMPS OWNERSHIP | (1) PRE IPO OWNERSHIP | (2) POST IPO OWNERSHIP | (3B) OFFICERS OWNERSHIP | (3),(6),(7) MGT & EMPS OWNERSHIP | (1) PRE IPO OWNERSHIP | (2) POST IPO OWNERSHIP | IPO VALUE $8.00 Per Share |
|---|---|---|---|---|---|---|---|---|---|---|
| f CEO | $135,231 | 27.3% | 12.6% | 5.4% | 4.6% | 950,000 | 950,000 | 848,106 | 848,106 | $6,784,848 |
| f VP-MS-Left | | 19.1% | 8.8% | 1.6% | 1.4% | 665,000 | 665,000 | 254,004 | 254,004 | $2,032,032 |
| VP-MKT | $95,163 | 2.0% | 0.9% | 0.4% | 0.4% | 70,000 | 70,000 | 70,000 | 70,000 | $560,000 |
| VP-SLS-Left | $100,173 | 2.0% | 0.9% | 0.1% | 0.1% | 70,000 | 70,000 | 21,001 | 21,001 | $168,008 |
| f VP-OPS | $101,173 | 19.1% | 8.8% | 3.8% | 3.3% | 665,000 | 665,000 | 600,000 | 600,000 | $4,800,000 |
| VP-QR | | 2.2% | 1.0% | 0.5% | 0.4% | 75,000 | 75,000 | 75,000 | 75,000 | $600,000 |
| f VP-ENG | $101,173 | 19.1% | 8.8% | 3.8% | 3.3% | 665,000 | 665,000 | 605,754 | 605,754 | $4,846,032 |
| f VP-FA | | 1.9% | 0.9% | 0.4% | 0.4% | 65,000 | 65,000 | 65,000 | 65,000 | $520,000 |
| f OTHERS | Avg = $89,191 | 19.1% | 3.3% | 1.6% | 1.4% | 251,751 | 251,751 | 251,751 | 251,751 | $2,014,008 |
| OFFICERS & EXECUTIVES | | 100.0% | 46.0% | 17.6% | 15.3% | 3,476,751 | 3,476,569 | 2,790,616 | 2,790,616 | $22,324,928 |
| ALL OTHER | | | 25.0% | 11.9% | 10.3% | | 1,887,818 | 1,887,818 | 1,887,818 | $15,102,544 |
| TOTAL COMMON BEFORE OPTIONS | | | 71.0% | 29.6% | 25.6% | | 5,364,569 | 4,678,434 | 4,678,434 | $37,427,472 |
| OPTIONS-Outstanding | | | 29.0% | 13.9% | 12.0% | | 2,195,530 | 2,195,530 | 2,195,530 | $17,564,240 |
| OPTIONS-Available | | | 0.0% | 0.0% | 2.4% | | 0 | 0 | 429,470 | $3,435,760 |
| OPTIONS-Total | | | 29.0% | 13.9% | 14.4% | | 2,195,530 | 2,195,530 | 2,625,000 | $21,000,000 |
| COMMON-Total | | | 100.0% | 43.4% | 40.0% | | 7,560,099 | 6,873,964 | 7,303,434 | $58,427,472 |
| Major Venture Capital | | | | 21.4% | 18.5% | | | 3,386,000 | 3,386,000 | $27,088,000 |
| OTHER | | | | 35.2% | 30.5% | | | 5,571,469 | 5,571,469 | $44,571,752 |
| VENTURE Total | | | | 56.6% | 49.0% | | | 8,957,469 | 8,957,469 | $71,659,752 |
| PRE-IPO: sum of all stock | | | | 100.0% | 89.0% | | | 15,831,433 | 16,260,903 | $130,087,224 |
| IPO shares | | | | | 11.0% | | | | 2,014,000 | $16,112,000 |
| TOTAL OUTSTANDING | | | | | 100.0% | | | | 18,274,903 | $146,199,224 |

| REVENUE $M | REVENUE $M |
|---|---|
| Last 12 mos | Prior Quarter |
| $17.1 | $6.0 |
| Growth/Year | Growth/Year |
| 136.9% | 33.8% |

Nr of employees: 232

(7) Vesting is usually 5 years and fair market value at time of grant.
Lead Underwriters: Morgan Stanley + Hambrecht & Quist

| | | | |
|---|---|---|---|
| 2,014,000 nr shares sold by company | $21,200,000 | | IPO TOTAL CASH RAISED BEFORE FEES AND EXPENSES |
| 636,000 nr shares sold by selling shareholders | $1,484,000 | 7.00% | IPO fee for underwriters |
| | $550,000 | 2.59% | Estimated expenses of IPO |
| | $19,166,000 | 90.41% | NET TO COMPANY |

*SOURCE: Saratoga Venture Finance © All rights reserved. See prospectus for data. The above contain certain estimates.*

**SARATOGA VENTURE FINANCE EQUITY TABLE ™**
WAGES AND STOCK OWNERSHIP AT INITIAL PUBLIC OFFERING (IPO)

## Microsoft Corporation

IPO DATE: 13 March 1986
$21.00   Price per Share

Microcomputer software
Inception: 1975
Redmond, Washington

| TITLE  f = Founder | (4) COMP | (3B) OFFICERS OWNERSHIP | (3),(6),(7) MGT & EMPS OWNERSHIP | (1) PRE IPO OWNERSHIP | (2) POST IPO OWNERSHIP | (3B) OFFICERS OWNERSHIP | (3),(6),(7) MGT & EMPS OWNERSHIP | (1) PRE IPO OWNERSHIP | (2) POST IPO OWNERSHIP | IPO VALUE $21.00 Per Share |
|---|---|---|---|---|---|---|---|---|---|---|
| f CEO | $133,000 | 56.4% | 46.8% | 44.2% | 40.2% | 11,222,000 | 11,222,000 | 11,222,000 | 11,222,000 | $235,662,000 |
| f EVP-Left | | 32.1% | 26.6% | 25.2% | 22.9% | 6,390,000 | 6,390,000 | 6,390,000 | 6,390,000 | $134,190,000 |
| VP-SysSW | $88,000 | 8.6% | 7.1% | 6.7% | 6.1% | 1,710,001 | 1,710,001 | 1,710,001 | 1,710,001 | $35,910,021 |
| COO | $228,000 | 2.0% | 1.7% | 1.6% | 1.4% | 400,000 | 400,000 | 400,000 | 400,000 | $8,400,000 |
| VP-ApsSW;VP-OEM SLS | | 0.0% | 0.0% | 0.0% | 0.0% | 0 | 0 | 0 | 0 | $0 * |
| VP-CDROM SW;VP-RtlSLS | | 0.0% | 0.0% | 0.0% | 0.0% | 0 | 0 | 0 | 0 | $0 * |
| VP-INTL;VP-LEGAL | | 0.0% | 0.0% | 0.0% | 0.0% | 0 | 0 | 0 | 0 | $0 * |
| VP-COM | $96,000 | 0.0% | 0.0% | 0.0% | 0.0% | 0 | 0 | 0 | 0 | $0 * |
| VP-HW DEVL | | 0.0% | 0.0% | 0.0% | 0.0% | 0 | 0 | 0 | 0 | $0 * |
| CFO | $109,000 | 0.0% | 0.0% | 0.0% | 0.0% | 0 | 0 | 0 | 0 | $0 * |
| OTHER=Avg of 6 | $67,571 | 0.8% | 0.7% | 0.6% | 0.6% | 158,001 | 158,001 | 158,001 | 158,001 | $3,318,021 * |
| OFFICERS & EXECUTIVES | | 100.0% | 82.8% | 78.3% | 71.2% | 19,880,002 | 19,880,002 | 19,880,002 | 19,880,002 | $417,480,042 |
| ALL OTHER | | | 6.0% | 5.7% | 5.1% | | 1,435,111 | 1,435,111 | 1,435,111 | $30,137,331 |
| TOTAL COMMON BEFORE OPTIONS | | | 88.8% | 83.9% | 76.3% | | 21,315,113 | 21,315,113 | 21,315,113 | $447,617,373 |
| OPTIONS-Outstanding | | | 11.2% | 10.6% | 9.6% | | 2,681,457 | 2,681,457 | 2,681,457 | $56,310,597 |
| OPTIONS-Available | | | 0.0% | 0.0% | 1.9% | | 0 | 0 | 539,896 | $11,337,816 |
| OPTIONS-Total | | | 11.2% | 10.6% | 11.5% | | 2,681,457 | 2,681,457 | 3,221,353 | $67,648,413 |
| COMMON-Total | | | 100.0% | 94.5% | 87.8% | | 23,996,570 | 23,996,570 | 24,536,466 | $515,265,786 |
| Major Venture Capital | | | | 5.4% | 4.9% | | | 1,378,901 | 1,378,901 | $28,956,921 |
| OTHER | | | | 0.1% | 0.1% | | | 21,099 | 21,099 | $443,079 |
| VENTURE Total | | | | 5.5% | 5.0% | | | 1,400,000 | 1,400,000 | $29,400,000 |
| PRE-IPO: sum of all stock | | | | 100.0% | 92.8% | | | 25,396,570 | 25,936,466 | $544,665,786 |
| IPO shares | | | | | 7.2% | | | | 2,000,000 | $42,000,000 |
| TOTAL OUTSTANDING | | | | | 100.0% | | | | 27,936,466 | $586,665,786 |

Average $553K *

(7) Vesting not disclosed in prospectus, typically over five years.

Lead Underwriters: Goldman + Alex. Brown

2,000,000 nr shares sold by company
795,000 nr shares sold by selling shareholders

| | | |
|---|---|---|
| $58,695,000 | | IPO TOTAL CASH RAISED BEFORE FEES AND EXPENSES |
| $3,661,450 | 6.24% | IPO fee for underwriters |
| $541,000 | 0.92% | Estimated expenses of IPO |
| $54,492,550 | 92.84% | NET TO COMPANY |

| REVENUE $M | REVENUE $M |
|---|---|
| Last 12 mos | Prior Quarter |
| $140.4 | $49.9 |
| Growth/Year | Growth/Year |
| 44.0% | 35.6% |
| | Nr of employes: 998 |

SARATOGA VENTURE FINANCE EQUITY TABLE ™
WAGES AND STOCK OWNERSHIP AT INITIAL PUBLIC OFFERING (IPO)

# MIPS Computer Systems, Inc.

IPO DATE: 21 December, 1989
$17.50 Price per Share

RISC computers
Inception: 24 August 1984
Sunnyvale, California

| TITLE f = Founder | (4) COMPENSATION | (3B) OFFICERS OWNERSHIP | (3),(6),(7) MGT & EMPS OWNERSHIP | (1) PRE IPO OWNERSHIP | (2) POST IPO OWNERSHIP | (3B) OFFICERS OWNERSHIP | (3),(6),(7) MGT & EMPS OWNERSHIP | (1) PRE IPO OWNERSHIP | (2) POST IPO OWNERSHIP | IPO VALUE $17.50 Per Share |
|---|---|---|---|---|---|---|---|---|---|---|
| Chair,, Pres,CEO | $311,863 | 10.9% | 2.6% | 1.5% | 1.2% | 295,654 | 295,654 | 295,654 | 295,654 | $5,173,945 |
| f Chief Scientist | Consultant | 14.8% | 3.5% | 2.0% | 1.6% | 400,000 | 400,000 | 400,000 | 400,000 | $7,000,000 |
| f VP Dev. Programs | | 14.8% | 3.5% | 2.0% | 1.6% | 400,000 | 400,000 | 400,000 | 400,000 | $7,000,000 |
| f VP VLSI Devel-Left | | 14.8% | 3.5% | 2.0% | 1.6% | 400,000 | 400,000 | 400,000 | 400,000 | $7,000,000 |
| f Director | | 6.5% | 0.0% | 0.0% | 0.0% | 176,338 | 0 | 0 | 0 | $0 * |
| EVP Field Ops | $564,086 | 4.7% | 0.0% | 0.0% | 0.0% | 127,000 | 0 | 0 | 0 | $0 * |
| SVP Eng & Mfg | $211,277 | 3.5% | 0.0% | 0.0% | 0.0% | 94,000 | 0 | 0 | 0 | $0 * |
| VP International | $215,949 | 1.2% | 0.0% | 0.0% | 0.0% | 31,250 | 0 | 0 | 0 | $0 * |
| VP Legal | $131,331 | 0.9% | 0.0% | 0.0% | 0.0% | 25,200 | 0 | 0 | 0 | $0 * |
| Others = 5 | Avg = $118,147 | 27.8% | 6.6% | 3.7% | 3.0% | 750,625 | 750,625 | 750,625 | 750,625 | $13,135,938 |
| OFFICERS & EXECUTIVES | | 100.0% | 19.8% | 11.1% | 9.0% | 2,700,067 | 2,246,279 | 2,246,279 | 2,246,279 | $39,309,883 |
| ALL OTHER | | | 43.5% | 24.3% | 19.8% | | 4,934,951 | 4,934,951 | 4,934,951 | $86,361,643 |
| TOTAL COMMON BEFORE OPTIONS | | | 63.3% | 35.3% | 28.8% | | 7,181,230 | 7,181,230 | 7,181,230 | $125,671,525 |
| OPTIONS-Outstanding | | | 36.7% | 20.5% | 16.7% | | 4,163,147 | 4,163,147 | 4,163,147 | $72,855,073 |
| OPTIONS-Available | | | 0.0% | 0.0% | 2.5% | | 0 | 0 | 628,565 | $10,999,888 |
| OPTIONS-Total | | | 36.7% | 20.5% | 19.2% | | 4,163,147 | 4,163,147 | 4,791,712 | $83,854,960 |
| COMMON-Total | | | 100.0% | 55.8% | 48.1% | | 11,344,377 | 11,344,377 | 11,972,942 | $209,526,485 |
| Major Venture Capital | | | | 23.1% | 18.9% | | | 4,696,531 | 4,696,531 | $82,189,293 |
| OTHER: Kubota, DEC, Investors | | | | 21.1% | 17.2% | | | 4,278,304 | 4,278,304 | $74,870,320 |
| VENTURE Total | | | | 44.2% | 36.0% | | | 8,974,835 | 8,974,835 | $157,059,613 |
| PRE-IPO: sum of all stock | | | | 100.0% | 84.1% | | | 20,319,212 | 20,947,777 | $366,586,098 |
| IPO shares | | | | | 15.9% | | | | 3,950,000 | $69,125,000 |
| TOTAL OUTSTANDING | | | | | 100.0% | | | | 24,897,777 | $435,711,098 |

Average of 8=$1.6M *

| REVENUE $M | REVENUE $M |
|---|---|
| Last 12 mos | Prior Quarter |
| $39.4 | $17.5 |
| Growth/Year | Growth/Year |
| 183.3% | 141.1% |
| | Nr of employees: 592 |

(7) Vesting for Stock Option Plans is usually 25% for the first year and 6.25% per quarter over 5 years and fair market value at time of grant.

Lead Underwriters: Morgan Stanley + Cowen

| | | | | |
|---|---|---|---|---|
| 3,950,000 | nr shares sold by company | $80,500,000 | | IPO TOTAL CASH RAISED BEFORE FEES AND EXPENSES |
| 650,000 | nr shares sold by selling shareholders | $5,198,000 | 6.46% | IPO fee for underwriters |
| 4,600,000 | IPO TOTAL | $900,000 | 1.12% | Estimated expenses of IPO |
| | | $74,402,000 | 92.42% | NET TO COMPANY |

307

**SARATOGA VENTURE FINANCE EQUITY TABLE ™**
WAGES AND STOCK OWNERSHIP AT INITIAL PUBLIC OFFERING (IPO)

## Nellcor Incorporated

IPO DATE: 19 May 1987
$16.00 Price per Share

Medical electronic instruments
Inception: 7 October 1981
Hayward, California

| TITLE f = Founder | (4) COMPENSATION | (3B) OFFICERS OWNERSHIP | (3),(6),(7) MGT & EMPS OWNERSHIP | (1) PRE IPO OWNERSHIP | (2) POST IPO OWNERSHIP | (3B) OFFICERS OWNERSHIP | (3),(6),(7) MGT & EMPS OWNERSHIP | (1) PRE IPO OWNERSHIP | (2) POST IPO OWNERSHIP | IPO VALUE $16.00 Per Share |
|---|---|---|---|---|---|---|---|---|---|---|
| f Chairman | $151,946 | 28.6% | 19.6% | 7.8% | 6.6% | 1,024,440 | 1,024,440 | 1,024,440 | 1,024,440 | $16,391,040 |
| f President | $169,279 | 29.3% | 20.1% | 8.1% | 6.8% | 1,051,280 | 1,051,280 | 1,051,280 | 1,051,280 | $16,820,480 |
| f VP,CFO | $159,278 | 10.7% | 7.4% | 2.9% | 2.5% | 384,360 | 384,360 | 384,360 | 384,360 | $6,149,760 |
| f VP Engineering | | 8.5% | 5.8% | 2.3% | 2.0% | 303,920 | 303,920 | 303,920 | 303,920 | $4,862,720 |
| f VP Human Res. | | 0.0% | 0.0% | 0.0% | 0.0% | 0 | 0 | 0 | 0 | $0 * |
| All Others* Avg of 6 = $113,959 | | 22.9% | 15.7% | 6.3% | 5.3% | 821,469 | 821,469 | 821,469 | 821,469 | $13,143,504 * |
| OFFICERS & EXECUTIVES | | 100.0% | 68.6% | 27.5% | 23.1% | 3,585,469 | 3,585,469 | 3,585,469 | 3,585,469 | $57,367,504 |
| ALL OTHER | | | 8.7% | 3.5% | 2.9% | | 453,913 | 453,913 | 453,913 | $7,262,608 |
| TOTAL COMMON BEFORE OPTIONS | | | 77.3% | 30.9% | 26.0% | | 4,039,382 | 4,039,382 | 4,039,382 | $64,630,112 |
| OPTIONS-Outstanding | | | 22.7% | 9.1% | 7.7% | | 1,189,098 | 1,189,098 | 1,189,098 | $19,025,568 |
| OPTIONS-Available | | | 0.0% | 0.0% | 5.5% | | 0 | 0 | 850,542 | $13,608,672 |
| OPTIONS-Total | | | 22.7% | 9.1% | 13.2% | | 1,189,098 | 1,189,098 | 2,039,640 | $32,634,240 |
| COMMON-Total | | | 100.0% | 40.0% | 39.2% | | 5,228,480 | 5,228,480 | 6,079,022 | $97,264,352 |
| Major Venture Capital | | | | 60.0% | 50.5% | | | 7,830,454 | 7,830,454 | $125,287,264 |
| OTHER | | | | 0.0% | 0.0% | | | 0 | 0 | $0 |
| VENTURE Total | | | | 60.0% | 50.5% | | | 7,830,454 | 7,830,454 | $125,287,264 |
| PRE-IPO: sum of all stock | | | | 100.0% | 89.7% | | | 13,058,934 | 13,909,476 | $222,551,616 |
| IPO shares | | | | | 10.3% | | | | 1,600,000 | $25,600,000 |
| TOTAL OUTSTANDING | | | | | 100.0% | | | | 15,509,476 | $248,151,616 |

Average of 7 = $1.8M *

| REVENUE $M | REVENUE $M |
|---|---|
| Last 12 mos | Prior Quarter |
| $46.2 | $21.5 |
| Growth/Year | Growth/Year |
| 250.9% | 59.6% |
| Nr of employes: 634 | |

(7) Vesting for Stock Option Plans is usually 4 years, with one year waiting period for 25%, 6.25% per quarter thereafter and fair market value at time of grant.

Lead Underwriters: Goldman Sachs + Robertson + Cowen

| | | | |
|---|---|---|---|
| 1,600,000 | nr shares sold by company | $38,400,000 | IPO TOTAL CASH RAISED BEFORE FEES AND EXPENSES |
| 800,000 | nr shares sold by selling shareholders | $2,688,000 | 7.00% IPO fee for underwriters |
| 2,400,000 | IPO TOTAL | $480,000 | 1.25% Estimated expenses of IPO |
| | | $35,232,000 | 91.75% NET TO COMPANY |

**SOURCE:** *Saratoga Venture Finance © All rights reserved. See prospectus for data. The above contain certain estimates.*

**SARATOGA VENTURE FINANCE EQUITY TABLE ™**
WAGES AND STOCK OWNERSHIP AT INITIAL PUBLIC OFFERING (IPO)

## Network Equipment Technologies

IPO DATE: 23 January 1987
$16.00  Price per Share

Telecommunications systems
Inception: 27 May 1983
Redwood City, California

| TITLE f = Founder | (4) COMPENSATION | (3B) OFFICERS OWNERSHIP | (3),(6),(7) MGT & EMPS OWNERSHIP | (1) PRE IPO OWNERSHIP | (2) POST IPO OWNERSHIP | (3B) OFFICERS OWNERSHIP | (3),(6),(7) MGT & EMPS OWNERSHIP | (1) PRE IPO OWNERSHIP | (2) POST IPO OWNERSHIP | IPO VALUE $16.00 Per Share |
|---|---|---|---|---|---|---|---|---|---|---|
| f  CEO,President | $113,279 | 40.3% | 13.1% | 4.4% | 3.9% | 534,513 | 534,513 | 534,513 | 534,513 | $8,552,208 |
| f  VP-ENG | $82,114 | 26.4% | 8.6% | 2.9% | 2.5% | 350,070 | 350,070 | 350,070 | 350,070 | $5,601,120 |
| VP-SLS | $103,154 | 11.4% | 3.7% | 1.3% | 1.1% | 151,141 | 151,141 | 151,141 | 151,141 | $2,418,256 |
| VP-MKTG | $74,193 | 9.2% | 3.0% | 1.0% | 0.9% | 122,070 | 122,070 | 122,070 | 122,070 | $1,953,120 |
| VP-OPS | $75,847 | 11.4% | 3.7% | 1.3% | 1.1% | 0 | 0 | 0 | 0 | $0 * |
| VP-FIN | $81,239 | 0.0% | 0.0% | 0.0% | 0.0% | 0 | 0 | 0 | 0 | $0 * |
| OTHER | | 12.8% | 4.2% | 1.4% | 1.2% | 169,761 | 169,761 | 169,761 | 169,761 | $2,716,176 * |
| OFFICERS & EXECUTIVES | | 100.0% | 32.6% | 11.0% | 9.6% | 1,327,555 | 1,327,555 | 1,327,555 | 1,327,555 | $21,240,880 |
| ALL OTHER | | | 43.0% | 14.5% | 12.6% | | 1,749,432 | 1,749,432 | 1,749,432 | $27,990,912 |
| TOTAL COMMON BEFORE OPTIONS | | | 75.6% | 25.5% | 22.2% | | 3,076,987 | 3,076,987 | 3,076,987 | $49,231,792 |
| OPTIONS-Outstanding | | | 24.4% | 8.2% | 7.2% | | 993,555 | 993,555 | 993,555 | $15,896,880 |
| OPTIONS-Available | | | 0.0% | 0.0% | 2.1% | | 0 | 0 | 294,033 | $4,704,528 |
| OPTIONS-Total | | | 24.4% | 8.2% | 9.3% | | 993,555 | 993,555 | 1,287,588 | $20,601,408 |
| COMMON-Total | | | 100.0% | 33.7% | 31.5% | | 4,070,542 | 4,070,542 | 4,364,575 | $69,833,200 |
| Major Venture Capital | | | | 34.7% | 30.2% | | | 4,185,025 | 4,185,025 | $66,960,400 |
| OTHER | | | | 31.6% | 27.5% | | | 3,806,975 | 3,806,975 | $60,911,600 |
| VENTURE Total | | | | 66.3% | 57.7% | | | 7,992,000 | 7,992,000 | $127,872,000 |
| PRE-IPO: sum of all stock | | | | 100.0% | 89.2% | | | 12,062,542 | 12,356,575 | $197,705,200 |
| IPO shares | | | | | 10.8% | | | | 1,500,000 | $24,000,000 |
| TOTAL OUTSTANDING | | | | | 100.0% | | | | 13,856,575 | $221,705,200 |

Avg of 2 = $912K *

| REVENUE $M | REVENUE $M |
|---|---|
| Last 12 mos | Prior Quarter |
| $8.7 | $10.7 |
| Growth/Year | Growth/Year |
| Not meaningful | Not meaningful |
| Nr of employes: 429 | |

(7) Vesting for Stock Option Plans is usually 5 years, with a one year waiting period, 1/60 per mo thereafter and fair market value at time of grant.

Lead Underwriters: Morgan Stanley & Alex. Brown

| | | |
|---|---|---|
| 1,500,000  nr shares sold by company | $40,000,000 | IPO TOTAL CASH RAISED BEFORE FEES AND EXPENSES |
| 1,000,000  nr shares sold by selling shareholders | $2,800,000 | 7.00%  IPO fee for underwriters |
| 2,500,000  IPO TOTAL | $680,000 | 1.70%  Estimated expenses of IPO |
| | $36,520,000 | 91.30%  NET TO COMPANY |

**SARATOGA VENTURE FINANCE EQUITY TABLE ™**
WAGES AND STOCK OWNERSHIP AT INITIAL PUBLIC OFFERING (IPO)

## Oracle Systems Corporation

IPO DATE: 12 March 1986
$15.00  Price per Share

Database software
Inception: June 1977
Belmont, California

| TITLE f = Founder | (4) COMPENSATION | (3B) OFFICERS OWNERSHIP | (3),(6),(7) MGT & EMPS OWNERSHIP | (1) PRE IPO OWNERSHIP | (2) POST IPO OWNERSHIP | (3B) OFFICERS OWNERSHIP | (3),(6),(7) MGT & EMPS OWNERSHIP | (1) PRE IPO OWNERSHIP | (2) POST IPO OWNERSHIP | IPO VALUE $15.00 Per Share |
|---|---|---|---|---|---|---|---|---|---|---|
| f Pres,CEO | $212,513 | 57.4% | 33.4% | 30.6% | 27.5% | 4,608,750 | 4,608,750 | 4,608,750 | 4,608,750 | $69,131,250 |
| f SVP Devel. | $122,551 | 28.0% | 16.3% | 14.9% | 13.4% | 2,246,668 | 2,246,668 | 2,246,668 | 2,246,668 | $33,700,020 |
| VP Sales Intl | | 4.1% | 2.4% | 2.2% | 1.9% | 326,000 | 326,000 | 326,000 | 326,000 | $4,890,000 |
| Employee | | 2.8% | 1.6% | 1.5% | 1.4% | 227,222 | 227,222 | 227,222 | 227,222 | $3,408,330 |
| Employee | | 2.7% | 1.6% | 1.5% | 1.3% | 220,000 | 220,000 | 220,000 | 220,000 | $3,300,000 |
| VP F&A,CFO | $111,524 | 1.7% | 1.0% | 1.5% | 1.3% | 140,000 | 140,000 | 140,000 | 140,000 | $2,100,000 |
| All Others | | 3.2% | 1.9% | 1.7% | 1.6% | 260,000 | 260,000 | 260,000 | 260,000 | $3,900,000 |
| OFFICERS & EXECUTIVES | | 100.0% | 58.2% | 53.4% | 47.9% | 8,028,640 | 8,028,640 | 8,028,640 | 8,028,640 | $120,429,600 |
| ALL OTHER | | | 19.5% | 17.9% | 16.1% | | 2,690,804 | 2,690,804 | 2,690,804 | $40,362,060 |
| TOTAL COMMON BEFORE OPTIONS | | | 77.7% | 71.2% | 64.0% | | 10,719,444 | 10,719,444 | 10,719,444 | $160,791,660 |
| OPTIONS-Outstanding | | | 22.3% | 20.5% | 18.4% | | 3,082,863 | 3,082,863 | 3,082,863 | $46,242,945 |
| OPTIONS-Available | | | 0.0% | 0.0% | 4.2% | | 0 | 0 | 707,841 | $10,617,615 |
| OPTIONS-Total | | | 22.3% | 20.5% | 22.6% | | 3,082,863 | 3,082,863 | 3,790,704 | $56,860,560 |
| COMMON-Total | | | 100.0% | 91.7% | 86.6% | | 13,802,307 | 13,802,307 | 14,510,148 | $217,652,220 |
| Major Venture Capital | | | | 8.3% | 7.4% | | | 1,246,666 | 1,246,666 | $18,699,990 |
| OTHER | | | | 0.0% | 0.0% | | | 0 | 0 | $0 |
| VENTURE Total | | | | 8.3% | 7.4% | | | 1,246,666 | 1,246,666 | $18,699,990 |
| PRE-IPO: sum of all stock | | | | 100.0% | 94.0% | | | 15,048,973 | 15,756,814 | $236,352,210 |
| IPO shares | | | | | 6.0% | | | | 1,000,000 | $15,000,000 |
| TOTAL OUTSTANDING | | | | | 100.0% | | | | 16,756,814 | $251,352,210 |

| REVENUE $M | REVENUE $M |
|---|---|
| Last 12 mos | Prior Quarter |
| $23.1 | $11.4 |
| Growth/Year | Growth/Year |
| 82.1% | 103.4% |
| Nr of employees: 425 | |

(7) Vesting for Stock Option Plans is usually 4 years, with one year waiting period, 1/4 per year thereafter and fair market value at time of grant.

Lead Underwriters: Merrill Lynch + Alex. Brown

| | | | |
|---|---|---|---|
| 1,000,000 | nr shares sold by company | $31,500,000 | IPO TOTAL CASH RAISED BEFORE FEES AND EXPENSES |
| 1,100,000 | nr shares sold by selling shareholders | $2,205,000  7.00% | IPO fee for underwriters |
| 2,100,000 | IPO TOTAL | $545,000  1.73% | Estimated expenses of IPO |
| | | $28,750,000  91.27% | NET TO COMPANY |

**SARATOGA VENTURE FINANCE EQUITY TABLE ™**
WAGES AND STOCK OWNERSHIP AT INITIAL PUBLIC OFFERING (IPO)

## Sigma Designs, Inc.

IPO DATE: 15 May 1986
$17.00 Price per Share

DOS micromputer boards and add-on hardware
Inception: 7 January 1982
Fremont, California

| TITLE f = Founder | (4) COMPENSATION | (3B) OFFICERS OWNERSHIP | (3),(6),(7) MGT & EMPS OWNERSHIP | (1) PRE IPO OWNERSHIP | (2) POST IPO OWNERSHIP | (3B) OFFICERS OWNERSHIP | (3),(6),(7) MGT & EMPS OWNERSHIP | (1) PRE IPO OWNERSHIP | (2) POST IPO OWNERSHIP | IPO VALUE $17.00 Per Share |
|---|---|---|---|---|---|---|---|---|---|---|
| f Chair,CEO,Pres | $77,000 | 23.3% | 7.4% | 7.4% | 6.4% | 424,634 | 424,634 | 424,634 | 424,634 | $7,218,778 |
| f VP Mfg | $67,000 | 23.3% | 7.4% | 7.4% | 6.4% | 425,634 | 425,634 | 425,634 | 425,634 | $7,235,778 |
| f VP Prod Devl | $67,000 | 22.5% | 7.1% | 7.1% | 6.2% | 409,962 | 409,962 | 409,962 | 409,962 | $6,969,354 |
| f VP Engineering | $72,000 | 21.7% | 6.9% | 6.9% | 6.0% | 395,634 | 395,634 | 395,634 | 395,634 | $6,725,778 |
| VP Fin, CFO | $73,886 | 4.3% | 1.3% | 1.3% | 1.2% | 77,726 | 77,726 | 77,726 | 77,726 | $1,321,342 |
| VP Marketing | $58,199 | 3.4% | 1.1% | 1.1% | 0.9% | 61,262 | 61,262 | 61,262 | 61,262 | $1,041,454 |
| VP Sales | $69,000 | 1.6% | 0.5% | 0.5% | 0.5% | 29,844 | 29,844 | 29,844 | 29,844 | $507,348 |
| OFFICERS & EXECUTIVES | | 100.0% | 31.7% | 31.7% | 27.6% | 1,824,696 | 1,824,696 | 1,824,696 | 1,824,696 | $31,019,832 |
| ALL OTHER | | | 49.1% | 49.1% | 42.8% | | 2,826,701 | 2,826,701 | 2,826,701 | $48,053,917 |
| TOTAL COMMON BEFORE OPTIONS | | | 80.8% | 80.8% | 70.4% | | 4,651,397 | 4,651,397 | 4,651,397 | $79,073,749 |
| OPTIONS-Outstanding | | | 11.9% | 11.9% | 10.4% | | 686,461 | 686,461 | 686,461 | $11,669,837 |
| OPTIONS-Available | | | 7.3% | 7.3% | 6.4% | | 421,001 | 421,001 | 421,001 | $7,157,017 |
| OPTIONS-Total | | | 19.2% | 19.2% | 16.8% | | 1,107,462 | 1,107,462 | 1,107,462 | $18,826,854 |
| COMMON-Total | | | 100.0% | 100.0% | 87.1% | | 5,758,859 | 5,758,859 | 5,758,859 | $97,900,603 |
| Major Venture Capital | | | 0.0% | 0.0% | 0.0% | | | 0 | 0 | $0 |
| OTHER | | | 0.0% | 0.0% | 0.0% | | | 0 | 0 | $0 |
| VENTURE-Total | | | 0.0% | 0.0% | 0.0% | | | 0 | 0 | $0 |
| PRE-IPO: sum of all stock | | | 100.0% | 100.0% | 87.1% | | | 5,758,859 | 5,758,859 | $97,900,603 |
| IPO shares | | | | | 12.9% | | | | 850,000 | $14,450,000 |
| TOTAL OUTSTANDING | | | | | 100.0% | | | | 6,608,859 | $112,350,603 |

| | REVENUE $M | REVENUE $M |
|---|---|---|
| | Last 12 mos | Prior Quarter |
| | $10.1 | NA |
| | Growth/Year | Growth/Year |
| | 57.9% | NA |
| | Nr of employes: 120 | |

(7) Vesting for Stock Option Plans is usually 5 years at 20% per year and fair market value at time of grant.

Lead Underwriters: Laidlaw Adams & Peck Inc.

| | | |
|---|---|---|
| 850,000 nr shares sold by company | $17,000,000 | IPO TOTAL CASH RAISED BEFORE FEES AND EXPENSES |
| 150,000 nr shares sold by selling shareholders | $940,000 | 5.53% IPO fee for underwriters |
| 1,000,000 IPO TOTAL | $300,000 | 1.76% Estimated expenses of IPO |
| | $15,760,000 | 92.71% NET TO COMPANY |

# SARATOGA VENTURE FINANCE EQUITY TABLE ™
WAGES AND STOCK OWNERSHIP AT INITIAL PUBLIC OFFERING (IPO)

## Silicon Graphics, Inc.
IPO DATE: 29 October 1986
$11.25 Price per Share

3D computer systems
Inception: 9 November 1981
San Jose, California

| TITLE | (4) COMPENSATION | (3B) OFFICERS OWNERSHIP | (3),(6),(7) MGT & EMPS OWNERSHIP | (1) PRE IPO OWNERSHIP | (2) POST IPO OWNERSHIP | (3B) OFFICERS OWNERSHIP | (3),(6),(7) MGT & EMPS OWNERSHIP | (1) PRE IPO OWNERSHIP | (2) POST IPO OWNERSHIP | IPO VALUE Per Share $11.25 |
|---|---|---|---|---|---|---|---|---|---|---|
| **f = Founder** | | | | | | | | | | |
| Pres,CEO,Dir | $156,057 | 26.6% | 11.9% | 3.9% | 3.1% | 400,050 | 400,050 | 400,050 | 400,050 | $4,500,563 |
| f CHAIR+CTO | $138,077 | 39.4% | 17.6% | 5.7% | 4.6% | 592,133 | 592,133 | 592,133 | 592,133 | $6,661,496 |
| VP-ENG | $108,655 | 0.0% | 0.0% | 0.0% | 0.0% | 0 | 0 | 0 | 0 | $0 * |
| VP-NA Sales | $104,705 | 0.0% | 0.0% | 0.0% | 0.0% | 0 | 0 | 0 | 0 | $0 * |
| VP-Fin&Admin | $125,000 | 0.0% | 0.0% | 0.0% | 0.0% | 0 | 0 | 0 | 0 | $0 * |
| VP-R&D | | 0.0% | 0.0% | 0.0% | 0.0% | 0 | 0 | 0 | 0 | $0 * |
| VP-MKTG;VP-OEM;Pres. Int'l | | 0.0% | 0.0% | 0.0% | 0.0% | 0 | 0 | 0 | 0 | $0 * |
| VP-HR VP-OPS VP-SLS | | 0.0% | 0.0% | 0.0% | 0.0% | 0 | 0 | 0 | 0 | $0 * |
| OTHER EMPS   Avg of 4 = $60,316 | | 33.9% | 15.1% | 4.9% | 3.9% | 509,662 | 509,662 | 509,662 | 509,662 | $5,733,698 |
| OFFICERS & EXECUTIVES | | 100.0% | 44.6% | 14.5% | 11.6% | 1,501,845 | 1,501,845 | 1,501,845 | 1,501,845 | $16,895,756 |
| ALL OTHER | | | 50.2% | 16.3% | 13.1% | | 1,692,225 | 1,692,225 | 1,692,225 | $19,037,531 |
| TOTAL COMMON BEFORE OPTIONS | | | 94.8% | 30.8% | 24.7% | | 3,194,070 | 3,194,070 | 3,194,070 | $35,933,288 |
| OPTIONS-Outstanding | | | 5.2% | 1.7% | 1.3% | | 174,400 | 174,400 | 174,400 | $1,962,000 |
| OPTIONS-Available | | | 0.0% | 0.0% | 7.9% | | 0 | 0 | 1,025,600 | $11,538,000 |
| OPTIONS-Total | | | 5.2% | 1.7% | 9.3% | | 174,400 | 174,400 | 1,200,000 | $13,500,000 |
| COMMON-Total | | | 100.0% | 32.5% | 34.0% | | 3,368,470 | 3,368,470 | 4,394,070 | $49,433,288 |
| Major Venture Capital | | | | 41.0% | 32.9% | | | 4,246,151 | 4,246,151 | $47,769,199 |
| OTHER | | | | 26.5% | 21.3% | | | 2,749,763 | 2,749,763 | $30,934,834 |
| VENTURE Total | | | | 67.5% | 54.1% | | | 6,995,914 | 6,995,914 | $78,704,033 |
| PRE-IPO: sum of all stock | | | | 100.0% | 88.2% | | | 10,364,384 | 11,389,984 | $128,137,320 |
| IPO shares | | | | | 11.8% | | | | 1,530,000 | $17,212,500 |
| TOTAL OUTSTANDING | | | | | 100.0% | | | | 12,919,984 | $145,349,820 |

Avg. of 7 = $819K *

| REVENUE $M | REVENUE $M |
|---|---|
| Last 12 mos | Prior Quarter |
| $41.5 | $14.2 |
| Growth/Year | Growth/Year |
| 92.6% | 106.0% |
| Nr of employes: 331 | |

(7) Vesting for Stock Option Plans is usually 5 years, with ten month waiting period, 2% per mo thereafter and fair market value at time of grant.
Lead Underwriters: Morgan Stanley + Alex. Brown

| 1,530,000 nr shares sold by company | $20,250,000 | | IPO TOTAL CASH RAISED BEFORE FEES AND EXPENSES |
|---|---|---|---|
| 270,000 nr shares sold by selling shareholder | $1,422,000 | 7.02% | IPO fee for underwriters |
| 1,800,000 IPO TOTAL | $460,000 | 2.27% | Estimated expenses of IPO |
| | $18,368,000 IPO TOTAL | 90.71% | NET TO COMPANY |

SARATOGA VENTURE FINANCE EQUITY TABLE ™
WAGES AND STOCK OWNERSHIP AT INITIAL PUBLIC OFFERING (IPO)

## Software Publishing Corporation

Software for microcomputers
Inception: 18 April 1980
Mountain View, California

IPO DATE: 15 November 1984
$7.00  Price per Share

| TITLE f = Founder | (4) COMPENSATION | (3B) OFFICERS OWNERSHIP | (3),(6),(7) MGT & EMPS OWNERSHIP | (1) PRE IPO OWNERSHIP | (2) POST IPO OWNERSHIP | (3B) OFFICERS OWNERSHIP | (3),(6),(7) MGT & EMPS OWNERSHIP | (1) PRE IPO OWNERSHIP | (2) POST IPO OWNERSHIP | IPO VALUE $7.00 Per Share |
|---|---|---|---|---|---|---|---|---|---|---|
| f Pres, CEO | $119,286 | 31.9% | 25.1% | 17.0% | 13.4% | 925,000 | 925,000 | 925,000 | 925,000 | $6,475,000 |
| f VP, Gen Mgr. | $107,094 | 32.8% | 25.7% | 17.5% | 13.8% | 950,000 | 950,000 | 950,000 | 950,000 | $6,650,000 |
| f VP R&D | $107,094 | 32.8% | 25.7% | 17.5% | 13.8% | 950,000 | 950,000 | 950,000 | 950,000 | $6,650,000 |
| VP F&A, CFO | $75,361 | 2.6% | 2.0% | 1.4% | 1.1% | 75,000 | 75,000 | 75,000 | 75,000 | $525,000 |
| OTHER | | 0.0% | 0.0% | 0.0% | 0.0% | 0 | 0 | 0 | 0 | $0 |
| OFFICERS & EXECUTIVES | | 100.0% | 78.6% | 53.3% | 42.1% | 2,900,000 | 2,900,000 | 2,900,000 | 2,900,000 | $20,300,000 |
| ALL OTHER | | | 12.1% | 8.2% | 6.5% | | 444,947 | 444,947 | 444,947 | $3,114,629 |
| TOTAL COMMON BEFORE OPTIONS | | | 90.7% | 61.5% | 48.5% | | 3,344,947 | 3,344,947 | 3,344,947 | $23,414,629 |
| OPTIONS-Outstanding | | | 9.3% | 9.3% | 5.0% | | 344,617 | 344,617 | 344,617 | $2,412,319 |
| OPTIONS-Available | | | 0.0% | 0.0% | 2.0% | | 0 | 0 | 139,063 | $973,441 |
| OPTIONS-Total | | | 9.3% | 6.3% | 7.0% | | 344,617 | 344,617 | 483,680 | $3,385,760 |
| COMMON-Total | | | 100.0% | 67.8% | 55.5% | | 3,689,564 | 3,689,564 | 3,828,627 | $26,800,389 |
| Major Venture Capital | | | | 29.7% | 23.4% | | | 1,616,000 | 1,616,000 | $11,312,000 |
| OTHER | | | | 2.5% | 1.9% | | | 134,000 | 134,000 | $938,000 |
| VENTURE Total | | | | 32.2% | 25.4% | | | 1,750,000 | 1,750,000 | $12,250,000 |
| PRE-IPO: sum of all stock | | | | 100.0% | 80.9% | | | 5,439,564 | 5,578,627 | $39,050,389 |
| IPO shares | | | | | 19.1% | | | | 1,315,000 | $9,205,000 |
| TOTAL OUTSTANDING | | | | | 100.0% | | | | 6,893,627 | $48,255,389 |

(7) Vesting for Stock Option Plans is usually 4 years, with 25% at end of a one year waiting period, 1/48th per month thereafter and fair market value at time of grant.

Lead Underwriters: Robertson + Rothschild

| | | | |
|---|---|---|---|
| 1,315,000 nr shares sold by company | $11,200,000 | | IPO TOTAL CASH RAISED BEFORE FEES AND EXPENSES |
| 285,000 nr shares sold by selling shareholders | $800,000 | 7.14% | IPO fee for underwriters |
| 1,600,000 IPO TOTAL | $375,000 | 3.35% | Estimated expenses of IPO |
| | $10,025,000 | 89.51% | NET TO COMPANY |

| REVENUE $M | REVENUE $M |
|---|---|
| Last 12 mos | Prior Quarter |
| $23.5 | $7.4 |
| Growth/Year | Growth/Year |
| 131.9% | 104.5% |
| | Nr of employes: 130 |

*SOURCE: Saratoga Venture Finance © All rights reserved. See prospectus for data. The above contain certain estimates.*

**SARATOGA VENTURE FINANCE EQUITY TABLE ™**
WAGES AND STOCK OWNERSHIP AT INITIAL PUBLIC OFFERING (IPO)

# Sun Microsystems, Inc.

IPO DATE: 4 March 1986
$16.00  Price per Share

UNIX workstations
Inception: 24 February 1982
Mountain View., California

| TITLE f = Founder | (4) COMPENSATION | (3B) OFFICERS OWNERSHIP | (3),(6),(7) MGT & EMPS OWNERSHIP | (1) PRE IPO OWNERSHIP | (2) POST IPO OWNERSHIP | (3B) OFFICERS OWNERSHIP | (3),(6),(7) MGT & EMPS OWNERSHIP | (1) PRE IPO OWNERSHIP | (2) POST IPO OWNERSHIP | IPO VALUE $16.00 Per Share |
|---|---|---|---|---|---|---|---|---|---|---|
| f CEO | $239,748 | 18.3% | 9.2% | 4.4% | 3.9% | 1,147,263 | 1,147,263 | 1,147,263 | 1,147,263 | $18,356,208 |
| f VP-TECH | | 25.1% | 12.6% | 6.1% | 5.3% | 1,571,093 | 1,571,093 | 1,571,093 | 1,571,093 | $25,137,488 |
| f Board Director | | 18.4% | 9.2% | 4.4% | 3.9% | 1,149,011 | 1,149,011 | 1,149,011 | 1,149,011 | $18,384,176 |
| VP R&D | | 14.1% | 7.1% | 3.4% | 3.0% | 884,077 | 884,077 | 884,077 | 884,077 | $14,145,232 |
| EVP | $122,987 | 5.4% | 2.7% | 1.3% | 1.1% | 336,875 | 336,875 | 336,875 | 336,875 | $5,390,000 |
| VP-SLS | $117,812 | 0.0% | 0.0% | 0.0% | 0.0% | 0 | 0 | 0 | 0 | $0 * |
| VP-FIN | $128,700 | 0.0% | 0.0% | 0.0% | 0.0% | 0 | 0 | 0 | 0 | $0 * |
| VP-EUR | $104,000 | 0.0% | 0.0% | 0.0% | 0.0% | 0 | 0 | 0 | 0 | $0 * |
| OTHER | Avg. of 8 = $60,554 | 18.7% | 9.4% | 4.5% | 4.0% | 1,170,248 | 1,170,248 | 1,170,248 | 1,170,248 | $18,723,968 * |
| OFFICERS & EXECUTIVES | | 100.0% | 50.2% | 24.2% | 21.2% | 6,258,567 | 6,258,567 | 6,258,567 | 6,258,567 | $100,137,072 |
| ALL OTHER | | | 34.1% | 16.4% | 14.4% | | 4,254,338 | 4,254,338 | 4,254,338 | $68,069,408 |
| TOTAL COMMON BEFORE OPTIONS | | | 84.4% | 40.6% | 35.6% | | 10,512,905 | 10,512,905 | 10,512,905 | $168,206,480 |
| OPTIONS-Outstanding | | | 15.6% | 7.5% | 6.6% | | 1,948,956 | 1,948,956 | 1,948,956 | $31,183,296 |
| OPTIONS-Available | | | 0.0% | 0.0% | 2.2% | | 0 | 0 | 660,383 | $10,566,128 |
| OPTIONS-Total | | | 15.6% | 7.5% | 8.8% | | 1,948,956 | 1,948,956 | 2,609,339 | $41,749,424 |
| COMMON-Total | | | 100.0% | 48.1% | 44.4% | | 12,461,861 | 12,461,861 | 13,122,244 | $209,955,904 |
| Major Venture Capital | | | | 41.1% | 36.0% | | | 10,654,885 | 10,654,885 | $170,478,160 |
| OTHER | | | | 10.8% | 9.4% | | | 2,786,514 | 2,786,514 | $44,584,224 |
| VENTURE Total | | | | 51.9% | 45.5% | | | 13,441,399 | 13,441,399 | $215,062,384 |
| PRE-IPO: sum of all stock | | | | 100.0% | 89.9% | | | 25,903,260 | 26,563,643 | $425,018,288 |
| IPO shares | | | | | 10.1% | | | | 3,000,000 | $48,000,000 |
| TOTAL OUTSTANDING | | | | | 100.0% | | | | 29,563,643 | $473,018,288 |

Avg. of 11=$1.7M *

| REVENUE$M | REVENUE$M |
|---|---|
| Last 12 mos | Prior Quarter |
| $115.2 | $42.2 |
| Growth/Year | Growth/Year |
| 196.6% | 73.5% |

Nr of employes: 1,223

(7) Vesting for Stock Option Plans is usually 4 years, with six month waiting period, 1/48 per mo thereafter and fair market value at time of grant.

Lead Underwriters: Robertson + Alex. Brown

| | | | |
|---|---|---|---|
| 3,000,000 nr shares sold by company | $64,000,000 | | IPO TOTAL CASH RAISED BEFORE FEES AND EXPENSES |
| 1,000,000 nr shares sold by selling shareholders | $3,920,000 | 6.13% | IPO fee for underwriters |
| 4,000,000 IPO TOTAL | $600,000 | 0.94% | Estimated expenses of IPO |
| | $59,480,000 | 92.94% | NET TO COMPANY |

SARATOGA VENTURE FINANCE EQUITY TABLE ™
WAGES AND STOCK OWNERSHIP AT INITIAL PUBLIC OFFERING (IPO)

# Vertex Pharmaceuticals Incorporated

IPO DATE: 24 July 1991
$9.00 Price per Share

Drug designer
Inception: 4 January 1989
Cambridge, Massachusetts

| TITLE f = Founder | (4) COMPENSATION | (3B) OFFICERS OWNERSHIP | (3),(6),(7) MGT & EMPS OWNERSHIP | (1) PRE IPO OWNERSHIP | (2) POST IPO OWNERSHIP | (3B) OFFICERS OWNERSHIP | (3),(6),(7) MGT & EMPS OWNERSHIP | (1) PRE IPO OWNERSHIP | (2) POST IPO OWNERSHIP | IPO VALUE $9.00 Per Share |
|---|---|---|---|---|---|---|---|---|---|---|
| f Pres,CSO | $162,880 | 80.4% | 33.3% | 7.8% | 4.9% | 520,000 | 520,000 | 520,000 | 520,000 | $4,680,000 |
| VP-BusDev | $83,807 | 0.0% | 0.0% | 0.0% | 0.0% | 0 | 0 | 0 | 0 | $0 * |
| Sr. Scientist | $92,054 | 0.0% | 0.0% | 0.0% | 0.0% | 0 | 0 | 0 | 0 | $0 * |
| OTHER | | 19.6% | 8.1% | 1.9% | 1.2% | 126,999 | 126,999 | 126,999 | 126,999 | $1,142,991 * |
| OFFICERS & EXECUTIVES | | 100.0% | 41.4% | 9.7% | 6.1% | 646,999 | 646,999 | 646,999 | 646,999 | $5,822,991 |
| ALL OTHER | | | 58.6% | 13.8% | 8.6% | | 915,343 | 915,343 | 915,343 | $8,238,087 |
| TOTAL COMMON BEFORE OPTIONS | | | 100.0% | 23.5% | 14.7% | | 1,562,342 | 1,562,342 | 1,562,342 | $14,061,078 |
| OPTIONS-Outstanding | | | 0.0% | 0.0% | 0.0% | | 0 | 0 | 0 | $0 |
| OPTIONS-Available | | | 0.0% | 0.0% | 9.4% | | | 0 | 1,000,000 | $9,000,000 |
| OPTIONS-Total | | | 0.0% | 0.0% | 9.4% | | | 0 | 1,000,000 | $9,000,000 |
| COMMON-Total | | | 100.0% | 23.5% | 24.1% | | 1,562,342 | 1,562,342 | 2,562,342 | $23,061,078 |
| Major Venture Capital | | | | 73.5% | 45.8% | | | 4,875,742 | 4,875,742 | $43,881,678 |
| OTHER | | | | 3.0% | 1.9% | | | 200,000 | 200,000 | $1,800,000 |
| VENTURE Total | | | | 76.5% | 47.7% | | | 5,075,742 | 5,075,742 | $45,681,678 |
| PRE-IPO: sum of all stock | | | | 100.0% | 71.8% | | | 6,638,084 | 7,638,084 | $68,742,756 |
| IPO shares | | | | | 28.2% | | | | 3,000,000 | $27,000,000 |
| TOTAL OUTSTANDING | | | | | 100.0% | | | | 10,638,084 | $95,742,756 |

Avg. of 4=$286K *

| REVENUE $M | REVENUE $M |
|---|---|
| Last 12 mos | Prior Quarter |
| $0.8 | $0.0 |
| Growth/Year | Growth/Year |
| Not meaningful | Not meaningful |
| Nr of employes: 53 | |

(7) Vesting determined by board of directors.

Lead Underwriters: Kidder + Cowen + BT Securities

| 3,000,000 nr shares sold by company | $27,000,000 | | IPO TOTAL CASH RAISED BEFORE FEES AND EXPENSES |
|---|---|---|---|
| 0 nr shares sold by selling shareholders | $1,732,500 | 6.42% | IPO fee for underwriters |
| | $600,000 | 2.22% | Estimated expenses of IPO |
| 3,000,000 IPO TOTAL | $24,667,500 | 91.36% | NET TO COMPANY |

SOURCE: Saratoga Venture Finance © All rights reserved. See prospectus for data. The above contain certain estimates.

315

**SARATOGA VENTURE FINANCE EQUITY TABLE ™**

WAGES AND STOCK OWNERSHIP AT INITIAL PUBLIC OFFERING (IPO)

## Worlds of Wonder

Electronic toys
Inception: March 1985
Fremont, California

IPO DATE: 20 June 1986
$18.00 Price per Share

| TITLE f = Founder | (4) COMPENSATION | (3B) OFFICERS OWNERSHIP | (3),(6),(7) MGT & EMPS OWNERSHIP | (1) PRE IPO OWNERSHIP | (2) POST IPO OWNERSHIP | (3B) OFFICERS OWNERSHIP | (3),(6),(7) MGT & EMPS OWNERSHIP | (1) PRE IPO OWNERSHIP | (2) POST IPO OWNERSHIP | IPO VALUE $18.00 Per Share |
|---|---|---|---|---|---|---|---|---|---|---|
| CEO | $332,641 | 71.5% | 51.2% | 25.6% | 20.5% | 4,918,356 | 4,918,356 | 4,918,356 | 4,918,356 | $88,530,408 |
| EVP-COO | $203,591 | 8.9% | 6.4% | 3.2% | 2.5% | 610,715 | 610,715 | 610,715 | 610,715 | $10,992,870 |
| EVP-DEV | | 2.7% | 2.0% | 1.0% | 0.8% | 187,500 | 187,500 | 187,500 | 187,500 | $3,375,000 |
| EVP-MKTG | | 0.0% | 0.0% | 0.0% | 0.0% | 0 | 0 | 0 | 0 | $0 |
| EVP-SLS | $199,096 | 4.4% | 3.1% | 1.6% | 1.2% | 300,000 | 300,000 | 300,000 | 300,000 | $5,400,000 |
| EVP-MFG/ENG | $199,096 | 5.4% | 3.9% | 2.0% | 1.6% | 375,000 | 375,000 | 375,000 | 375,000 | $6,750,000 |
| EVP-ADMIN | $167,243 | 3.2% | 2.3% | 1.1% | 0.9% | 217,500 | 217,500 | 217,500 | 217,500 | $3,915,000 |
| EVP-FIN/CFO | | 2.7% | 2.0% | 1.0% | 0.8% | 187,500 | 187,500 | 187,500 | 187,500 | $3,375,000 |
| EVP | | 0.0% | 0.0% | 0.0% | 0.0% | 0 | 0 | 0 | 0 | $0 |
| OTHER Avg. of 3=$115,186 | | 7.1% | 5.1% | 2.6% | 2.0% | 491,875 | 491,875 | 491,875 | 491,875 | $8,853,750 * |
| OFFICERS & EXECUTIVES | | 100.0% | 75.8% | 38.0% | 30.4% | 6,883,446 | 7,288,446 | 7,288,446 | 7,288,446 | $131,192,028 |
| ALL OTHER | | | 12.0% | 6.0% | 4.8% | | 1,151,639 | 1,151,639 | 1,151,639 | $20,729,502 |
| TOTAL COMMON BEFORE OPTIONS | | | 87.8% | 44.0% | 35.2% | | 8,440,085 | 8,440,085 | 8,440,085 | $151,921,530 |
| OPTIONS-Outstanding | | | 12.2% | 6.1% | 4.9% | | 1,174,750 | 1,174,750 | 1,174,750 | $21,145,500 |
| OPTIONS-Available | | | 0.0% | 0.0% | 3.4% | | 0 | 0 | 810,250 | $14,584,500 |
| OPTIONS-Total | | | 12.2% | 6.1% | 8.3% | | 1,174,750 | 1,174,750 | 1,985,000 | $35,730,000 |
| COMMON-Total | | | 100.0% | 50.1% | 43.4% | | 9,614,835 | 9,614,835 | 10,425,085 | $187,651,530 |
| Major Venture Capital | | | | 0.0% | 0.0% | | | 0 | 0 | $0 |
| OTHER | | | | 49.9% | 39.9% | | | 9,577,350 | 9,577,350 | $172,392,300 |
| VENTURE Total | | | | 49.9% | 39.9% | | | 9,577,350 | 9,577,350 | $172,392,300 |
| PRE-IPO: sum of all stock | | | | 100.0% | 83.3% | | | 19,192,185 | 20,002,435 | $360,043,830 |
| IPO shares | | | | | 16.7% | | | | 4,000,000 | $72,000,000 |
| TOTAL OUTSTANDING | | | | | 100.0% | | | | 24,002,435 | $432,043,830 |

Avg. of 3= $2.9M

| | REVENUE $M | REVENUE $M |
|---|---|---|
| | Last 12 mos | Prior Quarter |
| | $93.1 | $44.6 |
| | Growth/Year | Growth/Year |
| | Not meaningful | Not meaningful |
| | Nr of employes: 134 | |

(7) Vesting for Stock Option Plans is usually 4 years, with a three month waiting period, 1/48 per mo thereafter and fair market value at time of grant.

Lead Underwriters: Smith Barney + Dean Witter

| | | | |
|---|---|---|---|
| 4,000,000 | nr shares sold by company | $108,000,000 | IPO TOTAL CASH RAISED BEFORE FEES AND EXPENSES |
| 2,000,000 | nr shares sold by selling shareholders | $6,780,000 | 6.28% IPO fee for underwriters |
| 6,000,000 | IPO TOTAL | $755,000 | 0.70% Estimated expenses of IPO |
| | | $100,465,000 | 93.02% NET TO COMPANY |

SOURCE: *Saratoga Venture Finance* © *All rights reserved.* *See prospectus for data.* *The above contain certain estimates.*

*Appendix B*

# Resources for the Entrepreneur

The Internet now contains many excellent resources for the start-up CEO. A search on the words "list of venture capital firms" easily results in more than 500,000 web pages! To save time, below are several of our favorite sources of information. Remember to also be aware of how fast the information changes and to recheck your sources for the freshest facts.

## Sources of Venture Capitalists and Related Information

### Pratt's Guide to Venture Capital Sources

This standby, with its extensive information about venture capital firms, is probably already in your public library. ISBN: 0914470973; Author: Stanley E. Pratt; Publisher: Venture Economics.

### National Venture Capital Association

**www.nvca.org**

Here you can find an up-to-date directory of venture firms that are members, with links to the homepages of the venture firms.

### Venture Economics

**www.nvst.com/vcj**

This is what the venture capitalists read. This monthly magazine contains valuable data about trends and results of VC financing deals.

### Vfinance.com

**www.vfinance.com**

This Internet site is an extensive source of links to VC firms, along with many other kinds of investor information.

### Garage.com

**www.garage.com**

This Internet site is very worthwhile. It has good information for start-ups, including discussions and topical papers by lawyers and VCs.

## 'Zines, Magazines, Newspapers, and Periodicals

### Business2.0

**www.business2.com**

This Silicon Valley–headquartered Internet-era business magazine is focused on the news about the new companies of the new economy.

### Business Journal of San Jose

**www.amcity.com/sanjose**

This periodical has excellent lists ("Book of Lists") that show the top twenty-five of all sorts of Silicon Valley businesses that support start-ups, from law and PR firms to recruiters and real estate.

### BusinessWeek

**www.businessweek.com**

This must-read weekly business magazine covers private and public companies.

### CNET

**www.cnet.com**

This is standard reading for many start-up-focused thinkers interested in daily news about the Internet, computers, and technology.

### The Economist

**www.economist.com**

World-class coverage of global news, especially key political and economic issues driving private and public enterprises.

### Forbes

**www.forbes.com**

*Forbes* writes its frank reviews of start-ups in each issue in the section entitled "Entrepreneurs." It is an excellent source of learning about how the media looks at unfair advantage. The related Internet web site is very useful to entrepreneurs.

### Gilder Technology Report

**www.gildertech.com**

The report that tracks the disruptive technologies of our times and talks about the implications for private and public companies.

## *Inc.*

**www.inc.com**

*Inc.* magazine is a storehouse of tips and tricks and tools for CEOs of all kinds of start-ups. It starts with coverage of the smallest of companies and builds to large companies that go public.

## *The Industry Standard*

**www.thestandard.com**

This San Francisco–headquartered Internet-era business magazine is focused on the news about the new companies of the new economy.

## *Quarterly Venture Capital Survey*

**www.mercurycenter.com/svtech/companies/moneytree/**

The quarterly survey of funding of start-ups, mostly of Silicon Valley companies.

## *Red Herring*

**www.redherring.com**

Brings the buzz of venture news about the latest trends in venture-backed start-ups, tracking them from funding to IPO.

## *The San Jose Mercury News*

**www.mercurycenter.com/svtech/**

The newspaper of Silicon Valley, it has an excellent Internet site with the news of the day from the heart of high tech.

## *Technologic Partners*

**www.tpsite.com**

This respected publishing and services firm delivers daily news about fundings of start-ups, as well as related newsletters and conferences.

## *Upside*

**www.upside.com**

The magazine that pioneered coverage of venture capital, start-ups, Wall Street, and IPOs.

## *The Wall Street Journal*

**www.interactive.wsj.com**

In addition to excellent daily news in printed form, the Technology and Internet versions have additional coverage of technology-related news, including start-ups and IPOs.

# Legal Counsel

*Martindale-Hubbell*

**www.martindale-hubbell.com**

This is the standard reference for law firms. The Internet site allows free searches. Law firms have copies in their libraries.

*Lawoffice.com*

**www.lawoffice.com**

This Internet site is a good source to use to find a local lawyer when you are not sure where to start. It also has papers on subjects related to start-up law. Law firms in one city will recommend firms in other cities.

**The following lists the larger law firms in Silicon Valley.**

*Brobeck, Phleger & Harrison*

**www.brobeck.com**

*Cooley Godward*

**www.cooley.com**

*Fenwick & West*

**www.fenwick.com**

*Gray Cary Ware & Freidenrich*

**www.graycary.com**

*Morrison & Foerster*

**www.mofo.com**

*Wilson Sonsini Goodrich & Rosati*

**www.wsgr.com**

**The following are some new law firms in Silicon Valley.**

*Gunderson Dettmer*

**www.gunder.com**

*Venture Law Group*

**www.vlg.com**

## Intellectual Property Attorneys

*These are two of the top intellectual property firms in Silicon Valley.*

*Skjerven, Morrill, MacPherson, Franklin & Friel*

**www.skjerven.com**

*Townsend & Townsend*

**www.townsend.com**

## Accounting Firms

To request local assistance, call up the nearest office listed in the white pages of the telephone book and ask for the managing partner.

*Arthur Andersen*

**www.arthurandersen.com**

*Deloitte Touche Tohmatsu*

**www.deloitte.com**

*Ernst & Young*

**www.eyi.com**
This firm gives out annual awards called "Entrepreneur of the Year."

*KPMG*

**www.kpmg.com**

*PricewaterhouseCoopers*

**www.pwcglobal.com**
This firm lists data on quarterly venture fundings.

*Grant Thornton*

**www.gti.org**

## IPOs

*Securities and Exchange Commission*

**www.sec.gov**
The SEC's EDEAR database lists IPO filings by private companies that can be accessed for free.

## IPO.com

**www.ipo.com**

Focused on IPO news, this Internet site is for new IPO filings and offerings.

## IPO Information Details

**www.linux.agsm.ucla.edu/ipo**

This site contains educational information about an IPO.

## Investor Links

**www.investorlinks.com**

This Internet site includes many sources of information about Wall Street and stocks, including IPOs.

# Banks

## Silicon Valley Bank

**www.svbank.com**

This bank, focused on serving new enterprises, has branches across the United States and is a source of assistance to start-ups in many ways in addition to offering to provide capital.

# Wall Street

The following list includes the more prominent high-tech investment banking firms. Each site varies in the degree of information available for free to entrepreneurs. Most firms require an investment relationship in order to access the more valuable research information.

## Institutional Investor

**www.iimagazine.com**

This respected magazine for professionals ranks the top stock analysts and their investment bankers. Start by picking the top analysts for your industry and follow the path to the investment banker.

*The following five are new Internet investment bankers.*

## Charles Schwab

**www.schwab.com**

This site provides high-quality information for investors with free quotes and charts.

## E*OFFERING

**www.eoffering.com**

This investment banker is related to E*Trade, and its Internet site has information about the firm's related IPOs as well as comments from selected stock analysts.

## E*Trade

**www.etrade.com**

This Internet firm's site has a special IPO Center for IPO news.

## Wit Capital

**www.witcapital.com**

This Internet firm is an early leader of investment banking using the Internet.

## W. R. Hambrecht

**www.wrhambrecht.com**

This Internet firm is the newest creation of Bill Hambrecht, an icon of Silicon Valley.

***The following eleven are traditional investment bankers.***

## BancBoston Robertson Stevens

**www.rsco.com**

Bank Boston purchased Robertson Stevens.

## Bank of America (re: Montgomery)

**www.corp.bankofamerica.com**

Montgomery Securities was purchased by NationsBank, which merged with BankAmerica.

## Bear Stearns

**www.bearstearns.com**

## Credit Suisse First Boston

**www.csfb.com**

## Deutsche Bank (re: Alex Brown)

**www.db.com**

Alex Brown was purchased by Bankers Trust, which was purchased by Deutsche Bank.

## Goldman Sachs

**www.goldmansachs.com**

*Hambrecht & Quist*
**www.hamquist.com**

*Lehman Brothers*
**www.lehman.com**

*Merrill Lynch*
**www.ml.com**

*Morgan Stanley Dean Witter*
**www.msdw.org**

*Salomon Smith Barney*
**www.smithbarney.com**

# Investor Relations

National Investor Relations Institute

**www.niri.org**

The resource center for how to manage Wall Street and investor relations.

*Appendix C*

---

# *Three Venture Capital Firms*

---

## Sequoia Capital, Menlo Park, California

Sequoia Capital is one of the most successful venture capital firms. Started in 1972, it has funded many famous start-ups that went IPO in many high-tech industries. The firm invests in all stages, from the seed round through later stages. Below is a list of very helpful questions for the founder/CEO to use from the web site of the firm.

**Frequently Asked Questions:**

**How do I submit a plan to Sequoia?**

Thank you very much for considering Sequoia.
Please send an email to businessplans@sequoiacap.com with the following attached:
1. 15–20 page PowerPoint Presentation describing your business.
2. A copy of your executive summary.

**What sort of companies does Sequoia like to finance?**

Our favorite investment candidates are companies operating in the electronic and health-care segments of the economy. We like our investments to be well positioned in new and very rapidly growing markets where the customers have great enthusiasm for the company's products.

**At what stage does Sequoia invest?**

Most of Sequoia's investments are aimed at the very early stages of technology companies.

**Where does Sequoia invest?**

We prefer our early stage investments to be on the West Coast. We will invest in post–beta stage companies around Boston and Austin and will invest nationwide in more mature companies.

**What is the typical size of an investment?**

We invest anywhere from a $50,000 seed investment to $10 million.

**What is the most important investment characteristic for Sequoia?**

The first trait we seek are start-ups that will attack markets poised for rapid growth. We want to be investors in companies that can gain the largest market share in large markets. These companies invariably make the best investments. We cannot afford to wait for markets to develop and we do not have the money or inclination to educate customers to buy products they don't know they need. We like investment areas that show the potential to blossom into markets that are over $1 billion. That sort of size allows room for error and also provides enough headroom to build a substantial company.

**Does Sequoia always want a board seat?**

No. It depends on the stage of the company and the desire and wishes of the founders and management.

**What sort of people does Sequoia like to finance?**

Sequoia's most successful entrepreneurs possess some, or all, of the following attributes. Most have come from modest, if not humble, backgrounds. Many are immigrants or first generation Americans. All know the value of money and instinctively understand the crucial difference that separates need from want. Their confidence is tempered by an understanding of their shortcomings. They have a sense of urgency. They know that a combination of speed and stealth will usually help them beat large companies. They know too that other start-ups pose the greatest threat to their existence.

**What sort of products are attractive to Sequoia?**

The products that fuel start-ups fall into two categories. The first are difficult to duplicate and contain a lot of proprietary know-how. The second type do not contain tremendous science or technological know-how but have a first mover's advantage and allow a company to start rolling very quickly, garner a large market share, and turn that position into a powerful competitive weapon.

**What is Sequoia's attitude toward large amounts of equity?**

Dilution is our greatest enemy. Recognition of the corrosive force of dilution is what separates the wealthy entrepreneur from the successful one. We like to start companies with relatively small amounts of money and we like our investments to become profitable quickly. This allows the founders and management of a start-up to retain a large equity stake throughout the life of the company. We have discovered that founders and entrepreneurs clever enough to develop a large return from a small investment will frequently build significant companies.

**Does Sequoia usually control ownership of a company?**

No. Great investments usually occur when the founders and management of a company are the majority owners. All of our best investments have come in companies where we have been minority shareholders.

## What is Sequoia's role after an investment is made?

It varies. It can range from intensive involvement in an early stage company that, during its formation, can be housed in our offices to a far more detached role once the company has become mature. In an early stage company we tend to be very involved with key hiring decisions, major changes of strategic direction, company positioning, and financings.

## Does Sequoia have an entrepreneur-in-residence program?

Yes. Several companies have either started in our office or used it as a base during their early existence. Electronic Arts, PMC-Sierra, Yahoo!, and RedBack Networks are some of the better known examples. We also will house entrepreneurs who are nursing interesting ideas or who can be of help to our investment program.

## Does Sequoia get involved in the management of a company?

Venture capitalists often think they build companies. We disagree. Managements build companies. Sometimes venture capitalists help. At Sequoia we provide assistance when it is requested or needed, but we do not want to run companies. We have opinions. We are not shy about making recommendations. But, the decisions are yours.

## Who are Sequoia's investors?

The majority of Sequoia's institutional investors are large foundations, endowments, and universities. All of them are experienced venture capital investors and understand the long-term nature of our business. Many of them are in their third decade of investing with Sequoia Capital.

## What's the length of time Sequoia holds an investment?

We can offer our greatest help to companies during their formative years. However, on occasion, when the management of a magnet company asks us to stay involved, we do. In some cases we have remained as directors of companies for more than ten years.

## How many investments does Sequoia make every year?

We have no hard and fast rules about how many investments we make in a year or a quarter. During the last few years we have made between eight and twelve fresh commitments a year. We also make between twelve and fifteen follow-on investments a year in companies that are already within the Sequoia portfolio.

## How many business plans does Sequoia review?

Every day we hear about ideas for twenty new businesses. Some of these ideas come in the form of comprehensive business plans; some are executive summaries that arrive by fax or e-mail; and some are telephone inquiries. We try to review every idea that we hear about.

## What is the best way to get introduced to Sequoia?

The easiest and most effective introduction is from someone who knows you and knows us. We frequently get introduced to new companies and entrepreneurs by people employed by existing Sequoia companies, by lawyers, accountants, commercial bankers, investment bankers, and headhunters. We have an extensive web of contacts and like to think that we are only two telephone calls away from anyone with a good idea in and around Silicon Valley.

**How long does it take Sequoia to make an investment decision?**

We have made a few investment decisions within twenty-four hours, while others have taken us over a year. It usually takes us between three and six weeks from the time we first encounter a company to making a final investment decision.

**How does Sequoia make investment decisions?**

All the Sequoia Partners need to agree to make an investment. This means that they all have to be exposed to the prospective investment—either through a review of a business plan and reference checks or through attending a company presentation. Usually, all the partners will participate in both activities. For a company this means making between one and three presentations at Sequoia; providing a business plan or a summary of a business plan; and furnishing personal reference checks and, where appropriate, customer reference checks.

**What sort of executive summary format appeals to Sequoia?**

We like business plans that present a lot of information in as few words as possible. The topics that interest us the most in any business plan are a description of the market the company plans to attack; an overview of the company's initial product and planned products; a description of distribution channels; a summary of the backgrounds of the management team; a five-year summary of financial projections; and a capitalization table. We place more credence in a fifteen-to-twenty page business plan than a compendious compilation with attendant appendixes. We are very skeptical about placing too much faith in detailed financial projections beyond the first twelve-to-eighteen months of a company's operations and have a jaundiced view of reams of financial data.

**What makes for an effective presentation at Sequoia?**

We have found that the following format (see web site) provides a good overview of a prospective investment. It usually works best when limited to around fifteen-to-twenty slides (either in overhead foils or when driven from a PC.

# Kleiner Perkins Caufield & Byers, Menlo Park, California

In 1972 Kleiner Perkins Caufield & Byers began offering entrepreneurs a broader philosophy of value-added investing: not merely access to capital, but access to people. A partnership with experienced industry leaders who recognize, challenge, and even improve on a brilliant idea.

We believe we must earn the right to advise entrepreneurs on a daily basis, by intellectually committing to deliver the best ideas. We are here to build your vision. Strengthen strategic thinking. Tap the industry network. Access talent. Pull strings. Sew up financing. And stick with you through every challenge along the way.

That's what good ideas demand today. If they are to become breakthrough products and build successful companies, it takes more than money. It takes the right people. The right connections. And experience.

## Benchmark Capital Menlo Park, California

At Benchmark Capital, we're focused on one, and only one, mission: to help talented entrepreneurs build great technology companies. That's what drives us and everything we do—from how we organize our firm to our investment strategy.

When we created Benchmark, we rewrote the book on venture capital. We did away with the organizational bureaucracy of traditional venture firms and created a different kind of partnership that enables us to provide a superior level of service to our entrepreneurs.

Unlike other venture firms whose partners work independently and often even compete for resources, we function as a team. We have six equal general partners, all working together to help our portfolio companies succeed.

This fundamentally better architecture gives our portfolio companies the benefit of having all of our experienced, well-connected partners working for them, not just one. Each portfolio company has access to the combined resources of our entire firm—whether it's to help recruit for an exec staff position, facilitate a corporate partnership, or get advice on a strategic move.

Our emphasis on teamwork and providing quality service are big reasons why the industry's top entrepreneurs turn to Benchmark for funding. Entrepreneurs with proven track records like Mike Farmwald of Rambus, Chromatic, Epigram and Matrix Semiconductor; Brian Dougherty of Wink and GeoWorks; and Keith Krach of Ariba could get funding from virtually any firm. But they don't. Why? They say it's because Benchmark brings a lot more to the table than just money.

Our investment strategy is simple: be the first venture investor in technology companies that seek to create new markets. We focus on early stage investing and take a labor-intensive, service-oriented approach in markets where we have direct experience. These markets include consumer devices, e-commerce, application services, networking equipment, semiconductor, software, and telecommunications services.

And, to make sure that each of our portfolio companies gets the support it needs to succeed, we actively limit the number of companies we invest in. This strategy gives us an unusually high partner-to-capital ratio and ensures portfolio companies get the attention they deserve.

Our investments range in size from as little as $100,000 to as much as $10 million. Typically, we invest $2 million to $4 million initially and expect to invest $5 million to $7 million over the life of a company. We invest for the long haul, not "quick flips," and look for entrepreneurs with a similar perspective.

# Bibliography

Aaker, David A. *Building Strong Brands*. New York: Free Press, 1996.

Bennett Jr., Thomas E. "What Do Bankers Want?" *Inc.*, June 1987, pp. 149–150.

Berglas, Steven. "The Big Lie." *Inc.*, March 1996, pp. 70–75.

Brehm, Barbara A. "Exercise for Good Sleep and Health." *Fitness Magazine*, 1998.

Clifford, Donald K., and Cavanaugh, Richard E. *The Winning Performance*. New York: Bantam Books, 1985.

Coyne, Kevin. "Sustainable Competitive Advantage—What It Is, What It Isn't." *Business Horizons*, January/February, pp. 27–34.

Christensen, Clayton M. *The Innovator's Dilemma*. Harvard Business School Press, 1997.

Drucker, Peter. *Innovation and Entrepreneurship*. New York: Harper & Row, 1985.

Dunham, Kemba J. "Recruits Insist That Firms Hire Their Friends as Well." *Wall Street Journal*, June 22, 1999.

Engstrom, Ted W., and David J. Juroe. *The Work Trap*. Old Tappan, NJ: Fleming H. Revell, 1979.

Freudenberger, Herbert J. *Burnout: How to Beat the High Cost of Success*. New York: Bantam Books, 1980.

Harrell, Wilson. "Entrepreneurial Terror," *Inc.*, February 1987, pp. 74–76.

Hattlestad, Luc. "Diary of an Internet IPO." *Red Herring*, July 1999, pp. 53–61.

Hof, Robert D. "Inside an Internet IPO.", September 6, 1999, pp. 60–73.

Kaufman, Steve. "High-tech Survivalists." *San Jose Mercury News*, September 29, 1986.

Kroll, Luisa. "Dog Fight." *Forbes*, July 5, 1999, pp. 137–139.

Mamis, Robert A. "Great Companies That Were Started with $1,000 or Less: The Secrets of Bootstrapping." *Inc.*, September 1991, pp. 52–70.

Maran, Meredith. "How to Shrink an Engineer." *West* magazine, *San Jose Mercury News*, July 27, 1986.

Moore, Geoffrey A. *Inside the Tornado*. New York: Harper Business, 1995.

Peters, Tom. "On Excellence." *San Jose Mercury News*, March 27, 1986.

Porter, Michael. "How to Get a Competitive Edge." *The Economist*, January 15, 1987, p. 57.

Porter, Michael. "The State of Strategic Thinking." *The Economist*, May 23, 1987, pp. 17–22.

Ries, Al, and Ries, Laura. *The 22 Immutable Laws of Branding*. New York: Harper Business, 1998.

Ries, Al, and Jack Trout. *Marketing Warfare*. New York: Penguin Books, 1986.

Stout, Hilary. "Web Hotshots Learn The Dangers of Being Ahead af the Market." *Wall Street Journal*, July 30, 1999.

Sylvester, David. "The Ghosts of a Bull Market." In "Business Monday," *San Jose Mercury News*, August 10, 1987.

Trout, Jack. *The New Positioning*. New York: McGraw-Hill, 1996.

Uttal, Bro. "Inside the Deal That Made Bill Gates $350,000,000." *Fortune*, July 21, 1986, pp. 23–31.

# *Index*

Aaker, David, 84
Abraham, Lois, 57
Accountants
  business plans and,
    36–37, 85–87
  choosing, 86–87
  fees of, 87
  internal start-ups and,
    275–76
  IPOs and, 253–54, 255
  role of, 107
Acquisitions. See Mergers
    and acquisitions
Adler, Fred, 16, 186
Adobe Systems, 119, 189
Advanced HR, 130, 138, 139
Advance/Newhouse, 278
Agreements, 122–24. See
    also Contracts
AirFlash, 9
Akamai Technologies, 278
Alcohol use, 158
Alex Brown, 18, 237t, 238,
    255, 264, 265
Allen, Ken, 63
Allen, Paul, 24, 28
Alliant, 6
Altos, 7
Amazon.com, 156, 226, 273
Amdahl, Gene, 258
Amdahl Corp., 33
American Cardiovascular,
    268, 270, 273–74
American Institute of Certi-
    fied Public Accoun-
    tants (AICPA), 275
American Software, 80
America Online, 224
Analog Devices, 17

Anderson, Dave, 251
Anderson, Jerry, 259
Andreessen, Marc, 118
Angels, 9, 222, 223–24
Antidilution clauses, 111, 123
Appendices of business
    plan, 78
Apple Computer, 17, 24, 98,
    162, 180, 276
Arrillaga, John, 202
Arthur Andersen, 86
Arthur Rock, 16, 192t
Ascend, 17
Ashton-Tate, 7
Asia, 13, 188, 224–25, 229,
    281
AsiaTech Ventures, 192t
AT&T, 274, 277

Bad news, 163
Band of Angels, 223
Bank Boston, 237t
Bankers, 212–19. See also
    Commercial bankers;
    Investment bankers
  relatives as, 218–19
  role of, 212–17
Bankers Trust, 237t, 238
Bank of America, 19, 237t,
    238
Bankruptcies, 2, 47, 96, 180,
    181t, 185, 217
Barksdale, Jim, 224
BBN, 278
Bear, Stearns, 237t
Bell Laboratories, 18, 274,
    276, 277–78
Benchmark Capital, 192t,
    329

BenDaniel, David, vii
Big Company Counter-
    punch, 48
Bigler, Hal, 17
Bluebird Leasing, 209
Blue sky laws, 121
Board of directors, 45,
    123–24, 227, 228, 264
Bonuses, 135
Boom-to-bust cycles, 4, 10
Bootstraps, 8, 33, 218–20
Breakeven, 181t
Brentwood Associates, 192t
Bridge loans, 109
Brown & Bain, 57
*Building Strong Brands*
    (Aaker), 84
Burnout, 2, 11, 156–57
Burn rate, 5, 45, 46, 48, 111
*Business 2.0*, 25
*Business Horizons*, 82–83
Business model, 88
*Business Monday*, 208, 234
Business plans, 1, 68–90
  attention getters in, 70–71
  confidentiality and, 69
  creation of, 25t, 35–37,
    168t
  deal flow and, 71–72
  due diligence and, 72
  investor requirements,
    72–76, 99
  modifying, 104
  outline, 77t
  overview of, 76–78
  required material for, 69
  timing of, 69–70
  trends in screening of, 12
Business slips, 110

Business strategy and key
  milestones (business
  plan section), 76, 77t
*BusinessWeek*, 35, 74, 193,
  194, 220, 233, 265

Campaign, launching,
  101–2
Campbell, Gordon A., 42,
  117, 118, 202–3
Canion, 35–36
Capital
  closing, 25t, 41–42, 168t
  shortfall of, 162
  venture. See Venture
    capital
  working, 27t, 49–50, 169t
Capital Group, The, 264
Carry, 176
Case studies
  American Cardiovascular,
    273–74
  Bell Laboratories, 277–78
  Chips and Technologies,
    117–18, 202–3
  Compaq Computer,
    35–36
  of compensation, 142–45
  Critical Path, 265
  Crown Semiconductor,
    100–101
  Cypress Semiconductor,
    131–32
  Dell Computer, 220
  Devices Corp., 197–98
  Extro Electronics, Inc.,
    63–64
  Lucent Technologies,
    277–78
  Microsoft IPO, 265
  National Semiconductor,
    270–73
  Netscape, 118–20
  Network Equipment
    Technologies, Inc.,
    116–17
  New Software, Inc.,
    196–97
  Newtech Company, 59–62
  Plus Development, 277
  Quantum Corporation,
    277
  Range Semiconductor,
    209–11

Sigma Designs, 33
Tophill Systems, 208–9
work style, 152
Yourco, Inc., 121–22
Cash compensation,
  133–34. See also
  Wages/salaries
  just before IPO, 136t
  for management, 2
  tables of, 138–39
  for VPs, 2–3, 136, 138
Cavanagh, Richard, 68
CBS, 278
Chan, Jimmy, 33
Change, 159–62, 185–87
Chase Manhattan, 19
Chen, Jason, 33
Chief executive officers
  (CEOs), 10–11, 93
  founders with experience
    as, 3, 12
  outsourcing, 95–96
  ownership by, 1, 14, 127t,
    128–29
  risk/reward trade-offs for,
    177–78
  wages/salaries of, 2, 9,
    135
Chief financial officers
  (CFOs), 49, 93–94, 252,
  263
Chief operating officers
  (COOs), 38
Children, 160–62, 165, 217
China, 281
Chips and Technologies,
  Inc., 9, 42, 50, 132, 134,
  201, 224
  case studies, 117–18,
    202–3
  cash compensation in,
    136t, 138
  ownership of, 118, 127t
Cisco Systems, 17, 18, 180,
  226, 273, 278, 279
Claris Corp., 276
Clark, Jim, 9, 74, 118–19, 130
Classics, 9
Clifford, Donald, 68
Closing, 105, 124, 194–95
Closing capital, 25t, 41–42,
  168t
Cobalt, 118
Comcast Interactive

Capital, 278
Commercial bankers, 41
  conventions and prac-
    tices of, 212–13
  leasing from, 204, 210,
    214–15
Commercial possibilities, 75
Common stock, 112, 123,
  141–42
Company name, 65
Compaq Computer Corpo-
  ration, 23, 35–36, 37,
  42, 75, 98, 104, 180,
  204, 270, 272
Comparables, 257
Compensation, 136–46
  case study of, 142–45
  cash. See Cash compen-
    sation
  incentive, 274–75
  in internal start-ups,
    274–75
Competition
  excess, 45–46
  between venture capital
    firms, 3, 5
Conexant, 278
Conferences, 148
Confidentiality, 69
Conflict of interest, 107–8
Conrades, George H., 278
Consistency, 261, 262
Consultants, 36, 95–96,
  106–7, 166
Contractors, 95–96
Contracts, 105, 141. See also
  Agreements
Control, 120–22, 135, 262
Convex, 6
Copyrights, 56, 64
Core team, 12–13, 21, 91–92
Corporate finance staff, 235
Corporate venture capital,
  6, 225–27, 279–82
  finding, 279
  foreign, 280–81
  historical overview of,
    17–18
  mergers and acquisitions
    and, 267–70
  opportunities for, 281–82
  pricing of, 226, 279–80
  pros and cons of using,
    226–27

trends in, 13
Corrigan, Wilfred, 272
Costella Kirsch, 204
Cost of capital, viii, 6, 19, 170, 181, 185, 201, 205, 206, 279, 282
Costs
  of business plan creation, 36–37
  of closing, 42
  of filling management team, 39
  of finding a location, 43
  at founders' commitment stage, 32
  at idea stage, 28
  of incorporation, 42, 65
  of IPOs, 50, 240–44
  at kitchen table stage, 31
  of leasing, 205–6
  personal, 10–11, 139t, 150–57, 217
  of product launching, 48
  of pullout from employer, 34
  of raising seed capital, 40
  of raising working capital, 49
  of secondary capital rounds, 46
  at starting up stage, 45
Counselors, 166
Cowan and Company, 248
Cox Communications, 278
Coyne, Kevin P., 83
CPAs. See Accountants
Creative start-ups, 9
Creativity, 147–48, 153
Credit references, 214
Credit Suisse First Boston, 237t
Creeping close, 42, 194
Creeping elegance, 48
Critical Path, 265
*Crossing the Chasm* (Moore), 88
Crossroads, 17
Crowley, Jerry, 84, 189
Crown Semiconductor, 100–101
Customer need and business opportunity (business plan section), 76, 77t

Customers
  finding, 47
  tales for, 163
Cvietusa, Don, 216
Cypress Semiconductor, 127t, 131–32, 134, 136t, 203

Daisy Systems, 34
Data General, 16
Dataquest, 75
Davis, Tommy, 16
Day traders, 3, 19, 172, 244–45
Deal flow, 4, 71–72
Dean Witter, 237t
Dell, Michael, 220
Dell Computer, 204, 220
Deloitte & Touche, 86
Denver Stock Exchange, 228–29
Designer start-ups, 13
Deutsche Bank, 237t, 238
Devices Corp., 197–98
Diet, 158
Digital Equipment Corporation, 16
Diller, Jim, 34
Dilution, 6–7, 40, 99, 100, 101, 182f
  antidilution clauses, 111, 123
DiPietro, Dee, 130
DIRECTV, 278
Discovery Communications, 278
Divorce, 11, 160–62
Doctor visits, 159
Doer, John, 118–19
Dream, 30
Drucker, Peter F., vii, 68, 84, 172, 269
Drug abuse, 159–60
Due diligence, 21, 72, 104, 255

eBay, 8
*Economist*, 278
EDGAR database, 183
Eli Lilly, 273
E Loan, 265
Emerging incompetence, 74
Employees

benefits and perquisites, 145–46
  IPOs and, 249–50
  ownership by just before IPO, 134t
  personal loans to, 141
  relocation of, 141
  stock options of, 130–31, 140–41
  worth of stock owned by, 2
Employers
  pullout from, 24t, 33–35, 56–59, 168t
  trustworthy, 166
Employment contracts, 141
E*Offering, 19
Equipment leasing, 3, 203–7, 214–15
Equity, 126–27, 133–34. See also Ownership
  as cost of leasing, 205–6
  leveraging of, 46, 49
Ernst & Young, 86
Ethics, 56–59, 162–63
E*Trade, 3, 19, 224, 238
Europe, 3, 13, 188, 224–25
Evans, Barry, 63
Executive Fitness Center, 157
Executive summary, 71, 76, 77t, 89–90
Executives, 153
Exercise, 157–58
Exit strategy. See Liquidity
Exodus Communications, 9
Extro Electronics, Inc., 63–64

Fairchild Camera and Instrument Corp., 270, 271, 272–73
Families, 160–62
Fanyo, Dick, 255
Felsenstein, Lee, 30
Financial projections, 76–78, 87–89
Financial statements, 124
*Financial World*, 245
Financing rounds. See Funding rounds
Fire sales, 10, 181t
First capital round, 109–10
First mover advantage, 8, 21
Fitness, 157–59
Flipping, 237, 238

Floundering founder phe-
nomena, 150
Focus, lack of, 47, 48
*Forbes*, 6, 19, 20, 25, 79–81,
147, 225, 228, 233,
247–48
Foreign corporate capital,
280–81
Foreign stock exchanges,
13, 229–30
*Fortune*, 20, 265
Fortune 500 companies,
153, 224, 225–27, 279
49ers, 9, 96, 223
Founders, 36
cash invested by, 114
CEO experience in, 3, 12
at closing and incorpora-
tion stage, 41–42
commitment of, 24t,
31–32, 168t
floundering in, 150
IPOs and, 250
ownership by, 1, 127t,
129–30, 139–40, 184
Four Horsemen, The, 18, 19
France, 280–81
Freudenberger, Herbert J.,
156–57
Friends, 165
Funding. See also Capital;
Venture capital
impact of management
on, 96–97
key issues in, 114–15
setting objectives for, 99
Funding rounds
in Chips and Technolo-
gies, 117
first capital, 109–10
multiple capital, 110–11
in Netscape, 119
in Network Equipment
Technologies, Inc., 116
pricing of, 114, 181–85
secondary capital, 26t,
46–47, 169t
seed capital. See Seed
capital

Gates, Bill, 16, 24, 28, 74,
128, 250
Gateway, 204
Gazelle Microcircuits, 84, 189

Genentech, 17
General legal counsel,
55–56
Generally Accepted Ac-
counting Principles
(GAAP), 253
General Motors, 226, 278
Germany, 280–81
Goldman Sachs, 17, 19, 235,
236, 237t, 238, 242, 244,
248–49, 264
*Gorilla* (Moore), 84
Government-backed loans,
217–18
Green Shoe, 239–40
GTE, 278

*Hall* v. *Geiger-Jones*, 121
Hambrecht, Bill, 19, 238
Hambrecht & Quist, 16, 18,
19, 193–94, 235, 237t,
238, 264, 265, 278
Harrell, Wilson, 154–55
Harris, James M., 35
Hazle, Bill, 159–60
Health, 157–59
Health benefits, 145
Hearst Corporation, 119
Heart attacks, 11, 164
Heidrick & Struggles, 153,
160
Hewlett-Packard, 74, 130
Higgerson, Clifford, 194
Historical overview, 15–22
Home equity loans, 217
Home HBO, 278
Honesty, 11, 261
Hong Kong, 188, 224, 230,
281
Hours worked per day, 11
Huang, Philip, 137
Hurdle rate, 172
Hybrid start-ups, 9

IBM, 17, 63, 226
IDC, 75
Idea stage, 24–30, 168t
*Inc.*, 25, 154, 218, 220, 233
Incentive compensation,
274–75
Incentive Stock Options
(ISO), 141
Incorporation, 25t, 41–42,
64–66

India, 188, 224
Industry business acco-
lades, 148–50
Initial public offerings
(IPOs), 111–12, 232–66
average time to, 3, 7, 20t
cash compensation just
before, 136t
cost of doing, 50, 240–44
Critical Path, 265
decision to join during,
169t
employees and, 249–50
failure to reach, 180–81
foreign stock exchanges
and, 13, 229–30
founders and, 250
future trends in, 13
historical overview of,
18–20
importance of, 5, 249–51
investors and, 250–51
managing stage follow-
ing, 51
Microsoft, 128, 232, 242–
44, 250, 251, 252, 265
new issues and, 232–35
ownership by employees
and investors just be-
fore, 134t
ownership by founders
and CEOs following, 1,
127t
ownership by venture
capitalists at time of, 2
participants in, 252–54,
263–65
potential problems and
pitfalls of, 257–59,
261–63
practices and principles
in, 254–55
price of, 171–72
process of, 251–55
statistics on success and
failure of, 247–48
successful conclusion to,
259–65
time consumption in,
261–62
timing in, 251–52, 253t
value of one percent at,
132–34
venture capital formation

for, 27t, 50–51, 169t
windows for, 3, 51
*Innovation and Entrepre-
neurship: Practice and
Principles* (Drucker),
84
*Inside the Tornado* (Moore),
84
Inspection rights, 123
Institutional funds, 172–73
Institutional investors, 178,
244–46
Institutional sales people,
236
Integrity, 11, 247, 261
Intel, 9, 18, 53, 56, 201, 226,
261–62, 274
Intellectual property, 13–14,
31, 34, 53, 60, 102–3
of former employers,
56–57
protecting, 59t, 62–64
theft of, 162
Internal rates of return
(IRR), 178, 179f, 206
Internal start-ups, 4, 6, 13,
18, 274–78
expert help for, 276
first mover advantage of,
21
potential problems and
pitfalls of, 274
valuation of, 276
Internet start-ups, 6, 7, 17,
20, 128, 174
historical overview of, 19,
20
stock options in, 130, 131
Investment bankers, 13, 18–
20, 233, 252, 258, 259
choosing, 246–49
cost of IPOs and, 240–41
differentiating, 236–38
how money is made by,
238–40
institutional investors
and, 245–46
pricing of shares and,
256, 257
ranking of, 237t
role of, 235–38, 254
Investor relations man-
agers, 263
Investors

business plans and,
72–76, 99
institutional, 178, 244–46
IPOs and, 250–51
ownership by, 9–10, 134t
promises to, 162
tales for, 163
Israel, 224, 229–30, 281

Japan, 224, 225, 268, 281
Jaws, 48
JDS Uniphase, 54
Jobs, Steve, 16, 24
Juryproof prospectuses,
235, 253, 255

Kaufman, Steve, 33
Kidder Peabody, 19
Kitchen table stage, 24t,
30–31, 168t
Kleiner, Gene, 45
Kleiner Perkins Caufield &
Byers, 10, 45, 119, 192t,
328–29
Knight-Ridder, 119
Kodak, 17, 56, 227, 280
Korea, 224, 230, 281
KPM, 86
Kyocera Corporation, 225

L. F. Rothschild, Unterberg,
Towbin, 18
L. F. Rothschild, Unterberg
and Tobin, 238
Lam, Chih-Chao, 195
Landlords, 201–2
LaPine, Tony, 225
Lawrence Livermore Labo-
ratories, 34
Lawsuits, 31, 56
IPOs and, 234–35, 254,
258
management incom-
pleteness and, 94–95
pullout from employer
and, 35
shooting stars and, 79
Lawyers, 53–67
business plan and, 36
closing and, 41, 105
fees of, 124
general counsel, 55–56
incorporation and, 41,
64–65

IPOs and, 252–53, 255,
263–64
kitchen table stage and,
31
patent counsel, 56
pullout from employer
and, 34
start-up, 106–7
types required, 53–55
Lead spokesperson, 263
Lead venture capital firms,
39, 40, 104–5
Leaks, 39
Leasing, 3, 43, 200–211
cost of, 205–6
of equipment, 3, 203–7,
214–15
of real estate, 201–2
Lee Data Corp., 80
Legal limitations, 227–30
Lehman Brothers, 237t
Leveraging of equity, 46, 49
Liberty Digital, 278
Limited partnerships, 176
Linear Technology, 25, 34,
53, 73, 75, 95
Liquidity, 2, 5, 13, 19
Loans, 215–16
bridge, 109
government-backed,
217–18
home equity, 217
personal, 141, 217
working capital, 215–16
Location of business, find-
ing, 26t, 42–44, 169t
London Stock Exchange, 13,
228, 229
Lotus, 16, 56, 75, 98, 215,
270, 272
LSI Logic, 272
Lucent Technologies, 9,
274, 276, 277–78

MacPherson, Allen, 63
Malaysia, 230, 281
Management, 91–97
cash compensation for,
2
climbing and turnover in,
149–50
completeness in, 21,
92–95, 110
core, 12–13, 21, 91–92

Management *(Cont.)*
experienced, 73–74, 91
filling, 25t, 37–39, 168t
in investment banking, 247
lack of focus in, 47
stand-in, 12, 96
thinness of, 269
traits desired in, 193t
Management and key personnel (business plan section), 76, 77t
Marketing plan, 76, 77t
*Marketing Warfare* (Ries and Trout), 84
Markets
insufficient, 45–46
large, rapidly expanding, 75
poor acceptance from, 48
traits desired in, 193t
Marocco, William L., 117, 202–3
Marriage. See Divorce; Spouses
Martin, Gary, 202
McCracken, Edward, 130
McKenna, Joseph, 121
McKenna, Regis, 25, 148, 261–62
McKinsey & Company, 269
Media, 38, 148
Mentor Graphics, 34
Mentors, 165
Mergers and acquisitions (M&A), 3, 17
case studies of, 270–74
corporate venture capital and, 267–70
percentage of companies experiencing, 2
trends in, 12
Merrill Lynch, 19, 237t
MESBICs, 218
Meyers-Briggs Type Indicator, 167
Mezzanine, 111
Michaely, Roni, 239
Microsoft, 7, 16, 24, 28, 56, 63, 134, 218, 226, 279
case study, 265
IPO, 128, 232, 242–44, 250, 251, 252, 265
value of one percent, 132

Milestones, missed, 162
Million Clinical Multiaxial Inventory (MCMI), 167
Minnesota Multiphasic Personality Inventory (MMPI), 167
Monolithic Memories, 132
Montgomery Securities, 19, 238
Moore, Geoffrey, 84, 88
Morals, 162–63
Moran, Raymond, 248
Morgan Stanley, 19, 237t, 238, 264
Morrison & Foerster, 30, 54, 65
Mostek, 272
MP3.com, 19, 204
Multiple, 4, 5
Multiple capital rounds, 110–11
Murto, William H., 35

National Association of Securities Dealers Automated Quotations (NASDAQ), 171, 228, 229, 230, 233, 245, 281
National Investor Relations Institute, 262, 264
National Semiconductor Corporation, 34, 53, 73, 95, 189, 201, 270–73
Nationbanc, 19
NBC, 278
NEC, 56
Negotiation, 109–12
Netscape, 7, 9, 17, 74, 98, 114, 130, 132, 134, 146, 224
case study, 118–20
cash compensation just before IPO, 136t
ownership of, 120, 127t
Network Equipment Technologies, Inc. (NET), 116–17
Neuer Markt, 13, 228, 230
*New Positioning* (Trout), 84
New Software, Inc., 196–97
Newtech Company, 59–62
New Ventures Group, 277–78
New York Stock Exchange

(NYSE), 3, 233, 245
*New York Times*, 16
Nixdorf, 226
Nondisclosure agreements, 54, 102
Nonqualified Stock Options, 141
NTT, 227

Oak Micro Technology, 197
Objective personality testing, 167
Offshore investing, 12
Olivetti, 226
One percent, value of, 132–34
"On Excellence" (column), 83–84
Operations plan, 76, 77t
Osborne Computer, 20, 123, 254
Overperformance, 48
Over the Counter (OTC), 233
Ownership, 98, 120–22. See Equity
after IPO, 1, 127t
by CEOs, 1, 14, 127t, 128–29
of Chips and Technologies, 118, 127t
by employees, 134t
by founders, 1, 127t, 129–30, 139–40, 184
by investors, 9–10, 134t
just before IPO, 134t
of Netscape, 120, 127t
of Network Equipment Technologies, Inc., 116
at time of IPO, 2
by venture capitalists, 2, 141–42

Papers, technical, 148
Patent counsel, 56
Patents, 53, 55, 63, 64, 147–48
Payroll
missing, 162–63
services, 216
Peery-Arrillaga, 202
Penny stock, 228
Pension funds, 172, 173
Percent per annum (PA), 4–5, 10

Pericom, 224
Perot, Ross, 9, 224
Personal computers (PCs), 18–19, 178
Personal costs, 10–11, 139t, 150–57, 217
Personal growth, 149
Personal loans, 141, 217
Personal savings, 220–21
Peter Principle, 150
Peters, Tom, 68, 83–84
Phantom stock, 18, 276, 277–78
Philips Electronics, 278
Phillips, Mike, 30, 54–55
Phillips-Smith, 192t
Plus Development, 276, 277
PointCast, 251
Polaroid, 56
Porter, Michael, 68, 85
Positioning, 84–85
Post-money, 184
Preferred A stock, 110, 119
Preferred B stock, 110, 119
Preferred C stock, 119
Preferred stock, 110, 112–14, 119, 123, 141–42
    effective control and, 121
    typical terms of, 113t
Pre-money, 184
Presentations, 40, 191
    in business plan, 78
    elements of, 102–3
    feedback from, 103–4
*Prevention*, 157
Pricewaterhouse Coopers, 86
Pricing, 40, 112–20. See also Valuation
    of corporate venture capital, 226, 279–80
    of funding rounds, 114, 181–85
    of IPOs, 171–72
    of mergers and acquisitions, 269
    of Netscape, 120
    of stock, 122–23, 181–85, 255–57, 258–59
Printers, 254
Product launching, 27t, 47–49, 169t
Product schedule slips, 45,

48, 88–89, 110
Projective personality testing, 167
Prospectuses, 235, 253, 255
Prudential-Bache, 225
Psychological testing, 167
Public relations (PR), 148, 264
Purpose in life, 166

Quantum Corporation, 276, 277, 278
QuickUp™, 37, 184

Range Semiconductor, 201, 209–11
Ratios, 257
Raytheon, 17, 226, 278
Real estate brokers, 43
Recruiting, 163
*Red Herring*, 265
Registration rights, 123
Relatives, 218–19
Religion, 163–65
Relocation, 141
Repeatable technology, 45
Research analysts, 238, 246–47, 248, 261, 264–65
Research staff, 235
Resources (business plan section), 78
Return on investment (ROI)
    at business plan creation stage, 37
    at closing and incorporation stage, 42
    decrease in, 10
    at filling management team stage, 39
    at finding a location stage, 44
    at founders' commitment stage, 32
    at idea stage, 30
    measurement of, 4–5
    at product launching stage, 48–49
    at pullout from employer stage, 35
    at secondary capital rounds, 47
    at seed capital stage, 41
    at starting up stage, 46

technology versus, 279
for venture capitalists, 171, 172, 173, 174, 178–85
at working capital stage, 50
Rewards, 126–50
    financial, 126–46
    findings about, 9–10
    professional, 146–50
    for venture capitalists, 177–78
Ries, Al, 84
Ries, Laura, 84
Riordan, Dick, 122
Riordan & McKinzie, 122
Risks, 6–7
    at business plan creation stage, 37
    at closing and incorporation stage, 42
    at filling management team stage, 39
    at finding a location stage, 43–44
    findings about, 9–10
    at founders' commitment stage, 32
    at idea stage, 29–30
    at IPO stage, 51
    at kitchen table stage, 31
    at product launching stage, 48
    at pullout from employer stage, 34–35
    at secondary capital rounds stage, 47
    at seed capital stage, 40–41
    at starting up stage, 45–46
    venture capitalists and, 177–78
    at working capital stage, 49
Road shows, 246
Robertson, Colman & Stephens, 17, 18, 19, 238
Robertson, Sandy, 19, 238, 248
Robertson Stephens & Company, 19, 239
Robertson Stevens, 237t, 238, 248

Rock, Arthur. See Arthur Rock
Rockwell International Corporation, 278
Rogers, T. J., 131, 132
Rorschach Inkblot Test, 167
Rosati, Mario, 54
Rosen, Ben, 36, 75, 270, 272
Rosenberg Capital Management, 264
Rothschild, 19
Rule 144, 140

Salaries. See Wages/salaries
Sales department, 236
Sales revenue, 88
Salomon Brothers, 172
Salomon Smith Barney, 237t
*San Jose Mercury News*, 29, 33, 156, 159, 164, 208, 234, 267
Saratoga Venture Finance, 7, 9, 11, 37, 85, 96, 138, 177, 205
Saratoga Venture Tables™, 10, 40, 98, 120, 124–25, 128, 183, 283–316
Savi Technologies, 278
SBICs, 218
Schlumberger, 272
Secondary capital rounds, 26t, 46–47, 169t
Securities analysts, 263
Securities and Exchange Commission (SEC), 7, 19, 123, 124, 125, 228, 238, 252, 254, 263
Securities Industry Association, 172
Securities registration, 227–30
Seed capital, 25t, 39–41, 109, 111, 112, 168t, 220, 223
SEEQ, 25, 53
Sequoia Capital, 95, 192t, 325–28
Severins, Hans, 223
Sevin, L. J., 36, 272
Sevin Rosen Management, 36
Sha, James, 119
Shareholder relations, 260–61

Shooting stars, 79–81, 147, 209
ShoppingList.com, 195
Shopworn ideas, 40
Showtime Networks, 278
Siemens, 226
Sierra Semiconductor, 34, 44
Sigma Designs, Inc., 23, 33, 44
Signetics, 189
Silicon Graphics, 9, 74, 118, 127t, 129, 130, 136t
Silicon Valley, 3, 6, 201
Silicon Valley Bank, 216–17
Singapore, 188, 224, 230, 281
16-PF, 167
Sleep, 158
Small Business Administration (SBA), 218
Smith, Steve, 157, 159
Smoking, 158
Softbank, 224, 225, 268, 274, 281
Solids, 180, 181t
Sony Walkman, 75
Speaking forums, 265
Spin-ins. See Internal start-ups
Spirituality, 163–65
Sporck, Charles E., 74, 270–73
Spouses, 154, 160–62, 165, 217
Standard and Poors index, 173
Stand-in managers, 12, 96
Starting up stage, 26t, 44–46, 169t
Start-ins. See Internal start-ups
Start-up attorneys, 106–7
Start-up consultants, 106–7
Steeplechase effect, 81
Stock
    common, 112, 123, 141–42
    decrease in, 6–7
    investment bankers and, 237–38, 239–40
    penny, 228
    phantom, 18, 276, 277–78
    preferred. See Preferred stock

pricing of, 122–23, 181–85, 255–57, 258–59
undervaluing of, 40–41
worth of, 1, 2
Stock exchanges, 13, 228–30
Stock market, 171
Stock market crash of 1987, 18, 251
Stock options, 114, 130–32, 133, 140–41
Story investing, 21, 256
Strategic thinking, 85
Strategy
    creating, 83–85
    for raising capital, 99–100
Stress, 7–8, 40, 153–54
Strike price, 256
Structuring of venture deal, 112–20
Suicide, 165
Sun Microsystems, 227, 239, 240, 280
Super Venture Fund, 113–14
Support systems, 165–66
Sustainable competitive advantage (SCA), 1–2, 81–83
Sutter Hill, 251
Swanson, Bob, 34, 73
Syndication staff, 236

T. Rowe Price, 264
TA Associates, 192t
Taiwan Stock Exchange, 13, 188, 224, 228, 229, 230, 281
Task assignment, 101
Taxes, 50, 275
TCI, 119
Techfarm, 118
Technology
    business versus, 269
    repeatable, 45
    ROI versus, 279
Tel Aviv Stock Exchange, 229–30
Televideo, 7, 137
10-Ks, 254
10-Qs, 254, 263
Terror, 11, 154–55
Texas Instruments, 35, 56, 189
Theft, 162

Thematic Apperception Test, 167
Time commitment, 151–52
Times Mirror, 119
TiVo, 278
Tophill Systems, 201, 208–9
Toronto Stock Exchange, 188
Townsend & Townsend, 63
Trademarks, 56, 64
Traders, 236. See also Day traders
Trade secrets, 39, 64
Trends, 11–14, 21–22, 185–87
Trouble, 152–53
Trout, Jack, 84
TV Guide Interactive, 278
"22 Immutable Laws of Branding" (Reis and Reis), 84

Uhlman, Tom, 274, 277
Underperformance, 48
Underwriters, 50, 236, 255
commission of, 240
Unfair advantage, 1–2, 78–79, 89–90, 99, 193t
United Technology, 272
Uttal, Bro, 265

Vacations, 145, 166
Valentine, Don, vii, 95
Valid Logic, 34, 114, 259
Valuation, 40. See also Pricing
impact of management on, 96–97
of internal start-ups, 276
quantification techniques for, 115t
Vancouver Stock Exchange, 228, 229
Vector Capital, 278
*Venture*, 157, 158, 159
Venture capital
amount available each year, 12
amount committed to pools, 3
corporate. See Corporate venture capital
cost of, 170–72
critical issues in, 4–5

landlords as source of, 201–2
problems caused by surge in, 5–6
process of raising, 7–8, 190–99
sources of, 8–9, 222–31
Venture Capital Economic Services, 268
Venture capital firms
agreement of, 104–5
assistance provided by, 189
choosing, 190
comparisons of, 192t
competition between, 3, 5
control of investment by, 187–89
how money is made by, 176–77
lead, 39, 40, 104–5
motivation of, 178–81
profiles of, 325–29
Venture capital formation, 23–52
business plan creation stage, 25t, 35–37, 168t
closing and incorporation stage, 25t, 41–42, 168t
filling management team stage, 25t, 37–39, 168t
finding a location stage, 26t, 42–44, 169t
founders' commitment stage, 24t, 31–32, 168t
historical overview of, 15–17
idea stage, 24–30, 168t
IPO stage, 27t, 50–51, 169t
kitchen table stage, 24t, 30–31, 168t
learning the process of, 269
participants in, 29t
product launching stage, 27t, 47–49, 169t
pullout from employer stage, 24t, 33–35, 168t
secondary capital rounds stage, 26t, 46–47, 169t
seed capital stage, 25t, 39–41, 168t
starting up stage, 26t, 44–46, 169t

summary of campaign, 99–105
working capital stage, 27t, 49–50, 169t
Venture capitalists, 170–99, 250–51
on board of directors, 123–24
characteristics desired by, 192–94
at closing and incorporation stage, 42
corporate venture capitalists compared with, 280
cost of capital, 170–72
deals with famous start-ups, 124–25
differences among, 191
estimated earnings of, 1
finding, 190
life of, 174–76
ownership by, 2, 141–42
portfolio results for, 181t
risk/reward trade-offs for, 177–78
role of, 108–9
source of money, 172–73
*Venture Capital Journal*, 6, 16, 191
*Venture Economics Journal*, 17, 19, 174, 179, 191
Verdicom, 278
Vesting, 114, 124, 141
Veto rights, 113–14, 123
Vice presidents (VPs)
of business development, 93
cash compensation for, 2–3, 136, 138
of engineering, 93, 110
of finance and administration, 93
of manufacturing/operations, 93
of marketing, 93
of sales, 2–3, 93
Vietnam War, 16
VisiCalc, 215
Vision, 28, 29–30, 104
Vulcan Ventures, 278

W. L. Marocco Development Company, 202

W. R. Hambrecht & Co., 19, 238

Wages/salaries, 2, 133, 135. See also Cash compensation

Wall Street, 18–20, 232–66. See also Institutional investors; Investment bankers

*Wall Street Journal*, 15, 233, 259

Walt Disney Company, 278

Warnock, John, 189

Weather Channel, 278

Wechsler Adult Intelligence Scale-Revised (WAIS-R), 167

Welty, Bill, 193

*West* magazine, 156, 159

Western Technology Investment, 204, 207

Whisper numbers, 265

Whitman Breed Abbott & Morgan, 63

Wild Ones, 180, 181t, 185

Williams, Ray, 273

Wilson Sonsini Goodrich & Rosati, 54

Window for IPO, 3, 51

Winners, 180, 181t, 185

*Wired*, 251

Wit Capital, 19, 238

Wives. See Spouses

Workaholics, 155–56

Working capital, 27t, 49–50, 169t

Working capital loans, 215–16

Worlds of Wonder, 9, 223

Wozniak, Steve, 24, 162

Yahoo, 7, 18, 74, 98, 134, 180, 224, 226, 273

cash compensation just before IPO, 136t

ownership of just after IPO, 127t

Young, Arthur, 123, 254

Yourco, Inc., 121–22

Zachary, Paul, 29–30

ZDTV, 278

Zombies, 10, 180, 181t

# About the Author

John Nesheim is Chief Executive Officer of Nesheim Group, and an engineer and veteran of Silicon Valley. Since 1976, he has focused his research on how to do a high-tech start-up. Mr. Nesheim teaches entrepreneurship for Cornell University and other schools in Asia and Europe. His research findings are used by entrepreneurs, investors, governments, universities, corporations, and Wall Street to increase understanding of entrepreneurial effectiveness. Details can be found at *www.startupweb.com*.